THE
FIBROUS PLANTS OF INDIA

THE

FIBROUS PLANTS OF INDIA

FITTED FOR

CORDAGE, CLOTHING, AND PAPER.

WITH AN ACCOUNT OF THE

CULTIVATION AND PREPARATION

OF

FLAX, HEMP, AND THEIR SUBSTITUTES.

BY

J. FORBES ROYLE, M. D., F. R. S.

GYAN

Published by

GYAN

Gyan Publishing House
5, Ansari Road
Daryaganj, New Delhi-110002
Phone: 011-47034999, 9811692060
E-mail: books@gyanbooks.com

Distribution Network
gyanbooks.com
India, USA, Canada, UK, Australia, France

ISBN: 978-81-212-8304-5 (PB)
First Published, 1855

2nd Impression 2023

Printed at: Gyan Press, Delhi.

THE FIBROUS PLANTS OF INDIA
Author: J. FORBES ROYLE

FIBROUS PLANTS OF INDIA

THE FIBROUS PLANTS OF INDIA

FITTED FOR

CORDAGE, CLOTHING, AND PAPER.

WITH AN ACCOUNT OF THE

CULTIVATION AND PREPARATION

OF

FLAX, HEMP, AND THEIR SUBSTITUTES.

BY

J. FORBES ROYLE, M.D., F.R.S.,

FORMERLY SUPERINTENDENT OF THE HON. EAST INDIA COMPANY'S BOTANIC GARDEN AT SAHARUNPORE; PROFESSOR OF MATERIA MEDICA AND THERAPEUTICS, IN KING'S COLLEGE, LONDON, ETC., ETC.

LONDON:

SMITH, ELDER, AND CO., 65, CORNHILL.

BOMBAY: SMITH, TAYLOR, AND CO.

1855.

PREFACE.

Having a few years since paid attention to the subject of Fibres, and anticipating that the troubled state of Europe would cause a demand for those of India, I resumed the subject in the autumn of the year 1853.

In the following spring the distinguished senator, of whom the Indian Medical Service has reason to be proud, and whose loss the public has now to lament, Joseph Hume, Esq., M.P., having suggested Indian Fibres as a subject for inquiry to the Council of the Society of Arts, they did me the honour to ask whether I could prepare a paper on the subject. My time was then fully occupied with a general work on the 'Commercial Products of India,' several sheets of which were then, as they still are, in type, and the period for my Course of Lectures at King's College was approaching. I therefore found it impossible to devote sufficient time to the elaboration of a suitable paper, but offered to give a Lecture, which might be reported if thought desirable. This I did on the 11th of April, and, with the permission of the Honorable the Court of Directors, illustrated it with specimens of Fibre, Canvas, and Cordage, the property of the East India Company. The Report of it was published in the 'Journal of the Society of Arts,' on the 14th of April, 1854.

The Lecture having been reprinted, both in this country and in the Colonies, elicited much additional information, some of which came in time to be recorded in its proper place in the present work. The Lecture was also republished in the Pamphlet form, because, as was stated, it was out of print—though this is usually a reason for authors republishing their own productions. One editor complained that he had seen it reprinted more than a hundred times, and that it would never produce as much paper as it had been printed on. As I myself never sent it, either directly or indirectly, to any one for the purpose, I was happy to find that the aspect of the times made the subject appear sufficiently interesting to induce so many to republish so imperfect an account.

Having been requested to place the information respecting Indian Fibres in some permanent form, I commenced the present work at the conclusion, last summer, of my Lectures at King's College. It has extended much beyond the limits which I had prescribed for it, partly owing to the number of subjects to be treated of, but especially owing to the variety of points requiring to be attended to respecting each; in order that the culture of the plant and the preparation of the fibre—*e. g.*, of Flax—should be attended to according to the scientific principles and the improved practice of the present day. The object being that these should assist colonists and planters in escaping failure with the culture of Flax, at the same time that they might apply the information to the culture and preparation of other fibres.

Respecting Flax, I have been enabled to bring together much valuable information, in consequence of so much having been done and written: so it is because much has been done, though little is known regarding Indian Fibres, that my limits have been so much exceeded. This was necessary, in order that others might be able to make use of the information which is on record, and future experimentalists advance from points reached by their predecessors, instead of repeating as new what has long been known.

This copiousness of information is due partly to the Court of Directors of the East India Company having directed the culture of Fibres in India at the beginning of this century, as recorded in Wisset 'On Hemp, &c.,' and in Dr. Roxburgh's detached papers (*v.* p. 6); and partly to the subject having attracted the attention of many writers in the valuable 'Trans. and Journ. of the Agri-Horticultural Society of India.' The Great Exhibition of 1851 produced a fine collection of Indian Fibres. Many of Dr. Roxburgh's specimens are still in the India House, my own collection has afforded others, and the market has supplied such as are known in commerce.

The greatly increased Importation of Fibres from India proves the importance of the subject, and indicates, from the rapidity of the rise, how much more is still practicable. In successive editions of M'Culloch's 'Commercial Dictionary,' we find the following Imports into Great Britain; but, under the head of Hemp from India, are included the various Fibres described in this work, with probably no real Hemp, though this *may* be imported from thence.

Quantities of Hemp imported into the United Kingdom:

	1831.	1847.	1851.
From Russia	506,803	544,844	672,342
„ British Territories in East Indies .	9,472	185,788	590,923

If any effectual impediments had been interposed to the receipt of Hemp and Flax from the ordinary sources, a greatly increased supply of Fibres would have been received from India, and might be so at any time, if adequate notice were given of the expected demand before the seasons of cultivation—that is, before June and October. As the above increase in the Imports has been chiefly in the lower qualities of Fibre, it is reasonable to expect that some demand may arise for those which are superior in point of strength and equal fineness, to any which are imported, and that they will be able to bear the expenses of freight, &c., at least as well as the others.

While this sheet is passing through the press, a debate on "the Trade with Russia," has taken place in the House of Commons, on the 21st of February; when it was stated, that there had been recently a considerable importation of Hemp from India, but that ruinous losses had been sustained on the Linseed from India. This must have been of the ordinary produce of the country, and not the consequence of extended cultivation, produced by increased demand. A rise of price probably took place in the local markets, in expectation of higher prices prevailing in this country. Bombay Hemp, as observed at p. 288, usually sells there at from Rs. 5 to Rs. 8 in June; but in June, 1854, the price was Rs. 11 per cwt. But as this rise in price did not take place, the Linseed had to be sold at the ordinary rates; at which, however, Indian Linseed can compete with others, as is proved by the large and increasing imports from India. It was also asked, in the same debate, "Why does not he (the merchant) go to India now for it (that is, Flax), and the speaker replied, "on account of the difference of price." Little Flax is produced in India, for reasons which have been fully detailed in this work. But there is no reason to believe that it will be dearer than in other countries, when grown in suitable localities. In a letter from the Messrs. Noble, it was well stated, that a temporary stoppage of the trade "would give an impetus to the growers of fibres in the Colonies;" and that "the producers would be able to send it (after they were once fairly started), at prices that would compete with Russian Hemp, when at its lowest prices; and it would also be of great advantage in doing away with the prejudice now existing on the part of consumers about trying a new article."

In sending Fibres to the English market, it would greatly facilitate their employment, if the natives of India would prepare them in a cleaner state, and have them made up in the manner to which manufacturers here are accustomed. Most of the Fibres treated of have been examined by practical men of skill, who consider them to be well adapted for many purposes, and have assigned to them such prices as they seem to be worth. These appear to be sufficient to pay for their culture and export.

I have to acknowledge my obligations to Mr. Ord, of Threadneedle Street, who examined all the Fibres sent to the Exhibition of 1851; and also to the Messrs. Noble, who have recently examined the whole collection of Fibres.

It is often said that the only mode of ascertaining the value of a Fibre, or of any other product, is to see what it will bring in the open market. This is, no doubt, true of such things as are *known*. But if a new product is sent into the market, few of the regular purchasers will buy it, as they want that to which their machinery and manufactures are suited. I am told, that it is only by sending an article for some years into market, that it attracts notice. When worked up and found useful, inquiries are subsequently made for it, and by degrees its properties are determined, and its real value ascertained; as we may see on examining the present and former comparative prices of Jute. The process will be much expedited by employing brokers who pay special attention to particular classes of articles, and by giving them all the information possible. It would also be promoted by the more general establishment of Trade Museums, as these would assist in dispelling much of the ignorance which prevails respecting many valuable Natural Products.

Merchants and manufacturers in this country, on the

other hand, complain, that having written to India for particular Fibres, they are unable to obtain them in any quantity. But they can hardly expect that parties abroad should keep supplies of little-known articles for such accidental demands. It is very certain that if but moderate encouragement is given to such articles on their first appearance in the market, the supply will by degrees become very greatly increased; while of the Fibres which are already cultivated, the supply might at once become considerable, by sending orders for them before the season of cultivation. Indeed, it was observed in a recent Bombay paper, that the merchants there had been astonished at the quantity of Fibres which had been brought into the Bombay market.

The subject of Fibres has of late attracted considerable attention in India, as the Governor-General has issued instructions for the sending to England some of the stronger Fibres, both from the Northern and the Southern parts of that Empire. The Madras Government has also given directions for the investigation of the fibrous materials procurable in that Presidency. Dr. Clagham, in a letter dated 13th January 1855, states that Mr. Underwood has succeeded in separating them at a cheap rate. At Bombay a Company has been established for the collection of materials for paper-making, while individuals are paying attention to the preparation of Fibres. In Sindh and in the Punjab, the culture of Flax has been taken up and patronised by the Indian Government and the Court of Directors.

At the conclusion of this volume I have appended some Observations on Materials for Paper-making, as well as the Report which I wrote at the requisition of the Lords of the Committee of the Privy Council for Trade.

LONDON; *24th February*, 1855.

TABLE OF CONTENTS.

RUSSIA MATS.

JUTE.

THE SO-CALLED INDIAN HEMPS.

COROLLIFLORALS.

APETALOUS PLANTS

TRUE HEMP (CANNABIS SATIVA).

BREAD-FRUIT AND MULBERRY TRIBE.

NETTLES.

APPENDIX.

THE

FIBROUS PLANTS OF INDIA

FITTED FOR

CORDAGE, CLOTHING, AND PAPER.

THE combination of strength with flexibility makes many natural products so useful to man, that they attract his attention even in the earliest states of society. The necessity of sometimes tying up cattle, tethering a horse, or towing a raft, would readily lead to the twisting together of strips of skins or the tough bark of trees, so that length might be obtained, while strength was not sacrificed. Many of the same substances were early applied to the arts of platting and of mat-making; while the felting of wool was discovered at very remote periods in the northern parts of Asia. All these arts probably preceded the discovery of that of weaving, when textile fabrics, whether of wool or of vegetable fibre, came to be substituted, as clothing for man, for the skins and furs of animals or the primitive matting of rushes.

It has been very satisfactorily shown by Mr. Yates, in his 'Textrinum Antiquorum,' that in ancient times the inhabitants of Europe and of Western Asia were enveloped in skins and furs, or garments of wool and of goat's hair, while the Chinese were probably clothed in silk. Hemp was early employed for the same purpose by the Scythians. The Egyptian priesthood, we know, were allowed to wear only linen; while the Indians are described as wearing cloth made of fleeces from trees, which surpassed those of sheep in beauty and excellence. That cotton is meant, is evident not only from the description, but from the Indian name carbasus (from the Sanscrit kurpasum) being used to describe their dress—as "corpora usque pedes carbaso velant." But the natives of India were at still earlier periods acquainted with the arts of spinning and of weaving, as may be proved by a reference to their Vedas; while in the Institutes of Menu, written 800 years before the Christian era, we are told, that the sacrificial thread of a Brahmin must be made of cotton; that of a Cshatriya, of *sana*[1] thread only; that of a Vaisya, of woollen thread.

India is a country of such vast extent, and so diversified in soil as well as in climate, that we may readily believe it to be capable of producing almost every kind of natural produce, and among these every known variety of fibre. If we consider, moreover, how early India was civilised, how long the greater number of the useful arts have there been practised, we might safely infer that the country must long have possessed a variety of products fitted for the several purposes to which flax and hemp are elsewhere applied—that is, for platted or for twisted manufactures; as well as for the coarser and the finer textile fabrics, such as the construction of mats, the twisting of bow-strings, or lines for fishing, or for the making of nets; ropes for tow-lines, tethers for camels or other beasts of burden, or for harnessing cattle; yarn for the manufacture of canvas for sacking, or for sails for their shipping, or for the production of their "webs of woven air."

Cotton, was early, as it still is, employed in India for many of the purposes to which leather, hemp, and flax, are alone thought applicable in other countries; as for the coverings of carriages, the construction of tents, of canvas, and of cordage. And this, notwithstanding that India possesses, and its inhabitants are acquainted with, a vast number of fibre-yielding plants. These are little known to, or but slightly appreciated in other countries, though they are undoubtedly

[1] That is, of *sunn*, probably Crotalaria fibre, q. v.

possessed of very valuable properties. Further, by proceeding in such inquiries, we shall find that the natives of India, besides writing on the leaves of palm-trees and the bark of the birch, as well as engraving their records on rocks or on plates of metal, have long been acquainted with the manufacture of paper. We may, therefore, enquire whether cotton is the only material which they convert into this useful product, or whether there are not other substances which they themselves employ, and which we may also apply to the growing (I had almost said insatiable) wants of this manufacture, as necessary for our comfort and commerce, as for the continued and advancing civilisation of the world.

If we extend our inquiries only to the plants which are cultivated by the natives of India, many will no doubt be surprised to find among them not only the true Hemp but also the true Flax plant; and the more so when they learn, that both are extensively cultivated, not in one, but in almost every part of the wide-spread territories of the Indian empire. Still more curious is it, that in few places are these plants valued for their fibres, which in Europe are almost the sole objects of attention. But in India, the Hemp plant is esteemed for the intoxicating properties secreted by its leaves, and the Flax plant for the oil stored up within its seeds. The stems of both plants, which in Europe are valued for their fibres, are in India either thrown away or burnt. It will at once be concluded, as has more than once been the case, that countless loads of valuable fibre are thus yearly lost, either from the ignorance or the carelessness of the cultivators. Without denying that this may, in some degree at least, be the case, we may say in this, as in many other things, a little knowledge leads but to incorrect conclusions.

The Hemp plant being valued for its intoxicating secretions, it has been found by the people of India, that these are best produced when the plants are freely exposed to light and air, and therefore they place them at distances of nine feet apart from each other. This exposure to light, heat, and air, in a rich soil and brilliant climate, is so well suited to the plants, that they grow to a great size and throw out branches on all sides; but the fibres, instead of being flexible and strong, are found to be woody and brittle. And this is only what might be expected, for the fibrous product of plants is only the woody fibre in a younger state, and may be considered as wood in a separated form, while wood may be described as consisting chiefly of amalgamated fibres. Exposure to light and air is well known to be essential to the formation of good wood, by favouring the proper secretions of the tree and the thickening of the woody fibres. But this necessarily diminishes their flexibility, and therefore is not suited to plants which are grown on account of these fibres. Hence, to obviate this undue exposure of the plants to light and air, and to favour their shooting upwards, and to prevent the formation of lateral branches, the seeds of both the hemp and the flax plant are sown thick in Europe; and the plants grown closer as the fibre is required to be finer. But the Flax plant in India being cultivated for its seed, is, on the contrary, either sown in lines on the outside of and as an edging to, or broadcast and intermixed with, other crops. The seeds are collected when they are fully ripe, or when the other crops have been harvested. The effect is, that the plants are checked in their upward growth, and attain a height of only a foot or of eighteen inches, have numerous lateral branches, and are loaded with seed-vessels; each seed containing a larger proportion of oil than is found in those grown in Europe; but the fibre is short, brittle, and unfitted for the general purposes of flax.

It does not appear that the Indian climate is the best suited to the production of good flax and hemp; for it is one of comparatively short seasons, of great alternations of dryness and of moisture, as well as of considerable extremes of temperature. But the Creator of all has enriched the country with a variety of plants which do flourish well even within these extremes. The Indian mode of cultivation is better suited for the secretion of the resin in one case and of oil in the other, than for the production of strong and flexible fibre in either plant. For the production of this, both plants require a comparatively slow growth in a moderately moist and temperate climate. This it would be unreasonable to expect to find, either in the comparatively arid tracts of north-west India, or in the moist and warm plains of Bengal. In fact, if it were not that the autumnal and winter temperature of these districts approaches the summer temperature of European countries, flax plants could not be grown at all, so as to yield either oil, seed, or fibre. But, as it is, we may appropriately consider, under the respective heads of Flax and of Hemp, whether it may not be possible, by modifications of culture, or by selection of suitable sites, to grow both these plants, within the limits of India, so as to yield useful fibre.

On the other hand, it is now well known that India possesses, and indeed exports, various fibres which are produced by several fast-growing plants. Of these fibres, some, though long and fine in texture, are deficient in strength; others appear coarse in texture, or are harsh in feel, and yet not remarkable for tenacity. It has therefore been inferred by some very intelligent men, that the heat and moisture of the climates where these grow are favorable to rapid growth, which of itself is sufficient to account for the want of strength; and that therefore we cannot expect to find them suited to the production of good fibres. But here the conclusion come to is equally hasty, for no distinction is made between what is due to the nature of the plant itself, and what to its mode of cultivation, or to the preparation of its fibre, and what to the effects of soil and of climate. We do not in this country expect the willow to have the strength of the oak, nor that a rope of rushes will have the tenacity of even a cord of hemp. Yet all may be seen growing in the vicinity of each other. There is as little reason for expecting that the soft and silky Jute of India is to have the strength of either flax or of hemp; and because it does not have it, for inferring, that there cannot be produced in its vicinity other fibres possessed of greater strength. But, if we were to judge from the density and strength of some of the woods produced in the hottest and moistest, as well as in some of the driest climates, we might expect to find plants in the same localities which are equally conspicuous for tenacity of fibre. Instead, however, of inference, I hope to be able to prove to the satisfaction of even the most sceptical, that India grows plants in some of its dry and barren plains, yielding fibres which are as strong and tough as any produced in other parts of the world; but which are equalled in such qualities by others growing in some of its moistest and hottest valleys. Some of these, while possessed of the greatest strength, are also divisible to any extent of fineness. Most of them exist in sufficient quantities, or are so easily cultivated, as to be of great commercial and manufacturing value. Because it has been ascertained that they can be brought to the markets of Europe even from these distant fields, so as to contend in price, even in ordinary times, with the favoured products of the nearest countries.

Though India possesses so large a number of fibre-yielding plants, but few of them are objects of European commerce, or are known to the manufacturers of cordage or of textile fabrics in Europe. This is not because no efforts have been made to make them known; for Dr. Roxburgh, in consequence of orders from the Court of Directors of the East India Company, so long since as the beginning of this century, grew many of the plants in the neighbourhood of Calcutta, separated their fibres, twisted them into twine, and tried their strength, as well when plain as when tanned or tarred. He also sent specimens to the India House, where some of them are still in existence, and also to the Society of Arts, in whose 'Transactions' for the year 1804 many of them are described. The Court of Directors, indeed, must have made inquiries for substitutes for hemp in the latter part of the last century, for, in some of the publications quoted below,[1] references are made to the Board of Trade Consultations in Bengal of the date of 1792, which relate to the Reports of the Collectors of Districts. These give much valuable information respecting the culture of

[1] 'A Treatise on Hemp, including a comprehensive account of the best Modes of Cultivation and Preparation as practised in Europe, Asia, and America; with Observations on the Sunn Plant of India, which may be introduced as a Substitute for many of the purposes to which Hemp is now exclusively employed.' By Robert Wisset, Esq., F.R. and A.S., London, Clerk to the Committee of Warehouses of the East India Company. The first edition in 1804, the second in 1808.

'Observations on the Sunn Hemp of Bengal; with statements of Experiments made from 1802 to 1806 to ascertain its comparative Strength with Russian Hemp, and the advantages of encouraging its Culture and Importation.' London: 1806.

'Observations of the late Dr. William Roxburgh, Botanical Superintendent of the Honourable East India Company's Garden at Calcutta, on the various Specimens of Fibrous Vegetables, the produce of India, which may prove valuable Substitutes for Hemp and Flax, on some future day, in Europe.' Edited by a Friend, and published at the expense of the East India Company, for the information of the Residents, and the benefit that may arise therefrom throughout the Settlements in India. London: 1815.

Sunn Hemp in India. In a pamphlet, published anonymously in 1806, 'On the Sunn Hemp of Bengal,' p. 11, as well as in Macpherson's 'History of European Commerce with India,' p. 242, we are told that great losses were sustained in the years 1796, 1797, and 1798, by the East India Company, and "that their expenditure upon that object exceeded the amount of the sales by more than £45,000, and that all such imports were discontinued until the year 1800, when differences again occurred with the Northern Powers of Europe." But we learn from a letter of Dr. Roxburgh, dated 24th Dec., 1799, that the Court of Directors had sent out Mr. Sinclair to establish the cultivation of hemp; but he having died shortly afterwards, the experiment was continued by Mr. T. Douglas, and, according to Dr. Roxburgh, in a most expensive manner.

The Lords of the Privy Council for Trade and Foreign Plantations, in a letter dated the 4th of February, 1803, recommended to the Court of Directors of the East India Company, to encourage as much as possible the growth of strong hemp in such parts of their dependencies as might be best suited to the production of that article. On the 23d of the same month, the Court replied, that they would take the needful measures for accomplishing the object of their lordships' wishes (*v.* 'Product. Resources of India,' by the author).

Farms were accordingly directed to be established for the cultivation of hemp and of substitutes for it. Dr. Roxburgh, Superintendent of the Botanic Garden at Calcutta, was appointed to the charge of one of them. As above stated, he cultivated a great variety of the fibrous plants of India, made experiments with the fibres, and sent specimens of them to this country. Though Dr. Roxburgh published no separate work on the subject, he wrote letters and reports, and included detailed descriptions of the plants in his botanical works. His separate papers were collected together at his death into a small volume, entitled, 'Observations, &c., on the various specimens of Fibrous Vegetables, the produce of India, which may prove valuable substitutes for Hemp and Flax on some future day in India.' Dr. Roxburgh's exertions were acknowledged by the Society of Arts by the award of their gold medal.

Among the fibrous plants which Dr. Roxburgh submitted to

examination, was the Caloee of Sumatra, which he subsequently named *Urtica tenacissima.* He was informed by a friend at Canton, that the grass cloth of China was made from its fibres. The experiments were continued until 1811; for Dr. Buchanan, who was appointed to succeed Dr. Roxburgh, sent in that year three bales of the Caloee fibre of Sumatra to the India House. These the Court of Directors forwarded to Messrs. Sharpe, then of Mark Lane, who reported, that a thread spun of the fibres bore 252 lb., whereas the weight required to be borne by Russian hemp of the same size in her Majesty's Dockyard was only 82 lb. The Society of Arts, in the year 1814, awarded a silver medal to Capt. J. Cotton, then a Director of the East India Company—who had also paid great attention to the Sunn—for the introduction of this fibre, of which the reports were so favorable for strength and for other qualities. It has since been discovered to be abundant in Assam, and other parts of India.

Among the fibres subjected to experiment by Dr. Roxburgh, were the *Sunn* of Bengal (*Crotolaria juncea*), the Brown Hemp of Bombay (*Hibiscus cannabinus*), and the *Jute* produced by different species of Corchorus, which, though weak, has many valuable properties. Considerable quantities of the different kinds of *Sunn* and of *Jute* were imported by the East India Company. These were at times discontinued, and again resumed; but now we may consider them as trophies of the last war, inasmuch as they have become permanent and considerable articles of export. We may therefore fairly hope, as attention has, in the present war, been directed towards the Hemp of the Himalayas and the Rheea of Assam, that these also may become permanent sources of benefit to India, because they possess, in a superior degree, every quality required of fibres. Before proceeding, we may mention the quantities in which Jute and Sunn are now exported from India.

Though the accounts are imperfect of the export of these, at that time small matters, yet we perceive by the accounts of the Exports of India, given in to the Committee of the House of Commons for the Affairs of India, in 1831, that in the official year 1796-97, only 591 maunds of hemp, flax, and twine were exported from Calcutta to the United Kingdom, but 2883 maunds to the United States of America.

Of jute, at the same period, 521 maunds to the United Kingdom, 159 to America, and 1100 maunds to Hamburgh.

Gunny cloth, or sacking, which in Bengal is made of jute, is exported either in pieces or made up into bags; of these, besides considerable numbers to Penang, China, and New South Wales, 34,000 were exported to America in the year 1796. Since which, the quantity has gradually increased, having been, in 1849-50, 6,545,964, and of jute 33,302 maunds; so that India has contributed something to the success of the American cotton trade, as Bengal gunny bags are everywhere preferred in the Southern States for the packing of cotton. The following are the exports from the three Presidencies for the official year 1850-51; the maund being equal to 82 lb.:

	Hemp (Sunn).	Hemp (Sunn) twine.	Jute.	Gunny bags.	Gunny pieces.	Coir.	Canvass
	Maunds.	Maunds.	Maunds.	Number.	Maunds.	Maunds.	Bolts.
Calcutta .	7635	10,301	793,299	8,759,185	276,528	2654	
	Cwt.	Cwt.				Cwt.	
Madras .	2095	1372	—	58,950	—	109,288	470
Bombay .	11,793	274	—	188,540	—	4178	—

Besides these, as belonging to fibre plants, we may mention that, in addition to linseed oil, considerable quantities of linseed are exported from all three Presidencies, as will probably also soon be the case from Sindh.

	Maunds.	Cwt.	Cwt.
Linseed exported in 1850-51	From Calcutta, 765,497	Madras, 801	Bombay, 45,135.

The true Hemp is nowhere mentioned in these returns, though the plant is cultivated everywhere on account of its intoxicating properties. But Bombay being unable, from its insular situation, to produce enough for its own consumption, imported from the Concan 514 cwt. of *ganza*, or the dried leaves and flowers of the *true hemp*. In the above returns, by the word Hemp is no doubt intended the *Sunn* fibre of India, under which name, however, are probably included the fibres both of Crotolaria and of Hibiscus; while the gunny bags of Madras are probably made of Crotolaria fibre, as may be those of Bombay. But the latter also imports a large number of gunny bags from Calcutta, probably for packing some of the cotton produced in its own provinces.

As calculated to show the great importance of the commerce in fibrous materials, and also the extent of the interests involved in their growth and manufacture, as well as interesting for comparison with the exports from India, we insert here an account of the quantities of Hemp and of Flax imported into the United Kingdom for two years, that is, 1801 and 1853. A comparison of these will show the great increase in the imports of these two articles during the last half-century:

Years.	FLAX and TOW, or CODILLA of HEMP and FLAX.		
	From Russia.	From other Parts.	From all Parts.
	Cwt.	Cwt.	Cwt.
1801	188,106	85,613	273,719
1853	1,294,827	607,650	1,902,477
	HEMP UNDRESSED.		
1801	682,175	67,171	749,346
1853	806,396	412,374	1,218,770

Other fibres which were tried and made known at the above period, still remain unnoticed in Europe, and seem even to have been forgotten by the Indian community. This must be ascribed, on one side to the long peace having rendered manufacturers here indifferent to distant sources of supply; while in India the changing nature of European society, causes things familiar to all at one period, to become totally unknown only a few years afterwards. This effect is further promoted by the entire neglect of the Natural Sciences, which treat of these and other products as parts of general education. It would seem to be thought, that the earth we tread on, the air we breathe, and the animal and vegetable worlds by which we are fed and clothed, are not worthy objects of attention nor sources of valuable information. Not only are they so, but they are as well calculated as any other studies to train the mind to habits of correct observation, of careful induction, and of methodical arrangement. It is sometimes said, that these are subjects for professional rather than for general education.

Without admitting the truth of this opinion, we might yet have the evil rectified, if we found, that though soldiers and civilians neglected, some of these studies were pursued by planters and colonists, merchants and manufacturers. This is so far from being the case, that I was induced in another work to observe, that "the generality of modern experimentalists seem to be unacquainted with the labours of their predecessors, many of them commencing improvement by repeating experiments which had already been made, and announcing results as new which had long previously been ascertained."

We certainly now hear everywhere of the establishment of Schools where the principles of chemistry, of vegetable and animal structure, and physiology, are to be taught on account of their application to the improvement of gardening and of farming: while Trade Museums are being established to inform the manufacturer and merchant of the innumerable, to them useful substances, which nature everywhere produces, and which man so frequently neglects. From the general inattention, moreover, to such subjects, the short Reports and Essays which have been written on different useful products, are soon forgotten, and disappear from circulation. And, though great books have been pronounced to be great evils, small ones are like writings on the sand, which the waves of time obliterate, or remove so out of sight, as to be discovered only by the more diligent students of nature.

By some it has been said, that if these Indian fibres possess any useful properties, or can be afforded at reasonable rates, and there is any demand for them, that they will be sure to find their way to market. But others inquire, If there are such things, why don't they come to us? To this we may reply, that of the useful properties of many of these products there can be no doubt, as will be shown in the course of these pages. They are abundant, or may easily be cultivated, and can be supplied at rates to contend successfully with similar productions from other countries. Mr. Henley has lately shown, that fibrous materials may be supplied in Bengal at about four shillings a maund,[1] which is also the price of the *true hemp* in the Himalayas. Of the demand we may judge from the endless

[1] See Plantain, Jute, Sunn, and Hemp, for the prices at which fibres may be obtained in India.

inquiries, when there happens to be, from whatever cause, a dearth of the usual supplies. We may therefore infer, that as they are possessed of useful properties, and are purchaseable at reasonable prices, they ought to participate in the commerce of Europe in ordinary times. But there are great difficulties in their doing so at any time, for new articles are not enquired for, or even looked at, except in the above exceptional cases. And even in these, great indifference is displayed, unless you can say that large quantities are at once procurable. The colonists being seemingly expected to keep warehouses stored with raw products for the paroxysmal demands of European commerce; as if it were not enough to have within their reach the inexhaustible storehouse of nature, ready at all times to answer all legitimate demands. The Ryots of India are mostly too remote from the centres of commerce, or too apathetic to do anything different from what they have been accustomed to, while Europeans do not receive much encouragement in travelling out of the beaten track. For if we enquire into the history of many of the most important articles of commerce, we shall find that they were at first either neglected or abused. Large sums were expended, and much money was lost, before they came to be established as regular articles of commerce.

The difficulty in making new things known and appreciated as articles of commerce, arises chiefly from the habitual neglect of such things when sent for inquiry from abroad, in order to have their value ascertained at home. For if sent as specimens, I have seen many reports, in which they are pronounced to be of "no value," because they are "unknown in the market." The importer is sometimes advised to send the article in larger quantities to market for a few years, as it will then have a chance of being looked at and its true value ascertained. The planter is not often inclined to follow this advice. For if one more adventurous than his neighbours does send a quantity sufficient even for manufacturing purposes, it is not usually brought to the notice of the more inquiring manufacturer. The article being necessarily consigned by the planter to his agents, is by them transferred to a broker, by whom it is sold with other colonial produce, with little or no information respecting its properties, or the quantities in which, and the prices at which it could be supplied, if it should be approved of. Indeed,

I am informed, that the novelty of the appearance, or the strangeness of the name, is more often the subject of jest, than the article is one of serious enquiry. At all events, the result usually is, that the article is sold at a price which does not pay its expences, and the planter is deterred from sending any fresh quantities. Further progress is, in that quarter at least, thus stopped, even at its commencement.

Even without such impediments, the difficulties are considerable in bringing any new article into use in sufficiently large quantities to be an object of commerce. The natives of India, who are the universal cultivators or collectors of raw produce, being unwilling to enter upon practices or speculations unknown to their forefathers. Any European who, instead of following the established routes of commerce, endeavours to trace out a new one for himself, is, I am told, considered an unsafe man—certainly with some truth, as long as his labours in a new field are so little appreciated or requited by the consumers in Europe. He is, moreover, while the value of a new article is unknown, subjected to the inconvenience of not having advances made in India upon what he may have shipped, as is the case with the ordinary articles of commerce. The merchants in India, or agents as they are usually called, are unwilling or unable to engage in the export of new articles; for the Bombay Chamber of Commerce have described how difficult it is for the merchants resident in the capital to come in contact with the cultivators in the country, also that they are but a "small body," "in most cases the agents of others, whose orders they must comply with;" but Mr. Bracken explained that they are engaged in agency and banking in all its branches, as agents, and in making advances of money for commercial purposes.

One great objection which is frequently made against entering into any speculation for the cultivation of any particular product in India, is the necessity of making some advances of money before the natives can be induced to undertake any particular culture or preparation. This is, no doubt, true, but it is the fashion of the country, which it would be extremely difficult to alter, and certainly not for a great many years. The advance can be effected, however, without much trouble and with little risk, if respectable *dulals*, or native agents, are employed.

But under the operation of this practice have arisen, the great commercial products of India, such as indigo, silk, opium, &c. The practice, so far from being exclusively Indian, may be considered rather as Asiatic, and, indeed, much more general even than that. For, if we inquire into the history of some extensive articles of import, we shall find English agents established near the places of production, and English capital continually sent out to vivify the exertions of colonists or of the natives of the country. Indeed, it can hardly be otherwise, if we compare the wants of many countries with the enormous quantities of produce required to satisfy the demands of even a single large manufacturer: this being often equal to that of some kingdoms. The Russian trade in hemp and flax itself seems dependent for its great extension upon English capital, for I am informed that money is annually sent to different ports of Russia, agents are thence dispatched into the country districts; these buy up the quantities which each cultivator has been able to grow but cannot prepare before winter; so that the article is not delivered for six months afterwards. The Earl of Clarendon, in his speech on the Russian war, in the House of Lords, on the 10th of August, said: "We must consider, too, that the trade with Russia is usually conducted with English capital; that English capital has been indispensable for their production and for bringing them to market, and that that has entirely ceased; and that all the industry of the country has, to a great extent, been paralysed, while the want of markets has deprived the Russian proprietor of all that he had to depend on to meet the expenses to which he is subject." Indeed, I am happy to say that some of the capital, which used to be sent to Russia for the purchase of hemp and flax, has this year been sent to India for the purchase of its peculiar fibres, and among them, probably, of Indian-grown hemp.

Though the fate of the generality of experimentalists is to have their efforts unnoticed, and thus to be deterred from further attempts, there are, I am also glad to state, some, and among them not the least intelligent and successful of manufacturers, who do themselves inquire after new products likely to be useful in their special businesses, and who, having obtained, first make a scientific investigation of the properties of the new substance, and then having subjected it to the practical working of their factories, have in a few instances, which I myself have brought to their notice, given remunerative orders directly to the planter for his produce.

A manufacturer may justly object to employ a new thing, with the properties of which he is but partially acquainted; and which, having investigated, he has no information of the quantities or price at which it can be supplied, supposing that he found it suitable for his purposes. Because, unless obtainable in quantity, regularly and at reasonable prices, he is unable, he says, to do any *good* with it. Therefore, in sending a new product to market, it is essential that it should be accompanied with the necessary statistical information. It is not of this, however, but of the total neglect of their endeavours, which planters complain. These, if stimulated by enquiry, would be induced to collect or to cultivate, to prepare, and to send to the markets of Europe, a new or little-known article, and to take measures for keeping up a regular supply for such manufacturers as might be the first induced to employ it. Information, therefore, both of a practical and of a scientific nature, is essential for bringing new or comparatively little-known articles into use.

But the attempt to diffuse information, and to take advantage of the public attention being directed to this subject, seems to be objected to by some political economists. For it is said—"Some persons, amongst the rest Mr. Sharp, seem anxious to profit by present circumstances, to bring forward the fibrous productions of India, to the exclusion of those of other countries. Their object is not trade, but to give employment to our fellow-subjects in our colonies and dependencies, &c." This at the same time that others are enquiring—Why are not the resources of India more largely developed? If the object were only to give occupation to our fellow-subjects of the East, it would still be a laudable one, as many have been deprived of their hereditary occupations as weavers, by the gigantic progress made by the cotton trade of this country. But who the parties are who have attempted to give this occupation, without attending to the legitimate demands of trade, does not appear. Certainly not those who have been adopting very effective measures for securing, as an article of trade, ample supplies of fibrous material now produced in enormous quantities in different parts of the world, and allowed everywhere to go to waste, though capable of the most important applications, both here and elsewhere. It is also said, that the object in the main seems to be, "enriching some few hundreds or thousands of our countrymen, who have estates, or a pecuniary interest in the East and West Indies." The objections to enriching one party at the expense of another, was never thought of when thousands of the weavers of Dacca were ruined, at the same time that the manufacturers of cotton goods here were enriched. But this effect was inevitable, as the high state of mechanical invention in England produced machinery of which the products could undersell those of the Indian loom, even in the distant fields where the cotton was grown.

In the present, as in all other instances, the Indian ryot is quiescent and indifferent. It is the manufacturers and Chambers of Commerce of this country who enquire, that as war diminishes the ordinary supplies, why cannot their wants be supplied from India, as that country grows what they want? Opportunity has therefore been taken, and we trust wisely taken, to direct attention to the neglected riches of our Indian empire, and thus to remove some of the difficulties which impede the introduction of new things into market. Feeling confident, that as the country possesses many fibres which are of good quality, and the climate, where both land and labour are cheap, is favorable to their growth, that some of the success which eventually attended the efforts made during the last war, will attend the present attempts. Indeed, we trust to a still greater extent, as some of the fibres now available are possessed of the strength of the best of those then tried, but which, from their rarity, were not procurable in sufficient quantities for the purposes of commerce. All that is attempted is to inform the consumer here of what India is capable of supplying, and of enabling the producer there to send it in such a state to market as to attract the attention of the intelligent manufacturer. That is, to put information before him in its most complete form, and accompanied by specimens which can be handled, either in their raw state, or as converted into cordage; with accounts of the growth and culture of the plants, their productiveness, and prices. Thus it may be hoped, that the distant cultivator of India, himself in so different a state of society, may be placed on a footing to meet the demands of the more advanced manufacturers of Europe at the average prices of ordinary times. In so doing, though not imitating, we are only pursuing the path which has at last been taken in this country of forming Trade Museums for the exhibition of specimens, and the diffusion of information respecting the raw products of all parts of the world. We might go further, and yet have good precedents to adduce—as, for instance, the yearly grant of £1000 a year to the Royal Flax Improvement Society, for the culture of flax in Ireland, a measure which, though unnecessary in England, has certainly been most useful in that country.

THE NATURE OF VEGETABLE FIBRE.

Before proceeding to take into consideration the different kinds of fibre, or the plants which yield them, it is desirable to have some definite ideas respecting the nature of fibre, and in what kinds or parts of plants we may expect to find it.

Plants are found to be composed of CELLS only, or both CELLS and VESSELS.

Cells are completely closed vesicles, usually containing fluid, of which the sides are formed of excessively thin and pellucid membrane. This is their characteristic when young, but as they get older their sides become thickened by the deposit in their interior of more solid material. Though these cells are destitute of visible pores, they are necessarily permeated by fluids, which deposit the matters found within their interior; and among others of the secondary cell-membranes, which in certain states possess a fibrous structure. These are by some, indeed, supposed to be composed of primitive fibres, often arranged spirally, which are of extreme fineness and transparency, but which in time become thickened like the cells.

Vessels.—Cells may be short and varying in form, or oblong; sometimes much elongated, as is the case with Cotton. But at other times, several cells becoming joined end to end and the intervening partitions absorbed, form vessels, which, like the cells, become thickened on their sides, and have formed within them fibrous matter of different kinds. Neither cells nor vessels are fitted for yielding useful fibrous material, either for cordage or for textile fabrics; but, as many contain fibre as a part of their structure, they may be reduced into pulp for paper-making.

Woody Tissue or Fibre.—Within the cellular tissue are found the above-described vessels, and along with them what is called woody *fibre* or tissue. This, together with some vascular bundles, constitutes collectively the chief part of the wood of plants, and gives support to the whole vegetable fabric. These woody fibres consist of elongated cells or tubes with tapering extremities, which overlap each other, and by their union longitudinally form the fibres which are extracted for economic purposes. But when so obtained, they are seldom separated into their ultimate fibres, but, rather united together into bundles of fibres. These are found in the wood, in the inner bark, and in the leaves of plants.

These woody fibres are extremely slender and transparent, but tough. Like the membrane of the cells, that of the fibre is also without pores, but permeable to fluids, and becomes thickened by the internal deposition of layer within layer, of matter which surrounds the cavity of the cell. In length these constituent cells of the fibre do not exceed from one third to one line. The bast cells of flax and hemp are long, but it is difficult to measure them exactly, as it is impossible to ascertain where one cell terminates and another begins. When moistened, "considerable swelling takes place, principally in the direction of the breadth, and only in a small degree in the longitudinal direction."

The original membrane which forms the basis of the fibre-cell is composed of carbon, hydrogen, and oxygen. But, as Mohl has observed, "the combination of cell-membrane with inorganic substances, is a very general condition. In almost all plants, a skeleton (the ash), corresponding to the form of the membrane, and composed of the alkalies, earths, and metallic oxides which had been deposited in it, remains behind after the cell has been burnt. The younger an elementary organ is, the more abundant, in general, the alkalies appear to be; the older it is, the more exclusively the earths and metallic oxides seem to be combined with its substance." Hence the best fibres are found in the young bark of plants, or in fleshy leaves; and therefore, plants when grown for their fibre, are generally sown and grown close together. This is done in order to favour their shooting upwards, and to prevent their too great exposure to heat, light, and air, which favour the formation of the different secretions of the plant and the consequent hardening of the woody fibre.

PREPARATION OF FIBRE AND OF CORDAGE.

This woody or fibrous tissue, formed as it is by the junction, end to end, of elongated cells, is, when in its natural state in the living plant, adherent to the membranous sides of the cellular tissue, and surrounded with mucilaginous, resinous, or other vegetable secretions. It must, necessarily, be separated from all these before it can be applied to any economical purpose.

This separation of the fibre from the rest of the vegetable matter is effected, either by stripping the bark from trees, or taking fibre-yielding leaves, and pounding them between stones and subsequently washing; or simply picking the fibres by hand, and thus separating them from the rest of the vegetable mass. But it is more usual, and also more expeditious, to separate the fibres by previous maceration in water. Fermentation then takes place, much of the vegetable tissue becomes destroyed, the fibres loosened, and then easily separated by washing or beating. Various attempts have also been made to separate the fibres by mechanical means. These, as well as the other methods suited to different plants, will be described under their respective heads, but more especially in the section which treats of Flax, as that plant and its fibre has had much attention devoted to it.

But fibres, when thus separated for economical purposes, are rather bundles of fibres than in the separated state of the ultimate fibre. Sometimes the commercial fibre, or some portion of it, is in the state, as stripped from the stems, of narrow flat ribbons, and therefore with sharp edges. Hence the necessity of passing them between rollers, or of submitting them to a rough process of combing, called *heckling*. Thus, not only impurities are got rid of, but the fibres are divided, laid parallel, and the short ones separated, constituting *codilla* or *tow*.

The longest of these fibres being usually not more than from three to four feet in length, are obviously too short for conversion into ropes of any length, or for weaving into cloth, without first undergoing some preparation. The natives of the great Eastern Archipelago join the ends of different fibres together by means of some adhesive substance, and thus form the "invisible knots" of an old author and obtain a thread, which, without spinning or twisting, is long enough for weaving.

If this were practicable with all fibres, they might be joined together end to end, then laid side by side and formed into bundles, which might be wrapped round or tied at intervals, and form a rope in which the strength of each fibre would be retained. Some ropes thus made for the purpose of experiment by Duhamel, were found to be of great strength but of little durability. The outer case wore off, and the rope opened at the bendings, so as to let in water. This being retained, assisted the decomposition of the rope.

It has been long discovered that we may obtain length by twisting fibres together, when they press upon each other, so that any single fibre is unable to overcome the resistance, caused by the friction upon it of surrounding fibres. It will then break more readily than slip out from the mass. By this means, a certain degree of compactness is also obtained, so that the infiltration of water is prevented, and the rope preserved from decomposition. Though a certain degree of twist is essential, any excess is injurious; for a rope may be so twisted as to break in the operation. And therefore a rope, brought up to this point without breaking, would be unable to bear any further strain, or to support any weight at all, and consequently be useless. Great precautions are therefore necessary in twisting the fibres, so that they shall retain as much as possible of their original strength, and be preserved from sustaining any further injury.

In making a rope, the first operation is to twist a certain portion of the fibres into a thick thread, which is called a *yarn*. These yarns vary in size, from one twelfth to a little above one ninth of an inch in diameter. These yarns are then *warped*, or stretched so that they may bear any strain equally. The next process is to twist a number of yarns, say from fifteen to twenty-five, into a *strand*. The twist of the strand is in an opposite direction to that of the yarn of which it is composed, in order that any tendency in the yarns to untwist may be counteracted by an opposite tendency in the strand. Three of these strands are formed into a *rope*, and three ropes into a *cable*. The term rope is generally confined to those which are above an inch in circumference; those which are less being called *twine*, *line*, and *cord;* though some of the latter terms are used with less strictness, as *fishing lines* and *clothes lines* are of very different diameters. Other kinds are distinguished by the name of ratline or of lashing; sometimes they are distinguished by the weight of a certain quantity—thus, pound line signifies a line weighing 60 yards to the pound: 160 fathoms of white or untarred yarn weigh from two and a half to four pounds.

In a popular work by Mr. Tomlinson, the different operations of ropemaking are described as follow: 1. *Heckling*, or hackling, of which the object is to separate the short fibres or tow, and to straighten the long ones, in order to enable them to run freely in spinning. 2. *Spinning*, or twisting the fibres into threads or yarns. 3. *Tarring* the yarns. 4. *Twisting* the yarns into strands. 5. *Laying*, or twisting three strands together, so as to form what is called a *hawser-laid* rope. In this process, which is called the *first lay*, each strand consists of as many yarns as are found requisite to give the required thickness to the rope. 6. *Second lay*, or *shroud hawser-laid rope*. This consists of four strands laid in the same way and under the same conditions. This rope has a straight loose strand, consisting frequently of only a few yarns, running through its centre; the object of this core-piece being to render the rope solid. 7. *Third lay*, or *cable-laid rope*. This consists of three hawser-laid ropes, each formed of three large strands, twisted or laid together in one gigantic rope or cable.

A very important consideration is the due degree of twisting which ropes ought to receive in order to retain the utmost degree of strength. Another is the benefit or injury which is derived from a large or a small quantity of tar, because this, instead of being a preservative in all situations, as is generally supposed, is very often injurious, as is fully illustrated by the following experiments. The abridged account of these we have taken from Sir D. Brewster's 'Edinburgh Encyclopædia:'

It was long ago shown by Dr. Hooke, from several experiments on the strength of cordage in 1669, that the strength of the component parts of the rope was diminished by twisting. This fact, indeed, has been long practically known to sailors, who are familiar with the superior strength of rope yarns when made up into a *salvage*, which is nothing more than a skein without twisting. Salvages are invariably used for slinging great guns, rolling tackles, and for every kind of work where great strength and great pliancy are required.

In the 'Memoirs of the Academy of Sciences,' M. Reaumur has given an account of his experiments on the strength of ropes compared with that of their parts.

2. The yarn of a skein of white thread bore each, at an average, $9\frac{3}{4}$ lb. Two yarns twisted slack into a cord broke with 16 lb.

Hence we have the absolute strength of two yarns	$19\frac{1}{2}$ lb.
Real strength	16
Loss of strength by twisting	$3\frac{1}{2}$ lb.

3. The average strength of some thread was such, that each broke with 8 lb., whereas when *three* were twisted they bore only $17\frac{1}{2}$ lb.

Hence we have absolute strength	24 lb.
Real strength	$17\frac{1}{2}$
Loss of strength by twisting	$6\frac{1}{2}$ lb.

4. The average strength of some thread was such, that each broke with $7\frac{1}{2}$ lb., whereas when *four* were twisted they broke with $21\frac{1}{2}$ lb.

Hence we have absolute strength	30 lb.
Real strength	$21\frac{1}{2}$
Loss of strength by twisting	$8\frac{1}{2}$ lb.

5. The average strength of other four threads was such that each broke with 9 lb., whereas when twisted, they broke with 22 lb.

Hence we have absolute strength	36 lb.
Real strength	22
Loss of strength by twisting	14 lb.

6. A well made and small hempen cord broke in different places with 58, 63, 67, and 72 lb., so that its average strength was $\frac{58 + 63 + 67 + 72}{4} = 65$ lb. The cord consisted of three strands, and another part of it was untwisted, and its three strands separated. One of them bore $29\frac{1}{2}$, another $33\frac{1}{2}$, and the third 35.

Hence the absolute strength of the three strands, when separate, is	98 lb.
Real strength when twisted	65
Loss by twisting	33 lb.

7. Another part of the same cord, which broke with 72 lb., was separated into its strands, when they bore 26, 28, and 30 pounds.

Hence we have absolute strength	84 lb.
Real strength	72
Loss by twisting	12 lb.

Dr. Robison has given an account of a very interesting experiment by Sir Charles Knowles, upon a piece of white or untarred rope, $3\frac{1}{3}$ inches in circumference. It was cut into many portions, and from each of those portions a fathom was taken off, and carefully opened out. It consisted of 72 yarns, each of which was examined separately, and found to bear 90 lb. at an average for the whole. Each piece of rope corresponding to these was examined separately, and the mean strength of the same pieces was 4552 lb.

Hence we have absolute strength of yarns . . .	6480 lb.
Real strength	4552
Loss of strength by twisting . . .	1928 lb.

As the diminution of strength in the yarns, demonstrated by the preceding example, obviously arises from their position when twisted, in consequence of which they do not all bear the load at the same time; and not from any permanent weakness produced by the twisting it became reasonable to believe, that the twist given to ropes should be as moderate as possible.

* * * * *

The degree of twist commonly employed was such that the rope was *two thirds* the length of the yarns which composed it. M. Duhamel,[1] who made many valuable experiments on this subject, in the royal dock-yards of France, caused some rope, to be worked with only *three fourths* of the length of the yarn. This last rope with the inferior degree of twist, bore 5187 lb., whereas the other bore only 4321 lb. He next caused these ropes to be made with different twists, and obtained the following results:

Degree of twist.	Weight borne by each. One experiment.	Another experiment.
$\frac{2}{3}$	4098	4250
$\frac{3}{4}$	4850	6753
$\frac{4}{5}$	6205	7397

So far these experiments were highly satisfactory; but it still remained to be seen, whether or not the ropes which had an inferior degree of twist, had not also an inferior degree of useful solidity, notwithstanding their superiority of strength in carrying weights.

In order to determine this point, M. Duhamel had a considerable quantity of rigging made with yarns, wrought up into only *three fourths* of their length, and got them put into actual use on ship-board, during a whole campaign. The report given by the officers of the ship was highly satisfactory. They proved that the ropes thus manufactured were *one fourth* lighter than the common kind; that they were nearly *one eighth* more slender, so as to give less hold to the wind; that, from their being more pliant than the common ones, they run easier through the blocks, and did not run into what are technically called kinks; that the new cordage required fewer hands to work it, in the proportion of *two* to *three;* and that it was at least *one fourth* stronger.

* * * * *

Wherever ropes are not exposed to short bendings, as in the case of standing rigging, where they can be defended from water by tarring, &c., the least twisted cordage may be advantageously employed, and should, according to M. Duhamel's experiments, be made from strands; for it is demonstrable that in fine stranded cordage, when the twist of the strands is

[1] 'Traité de la Fabrique des Manœuvres pour les Vaisseaux, ou l'Art de la Corderie perfectionée.'

exactly equal to the twist in the laying, the strands lie less obliquely to the axis than in other ropes, and therefore bear a greater load.

* * * * *

In examining the strength of cordage, $3\frac{1}{2}$ inches in circumference and under, M. Duhamel found that the strength increased a little faster than the number of equal threads, thus:

Ropes of	bore	instead of
9 threads	1014	946 lb.
12	1564	1262
18	2148	1893

According to the experiments of Mr. Huddart, no strength is lost in the common way when there are only three yarns in the strand. When there are more than three yarns, the loss is one sixth, and with a hundred yarns it is about one half. His registered cordage, according to theory, loses nothing, but by actual experiment it loses one eighth.

The following rule is given by Dr. Robison for obtaining the strength of ropes:

Multiply the circumference of the rope in inches by itself, and the fifth part of the product will be the number of tons which the rope will carry.

For example, if the rope is 6 inches in circumference, we have 6 times 6 = 36, the fifth of which is $7\frac{1}{5}$ tons.

Tarring Ropes.—There is no branch of the rope manufacture more important than that which relates to the tarring of the cordage. The following experiments were therefore made by M. Duhamel on the relative strength of tarred and white or untarred cordage.

	Untarred Rope.	Tarred Rope.	Difference.
August 8th, 1741.			
Broke with	4500 pounds.	3400 pounds.	1100
	4900	3300	1600
	4800	3250	1550
April 25th, 1743.			
Broke with	4600 pounds.	3500 pounds.	1100
	5000	3400	1600
	5000	3100	1900
Sept. 3d, 1746.			
Broke with	3800 pounds.	3000 pounds.	800
	4000	2700	1300
	4200	2800	1400

The ropes with which the preceding experiments were made, were three French inches in circumference, and were made of the best Riga hemp.

M. Duhamel next examined the relative strength of a parcel of tarred and untarred cordage, which had been manufactured on the 12th of July, 1746. It had been laid up in the storehouse, and the following results were obtained at the dates mentioned.

	Difference of time in Months.	Untarred Rope.	Tarred Rope.	Difference.
		Pounds.	Pounds.	Pounds.
1746. April 14th .		2645	2312	333
1747. May 18th .	11	2762	2155	607
1747. Oct. 21st .	6	2710	2050	660
1748. June 19th .	9	2575	1752	823
1748. Oct. 2d . .	4	2425	1837	588
1749. Sept. 25th .	12	2917	1865	1052

From these results M. Duhamel concludes:

1. That *untarred cordage* in constant service is *one third* more durable than the same cordage when tarred.

2. That *untarred cordage* retains its strength for a much longer time when it is kept in store.

3. That *untarred cordage* resists the ordinary injuries of the weather *one fourth* longer than when it is tarred.

These results of direct experiments have been confirmed by the observations of seamen; but they have invariably found, that untarred cordage is weaker than tarred cordage, when it is exposed to be alternately wet and dry; that tarred cordage is chiefly useful for cables and ground tackle, which must be constantly soaked in water; and that cordage, *superficially tarred*, is always stronger than what is thoroughly tarred, and resists better the alternate conditions of dryness and wetness.

Several important experiments on the relative strengh of tarred and untarred ropes were made by Mr W. Chapman,[1] chiefly with the view of determining the effects of his method of preserving ropes with purified or washed tar. Three pieces of rope were made on the 10th of August, 1808, of 12 threads in each strand. The first was an untarred rope, the second a rope made of washed tarred yarn, and the third a common tarred rope. A part of each of these ropes had their strength tried on the breaking machine; and another part was steeped in water for about three months, and then taken to a foundry stove, which is supposed to have been at about 130° of Fahrenheit. They remained in the stove about three months. After that they lay at Mr. Chapman's ropery till Nov. 3d, 1803, when the following experiments were made with them:

	When made. Aug. 10th, 1802.	Nov. 3d, 1803.	Portion of original Strength retained.
	Cwt.	Cwt.	Cwt.
White rope	33·4	1·9	5·7 pr. cent.
Common tarred rope . .	22·2	7·35	33·0 pr. cent.
Washed tarred rope . .	29·1	12·35	43·8 pr. cent.

The tarred ropes were both brittle; but the latter was more so, and they both cracked on bending.[1]

[Mr. Chapman has also observed that though cordage is injured by tarring in cold climates, it is much more rapidly so in hot climates.]

The following experiments were made in 1807, by Mr. Chapman, for the purpose of showing the injury arising from the retention of that portion of the essential oil which cannot be dispensed with, and also the injury which arises from the progressive disengagement of the acid of essential oil.

	Weight with which it broke when Moist.	Weight with which it broke after exposure to a Stove for four months.
	Cwt.	Cwt.
Untarred rope	45·75	38·97
Rope tarred with cold tar .	51·29	26·40
Ditto with boiled tar.	38·94	25·07

[1] Author of 'Treatise on the progressive endeavours to improve the Manufacture and Duration of Cordage;' London, 1808.

The first column shows the strength of the rope when made; and the second after having been exposed to the heat of a stove from 85° to 100° Fahr.

The following experiments, also made by Mr. Chapman, confirm those of Duhamel, respecting the diminution in the strength of cordage produced by tarring. The ropes were registered on the improved principle, and were made with the same yarn, and with 17 threads in each strand.

	Girt in inches.		Comparative Strength.
		Cwt.	Cwt.
1806. Oct. 2. White rope .	2·75	Broke with 75	100
„ Oct. 24. Tarred rope .	2·8	„ 55	73·3
1807. May 8. Same rope .	2·8	„ 41·4	55·2

The following experiments were made with ropes made of the same yarns, and of nine in each strand.

	Girt in inches.		Comparative Strength.
		Cwt.	Cwt.
White rope . . .	1·7	Broke with 27·5	100
Tar of whale oil .	1·85	„ 22·5	83·7
Tar and tallow . .	1·8	„ 17·5	63·6
Tar unpurified . .	1·7	„ 15·95	57·7

Whale oil and tallow have therefore an excellent effect, particularly the former.

* * * * *

The following experiments were made by Mr. Chapman on the elasticity of ropes of different kinds, when strained with $\frac{7}{8}$ths of their breaking stress:

	Original Length.	Length when Strained.
	Inches.	Inches.
Registered primary strands . .	24	24¾ to 25
Registered shroud laid ropes . .	24	26 to 26½
Common made shroud laid rope .	24	27½ to 28
Registered cable laid rope . .	24	27 to 27½

The three kinds of rope last mentioned, stretched on an average 1 inch in 24 with a fifth of their breaking stress, which is from $\frac{1}{3}$ to $\frac{2}{5}$lb. of the whole stretching of the registered shroud laid ropes, but only from $\frac{2}{7}$ths to $\frac{1}{4}$th of the stretching of the common made shroud ropes.

In May, 1805, Sir Joseph Banks, being anxious to try teak tar for ropes, two three-inch ropes were made of the same yarns, one with teak tar, and the other with common tar. They were then placed in the same storehouse, and were broken Sept. 28th, 1807.

Common tarred rope broke with 3848 pounds.
That made with teak tar broke with 5980
The common tarred rope being only about *two thirds* the strength of the other.

It is interesting to conclude with a notice of the efficacy of an Indian product. It will probably be found that the Indian practice of tanning ropes is also efficacious, and has the advantage of not injuring the texture of the fibre, as will be mentioned when noticing Dr. Roxburgh's experiments.

ARRANGEMENT OF FIBROUS PLANTS.

In treating of the different Indian fibres, it is desirable to adopt some methodical, instead of an accidental arrangement. For such, as for instance, the alphabetical, would necessarily be irregular, when the selection of the names must be made from a variety of languages, according to the places where a fibre or the plant yielding it is best known. Preference will of course always be given to any name known in commerce. But some of the articles to be treated of are unknown in the markets of Europe, and a few, though common in every part of India, are yet not known there by any common name. A selection must, therefore, be made of one of the names, as this is essential for distinguishing the articles one from another, and to assist in fixing the attention upon each individually. Thus we shall avoid calling every new fibre, *hemp*, when one only can properly be so named. In the same way, the South Sea Islanders called every new animal they saw, a pig, because that was the only one with which they were acquainted.

Without entering into minute details, we shall adopt an arrangement founded upon the botanical affinities of plants, not purely because it is scientific, and therefore more satisfactory; but because it will enable us to make a number of comparisons with fibres obtained from plants of the same family in other parts of the world. It will also enable us to draw some practical deductions from the information we may thus bring together. Though I have no doubt that some who consider themselves eminently practical, will sneer at the idea of a scientific arrangement being productive of such results.

Botanists have for some time arranged all plants into a few large divisions, from characters derived from their internal structure: thus, some being composed of cells only, are called *Cellular;* others are called *Vascular,* because, in addition to cells, they also contain vessels usually accompanied by woody tissue. The cellular tissue being developed in every direction, is sometimes called the *horizontal* system, while the vascular growing vertically, is distinguished as the *longitudinal* system. It is in this direction that the fibres of which we have to treat are placed in the plant. The development and arrangement of these two systems produce three distinct forms of growth and of internal structure.

Acrogens, or summit growers, so called from the growth of the stem taking place by the junction of the bases of the leaves at the top of the stem, as in Tree Ferns. Under this—used as a general term—cellular plants, such as Mosses, &c., are included; but none of them yield fibre, either for cordage or for textile purposes, though it is possible that some of the ferns contain fibre enough to form pulp for paper-makers.

Endogens, or inside growers, are so called because the bundles of vessels and fibres proceed from the bases of the leaves into the cellular centre of the stem, and are thence pushed outwards by the new growths, so that the outside of such stems, as of Palms, is harder than the inside. These plants have no regular bark which can be stripped off, and their leaves have the veins running parallel to each other. It is these leaves which abound in fibre, which may be separated by simple pressure and washing, as in the Pine-apple, Agave or American aloe, Plantain, and many others. In Palms, the structure of the leaves is too dense for the fibres to be separated so easily.

Exogens, or outside growers, are so called from additions to their stems being made on the outside of the growth of former years, as seen in the rings of wood on a transverse section of the trunk of any of the ordinary trees of Europe. There is also a distinct bark, of which the outer part is composed of cellular, but the inner contains the woody tissue. From this the fibres are separated for various economic purposes, usually by stripping off the bark and then steeping it in water, as with Flax and Hemp, Jute and Sunn. The leaves of Exogens have a reticulated or net-like, instead of a parallel venation.

The above characters, taken from the parts of vegetation, are found to be accompanied by others equally characteristic, in the parts of fructification. Thus the spores of Acrogens, in germinating, are unaccompanied by anything like a leaf; the Endogens have a single seed-leaf, as may be seen in Wheat and other Cereals, as the Rice; while Exogens, in sprouting display two of these seed-leaves, as in Peas and Beans.

From these peculiarities other names are given to the above divisions, but which it is needless for our purposes to notice.

PREPARATION OF THE FIBRE OF ENDOGENS.

Though both the stem and the leaves abound in fibre, it is from the latter chiefly that this is separated for practical purposes. The fibres of some plants are not separated from the rest of the vegetable matter, but the stems and leaves are simply dried and twisted, as in the case of some Grasses, Sedges, Rushes, and even the leaves of Palms. The leaves of others are simply beaten with a stone on a flat board or on another stone, and afterwards the rest of the vegetable matter washed away. Occasionally such fleshy leaves have been passed between rollers, as those of a sugar-mill, and with the consequent saving of both time and labour, also with a diminution of cost. Very frequently, however, these leaves are steeped in water until fermentation takes place, when the labour of separating the fibre is much diminished. But this often takes place with great loss of strength as well as of the beautiful white colour, for which most of these endogenous fibres are particularly distinguished.

Dr. Hunter, who has paid much attention to the separation of this class of fibres, has observed that the ordinary modes of separating the fibres of plants in India, that is, steeping them in water, are exceedingly faulty. Every day's steeping of a vegetable substance in water takes from its strength, and communicates a tinge to the fibres which can only be removed by the subsequent application of some chemical agent, such as lime, the alkalies or chlorine, which in some cases, no doubt, diminishes their strength. He observes that in most parts of India the fermentation which takes place in plants heaped together or steeped in water proceeds so rapidly, that it is extremely difficult to prevent the accession of putrefactive decomposition. This, he says, commences in succulent plants, when immersed in water, in twenty or twenty-two hours, during warm weather. The sooner, therefore, that the decomposing parts of a plant—that is, the mucilaginous, saccharine, and other constituents of the sap and pulp—are removed, the whiter are the fibres, and they retain more of their original strength. The fibres cleaned within a day or two after the plant or leaf had been cut, were found to be white, strong, and silky. On wetting the same repeatedly and exposing them to the dew, it has been found that their strength is impaired.

Those fibres that were steeped in water for a few days acquired somewhat of the colour of English tow. Those steeped for three weeks became quite rotten, brown, and brittle. Dr. Hunter has further ascertained by experiment that the partial drying of the leaves or bark of plants in the sun, as recommended and practised by the natives, does more harm than good, as it makes the process of cleaning more tedious, and is apt to tinge the fibres. Such as have been thoroughly dried in the sun before being cleaned, give brittle and often brown-coloured fibres, unless there be naturally very little moisture to be dried up. The only way he found of preparing fibres by rotting, is that followed by the natives in a few localities near large rivers, where the leaves of the Agave, from their outside hardness, are sometimes buried under wet sand below the level of the water in the river.

GRASSES (*Gramina*).

The grasses so extensively diffused, and in different forms as pasturage for cattle and corn for man, so essential for the continued existence of the animal kingdom, are seldom thought of as materials for cordage. Yet they were probably the first substances which were converted into rope; for the simple twisting between the hands of the flexible leaves and pliant stems of many of the grasses will form a rope, as is daily practised with bands of hay or those of straw. In the chairs of the Crystal Palace, we may see the rush-like bottoms are formed of the twisted straw of rye. Others are employed for thatching, and some for platting, screen- and mat-making. All purposes which indicate the presence of fibre of sufficient tenacity to bear at least a certain degree of strain and of pressure. But in these plants, as well as in sedges and rushes, the fibre is not always separated from the rest of the vegetable matter, but the whole leaf or stem is dried, and used in its entire state. As the fibre, however, possesses the requisite degree of tenacity, it can be separated in the form of pulp and used for paper-making, as will be again mentioned in the subsequent pages.

The grasses abound in India; in the plains are numerous species of genera little known in Europe; with the cultivation of rice, maize, joar, and many millets in the rainy season; and in the cold weather, of wheat, barley, oats, and millet; while in the Himalayas the pasture-grasses are many of them the same as in Europe, and the cereals are cultivated in the spring and summer, with some rice in the rains. (*v.* Author's paper 'On the Corn and Pasture-Grasses of India, in Illustrations of Himalayan Botany,' pp. 415—427; reprinted in 'Trans. Agric. Soc. of India,' viii, p. 91.)

Though the grasses were probably among the first substances used for cordage, none of them seem ever to have been objects of export commerce; partly because they are so universally diffused, and partly because they are bulky and deficient in strength. One or two have, however, been sufficiently distinguished to have been noticed by the ancients. One of these is the Esparto of the Spaniards, supposed to be the Spartum of the Romans. It is probable, however, that a very different plant (*Spartium junceum*) was also sometimes included under this name, for it was not uncommon for what we consider very different plants to be included under one general name, if they were used for the same purposes. Indeed, it is not unusual, even in the present day, for very different substances to be included under one general term; as is the case, for instance, with the word *hemp*, of which we shall have to mention several instances. The *Esparto* of the south of Spain, especially of the provinces of Huesca, Murcia, and Almeria, is *Stipa* (or Macrochloa) *tenacissima*, called "mat-weed" by Ray, and supposed to be "the rush of a dry soil" of Pliny. It grows in tufts, with long leaves, and is still used by the Spaniards for making sandals, mats, baskets, and ropes; and also sacks, nets, and toils, which the shepherds use as hurdles for their sheep. Some seems to have been exported both to the South of France and into Italy, for making baskets, sacks, and ropes, as this was prohibited in 1783 and 1790. It is also employed for stuffing palliasses; and some paper made of it was sent to the Exhibition of 1851. *Lygeum Spartum* is supposed by others to be one kind of Spartum, as it is also called

Esparto by the Spaniards. *Arundo arenaria* is used in the Hebrides for many of the same purposes as Esparto is by the Spaniards.

In India several of the indigenous grasses are employed for the same purposes as the above. Thus the *Moonja* of the natives (*Saccharum Munja*) is collected after the rainy season and kept for use, as it is employed in tying up their cattle at night and for ropes for their Persian wheels. It is said also to be one of the grasses employed for making tow-ropes by the boatmen about Benares. The *Shur* or *Sara* of Bengal (*Saccharum Sara*), or the Pen reed grass, Mr. Henley informs me is another species employed by the boatmen about Allahabad and Mirzapore, and esteemed as a tow-line for its strength and durability even when exposed to the action of water. It is said to be beaten into a rude fibre and then twisted into a rope.

Besides the above, the sacred grass of the Hindoos, the *dab* or *koosha* of the Brahmins (*Poa cynosuroides*), is also made into rope in North-West India. Other species of Saccharum are used for thatching and for screens, and some for making writing-pens and for arrows. The fibres of the *Khuskhus* or Vetiveyr are more remarkable for their agreeable odour than for their tenacity, while the Bamboo, the most gigantic of grasses, might be enumerated with timbers rather than with fibres, though its split stems are often employed for making mats in India, and the young shoots for paper-making by the Chinese. Many others of the grasses might be converted into half-stuff for paper-makers, and have the great advantage of affording large quantities of a cheap material.

The *Nul* or *Nar* of Bengal is described as being employed for making the mats known by the name of Durma, which are formed of the stalks split open. Dr. Stocks informs me that in Sindh the grass called *Sur*, which perhaps is *Arundo karka*, has its culms, *sur jo kanee*, made into chairs, and its flower-stalks beaten to form the fibres called *moonyah*. These are made into string or twine (*moonyah jo naree*), and into ropes (*moonyah jo russa*).

While this sheet is passing through the press, I have been informed by Mr. Burns, of the Indus Flotilla, who has been several years in Sindh, that the boatmen of the Indus universally employ the Moonj (probably the above *Saccharum*

Munja) as a towing rope and for the rigging of their vessels, in all places above Sukkur. But below that place Coir rope is very generally employed, being better able, I believe, to stand the action of salt water. The Moonja, however, is possessed of great tenacity, as is evident from two-inch ropes, often fifty fathoms in length, made of its fibres, being sufficient for dragging their largest or 1200-maund boats up the Indus, and consequently against the full force of the stream, even round projecting points. The rope is also possessed of lightness, so advantageous for rigging, and is capable, also, of bearing, without injury, alternate exposure to wet and to subsequent drying. Both qualities being essential for a tow-rope. Mr. Burns has also informed me that plants growing beyond the range of the overflowings of the river, or of the influence of the tides—that is, in the interior of the country, where, indeed, it grows in vast abundance—are possessed of the greatest strength. The upper leaves, about a foot or so in length, are preferred and collected. Having been made up into bundles, they are kept for use. When required for twisting into rope, they are first moistened in water: two men then, sitting opposite to each other, take one of these moist bundles and beat it alternately with mallets, until the loose cellular are separated from the fibrous parts. These are then ready for twisting into the ropes which are so extensively employed on the Indus. It is evident that a continuation of the same process, or the employment of the *Dhenkee* of India, would afford a very ample supply of half-stuff for paper-makers, and at a cheap rate.

SEDGES (*Cyperacæ*).

Sedges nearly resemble grasses in appearance, but grow usually in moist situations, and are distinguished from them by their angular stems. They are remarkable for so few of them being useful for any purpose—not even for fodder. One of them, however, is famous as having yielded the Papyrus of the Egyptians, employed by them for making paper, ropes, and even boats; and of which the plant is so frequently represented in their sculpture and paintings. An Indian species of Cyperus (*C. tegetum*, Roxb.; called *Papyrus Pangorei* by Nees von Esenbeck), the *Madoorkati* of the Bengalees, which is extremely common about Calcutta and in Bengal, is very extensively employed for making the elegant, shining and useful mats for which the capital of India is famous, and which are frequently imported into Europe. Dr. Roxburgh states that the culms or stalks of the plant when green are split into three or four pieces, which in drying, contract so much as to bring the margins in contact, in which state they are woven into mats, and thus show a nearly similar surface on both sides. Specimens of the strips of this sedge were sent to the Exhibition of 1851, as well as mats made of them. These strips are tied up in bundles about four inches in diameter and four feet in length, and seem, besides their extensive use for mat-making to be well adapted for platting.

The cotton-grass (*Eriophorum*) of Europe is a conspicuous ornament of turf-bogs and marshy moors, from having its seeds clothed at the base with a silky or cotton-like substance. With this, pillows are sometimes stuffed, and wicks of candles as well as paper, made. There is a species of the genus very common in the Himalayas, both in low valleys and at considerable elevations. This, I named *Eriophorum cannabinum*, in consequence of my finding it everywhere employed in making ropes for all ordinary purposes by the mountaineers. Its name, *bhabhur* and *bhabhuree*, has a considerable resemblance to that of the papyrus, considering that the *b* and *p* are letters so frequently interchanged for each other. All who have scrambled up the steeps of the Himalayas are sensible of the great support they have received from the toughness of the tufts of the bhabhur. Specimens of the dried leaves, made up into bundles about three feet in length, were sent to the Exhibition of 1851, from Beerbhoom. Also twine made from it: this, though rough, is strong and well fitted for ordinary purposes.

Capt. Huddleston, in a paper on the Hemp and other fibres of Gurhwal, in the Himalayas ('Trans. Agric. Soc. of India,' viii, p. 272), mentions the Bhabhur as holding a conspicuous place, "from its extensive use and most abundant supply throughout the whole of the hills, affording a most economical substitute as an article of cordage, in lieu of others of a more costly and durable nature. All the jhoolas or rope bridges, which are erected over the large rivers, where sanghas or wooden-planked bridges cannot be made, on all the principal thoroughfares of this district, are constructed of this silky species of grass, the cables of which are of a considerable thickness. These rope bridges are a very safe means of communication over the large and rapid rivers intersecting different parts of the country, both for travellers and men with loads; and, where the footway and sides are properly laced with brushwood, afford an easy enough roadway for loaded sheep—but neither ponies nor cattle can travel over them. This grass grows abundantly in all the ravines up the sides of the mountains, and is to be had only for the cutting—but it is not of a very durable nature, though pretty strong when fresh made into ropes. It lasts about a twelvemonth only, or a little more, and the people in charge of the rope bridges are constantly employed in repairing and annually renewing the ropes and stays. The 'chinkas,' or temporary bridges of a single cable, upon which traverses a seat in the shape of an ox-yoke, are also sometimes made of this grass."

Bulrushes (*Typhaceæ*).

Bulrushes, so conspicuous in the marshes of Europe, extend also to similar situations in most parts of India. The leaves are in some parts of Europe employed in making mats and winter coverings for plants, as well as for stuffing chairs. I have already recorded that the leaves of *putera* and *reree* (or *Typha elephantina* and *T. angustifolia*) are employed in making mats in North-West India. Dr. Stocks informs me that in Sindh the former is called *pun*, and its leaves employed for making mats and baskets. The pollen, like that of Lycopodium, is inflammable, and used as a substitute for it in Europe. It is also collected in Sindh, and there called *booree*.

Vacoa or Screw Pines (*Pandanaceæ*).

The Screw Pines, having fruit something like that of pines, and flowers not more developed than those of the Bulrush, are remarkable for their gigantic Bromelia-like leaves, arranged in a spiral manner. Though abounding most in

Mauritius and Bourbon, species are also found in the southern parts of India, as well as in the Straits and Burma. "The leaves are composed of tough longitudinal fibres, white and glossy, which enable them to be employed for covering huts, making matting, as well as for cordage, in the South Sea Islands; and in Mauritius for making sacks for coffee, sugar, and grain." ('Himal. Bot.,' p. 408.) The species which is best known in India is the *Keora* or *Ketgee*, the Kaldera bush of the Madras Peninsula, called *Pandanus odoratissimus* by botanists, on account of the exquisite perfume of its flowers. Dr. Roxburgh ('Fl. Indica,' iii, p. 741) has, under this plant, mentioned the uses to which the species most common in the Mauritius is applied; which, as well as some of the other species, is known there by the name Vacoa or Baquois. It appears to be the *Pandanus sativus* of Du Petit Thouars, but which Mr. Henley mentions as *P. Vacoa*. He having observed the valuable uses to which the plant was applied in the Mauritius, recommended its introduction into India; in some of the dry southern parts of which, it would, no doubt, though slow of growth, be a valuable acquisition, from the facility with which good sacking may be manufactured from its leaves. Mr. Henley describes this most useful Vacoa of the Mauritius to grow to the height of thirty feet, when permitted to do so; but, in general, the cropping of the leaves, which commences in the third year, keeps the plant down to the height of from six to ten feet. The plant is remarkable for the aerial leafless roots which it sends down as supports for its stem, and which are of so fibrous a nature as to be employed for making paint brushes for common purposes. The leaves are cut every second year, beginning when the plant is three years old, and each plant yields enough for two large bags. The preparation must begin with the leaves immediately they are removed from the trees, and consists, first, in splitting the leaves into fillets, which are from three fourths to one inch broad at the base, but taper to a point, and are from three to four feet in length. One of them will support the weight of a bag of sugar, or about 140 lb., without breaking. Mr. Henley states that the leaves of the other species with which he is acquainted are comparatively weak. ('Jour. Agric. Soc. of India,' 1843, p. 92.)

The Nipah Palm (*Nipa fruticans*), which, from the appearance of its foliage, is generally supposed to be a Palm, though stemless, but which, in the nature of its flowers, approaches the Screw Pines, is a plant of which the leaves are applied to mat-making and thatching. It is a native of the Indian Archipelago, which extends northwards to the Mergui River, where it is found in perfection, but only a few specimens as far north as Moulmain. It flourishes in brackish water, along with the Mangrove, and its lower parts are inundated when the tide rises. It abounds in saccharine sap, which may be evaporated into an excellent sugar, or fermented into a kind of "Palm wine." Its leaves are those chiefly employed in the Tenasserim provinces for covering the roofs of houses, and large quantities are sent northwards from Mergui for this purpose. They are also made into mats, and no doubt abound in fibre, though this is not separated for economic purposes.

The Pine-apple Tribe (*Bromeliaceæ*).

The Pine-apple, or Ananas, is so well known as an object of the most careful culture in Europe, on account of its pleasantly sweet and aromatic fruit, that we should not expect to find it included among cordage plants. But its long and rigid leaves, which are thorny at the edges and point, abound in a quantity of fine white fibres, which are, in some countries, woven into the finest fabrics, netted, or twisted into lines for fishing and into ropes possessed of considerable strength. These are said not to be injured by constant immersion in water—a property which the natives increase by tanning them. Not only the cultivated Pine-apple, but others of the genus and family, are possessed of similar properties, as the Penguin, or broad-leaved wild ananas (*Bromelia Penguin*), which is common on the rocky hills in Jamaica and other West India islands. It is employed in making fences to their fields; and its leaves, after being steeped in water and beaten with a wooden mallet, yield a strong fibre, which is twisted into ropes, and manufactured by the Spaniards into cloth, of which they make hammocks, &c. So *B. Karatas*, or upright-leaved wild ananas, which includes the Caraguata of Piso, and is common in South America; and the Curratow or Grawatha (*B. sagenaria*), probably the same as the Craute de rede, common on the coasts near Pernambuco, and other parts of Brazil. So also *B.* (now *Bilbergia*) *variegata*, or Caroa, which grows in wild luxuriance for miles, and yields excellent twine for nets in Brazil; and the so-called New Orleans moss or "long beard" (*Tillandsia usneoides*), of which a bale was sent to the Exhibition of 1851, and proposed as a substitute for hair, for stuffing chairs, cushions, and mattresses.

The fibre commonly called Curratow, is twisted into thick rope; one of these is said to have been in use for many years at the city of Paraiba, for hoisting in merchandise. Large anchors are said to have been dragged up with this rope, when those of hemp parted. (*v.* Koster's 'Travels in Brazil,' ii, p. 341.)

The cultivated Ananas, or Pine-apple, like the other species of Bromelia, is a native of the warm parts of the continent, or of the islands of America. The Spaniards and Portuguese, when introducing the plants of the Old World into the countries they discovered, also transferred some of those of America into the parts of the Old World with which they were connected, such as the west coast of Africa, the south of India, and the Phillipine Islands. In all of which, the pine-apple has become so established and apparently wild, as to be by some considered even to be indigenous.

The Pine-apple (*Ananassa sativa*, formerly Bromelia Ananas), being a native of the moist forests of South America, from the level of the sea to elevations of about 1800 feet, requires, for its successful culture as a fruit, a warm and moist climate; but, like others of the family, the species are capable of existing in a warm, dry air.

The Pine-apple is said to have been introduced into India by the Portuguese, in the year 1594. It has, in some parts, become so naturalised, as to appear indigenous. Capt. Turner, in his journey to Teshooloomboo, mentions it as very abundant at the foot of the Himalayas. It flourishes in Assam, and forms thickets near Rangoon, producing, also, according to the accounts of different visitors, very juicy, well-flavoured fruit. Dr. Wallich, in the year 1836, presented to the Agricultural Society, a bag made on the Khasia Hills, of Pine-apple fibre, having purchased it for a trifle at Cherapoujee. He mentions the enormous quantity of Pines grown on that range, and that the plant appears as if it were quite a natural production. Dr. Helfer describes the Pine-apple as so abundant in the Tenasserim provinces, as to be sold in Amherst Town in the months of June and July at the rate of one rupee for a boat-load. It chiefly abounds in low grounds, though it is also to be found in the hills amongst the Kareans. The natives know it only by the American name, which they transform into *Nannah thi*—thi designating fruit. They do not seem to be acquainted with the beautiful fibre yielded by the leaves.

The Pine-apple is described as growing in great abundance in the Phillipine Islands, but as producing only a small, rather dry fruit. But we require some precise information to enable us to judge whether this is actually the plant escaped from cultivation. M. Perrotet considers it a distinct species, and has named it *Bromelia Pigna,* from the Spanish name *Pigna* or *Pina,* signifying a cone. There, this wild plant is valued on account of the fine hair-like fibres which are separated from out of the leaves. Of these fibres, the celebrated pine-apple cloth of the Phillipines, sometimes called "batiste d'ananas," and resembling the finest muslin-like fabric, is woven. This is embroidered by the nuns of the convents in Manilla, with great skill and taste. Some beautiful specimens of these, under the name of Pina muslin, were to be seen in the Exhibition of 1851. This is sometimes called grass-cloth, but erroneously. With a magnifier the fibres may be seen to be very numerous and fine, but not twisted at all, as in grass-cloth or the finest muslins and cambrics. Mr. Bennett, in his 'Wanderings,' observes that one of the coarser fibres may be subdivided into threads of such fineness as to be barely perceptible, and yet sufficiently strong for any purpose.

Mr. Bennett mentions visiting a plantation near Singapore, made by a Chinaman, for the preparation of the fibres of the ananas or wild pine-apple, which are exported to China, being used there "in the manufacture of linens." The Chinese said he got $1\frac{1}{2}$ rupees the catty, for the fibre. The leaves recently gathered—and the largest are preferred—are laid upon a board and the epidermis is removed with a broad knife. Upon its removal from the upper surface of the leaf, the long and beautiful fibres were seen lying upon the lower and denser epidermis, running in a longitudinal direction; the fasciculi of fibres were then readily detached by the hand on being raised with the broad knife.

The separation of the fibre of the ananas is practised in other places besides the Phillipine Islands. The Singapore Committee forwarded specimens (*Tali nanas*) from Malacca, as well as some of three different qualities prepared at Singapore, and a portion as ready for weaving, that is, with the ends gummed, or joined together by some adhesive substance; thus forming the "invisible knots" of an old author. Specimens were also sent from Java and the island of Celebes.

Dr. Roxburgh does not appear to have paid much attention to the separation of the ananas fibre; but in the year 1839, a lady (Miss Davy) sent specimens of a thread prepared from the wild pine-apple plant of Assam, of various degrees of fineness, observing that the thread must be prepared when the leaves are green, as nothing can be done with them in a dry state. Miss Davy subsequently sent specimens of cloth manufactured from this thread to the Agricultural Society of Calcutta, observing that she had had much difficulty in getting it woven, as the principal manufacturers in Dacca positively refused to undertake making it into cloth. A weaver in the jungles near Dacca, afterwards undertook to do so, and wove the cloth which was sent. Of this, Miss Davy had some embroidered in silver,—a style of work in which the natives of that part of the country excel. The specimens of the fibre were shown by Mr. E. Solly to spinners in this country, but who did not consider it could be substituted for flax in the manufacture of textile fabrics. A patent was, however, taken out by Mr. Zincke, for the manufacture of thread from this fibre, because, when bleached, it could be spun in the same way as flax. The process of bleaching, by destroying the adhesion between the bundles of fibres, renders it much finer; and hence enables it to be extended between the rolls in the process of spinning. He considers that, from its beautiful silky lustre, combined with considerable strength, it is well adapted to form a substitute for linen.

These pine-apple fibres (*anasa nara*), and the tow or oakum from them, were also sent from Madras and from Travancore, showing that the art of separating these fibres is extensively diffused. Dr. Hunter received some very fine, strong, and silky fibres from Porto Novo, prepared by Mr. Lima. But as the plants are not so abundant as in some other localities, we cannot therefore expect the fibres to be prepared so cheaply as elsewhere.

Besides the fibre, some twine and cord made with it was also sent from Madras and from the eastward.

Two skeins of the Pine-apple fibre were sent by the Court of Directors to the Society of Arts for a report on their properties, as long since as January, 1836, but the specimens were too small for a trial of their tenacity.

Mr. Bennett says, that at Singapore, from the expense attending labour, the pine-apple fibre could not be prepared under thirty-eight or forty dollars the pecul; but in Penang, or other places where labour is cheap, and women and children could be employed upon it, the expense would hardly exceed ten dollars per pecul.

In the experiments which I have had made with these various fibres, a certain quantity of those prepared at Madras bore 260 lb., while a similar quantity from Singapore bore 350 lb. before they broke; but New Zealand flax in the same proportions bore only 260 lb.

In a report from the Arsenal of Fort William, dated June 3d, 1853, the results are given of some experiments made by Conductor Wilkins on several kinds of rope manufactured by Messrs. W. H. Harton and Co., of Calcutta; and among these there is one of Pine-apple fibre, of three inches and a quarter in circumference. The Government proof is that a rope of this size should bear a weight of 42 cwt., but it bore no less than 15 cwt. more, that is, it broke with a weight of 57 cwt. ('Journ. of Agric. Soc. of India,' vol. viii, p. 182); proving incontestably that Pine-apple possesses strength for cordage, as well as fineness for textile fabrics.

Pita or Agave, commonly called Aloe (*Agaveæ*, a tribe of *Amaryllideæ*).

Hindee—Cantala and Bans-keora. *Tamul*—Petha-kalabuntha.

The species of Agave, commonly called aloe plants, are natives of America, which have become so naturalised in many parts as to appear to be indigenous in Africa, parts of India, and in the south of Spain. So much is the latter the case, that some authors take this American plant to be the aloe wood mentioned in Scripture. But there is not the slightest foundation for this opinion, nor indeed for the true aloe plants of which the agaves so frequently assume the name.[1] But, as they also yield some fibre, it is better to retain for them their appropriate name of Aloe.

The Agave plants, to which the name of American aloes is so frequently applied, resemble the true aloes in their sword-shaped leaves with parallel veins, which, however, grow to a gigantic size—that is, from eight to ten feet in length—in a cluster from the root, with their margins usually armed with short thorns, and their points with a hard and sharp thorn. This makes these plants so useful in the construction of hedges; a use to which they are applied in the south of Spain and of Italy, as also in Sicily. These plants come to perfection in about three years, though they do not flower for eight, and, in some situations, perhaps not for twenty years, when they throw up a tall candelabra-like flower stalk. This has, no doubt, given origin to the fable of their flowering only once in a hundred years. It is the leaves of these plants which abound in fibres of great length, and of considerable strength. Being also tough and durable, they are separated for the purpose of making string and rope, not only in their native countries, but also in those into which they have been introduced.

The author, in his 'Illustrations of Himalayan Botany' (p. 375), observed, respecting these plants: "The species of agave are not only ornamental as plants, and useful as hedges, but are important for their products. The roots, as well as leaves, contain ligneous fibre (*pita thread*), useful for various purposes: these are separated by bruising and steeping in water, and afterwards beating; practices which the natives of India have adopted, either from instruction or original observation. The Mexicans also made their paper of the fibres of agave leaves laid in layers. The expressed juice of the leaves evaporated, is stated by Long, in his 'History of Jamaica,' to be also useful as a substitute for soap. But the most important product of

[1] The Aloes wood of Scripture is the *Ahila* wood of the East, so famed for its fragrance, yielded by *Aquilaria Agallochum*, &c. (*v. Ahalim* by the author in Kitto's 'Cycl. of Biblical Literature,' i, p. 95.)

agave, and especially of *A. americana*, the species now most common in the South of Europe, is the sap, which exudes upon the cutting out of the inner leaves, just before the flower scape is ready to burst forth; of this a very full account is given by the illustrious Humboldt, in his 'Political History of New Spain' (book iv, c. 9).

The fibres of these Agave leaves are, in Mexico, converted into twine, cord, or rope; the last used in mines, and on the western coast, towards Guayaquill, for the rigging of ships. Humboldt describes a bridge over the River Chambo, in Quito, 131 feet in span, of which the main ropes, four inches in diameter, were made of the fibres of the agave; and upon these ropes the roadway was placed. In the West Indies, the negroes are described as making ropes, fishing-nets, and hammocks of agave fibres. The fibre is thus prepared: the longest and most perfect leaves being cut off, are laid upon a board and scraped with a square iron bar, which is held in both hands, until all the juice and pulp are pressed out, the fibres only remaining. Stedman says, the fibre is like white silk, and hence it obtains the name of silk-grass; though this name seems to be also applied to the fine fibres of *Agave vivipara*, and of *A. yuccæfolia*. But others of these white endogenous fibres are better entitled to the name, as they are softer and more flexible. Stedman says, ropes made of this material are stronger than any in use in England; but that they are liable to be sooner damaged by immersion in water. In Portugal the fibre is called *filo de pita*, and applied to various purposes. In Spain, also, the fibre is called Pita, and used for making string and rope, the plant being abundant in the southern provinces. In Sicily, the fibre is said, by Dr. Balfour, to be called Zambarone, where cordage and mats are made of it. Pita fibre is extensively used in South America for even considerably sized rope.

Pita fibre and rope have been stated to be prepared from the Agave so common in the south of Spain, though not to the extent at which the manufactory might easily be carried on. M. Ramon de la Sagra recommends the introduction of other kinds from Guatimala and Columbia, which are known there by the names of "Cabulla" and "Cocaiza." Species of Fourcroya also yield excellent fibre. *F. gigantea* is common at St. Helena, and has been introduced into Madras.

Pita fibre was sent to the Exhibition of 1851 from the island of Madeira, and also from Barbadoes and Demerara. Thread and paper made from *Agave americana* were also sent from Mexico, and fibre is also said to be obtained there from a species called "*Moogai*"—*A. diacantha* by botanists.

The name Pita seems to be also applied to similar fibres obtained from species of Bromelia and of Yucca, as well as of Agave, according to Dr. Hamilton, of Plymouth; and it is probable that it is so, for these are all very similar to each other. Dr. Hamilton further states, that the weight of Pita fibre being one sixth less than that of hemp, the difference would be very considerable for the entire rigging of a ship and produce a sensible reduction in the top weight, and thus increase the stability of the hull. He considers it also more durable than hemp, and that it bears the alternate action of humidity and of dryness with little injury; hence it is preferred for cables, standing rigging of vessels, nets for fishing, &c. The difference in hygrometric action is also in favour of the pita. In a few months' trial in H.M.S. Portland, a log-line, 300 feet long, of Pita, contracted sixteen feet two tenths, whilst a similar one made of hemp contracted twenty-one feet six tenths; the contraction, moreover, of the Pita ceased on the third day, while that of the hempen cord continued the whole time. The two lines have been deposited in the stores of the dockyard at Plymouth.

At Amboyna, says Labillardiere, the natives produce threads from the bastard Aloe, called *Agave vivipara:* the master of the house went and cut a leaf off this plant, and, resting it on his thigh, in order to scrape it with his large knife, he took off its pulp, and obtained from it a fascicle of threads as long as the leaf, and as strong as those of our best hemp.

The Agave grows well on the north coast of Africa, and its fibre has been paid much attention to by the French since their occupation of Algeria. There, it is stated, when fodder is scarce, cattle will eat the younger leaves when cut into transverse slices. A cloak and paper made of this fibre were sent to the Exhibition of 1851; and ropes have been made of the fibres—of these the strength is very considerable.

The Agave or Pita fibre being so extensively employed in different parts of the world, there is no doubt that it would be a valuable culture for many parts of India. It was probably introduced into India by the Portuguese, and is now common in both the northern and southern parts of India. The species which I found most common in the north-west of India was *Agave vivipara*. This seems to be the same as the *Agave americana* of Roxburgh ('Herb. Amb.,' v, 94). I observed that on rich soils, the plant invariably produced bulbs, but no seeds; while on a poor stony soil and dry climate, like that of Delhi, seeds alone are produced. This species must be closely allied to the *A. Cantala* of Dr. Roxburgh, which is, no doubt, a naturalised plant. These species or varieties flourish in dry parts of the country, where few fibre-yielding plants succeed so well, such as in the Deccan and in Mysore. Far in the north-west, the outer hedge of the Saharunpore Botanic Garden was formed of the Agave, and the fibres were commonly used for all garden purposes. Dr. Buchanan, at the beginning of the century, found the villagers in Mysore employing it for making strong hedges, and separating the fibres for cordage; and Mr. Webb, who was employed with Dr. Anderson in cultivating the Nopal for the Cochineal insect, had a plantation of the Agave, near Madras. Of this the fibres were made into rope, and reported upon at the arsenal of Fort St. George, as long since as the year 1798.

Mr. William Webb having made a plantation of the Agave plant, in the year 1798 manufactured ropes from its fibres, which he considered superior in strength to that made in Europe. He also stated that he believed rope without tar is preferable for all military purposes. He submitted a coil of this rope to the Military Board of Fort St. George, with a suggestion that he should be allowed to supply it in lieu of rope made in Europe. Capt. P. Malcolm, of H.M.S. Suffolk, writing from Cochin, reported upon it, "as strong, if not more so, than Coir, and as having the advantage in pliability." A Committee of the Military Board were "of opinion, that its appearance promises well, and that from a trial that has been made of it, it is at least equal when new to the best Europe rope of the same size in point of strength. Sixteen of the battering guns having been mounted with it before it gave way, while Europe rope of a larger kind failed after it had been employed in mounting only four guns." But it was observed that the yarns were made too large, and that diminishing their size would augment their strength. With respect to its durability, the Committee had no experience, but reported, that part of a coil which Mr. Webb stated "had been fixed to the anchor of his boat at Ennore, and kept constantly under water for six months, appears to have undergone no other alteration than Europe rope would have done in the same situation."

In another report made by the Commissary of Stores, Fort St. George, dated 27th July, 1801, on a coil of Aloe rope manufactured at Seringapatam, it is stated that "the coil of Aloe rope was, on its being received at the Arsenal, the 10th of June, immersed in a tub of water for twenty-four hours, and then exposed to the open air in the yard; since which date, a few showers of rain have fallen, after each of which the coil was turned; and upon being examined and tried the 27th instant, it was found to be quite rotten." From this it was inferred that Aloe rope will not stand wet; and it was stated that this was also the result of similar rope supplied to H.M.'s squadron then in India. ('Madras Artillery Records' for 1839.)

Though nothing is so objectionable in a rope for naval purposes as inability to bear exposure to wet, the above experiments are inconclusive, because we are without any information respecting the species of Agave which was cultivated, and also respecting the soil and climate where it was grown, as well as the time which the fibre was macerated before it was separated. All which influence not only the strength of fibre, but its capability of bearing moisture. The result of the experience in India is, moreover, contrary to that of South America.

The employment of the fibres of this plant seems very general, as it has since become widely distributed through the Madras Presidency. Thus, it is so employed at Masulipatam and at Bellary. At Cuddapah, the natives make ropes of it thirty cubits in length. The plant is abundant about Madura, whence fibre and cordage were sent. The fibres are prepared by pressing the leaves between two horns and then washing the pulp away. The ropes are described as being manufactured in great abundance, and at a trifling expense; and that they are much used for lashing bales of calico. The fibres are also separated on the Malabar coast, and specimens were sent from the prisoners in the jail. But the most varied assortment of specimens was sent from Madras, prepared at the instigation of Dr. Hunter in his School of Arts, and by the prisoners in the jails at Madras. Of these, the Agave was in the state both of fibre and of oakum; also made into string, cord, and rope, and dyed orange, red, maroon, and green, showing how well this fibre takes these colours. Also, some good paper, made with this fibre, mixed with that of gunny bags. In Madras, this plant is called *petha kalabuntha.* The usual way of preparing these fibres is to steep them in water for three days, and then to clear away the herbaceous parts. But the best way of steeping is that practised by the natives in some places; that is, of sinking the leaves in wet sand. But the fibres may also be separated by first beating, and then scraping away the rest of the vegetable tissue. The beating is required on account of the hardness of these agave leaves. Pressing them through grooved cylinders, would, no doubt, be efficacious and also expeditious.

The Agave is also common in the Bengal Presidency, where it is called *cantala;* and also *bans keora,* or "Bamboo Pandanus." Though, probably most valuable in the upper provinces, yet, in December, 1839, Mr. Bond, master-attendant at Balasore, sent to the Agricultural Society of Calcutta, a piece of cloth manufactured by him from a species of the Aloe plant, of which he sent a leaf; and stated that the cloth had been woven without the thread having been spun. I have already mentioned that the fibre was constantly employed for garden purposes at Saharunpore.

Mr. Tonnochy, B.C.S., succeeded in spreading the culture in the Boolundshuhur district, by exposing, in his office, some of the dressed fibre, and also a couple of sattranjees or carpets made of them, together with heaps of seed. These all disappeared. Mr. Tonnochy encouraged the culture as a hedge-plant, because it was not only valuable on its own account, but also, because enclosing the fields so much enhances the value of land. The long, flowering stem was, moreover, found useful as a ridge-pole for cottages.

In the year 1852, Sir R. C. Hamilton, resident at Indore, forwarded some specimens of the fibre of the *Agave Cantala* which grows freely in Malwa, and to which attention had been directed during the temporary want of "Bakkul," the fibrous bark of the roots of certain trees, which is used in that part of India as a cheap substitute for string and cord. Dr. Tranter found he could pull out single fibres, measuring from twenty to thirty inches in length; but he separated a larger quantity by macerating the leaves in water for a week and then beating them with a stick. Capt. A. Thompson, of Messrs. T.'s rope-manufactory at Calcutta, having tested the fibres, found the strength quite equal to the best Russian hemp. He also states, in June, 1852, that a considerable quantity of fibre, exactly similar, had lately been imported from the Malabar coast, and that he had some made into rope, which very much resembled Manilla rope: but time was required to test its durability. It was then worth about four rupees per bazar maund in the Calcutta market.

Though this Pita or Agave fibre is so much employed in different parts of the world, its great merits seem to be, generally, but little known. We have seen that in South America, ropes made with it are considered both strong and durable. The ropes made at Algiers have been found to possess great strength; and the log-lines in H.M. ship Portland to be both durable and not shrinking after the third day. In lightness and colour they resemble ropes of Manilla hemp, though they are not usually so strong. But in a "comparative trial made at Paris, between ropes made of hemp and of the aloe from Algiers, the latter was found to bear 2000 kilogrames, while the former, of equal size, bore only 400." So, in some comparative trials made at the French dock yard at Toulon, on ropes made from these fibres and from hemp, the following results were obtained, both being immersed in the sea for six months, and exposed to the atmosphere for the same time.

PITA.	Weight supported.	HEMP.	Weight supported.	Difference in favour of Pita.
	Pounds.		Pounds.	Pounds.
Plunged in sea . .	3810	Plunged in sea . .	2538	1272
Exposed to air . .	3724	Exposed to air . .	3022	702

In the year 1841 some rope was made under the direction of Mr. Hornby at the Allipore Jail rope-walk, of Aloe, or rather Agave fibre, obtained from plants which had been grown by the convalescent insane, near Calcutta. Mr. Hornby tested this rope against others made of Country Hemp (that is *Sunn*), Jute, and Coir, and he found the Agave rope exceed the others in strength, as appears from the following statement sent by him to the Agricultural Society of India:

CALCULATION OF THE POWERS OF ALOE FIBRE ROPE, COUNTRY HEMP, JUTE, AND COIR ROPE, TRIED AT THE ALLIPORE JAIL ROPE-WALK.

				lb. Troy.
Aloe Fibre Rope, 1 fathom long, and 3 inches in circumference, broke in a weight of				$2519\frac{1}{2}$
Coir	do.	do.	do. . .	2175
Country Hemp	do.	do.	do. . .	$2269\frac{1}{2}$
Jute	do.	do.	do. . .	$2456\frac{1}{2}$

In some experiments which I had made, I found a bundle of the fibres bore 270 lb., when a similar bundle of Russian hemp bore only 160 lb. Dr. Wight had some cord prepared with the Agave fibre in Coimbatore, and found it bore 362 lb.; when similar rope, made from Crotolaria juncea broke with 407 lb. The following are the results of—

EXPERIMENTS MADE IN ARSENAL AT FORT ST. GEORGE, JULY 30TH, 1850, ON ROPES MADE IN JAIL AT MADRAS, IN 1850.[1]

	Circumference.	Length.	Weight required to break.	After 24 hours in water, and used 7 days aft.	Immersed in water 10 days, and dried.	Manilla Rope.	English Hempen Rope.	Weight of one fathom of each.		
								Pita.	Manilla.	Europe.
	In.	Fms.	lb.	lb.	lb.	lb.	lb.	oz.	oz.	oz
Rope .	$1\frac{7}{8}$	2	2218	1994	2016	—	—	$19\frac{11}{16}$	—	—
Ditto .	$1\frac{3}{4}$	2	1154	—	—	1490	1184	$8\frac{14}{16}$	$9\frac{1}{2}$	13
Line .	$0\frac{3}{8}$	1	$86\frac{1}{4}$	—	—	—	—	$0\frac{7}{16}$	—	—
Cord .	$0\frac{3}{16}$	1	$39\frac{1}{2}$	$34\frac{1}{2}$	$37\frac{14}{16}$	—	—	$0\frac{2}{16}$	—	—

These experiments prove incontestibly, that the Pita fibre is possessed of very useful properties; and we have seen that the Agave plant has become naturalised in many widely separated parts of the Indian territories. Its characteristics have been dwelt upon in detail, because it seems calculated to prove extremely useful in India. First, because it grows in dry climates and poor soils, such as may be met with both in the Deccan and in Mysore. It will, in such situations, form a very effective hedge—useful, not only in keeping off from the crops the innumerable

[1] For similar experiments on rope, &c., made from Plantain fibres, *v.* p. 78, &c.

herds of deer, &c., but also in assisting in saving the soil, a road or a railway, from being covered with the sand blown from the desert. The leaves would form a continual source of employment for the people, in separating an abundant supply of material for cordage. This will, at all events, be sufficiently good for all agricultural purposes, for the harnessing of cattle, the baling of produce, and for the rigging of vessels employed in river navigation. The fibre is also sufficiently good to form an exportable article of considerable value, especially as the prejudice against white cordage will by degrees be removed, and the tow will be invaluable for the manufacture of paper. It is desirable that some comparative experiments should be made on the age at which the leaves should be collected, and on how long they should be steeped. Also, whether this process is necessary at all; that is, whether the fibre may not be separated by mechanical means. The climate best suited to the growth of the strongest fibre should be ascertained, as well as what are the differences of quality between the fibre of different species of Agave. Also, the susceptibility of different kinds to the effects of moisture, either with or without superficial tarring. In the preparation of the cordage submitted to trial, care should be taken that the fibres are so prepared as to cut each other as little as possible when twisted; and also that the cordage is made by a regular rope-maker. Under the head of Plantain and of Moorva (v. p. 53) fibre, we shall consider the quantity of fibre producible from a certain number of such plants, and also the price at which it may probably be produced.

Liliaceous Plants.

Liliaceous plants, from their generally ornamental nature, have attracted attention from the earliest ages to the present time, and Our Saviour selected the flower of one of these (*Lilium chalcedonicum*) as a type of the beautiful productions of nature. The plants are usually herbaceous, though some few are shrubby, and even arboreous; most are distinguished by their narrow parallel-veined leaves: of these, some are soft, herbaceous, and succulent; others hard and perennial. Of the latter many abound in fibre, which may be, and is, extracted for useful purposes; as Aloe, Sanseviera, Phormium, &c.

True Aloes (*Aloe vulgaris, Barbadensis*, &c.)

The true genus *Aloe*, or the plants which yield the medicinal drug of that name, abound at the Cape of Good Hope, on the west coast of Africa, and on that of Arabia, with one or two species in India. They might be supposed to yield much fibre from the frequency with which we find the name applied to some of those met with in commerce; but these we have seen are the produce of a species of Agave, commonly called American Aloe (*v.* p. 41, &c). The leaves of the true Aloes are, in all the countries where the species are indigenous, as well as in the West Indies, where one or two of them have been long introduced, cut up and boiled down to yield the *extract* called *Aloes*. In some cases the yellow juice is allowed to exude from the cut leaf to form what is called Socotrine Aloes; but nowhere is the fibre which these leaves undoubtedly contain turned to useful account. It is probable, however, that it might, even when the leaves are cut into small pieces, be separated at little expense, for the use of the paper-maker.

That the fibre, as well as the tow, of the true Aloes is of a good and useful quality, is satisfactorily proved by the specimens of both sent from Madras by Dr. Hunter, as those of the *kala-buntha*, or of the species which is there called *Aloe perfoliata*, and which is, probably, the same plant with red flowers which I named *Aloe indica*, and found in dry situations in North-West India. The fibre is white in colour, fine in quality, with sufficient tenacity for textile fabrics, and readily takes colours, as shown by the orange, red, and crimson-coloured specimens sent by Dr. Hunter. The fibres are about two feet in length, and have considerable strength. A bundle of the fibres bore 160 lb., when a similar one of Petersburgh hemp broke with the same weight.

Moorva Fibre, Marool of Madras (*Sanseviera zeylanica*).

Bowstring Hemp. *Sans.*—Mūrva. *Beng.*—Moorga and Moorgavee. *Tamool*—Marūl.

Sanseviera is a genus of Liliaceous plants, of which individuals are very abundant on the coast of Guinea and of other parts of

Africa; also around Ceylon, and all along the Bay of Bengal, extending thence to Java and to the coasts of China.

The leaves are succulent, and abound in fibre remarkable for fineness and tenacity. Dr. Roxburgh proposed that the fibres might be called *Bowstring hemp* in England, because the natives of the Circars make their best bowstrings of them.

Sanseviera zeylanica is the best-known species, and has been so called as being common on the Ceylon coast. From it has been distinguished *S. Roxburghiana,* common on the coasts of the Bay of Bengal, apparently on insufficient grounds. It is figured by Dr. Roxburgh himself under its former name in his 'Coromandel Plants,' ii, tab. 184. *S. lanuginosa* is probably a distinct species, the *katu-kapel* of Rheede ('Hort. Mal.,' vol. xi, tab. 42), which grows on the sands of the Malabar coast. All are closely allied to each other, and to the African *S. guineensis.* Of this the fibres have been occasionally introduced into the markets of Europe, and by some thought superior to New Zealand Flax. They have been called African Bowstring Hemp. (The author's 'Himal. Bot.,' p. 391.)

The Indian species of Sanseviera was first described by Sir William Jones, in the 'Asiatic Researches,' vol. iv, p. 271, under its ancient Sanscrit name of *Moorva,* and he says, that—"From the leaves of this plant the ancient Hindoos extracted a very tough elastic thread called Maurvi, of which they made bowstrings; and which, for that reason, was ordained by Menu to form the sacrificial zone of the military class." Dr. Roxburgh describes the plant as common on the jungly salt soils along the coasts, growing under the bushes, and easily propagated on almost every soil, from the slips which issue in great abundance from the roots, requiring little or no care, and not requiring to be renewed often, if at all, as the plant is perennial. The leaves, when thus cultivated, are from three to four feet long. The fibre, which extends their whole length, is separated from the pulpy part of the leaves. The natives place them on a smooth board; then press one end of the leaf down with one of their great toes, and with a thin bit of hard stick held between the two hands, they scrape the leaf from them, and very quickly remove every part of the pulp. This can also be removed by steeping the leaves in water till the pulpy parts rot, &c.

Dr. Buchanan found apparently the same plant, but which he calls *Aletris nervosa*, employed for making cordage near Bangalore. Before the leaves are beaten to separate the fibres, they are steeped in water fifteen (others say five) days, in order to rot the useless parts; but with Dr. Roxburgh the fibres became discoloured by this process.

Dr. Roxburgh sent drawings of the plant and specimens of the fibre (*v.* 'Obs.,' p. 18) as early as the year 1790 to the Court of Directors, and again in 1800 by Mr. Bebb; after he had cultivated a begah (*i. e.*, third of an acre of ground) with this plant. As full-grown leaves of three to three and a half feet long yielded about one pound of the clean fibre for every forty pounds of the fresh leaves, Dr. Roxburgh concluded that this plant might be cultivated with advantage. By another calculation he found that one acre would yield 1613 pounds of clean fibre at a gathering, two of which may be reckoned on yearly, in a good soil and a favorable season, after the plants are of a proper age. He also ascertained that a line four feet long, made of *moorva* fibre, bore a weight of 120 lb., when a cord of the same size, made of Russian hemp, bore only 105. The former, moreover, after 116 days' maceration, bore a weight of 30 lb., when the latter was completely rotten.

Dr. Roxburgh further observes: "Should it ever become an object of culture, a less expensive and more expeditious method of clearing the fibres from the pulpy parts of the leaves, than that of the natives above mentioned, must be contrived." This seems to have been since done. For the Rev. J. Garrow, as quoted by Mr. Murray, states that, in the year 1831, during his residence in Cuttack, in the province of Orissa, he first by mere accident discovered that the leaf of the *Aloe angustifolia*[1] of Linnæus, contained a quantity of long white fibres. Perceiving that this material possessed great strength, clearness, and tenacity, he caused some quantities of the leaf to be beaten out with mallets, and the fibres to be withdrawn, and in this way collected about three hundredweight of fine grass, the fibres severally running about three feet long. On taking this to Calcutta, Mr. Tapley, chief officer of the Thalia East Indiaman, then lying off that

[1] It is not easy to ascertain what plant is meant, but it is probably only a variety of Agave, as no species of Aloe is known to be indigenous on that coast.

port, had some of it manufactured into ropes. On a fair trial of a three-stranded rope of this material with a similar one of Russian hemp, in raising two and a half hundredweight of spelter from the hold, the grass faithfully brought it up on three successive occasions; whereas, in applying the hempen rope, twice out of three times it gave way, and in the third trial lost one strand. Both Mr. Tapley and Capt. Biden, the commander, highly approved of the article, as did many commanders of ships of other nations then frequenting the port of Calcutta.

"On the writer's return to Cuttack he laid waste the whole of the aloe plant he could discover, without respect to species; and to save time and labour, passed the leaves through a *pressing mill* similar to that used for expressing the juice from the sugar-cane. He then caused them to be laid in heaps under water for some days, till the fleshy portion of the leaf was decomposed, by which means the fibres were more easily collected; they were then hackled and baled. In the course of a short time afterwards he discovered a short species of aloe, growing wildly and profusely in all the moist woods of the neighbourhood, which the natives called *Moorgubbee*. On experiment, this plant produced a most beautiful fibre, as soft and as fine as human hair, but possessing, notwithstanding, extraordinary strength and tenacity. He derived a great quantity of flax from this plant, which, when portioned off in hanks, bore a strict resemblance to raw silk; indeed, side by side, the difference could not be distinguished. It was this article that first induced the writer to turn his attention to the manufacture of cloth. He engaged two native 'Tantees,' or weavers, to construct a narrow loom for this purpose. They at first found some difficulty in the undertaking, but in the course of four or five days they produced as fine a piece of cloth as was ever beheld: one portion of it the writer presented to Sir Charles (afterwards Lord) Metcalf."

The fibres of the Sanseviera may, from their fineness, combined with tenacity, be applied to a variety of purposes. Dr. Roxburgh at one time supposed, though erroneously, that they were identical with China grass. They are usually about two feet in length, but may easily be obtained longer, if plants are cultivated. The fibres are firm, hair-like, and silky, and resemble those of the pine-apple most closely. The tow is excellent for paper-making. The natives of Bengal twist the fibres into a fine thread, upon which they string ornaments to be hung round the neck; those of the coast employ them for making bowstrings; and the Rajpoot thread is sometimes made of its fibres. They readily take dyes, as was some years ago shown by Miss Davy, and specimens dyed red, orange, maroon, and green, were sent to the Exhibition by Dr. Hunter. Miss Davy, moreover, had some cloth woven with the fibres, after some difficulty, but the fibre was still too wiry, from imperfect preparation. The weaver, moreover, having neglected to separate the coarse from the fine fibres, gave the cloth an uneven and irregular appearance. But if the necessary care was taken with this, as with all other fibres, there seems no reason to doubt that it might be applied to the fabrication of fine cloths, in the same way as pine-apple fibre. The fibre has been proposed for the packing of steam-engines, and its tow used to be, and perhaps still is, converted into very good paper at Trichinopoly.

As the Moorva fibre is employed by the natives for their bowstrings, there can be no doubt of its possessing sufficient strength for rope-making. In some recent experiments, this fibre, in its untwisted state, bore 280 lb., when Agave fibre broke with 270 lb. Dr. Wight found some string made of the latter, broke with 362 lb., while the Sanseviera broke with 316 lb., so that these two may be considered as nearly equal to each other in strength.

Attention was called to the fibre of Moorgavie by Mr. A. Bond, Master-Attendant at Balasore, who sent to the Marine Board of Calcutta some of the fibres prepared from the leaves of plants growing in the jungly salt soils along the coast from Kedgeree southward, informing the Board that he had found the fibre useful on board the Hon. Company's schooner Orissa, as it answered excellently for running gear.

On the receipt of the samples, the Board having desired the Master-Attendant at Calcutta to submit them to trial, the latter reported that it was "not equal in strength to the Europe or Manilla hemp, but that it seemed to take hot tar as well as the latter, and would answer generally for the same purposes as those to which the Europe and Manilla cordage is applied." The following were the results obtained:

Europe hemp, made of sewing twine (untarred) . .	broke at	212 lb.
Harris's patent colonial bolt rope (tarred)[1] . . .	"	204 "
Manilla hemp (untarred)	"	188 "
Europe bolt rope (tarred)	"	168 "
Balasore fibre (untarred), at Calcutta	"	137 "
Ditto, spun by Capt. Bond (thumb line)	"	135½ "
Europe rope (tarred)	"	88 "

In a further report, Capt. Bond stated, that forty maunds of the fresh plant produced one maund of fibre. The expenses of the experiment were high, as the plant had to be brought to him from some distance (four miles) to the place where it was dressed, and the best methods of separating the fibre had not been followed. The natives being averse to a work which their forefathers had never taken in hand. The plants having been steeped for eight days, were beaten out on a stone or plank, and then taken to another tank of water to be washed, and then dried and combed. All these processes necessarily increased the expenses. Mr. Bond further ascertained that the steeping spoiled the colour of the fibre, at the same time that it diminished its strength. With some fresh specimens of the fibre he also sent two pieces of cloth, which had been woven from threads spun by fishermen, which were irregular in thickness, and so, consequently, was also the cloth.

From the abundance of this plant in many situations, from the ease with which it may be cultivated, and the facility with which the fibre may be separated and cleaned, there is no doubt that it could be produced as cheaply as any of the other fibres; and it has been shown that it is capable of being used for a variety of purposes, as for textile fabrics, and for string and cordage, as well as for paper-making. It is abundantly diffused, especially along the coasts, and its fibre was sent to the Exhibition from Assam and Cuttack, as well as from Madras, Coimbatore, and the Malabar coast.

Besides the foregoing, many other Liliaceous plants might be adduced, as yielding useful kinds of fibre, and in quantities sufficient to repay the trouble of their extraction. But they

[1] Probably made of New Zealand Flax, *v.* p. 58.

are not indigenous or sufficiently abundant in India, though the fibres of some have been separated, and sent as specimens. As, for instance, of—

YUCCA, OR ADAM'S NEEDLE FIBRE.

Adam's Needle, or *Yucca gloriosa*, *&c.*, like others, seems sometimes to be called an Aloe. The species of *Yucca* are natives of the southern provinces of the United States, and being there exposed to extremes, are capable of living in the open air, both in Europe and India. They are conspicuous for their noble show of lily-like white flowers, as well as for their long sword-shaped leaves, terminated by a thorny point. They, no doubt, all abound in fibre, as some of a fine quality and strong in nature, has been sent from Madras, separated from the leaves of the *Yucca angustifolia*. Other species flourish as far north as in the Botanic Garden at Saharunpore. The fibres also take colour, as in the specimens sent from Madras, dyed red, orange, purple, and green. Fibre has also been separated from other species of Yucca, as *Y. aloifolia* and *Y. filamentosa*, These are amongst those which have received the name of silk-grass. Those sent from India are from two to four feet in length, and are rather wiry, or resemble those of the Agave more than they do the fibres of Bromelias.

NEW ZEALAND FLAX (*Phormium tenax*).

New Zealand Flax, or *Phormium tenax*, belonging to this family of plants, may here be noticed, though it is not so well suited as many others, to the general nature of Indian climates, but it will enable us to make some useful comparisons. It was discovered by the celebrated Cook in New Zealand—as he says "the country produced a grass plant, like flags, of the nature of hemp or flax, but superior in quality to either; of this the natives make clothing, lines, nets, &c." It grows both on the north and the south coast. It was introduced in the year 1798 into the south of Ireland, and has been found to flourish on the west coast of Scotland, though European winters are occasionally too severe for it. The native name of the plant is *koradi* or *korere*, while the fibre is called *muka*. The leaves of the plant are perennial, hard, sword-shaped, from five to seven feet in length, with a flower-stalk rising four or five feet above them, and bearing a profusion of yellow flowers, followed by triangular seed-vessels, filled with flat and thin black shining seeds. According to Salisbury, three-year old plants yield on an average, thirty-six leaves, beside offsets from the roots. Six leaves produced one ounce weight of dry fibres, after being scutched and cleaned; and he calculated that an acre cropped with these plants, three feet apart (but they could not be placed so near without interfering with each other), will yield more than sixteen cwt. "The leaves are cut when full-grown, macerated in water for a few days, and then passed under a weighted roller." The natives of New Zealand cut the leaves when full-grown, and separate the fibres while yet green. Mr. G. Bennett states that a lateral incision is made with a large shell on each side of the leaf, merely to cut through the epidermis, which is first removed, and then, what he calls the internal epidermis, probably a part of the cellular tissue, "which agglutinates the fibres, and, if not removed, deteriorates the flax." The principal operation is scraping with the shell, and then separating the fibres with the thumb-nails, and then employing combs for a more minute separation. The fibres are subsequently dried in the sun, and are perfectly white; some stout and strong, others fine and silky. It is said that "the plant may be shorn of its leaves in the morning, and before the sun has set be ready for weaving into cloth." The same thing may, no doubt, be done with others of these naturally white endogenous fibres. Considerable quantities were at one time imported, and a factory was established by Capt. Harris for their manufacture, but the supply seems to have been irregular, and now to have fallen off rather than increased.

Mr. J. Wood, in the year 1844, in a communication to the Agricultural Society of India, called attention to the New Zealand Hemp, as a plant which was very hardy and would thrive in any soil or climate, but that it preferred swampy lands. He stated that it was often met with in New Zealand, thriving three or four feet under sea-water, (but it is also found at some distance from the sea-shore). He therefore thought the locality of the Soonderbunds, extending from near Calcutta to the sea, to be well adapted for this plant; and which would be profitable in a country where labour was so cheap. But it seems to have been forgotten, in this, as well as in a paper in the first volume of the 'Transactions of the Society,' that a plant which flourishes so far south as New Zealand, and succeeds well both in Scotland and in Ireland, is not likely to do well in so tropical a situation as that of the Soonderbunds.

An interesting set of specimens of New Zealand Flax, showing the native method of preparing the fibre and of dyeing it black, were sent to the Exhibition of 1851, by Taohui, a New Zealand chief; and another, a very valuable and suggestive set of specimens of the fibre and its tow, by Mr. E. W. Trent (*v.* 'Illust. Col.,' xli, p. 197), which he described as having been separated entirely by machinery invented by himself. If this fibre can be so prepared, then it is evident that others of the same nature may be successfully treated in a similar manner.

These fibres are applicable to a variety of purposes, either of a textile nature or for cordage, and will, like the other white fibres we have mentioned, take colour. The strength of the fibres is considerable, for in some experiments by De Candolle, in which, however, that of Agave is understated, there is no doubt that the New Zealand Flax, which bore 23·7, was stronger than either Flax or Hemp, which bore respectively 11¾ and 16¾. It has also the advantage of being lighter, but has the disadvantage of many of the white fibres of breaking at a knot. Mr. J. Murray, in his pamphlet on this plant, printed on paper made from its leaves, states that the ship Atalanta, which plied between Southampton and the Channel Islands, was completely equipped with cordage and rigging made of *Phormium tenax*. He further continues—

"I have seen specimens of ropes, twine, yarn, lines, sailcloth, sacking, bedtick, &c., made of *Phormium tenax;* also fine fabrics of various kinds, affording demonstrable evidence that its fibre is susceptible of being woven into tissues of the most delicate description, or manufactured into materials of the strongest and coarsest kind. The sails, cables, and running rigging of the beautiful model of the frigate presented by his late Majesty William the Fourth to the King of Prussia, were entirely formed of *Phormium tenax*. Capt. Harris's yacht, a perfect gem in naval architecture, was supplied with a mainsail composed of three different varieties of New Zealand flax, and the cordage made of *Musa textilis*," that is, of Manilla hemp, of which we have immediately to treat.

Rushes (*Juncaceæ*).

Rushes have so long been employed for some of the same purposes as other fibres that we can hardly omit noticing them, as they are found in moist places on the mountains of India. But the author may quote what he has formerly said:

"The *Juncaceæ*, or true rushes, are insipid and inodorous; several are employed for mechanical purposes only, as the common rush, for making mats, baskets, and the bottoms of chairs, while the pith is employed for the wicks of rushlights. *Juncus effusus*, which is the common European species, is, according to Thunberg, cultivated in Japan for making floor-mats. *J. glaucus* a European species found in the Himalayas, and closely allied to *J. effusus*, might be employed for all the purposes of the common rush." ('Illust. Himal. Bot.,' p. 401.)

Arrow-root Tribe (*Marantaceæ*).

These plants are celebrated for several of the species storing up large quantities of fecula in their tubers or root-stocks, and which is separated and known by the name of Arrow-root powder. They are little known for their herbaceous parts containing any useful quantity of fibre. But one of the South American genera has been named Calathea, in consequence of its leaves being employed in basket-making. So in India, the stems of *Moocta patee* of the Bengalees, *Maranta* (*Phrynium*, Roxb.) *dichotoma* of botanists, which are straight and tapering, about as thick as a man's thumb, and from three to five or six feet high, of a beautiful highly polished green colour, are said to be employed in making some of the mats for which Calcutta is famous. Mr. Colebrooke says: "Mats made of the split stems of this plant being smooth and particularly cool and refreshing, are termed in Hindoo *sital-pati*, which signifies a cool mat, whence the plant itself is said to bear the name. Suspecting, however, this to be a misappropriation of the term, I have inquired of natives of the eastern parts of Bengal, who assure me that the plant is named *mucta-pata* or *patti-pata,* and the mat only is called 'sital-pati.'" The split stems, as prepared for making mats, are about four feet in length, one twentieth of an inch in breadth, thin as paper, greyish coloured, compact and shining almost like cane on the outside; finely striated on the inside, and apparently made up by the agglutination of very fine fibres. They seem admirably adapted for platting of all kinds.

The plants of this family, however, deserve attention, rather on account of what may be, than for anything that has yet been done with them; for the Marantas yielding arrow-root, and the Cannas which yield "Tous les mois," have, with perennial root-stocks, only annual stems and leaves. Many of these, no doubt, contain a sufficient quantity of fibre to be usefully extracted for the paper-maker.

The same may be said of the innumerable plants of Ginger, Turmeric, Cardamom, and others of the nearly allied family of Zingiberaceæ, which are similarly cultivated entirely for their roots and seeds, and the herbaceous plants thrown away. These from their nature cannot but abound in useful fibre, applicable to the same purpose—that is, of the paper-maker.

THE PLANTAIN AND BANANA TRIBE (*Musaceæ*).

The name of this family of plants, derived from *Musa,* is, as the author has already observed,[1] so classically sounding, that we are apt to forget its probably oriental origin. For being natives of tropical countries, though often extending beyond such limits, and having the name of *mauz* or *moz* applied to one of the species by old Arabic writers, there is very little doubt of this being the source of the name *Musa.* This is now applied to the genus which produces the fruits commonly known as Plantains and Bananas; as also the fibre so well known under the name of Manilla Hemp. The Plantain was undoubtedly known by description both to the Greeks and Romans, for Theophrastus, among the plants of India, describes one as having fruit which serves as food for the wise men of

[1] 'Illustrations of Himalayan Botany,' p. 354.

India; and which was remarkable both for its sweetness and for its size, as one would suffice for four men—referring most probably to a bunch of plantains. Pliny, evidently describing the same plant, informs us that its name was *Pala*. Garcias, in comparatively modern times, describing the plantain, states that its name on the Malabar coast was *Palan*.

The plants of Musa are conspicuous for their size among herbaceous plants. They are devoid of true stems, but form a spurious stem, often of considerable thickness, from the leaves, as they rise from the root-stock, being sheathing at their base, encircling each other, and enveloping, layer within layer, the slender flower and fruit-stalk. This, rising through the centre, projects and hangs down from the top of the sheathing part of the leaves. These, at this point, expand into broad, and at the same time long laminæ or blades, in which numerous parallel veins proceed at right angles from the thick midrib to the margin of each leaf. As these veins do not anastomose and form a network as in ordinary leaves, the leaves are apt, when blown about by the wind, to be divided into innumerable narrow shreds, which are still attached to the midrib. This appearance, no doubt, suggested and justifies the leaves being said to be like ostrich feathers. Every part, both of the sheathing and the exposed parts of these leaves, abounds in fibre.

The species of Musa are found in hot and tropical parts of the world, as in the Phillipine Isles, where *Musa textilis* is indigenous, as well as in those of the Indian Archipelago, where the edible species are common. From thence they extend northwards as far as Japan; while in China are found *Musa coccinea* and *Cavendishii;* also along the Malayan Peninsula to Chittagong—*M. glauca* being indigenous in the former, and *M. ornata* in the latter locality. In the valleys of the south of the Peninsula of India and of the Dindygul Mountains, *M. superba* is found. The common edible varieties of *M. paradisiaca* flourish even in the poorest soils, and also near brackish water. They are extensively cultivated at stations in the interior. On the Malabar coast, the Plantain is everywhere at home. The fruit of those at Bassein is especially well-flavoured, and the plant is particularly abundant in the district of Broach.

If from the west we return to the east of India, we find the

Plantain and Banana most extensively cultivated. The Plantain, according to Dr. Helfer, is to be found in the highest perfection in Tenasserim, especially in province Amherst. More than twenty varieties are known, of which several are peculiar to the country, and the greatest part of them are superior to any to be got in Bengal. They thrive well everywhere without the slightest care. No Burmah or Karean house is to be found without a plantation of Plantains. As the latter leave their abodes, at least every three years, in order to migrate to fresh localities, they are, of course, obliged to leave their Plantain gardens behind them, and therefore these may be found growing luxuriantly in many uninhabited places, until they become choked up by the growth of the more vigorous jungle trees.

With the Plantain, as with other long-cultivated plants, many distinct varieties are recognised and named; but which it is extremely difficult to arrange in suitable order. But the natives of Bengal generally prefer the large and coarse-fruited kinds, called Plantain; while the smaller and more delicately tasted fruit, known as the Banana, is alone esteemed by Europeans. These are cultivated in the most northern, as well as in the southern parts of India; while along the jungly base of the Himalayas there is a suitable climate as far as 30° of north latitude, for plants of this genus growing in a wild state. That growing in Nepal has been called *M. nepalensis*. A similiar species may be seen growing below the Mussoore range, as well as near Nahn. The fruit, however, in all these situations, consists of little else than the hard dry seeds.[1] In Kemaon and Gurhwal it is cultivated at as great an elevation as 4000 and 5000 feet above the sea, and has been seen as far north as the Chumba range at an equal elevation. Major Munro has seen the wild Plantain at 7000 feet above the sea, in the Khondah slopes of the Neilgherries. Though many of the above have been mentioned as distinct species, it is probable that some, at least, are only varieties.

"Baron Humboldt has suggested, that several species of Musa may possibly be confounded under the names of Plantain

[1] A similar variety of *Musa sapientum*, having seeds surrounded with a gummy substance, instead of fruit-like pulp, was found by Dr. Finlayson, on Pulo Ubi, near the southern extremity of Cambodia. In Batavia also, there is stated to be a variety full of seeds, which is called *Pisang batu*, or *Pisang bidju*—that is, Seed Plantain.

and Banana, and that some of these may be indigenous to America; but as stated by Mr. Brown, nothing has been advanced to prevent all the cultivated varieties being derived from one species, *Musa sapientum* (also called *M. paradisiaca*), of which the original is the wild Musa, described by Dr. Roxburgh as grown from seed received from Chittagong. Mr. Brown further adds, that it is not even asserted that the types of any of those supposed species of American Banana, growing without cultivation and producing perfect seed, have anywhere been found." ('Illust. of Himal. Bot.,' p. 355.)

If the Plantain and Banana are therefore natives of Asia, which have been introduced, probably, by the Spaniards into America, no plants can more strikingly display the benefits derivable to one country from introducing the useful plants of another which is similar in climate. For Plantains and Bananas are now extensively cultivated in various parts of South America, and at an elevation of 3000 feet in the Caraccas. They are abundant in the West India Islands, as well as at considerable elevations in Mexico. To the negroes in the West Indies, the Plantain is invaluable, and like bread to the European, is with them denominated the staff of life. In Guiana, Demerara, Jamaica, Trinidad, and other principal colonies, many thousand acres are planted with the Plantain.

But, before proceeding to treat of the Plantain and Banana, it is desirable to notice the species which yields Manilla Hemp, showing how valuable some of these plants are, on account of their fibres.

Manilla Hemp (*Musa textilis*).

Among the various substitutes for hemp, few have hitherto attracted more attention than Manilla Hemp, and this from the elegance of its appearance, combined with the power of bearing great strains, as well as from being very durable, lighter, and also cheaper than Russian hemp. It has of late years been much employed for cordage of various kinds, especially where considerable strain is required, as in ropes for raising goods into warehouses or out of mines. Some yachts, as well as many American vessels, have the whole of their rigging composed of Manilla Hemp, and this cordage, when worn out, can be converted into an excellent quality of paper. Though the plant yielding this fibre is not indigenous in India, nor extensively cultivated, it is yet extremely interesting, not only because it may easily be cultivated there, but because there are other species of the same genus which may be turned to the same useful account.

The plant which yields Manilla Hemp is called *Abaca*[1] by the natives of the Philippine Islands, who are said to apply the same name to its fibre. The plant is sometimes called a tree, but it is, in fact, only a large herbaceous plant, which belongs to the same genus, and is, in fact, a kind of plantain or banana, which is named *Musa textilis* by botanists. It was first called *Musa sylvestris* by Rumphius in his 'Herbarium Amboinense.' It was thought to be a variety of *M. troglo-ditarum* by Blanco, but called *Musa textilis* by Don Luis Nee, in a memoir which has been translated into English, and published in the 'Annals of Botany,' vol. i; where there may also be seen another memoir, which was sent in French to Sir Joseph Banks. These have been republished in the 'Trans. of the Agric. Soc. of India,' vol. viii, p. 87, together with a translation by Mr. Piddington, of Calcutta, of a notice by Father Blanco, in his 'Flora de las Filipinas.' In addition to these we have a notice in the first volume of the Trans. of the above Society, 1828, by Mr. Piddington himself, one of the gentlemen who escaped the massacre of the English at Amboyna.

From these authors we learn that the Abaca is abundant in the volcanic region of the Philippine Islands, from Luzon, in the northern province of Camarines especially, to Mindanao; also in the neighbouring islands, even as far south as the Molucca Islands, that is, in Gilolo. Hence this species may be stated to extend from the Equator to nearly 20° of north latitude. It may, therefore, very probably be easily cultivated in other coun-

[1] The natives distinguish several varieties of the Abacà:

1. *Abacà brava* (the wild Abaca), called *Agotaï* by the Bicoles.

2. Mountain Abacà, the fibres of which only serve for making ropes, that are called *Agotàg* and *Amoquid* in the Bicol language.

3. The *Sagig* of the Bisayas.

4. The *Laquis* of the Bisayas, by whom the fibres of the original Abacà are called Lamót. Rumphius states that the Malay name is *Pissang utan;* that it is called in Amboyna, *Kula abbal;* in Ternate, *Fana;* and in Mindanao, *Coffo*, as also the cloth made from it. He distinguishes the Mindanao kind from that of Amboyna.

tries, where there is some similarity of soil, and warmth with moisture of climate; as in India in the province of Travancore, and on the Malabar coast, also in that of Arracan, in Chittagong. Assam, in parts of Bengal, and in the northern Circars. This was one of the plants subjected to experiment by Dr. Roxburgh, in the beginning of the century. His specimens are still in the East India House. Mr. Leycester, one of the founders of the Agricultural Society of India, called the attention of its members to its fibres as early as the year 1822, when he presented the fibres of three species of Musa. These were *Musa sapientum, M. ornata,* and the present species, *M. textilis.* That of the latter he describes as having been formed from a coat stripped off about sunrise on that day, and having been brought into the house about ten o'clock, had received no further bleaching from the sun or in any other way; and that he had had some of it made into a neat cord, which was in no way inferior to English whipcord. He concludes his letter by congratulating the members on the fibre of their common overgrown plantains being sufficient for all the purposes of twine required in their gardens. Some time after this was written we find it stated in the 'Proceedings of the Agricultural Committee of the Society,' 1st October, 1836, that "a row of the Musa plant, from which the China grass cloth is made, is in a flourishing condition." But, on 12th August, 1840, the Committee notice the favorable appearance of some plants of the Manilla hemp-tree (the Abaca or *Musa textilis*).

Musa textilis is the *Abaca* of the natives of the Philippine Islands. It is found both in a wild and cultivated state, but the natural groves are considered as property. The fruit is green and hard, and of a disagreeable taste. Several villages formerly furnished yearly 1500 arobas each of the fibre, and others exported nearly as much cordage. With the produce of this plant, the natives of these villages pay their tribute, parish dues, purchase the necessaries of life, and clothe themselves.

The Abaca is cut when about one year and a half old, just before its flowering or fructification is likely to appear, as afterwards the fibres are said to be weaker. If cut earlier, the fibres are said to be shorter and finer. It is cut near its roots, and the leaves cut off just below their expansion. It is then slit open longitudinally, and the central peduncle separated from the sheathing layers of fibres, which are in fact the petioles of the leaves. Of these layers the outer are harder and stronger, and form the kind of fibre called *bandala*, which is employed in the fabrication of cordage. The inner layers consist of finer fibres, and yield what is called *lupis*, and used for weaving the *nipis* and other more delicate fabrics; while the intermediate layers are converted into what is called *tupoz*,[1] of which are made web-cloths and gauzes, four yards long, of different degrees of fineness. These are universally used as clothing. Some being so fine, that a garment may be enclosed in the hollow of the hand. Mr. Bennett says, at Manilla there is an extensive manufacture of muslin and sinamaya or grass-cloth; as if, like in the notice at Calcutta, the Abaca was supposed to yield China grass.

The stem-like mass consists of cellular tissue and fibres, with much thickish, watery fluid, which requires to be pressed out.

The fibrous coats, when stripped off, are left for a day in the shade to dry, and are then divided lengthwise into strips, three inches wide. Blanco says the petioles are stripped off one by one, and an incision is made across inside with a knife, to take off the bark which covers them. They are then scraped with an instrument made of bamboo, until only the fibres remain. Sometimes they require much pressing while being scraped. Blanco says the strips are placed beneath the cutting edge of a knife fixed in a long bamboo, which acts as a spring; and the Abaca being placed beneath the knife, is drawn through strongly by one end. This must act as a scraper, but much of the Abaca is said to be spoiled. When sufficiently scraped, the bundle of fibres may be shaken into separate threads; sometimes they are washed, and then dried and picked—the finest being separated by the women with great dexterity. Those for cordage require no further preparation. Those for fine weaving are rendered soft and pliable by beating them with a wooden mallet, after having been made up into a bundle. They are then fastened to each other by "almost invisible knots"—but rather, have their ends gummed together, as in the case of the Pine-apple fibre—then wound into balls, and afterwards committed to the loom.

[1] Besides Pina fibre, already mentioned at p. 39, fibres of "Jussi" and striped Jussi dresses were sent from Manilla to the Exhibition of 1851, and "Bijuco" fibre is mentioned. The plants yielding these fibres are not known.

Don Luis Nee describes the Abaca as being dressed like flax on a kind of heckle—a sort of saw which operates like the heckle (Blanco). Mr. Piddington describes it as a bamboo scraper, into the slit of which the Abaca is introduced, and which being dragged downwards, acts as a scraper on both sides. The stuffs, when woven, are soaked in warm water (lime-water, Blanco) for twenty-four hours, after which they are soaked in cold water, then put into rice-water, and, lastly, washed as before—by which means they acquire lustre, softness, and a white colour. Some are also dyed, and take different colours (as blue and red). Others are embroidered.

Few are imported into Europe, but seem often to be confounded with grass-cloth.

These details have been given in order that the proper treatment may be followed if the plant is cultivated in India; or some of them may be applied to the other kinds of Musa cultivated in India—the fibres of some of which may have a portion of the properties of the Manilla Hemp as cordage. Mr. Piddington had no doubt that when the Manilla Hemp was better known, it would be more appreciated, especially if properly manufactured: the great defect of Manilla-made rope being its stiffness in rainy weather, arising from the coarseness of the yarns—not more than three being used to a strand, which should have nine or twelve. This, Mr. Piddington had ascertained in a vessel commanded by himself, in which both kinds were used; and the latter (made by himself) was at all times as pliant as hemp. It bears tarring well, and he had known it used for lower rigging with success.

In a subsequent volume of the 'Transactions,' in the year 1840, Mr. Stewart Mackenzie, then Governor of Ceylon, forwarded to the Agricultural Society of India, a specimen of Manilla rope, with a note from Mr. Higgs, Master-Attendant at Trincomalee. In this the latter observes, "that shortly after the arrival of the Melville in this country, in 1832, Sir John Gore procured rather a large supply of the different sizes (of Manilla rope) for the squadron, from seven inches to one inch. In that ship we made extensive use of it, reeving it on one side of the ship against Europe rope on the opposite side, and it is from a close observation of its merits, that I have formed the opinion of its being very superior to Europe rope in this country, particularly if this has been long in store here." Mr. Higgs regrets that the Manilla rope is not better laid; and observes that Capt. Neish, one of the oldest captains in the China trade, was in the habit of bringing the large rope from Manilla, and laying it up afresh at Bombay, and tarring the yarns; when it became excellent rope for shrouds. The price of Europe rope at the Naval Yard at Trincomalee, was then £2 *7s.* *3d.* per cwt., while the price of the Manilla rope (without freight) was £1 *12s.*, and it was one fifth lighter than Europe rope. The price at which Manilla Hemp was sold in England will be mentioned at the end of the following article.

Plantain Fibre (*Musa paradisiaca*).

The Plantain and Banana, though probably only varieties of one species, are yet sufficiently distinguished by the size and flavour of their fruit, to be considered familiarly as distinct. They are, from their luxuriant-growing and large overhanging leaves, considered among the most characteristic forms of tropical vegetation. They are also among the most valuable of plants, inasmuch as in some countries they supply the place of bread, and form the chief nutriment of the people. But not only does the Plantain supply the place of bread and serve as fruit, but also in a preserved state as dessert. The farinaceous parts may, moreover, be separated in the form of flour, and are probably as nutritious as rice. The shoots or tops of the young plants, both in the East and the West, are occasionally given as fodder to sheep and cattle, and are described by some as a delicate edible. The leaves, in a dried state, are used for thatching and bedding. Both the stem and leaves abound in fibre, useful for textile or cordage purposes, while the tow which is separated in preparing the fibres, forms an excellent material for the finest or the toughest kinds of paper. The illustrious Humboldt has long since remarked, that the Banana is for the torrid zone what the Cerealia are for Europe and Western Asia, or rice for Bengal and China, forming a valuable cultivation wherever the mean temperature of the year is about 75°. He has also calculated that the same extent of ground, when planted with the Banana, will support a far greater number of people than when planted with wheat. As this is a point of great economical interest, it has been a subject of subsequent investigation. The productiveness has been found to differ with the mean temperature of the place. Boussingault has given the following as the produce, per imperial acre, of the raw fruit in three places, according to Humboldt's (1), Gondot's (2), and his own observations (3):

	Temperature.	Produce, per imperial acre.	Or of dry food, per acre.
(1) In warm regions . .	81½ Fah.	72 tons.	19½ tons.
(2) At Cauca . . .	78⅘ „	59 „	16 „
(3) At Hague . . .	71⅗ „	25 „	6¾ „

Professor Johnston is the authority for the last column, or that of dry food per acre, as he had, from his analysis, obtained 27 per cent. of nutritive matter from the Banana. He justly observes, that all these quantities are very large, and show how easily life may be supported in tropical countries. And further, that as potatoes contain about one fourth their weight of dry nutritive matter, it would require a crop of twenty-seven tons of potatoes per imperial acre, to yield the smallest of the quantities above mentioned as the yield of an acre of Plantains; while only twenty to twenty-four tons of potatoes are obtained in favorable seasons and localities.

Though it is not probable that the Plantain is cultivated in India with the care to enable the largest possible quantity of produce to be obtained, yet there is no doubt that the produce is large and the culture most simple. It would be an interesting subject of experiment for the Agricultural Societies of India, to ascertain which are the most productive varieties; whether the modes of cultivation adopted in that country have attained the highest limits of productiveness; and also to determine the best methods for preserving the fruit in different places; and also, when superabundant, whether its meal might not be preserved for periods of scarcity, or for the season of the year when the fresh fruit is not procurable. In South America the fruit is not only used as an article of diet in its fresh state, but, when dried, forms an article of internal trade, besides having its flour separated, and cooked or made into biscuits. It is also preserved in the Society Islands.

The preservation of the fruit and the preparation of the meal has already been introduced into India. Some Plantain meal was sent to the Exhibition of 1851, from Madras, as well as baked Plantains from Jessore, by the Rev. J. Parry. These, after some years, are still in good preservation and well tasted. The late Dr. Stocks[1] informed the author that the Plantains at Bassein, where the cultivation is most extensive, are delicious in flavour, and that there the people had acquired the art of preserving them. But this was practised many years ago in Central India, and in Ceylon in 1840.

The late Sir John Robison, Secretary of the Royal Society of Edinburgh, wrote to the author some years since: "Among the products of India which, I think, might be easily brought into general sale in this country, are some of the fruits, which, if cut in slices and dried in the sun, would become susceptible of transport, as those of the Levant and the South of France. Above all, the Banana, of which the varieties, which are rich in saccharine matter, make an admirable preserve, on being skinned and split longitudinally and dried in the sun, by which process they immediately acquire a consistence like Turkey figs, and become capable of being packed and preserved in the same way." He concludes by stating: "I was in the habit of having large quantities preserved every year in this way at Hyderabad, and of using them as an article of dessert at table."

In treating of the cultivation of species of Musa or Plantain in India for fibre, it is desirable to advert to the cultivation of the edible species, or the numerous varieties included under the names of Banana and of Plantain, and suggesting them as above as subjects of experiment to members of the Agricultural Societies in India, to ascertain whether the modes of cultivation adopted in India have attained the highest limits of productiveness; and also whether the fruit might not be preserved in different forms. The author has already observed that a remarkable instance of the great length of time for which these Plantains may be preserved in an eatable state, occurred at the Exhibition of 1851. These were some preserved Plantains, "Platano pasado," which had been brought home by

[1] While this sheet is going to press, the author has heard, with deep regret, of the loss which Science and the East India Service have sustained, in the death of this accomplished naturalist, who was as remarkable for the variety of his attainments, as for his zeal for botanical science and its application to practical purposes.

Lieut.-Col. Colquhoun, R.A., from the province of Jatisco (Guadalagara), Mexico, in the year 1835, and which since then had remained neglected in a baggage warehouse. The specimen exhibited was the remainder of a package of 75 lb. weight, made up, as customary, in the leaves and fibre of the plant, after having been subjected to considerable pressure. The state of preservation, after sixteen years, was favorably reported on by Dr. Lindley, and no signs of decomposition are yet perceptible in the specimens given to the author by Colonel, now Sir W. Reid; the sugar of the fruit having been sufficient to preserve them. They are prepared in considerable quantities in the hot region (tierra caliente) of the western coast of Mexico, for consumption in the elevated districts of the interior. The Silver Medal of the Society of Arts was awarded for the first samples brought to England. *See* the 'Transactions,' vol. 1, p. 43, for the method of preparation, reprinted in 'Trans. Agric. Soc. of India,' viii, p. 60.

Before, however, proceeding to detail the methods of preservation of the fruit, or the preparation of the meal, it is desirable to notice the relative values of these as compared with other kinds of fruit. This we are enabled to do from an excellent Report 'On the composition and nutritive value of Plantain Meal,' by Professor Johnston, published in the 'Journal of the Highland and Agricultural Society of Scotland,' in 1848, and to which attention has already been called by Professor Key, of Madras. By this we shall see that, in extending the culture of the Plantain, on account of its fibre, there is no probability of this ever becoming so extensive as for its fruit to become valueless.

CHEMICAL ANALYSIS OF PLANTAIN FRUIT AND MEAL.

Extracts from a Report upon the 'Properties of the Plantain Meal.'—This meal is of a slightly brownish colour, and has an agreeable odour, which becomes more perceptible when warm water is poured upon it, and it has a considerable resemblance to that of Orris root.

When mixed with cold water, it forms a feebly tenacious dough, more adhesive than that of oatmeal, but much less so than that of wheaten flour. When baked on a plate, this dough forms a cake which is agreeable to the sense of smell, and is by no means unpleasant to the taste.

By washing with water this dough leaves no residue of insoluble tenacious gluten, as that of wheaten flour does. When filtered from the starch, the wash water gives no cloudiness when rendered slightly sour by Acetic Acid, when boiled yields a little coagulated albumen. Whether this is the case in the fresh fruit, or only in the dried meal prepared from it, I have had no opportunity of determining.

The addition of Alcohol to the same watery solution renders it more or less distinctly gelatinous, as it does similar solutions obtained from other fruits, and from the turnip, parsnip, &c. This shows the presence of pectin, or pectic acid, the substance which in fruits, in the turnip, and in many other bulbous roots, takes the place of the starch found in grain, and in the tubers of the potato.

When boiling water is poured over the meal, it is changed into a transparent jelly, having an agreeable taste and smell. If it be boiled with water, its forms a thick gelatinous mass, very much like boiled sago in colour, but possessing a peculiar pleasant odour.

Composition of the Plantain Meal.—By a careful analysis, the composition of the plantain meal was found to be nearly as follows:

a. The water.—Mr. Law states that 59 parts of the fruit yielded only 30·85 of eatable parts, which, on drying in the air, were reduced to 12·32 parts. The fruit, therefore, consisted in 100 parts of—

	Per cent.
Husks, &c.	47·71
Water evaporated by the sun	20·88
Meal dried in the sun	31·41
	100·00

The meal thus dried in the open air, when dried again in the laboratory at 212° Fahr., lost 14·07 per cent. of water in addition; or one hundred parts of the recent fruit contain 27 of dry nutritive matter.

b. The albumen, &c.—By combustion the proportion of nitrogen in this meal, in its ordinary state, was found by Dr. Fromberg, in two experiments, to be 0·88 and 0·97 respectively, equal as a mean to 5·82 per cent. of protein compounds. These, as we have already seen, are most probably in the state of soluble albumen taken up by cold water, and of coagulated albumen attached to, or mixed with, the starch, cellular fibre, &c. In the perfectly dry meal the proportion is 6·75 per cent.

c. The ash.—When burned in the air, the proportion of ash left behind amounts to 2·33 per cent., or in the dried meal to 2·71 per cent.

The entire composition of the plantain meal is represented in the following table:

	Dried in the air.	Dried at 212° Fah.
Water	14·07	
Starch	67·42	78·43
Gum and Pectin	4·47	5·21
Cellular fibre	4·84	5·62
Sugar	2·03	2·40
Oil	0·41	0·48
Albumen (soluble)	1·21	1·41
Albumen (coagulated gluten, &c.)	3·23	3·74
Ash	2·32	2·71
	100·00	100·00

On comparing the above composition with that of other kinds of food commonly eaten by man, we find the plantain *fruit* to approach most nearly in composition and nutritive value to the potato, and the plantain *meal* to those of rice. Thus, the fruit of the plantain gives 27 per cent., and the raw potato 25 per cent. of dry matter.

Again, the dry mealy matter of the plantain, of the potato, and of rice consists respectively of—

	Rice.	Potato.	Plantain.
Starch	86·9	65·0	78·4
Sugar, Gum, &c.	0·5	15·0	7·6
Fat	0·8	1·0	0·5
Cellular fibre	3·4	8·0	5·6
Protein compounds	7·5	8·0	5·2
Ash	0·9	3·0	2·7
	100·0	100·0	100·0

or, comparing only the Starch, Sugar, &c., and the protein compounds, on which the nutritive quality of these different vegetable productions principally depends, we have the following numbers:

	Rice.	Potato.	Plantain.
Starch, Sugar, &c.	87·4	79·0	86·0
Protein compounds	7·5	8·0	5·2

These numbers show that it approaches, as I have said, nearest in its composition to rice, containing nearly as much starch, but a sensibly smaller proportion of the protein compounds, on which the sustenance of the muscles is supposed chiefly to depend.

In regard to its value as a food for man in our northern climates, there is no reason to believe that it is unfit to sustain life and health; and as to warmer or tropical climates, this conclusion is of more weight.

The only chemical writer who has previously made personal observations upon this point (M. Boussingault) says: "I have not sufficient data to determine the nutritive value of the banana, but I have reason to believe that it is superior to that of potato. I have given as rations to men employed at hard labour about 3 kilogrammes (6½ lb.) of half-ripe bananas, and 60 grammes (2 ounces) of salt meat." Of these green bananas he elsewhere states that 38 per cent. consisted of husk, and that the internal eatable part lost 56 per cent. of water by drying in the sun. The 6·6 pounds, therefore, were composed of—

Husk	2·5 lb.
Water	2·3 „
Heart dried in the sun	1·8 „
	6·6 lb.

so that less than two pounds a day of this dried banana fruit, which we may suppose to be equal in quality and composition to the sun-dried plantain meal, above described, with two ounces of salt meat per day, were found sufficient to maintain men, *not slaves*, at moderately hard labour. This was equal to 12½ lb. dried eatable banana, and 1 pound of salt meat (query fish) per week.

*   *   *   *   *

The composition of the ash of the Plantain also bears a close resemblance to that of the potato. Both contain much alkaline matter, potash and soda salts, and in both there is nearly the same per centage of phosphoric acid and magnesia. In so far, therefore, as the supply of those mineral ingredients is concerned, by which the body is supported as necessarily as by the organic food, there is no reason to doubt that the banana, equally with the potato, is fitted to sustain the strength of the animal body. It must not be denied that our present knowledge indicates the advantage of a mixture of food, as the most conducive to health and strength, but experience shows that, however desirable, this is not absolutely necessary. The oat alone in Scotland raises and supports strong men; rye alone does so in the north of Europe; and the potato alone does so in Ireland. This result of experience in the case of the potato justifies us, were there no experience on the subject in tropical countries, in believing that the banana, which resembles it, will do the same. Whatever other reasons may lead us to recommend a mixture of other food with it, especially where *hard* labour, perhaps not a natural condition of things, is required of him, we ought not to base this recommendation upon any belief that the banana, when eaten alone, will not fully supply all the ordinary wants of the living animal.

Cultivation.—The Plantain has thus been proved to be valuable on account of its fruit, both in its unripe and ripe state, the latter both when fresh and when preserved, and for yielding nutritious meal. The plant is also to be esteemed on account of the fibre with which every part of it abounds. Though both the Plantain and the Banana are to be found near the huts of the poor and in the gardens of the rich, the most profitable mode of culture has, probably, in few places been as yet ascertained. In the first place, of the great varieties to be found in cultivation, it would be necessary to select those which abound most in the products we chiefly require.

The small Banana is most esteemed as a fruit by Europeans, but the large-fruited and, in comparison with the other, coarse-tasted Plantain is preferred by the natives of India, as is the long yellow Plantain in Jamaica. Both of the latter abound in fibre, and are therefore to be preferred when both this and the fruit are objects of desire.

The culture of the Plantain is, upon the whole, very simple, as it will succeed in almost any soil where the climate is warm and moist. The vicinity of water, for cleansing and washing the fibre, will, of course, be an essential. Professor Key, of Madras, has stated that in India the Plantain will flourish in the poorest soil and near brackish water, and that its culture might be extended with very little trouble and expense. A sucker being planted, rapidly attains maturity; some varieties in eight months, others within the year. Each producing a bunch of fruit which may weigh from twenty-five to forty, and even ninety pounds; and each throwing out from its roots and around its stem, from six and seven to eight and ten fresh suckers. These will each form a distinct plant, producing its own bunch of fruit; all requiring to be cut down annually, in order to make room for the fresh suckers which spring up. This may go on for fifteen or twenty years, though some think that it is better to renew the plantation entirely or partially at shorter periods. A chief consideration is the distance at which the original plants should be placed, in order to give room for the secondary suckers, as well as to allow of free ventilation. Some place them at distances of six feet, but it is better to have them ten feet apart, either around the boundaries of fields or of gardens, or in rows as a separate plantation. In the latter case, it is recommended that there should be space enough between the rows to allow of the culture of other crops. In some parts of India, the Plantain is employed as a nurse, or to afford shade, to the Betel Vine (itself one of the most valuable of crops), or to young Areca-nut and to Cocoa-nut Palms. By cutting away some of the suckers as they arise at different periods, and allowing others to remain, a supply of fruit, and also of stems for fibre, may be obtained for a great part of the year.

In Demerara and Guiana, the Plantains have been injured by some disease, which has impaired their fruitfulness, and, consequently, the profits of their culture. It has been recommended to plant them at sufficient distances (as eighteen feet) to allow of free ventilation, accompanied with good tillage in the intervals and the cultivation of annual crops of Maize, Yams, Sugar-cane, or Eddoes. (Arum.) According to the distances, there may be from 300 to upwards of 400 plants in an acre, each producing, say, on an average, seven suckers; making in all from 2100 to 3200 plants in an acre.

Preservation of the Fruit.—The fruit of the Plantain, when ripe, containing a sufficient proportion of nutritive matter, may well serve as a portion of the food of the natives of warm countries. But it is probably as much employed by them before being perfectly ripe, as it is sometimes stewed, and at other times fried; and, by the natives of India, dressed in various ways to eat with rice. In the West Indies, the fresh Plantain, when boiled whole, forms a mass of considerable toughness, and which, when beaten in a mortar, constitutes the *foo-foo* of the negroes. (Simmonds.) When nearly or perfectly ripe, it is pleasantly, or even lusciously sweet, and it is in the former state that it is preserved.

Col. Colquhoun describes the mode of preparation as very simple: "The fruit is gathered when fully ripe, and is laid on light cane frames, exposed to the sun. When it begins to shrivel, the outer skin is stripped off. (This is stated to be a very essential part of the process, as without it the fruit acquires an unpleasant flavour.) After this, the drying is completed. During this process it becomes covered with a white, mealy efflorescence of sugar, as the fig does under similar circumstances. For convenience of transport it is pressed into masses of about 75 lb. each, and is wrapped in plantain leaves. The masses are twenty-four inches long by fourteen wide, and four inches thick. The samples presented to the Society of Arts were about two years old, sufficiently moist, of a consistence and flavour between the date and the fig, very sweet, and without any acidity. It is evident that this process of preservation will be found to be of considerable value in other parts of the world, and especially in situations where it is cultivated in larger quantities than the fruit can be consumed. The drying in the sun would be sufficient in dry climates, but baking in ovens seems to be necessary in moist climates, such as Dacca and Jessore. The process seems to be sufficiently well understood in several parts of India. When the fruit is of a good kind, no addition of sugar can be necessary. This subject seemed so worthy of a fair trial in the British West Indies to the Society of Arts, that they offered, in the year 1834, a premium for its encouragement. It seems no less important for the East Indies, especially if any planters should be induced to cultivate the Plantain in large quantities, on account of its fibre, or for the preparation of half-stuff for paper-makers.

Plantain Meal.—Mr. Simmonds describes this meal as prepared by stripping off the husk of the fruit, slicing the core, and drying it in the sun. When thoroughly dry it is powdered and sifted. It is known among the creoles of the West Indies under the name of *Conquin tay.* It has a fragrant odour, which it acquires when drying, and which somewhat resembles that of fresh hay or tea. The flavour of the meal is, moreover, said to depend a good deal on the rapidity with which the slices are dried. Hence, the operation is only fitted for dry weather, unless where a kiln or stove is had recourse to. Above all, the Plantain must not be allowed to approach too closely to yellowness or ripeness, otherwise it becomes impossible to dry it. The colour of the meal is, moreover, injured, when steel knives are used in husking or slicing; but nickel blades or Bamboo slicers would not injure the colour. On a large scale, some single machine might be adapted to the husking and slicing processes, and the mode tried by which arrow-root is obtained, by scraping and suspension in cold water.

It is calculated that the fresh core will yield forty per cent. of dry meal, and that 5 lb. may be obtained from an average bunch of 25 lb. weight; and an acre of Plantain walk of average quality, producing even during the year 450 such bunches, would yield upwards of a ton of meal, the value of which must of course vary in different countries according to the price of other articles of food. In the West Indies it is largely employed as the food of infants, children, and convalescents. In point of nutritious value, we have seen that the fruit approaches the potato, and the meal to that of rice. There can be no doubt, therefore, of the value of this meal, and of the benefit of preparing it, wherever the fruit is preserved in larger quantities than it can be consumed.

Preparation of the Fibre.—The Plantain has been stated to abound in fibre—indeed, almost every part of the plant may be said to be available for this product. It is related, that from the upper part of these spurious stems, spiral vessels may be pulled out in handfuls, and are used as tinder in the West Indies. De Candolle has described them as consisting, in Musa, of seven distinct fibres lying parallel, formed into bands; and La Chesnaye of upwards of twenty, arranged in a spiral manner. M. Mohl describes the secondary cell-membrane as divided into as many as twenty parallel spiral fibres. But these are not the fibres which are separated for economic purposes, nor are they situated on the same side of the vegetable structure. For instance, if we take any separate layer of the Plantain stem—that is, a part of the sheathing footstalk of a leaf—we may observe on its outer side a layer of strong longitudinal fibres, which form a kind of framework or ribs for the support of the structure, which is cellular on its inside. It is on this side that spiral vessels are placed, and next the pith in exogenous plants. They are abundant in the peduncle, or core, as it is often called, of the Musa.

As in the Manilla, so in the common Plantain, the fibre is found to be coarse and strong in the outer layers of the sheathing footstalks, fine and silky in the interior, and of a middling quality in the intermediate layers. This fibre is separated by the natives of Dacca, for instance, and is used by them for making the string of the bow with which cotton is teazed (bowed). Much of it is well adapted for cordage. Mr. Leycester (*v. supra*), when calling attention to the fibre of the *Musa textilis* grown in Calcutta, directed attention to the fibres of *M. sapientum* and of *M. ornata*, as fitted to answer as string for all gardening purposes. Mr. Crawford is of opinion that the common Plantain most probably afforded the Indian Islanders the principal material for their clothing, in the same way that the indigenous species does in the Philippine Islands. The art of making cloth from these fibres seems also to have been known in Madagascar. There is no doubt that the large cultivated Plantain of India contains a considerable quantity of strong fibre, in the same way that the common yellow Plantain does in Jamaica. But it seems well worthy of inquiry, whether the wild, and at present useless Plantains, growing along the foot of the Himalayas and on the Neilgherries, may not yield a stronger fibre than any of the cultivated kinds.

The fibre may be easily separated from any part, by simply scraping it on a stone or flat board, with a piece of hard wood; iron, though frequently used, no doubt injures the colour. In the following directions given by Dr. Hunter ('Art Journal,' Madras, i, pp. 108 and 376) the essentials are attended to, and the fibre is separated in an uninjured state, but the process is probably not the most economical.

To prepare the fibres of the Plantain, he rejects the outer, withered layer of leaves, and then strips off the different layers, and proceeds to clean them in the shade, if possible soon after the plant has been cut down. Lay a leaf-stalk on a long flat board, with the inner surface uppermost, scrape the pulp off with a blunt piece of hoop-iron fixed in a groove in a long piece of wood. When the inner side, which has the thickest layer of pulp, has been cleaned, turn over the leaf and scrape the back of it. When a good bundle of fibres has been thus partially cleaned, it ought to be washed briskly in a large quantity of water, so as to get rid, as quickly as possible, of all the pulpy matter which may still adhere to the fibres. It may be readily separated by boiling the fibres in an alkaline ley or in alkaline soaps, but not in the Indian soaps made with quick-lime, as these are too corrosive. When the fibres have been thoroughly washed, they should be spread out in thin layers or hung up in the wind to dry. If exposed to the sun when in a damp state, a brownish-yellow tinge is communicated, which cannot be easily removed by bleaching. Exposure during the night to the dew bleaches them, but it is at the expense of part of their strength.

If we attend only to what is essential in the above process, we find that all that is required is scraping or pressure to separate the cellular and watery from the fibrous parts. This is followed by careful washing, and sometimes by boiling in an alkaline ley, but the latter part of the process does not appear to be essentially necessary.

In the West Indies, according to the complete account of a practical correspondent in Jamaica, as given in Simmonds' 'Commercial Products of the Vegetable Kingdom,' the fibre is separated, either by crushing under rollers in a mill, or by fermentation. If by the latter process, there is considerable saving in carriage, as the stems, when cut down, are heaped together near where they have grown, and are shaded from the sun by laying the leaves over them. A drainage of the sap takes place, which is described as having a tanning property, and as discolouring the pieces which lie at the bottom. But several weeks elapse before decomposition is complete, when the fibres can be easily separated from the rest of the vegetable mass. There is little doubt, that besides discoloration, there must be some weakening of the fibre by this process, as we know takes place in India when the stems are steeped in water until some decomposition takes place.

It is usual not to cut the stems until fruit has been produced; "for two reasons—first, that the fruit be not lost, and secondly, that the tree will not have arrived at its full growth and ordinary size, and the fibres will be too tender." This is the reverse of the practice in the Philippines, where the stem is cut before the fruit appears, in order to ensure a better quality of fibre. It would be an interesting experiment for those favorably situated, to ascertain the mode by which the best kind of fibre is produced, and what would be the loss of profit, supposing that the fruit is sacrificed for the sake of the fibre.

The stem is described as being cut off about six inches above the ground, and being tender, it may, on being bent down, be cut asunder with a single stroke of a hatchet or cutlass. It is then divided, longitudinally, into four parts, the centre taken out and left to serve as manure, and the pieces conveyed at once to the mill to be crushed. It is said that "one man can cut down 800 trees, and split them in a day." A very convenient size for the rollers of the mill, will be found to be about three feet in length and one foot in diameter. In the process of crushing, care should be taken to separate the tender from the harder layers of fibre. This may be attained by having the rollers of the mill placed horizontally; and if the pieces of Plantain are passed lengthways through the mill the pressure will be uniform, and the fibre uninjured. "In this manner, pass the different sorts of layers separately, and the produce will be about four pounds of fibre from each tree. The stalks of the branches of the Plantain (no doubt the mid-rib of the leaf is meant) give the best fibre, and a large quantity as compared with the body of the tree; 100 lb. of the stalk will give 15 lb. nett of fibre. In general, if a tree will give 4 lb. nett of fibre, the stalks will give 1 lb. out of the 4 lb. The stalks ought also to be crushed separately, because they are harder than the exterior layers of the tree. About 3000 trees may be passed through the mill in a day. Whilst the experiments were in progress, it was ascertained that, with a single horse, 100 Plantain trees, on an average, were crushed in twenty minutes—giving five minutes' rest for the horse."

The quantity of produce from each plant, is the point of greatest discrepancy between the West Indian practice and Dr. Hunter's experiments, as he mentions only a few ounces of fibre as procurable from each plant. But as he rejected the outer parts, and did not include the midrib of the leaves, the discrepancy may be partly accounted for. The combings or tow, separated from the fibres during their preparation, are also of value as a substitute for horse-hair, for stuffing mattresses, &c.; and also the peduncle or core, if pounded into half-stuff for paper-makers. Some of the cellular tissue containing much fibrous matter, might, probably, be converted to the same purposes.

In addition to the above processes of crushing and washing, the West Indian account also gives the details of the process of boiling the fibre with carbonate of soda and quick-lime, in order, it is said, to get rid of the remaining vegetable matter, and to bleach the fibre. The different qualities of which, having been crushed separately, are of course to be kept so, and boiled separately. The proportions given in the above account are for making three tons of fibre per day. For this, four large (800-gallon) boilers are required, and about 360 lb. of soda would be consumed, with a proportionate quantity of lime; or the soda, that is, its carbonate, may be first deprived of its carbonic acid. This may be done by preparing, in a small separate boiler, the quantity of liquid necessary for a day's consumption, which may be done in about an hour, by taking, by weight, ten parts of soda, six parts of quick-lime, and not less than seventy parts of water. The operation of boiling in the soda ley is said to be important in separating the gluten and colouring matter from the fibres, and also to facilitate their bleaching. The lightest coloured fibres do not require more than six hours to bleach, whilst the darkest will probably take from twelve to eighteen hours. It is advisable to place over each boiler the means of lifting the mass of fibre when boiled, and suffering it to drain into the boiler before it is carried away to be washed. The machinery necessary for cleansing and washing may be of various descriptions—as that used by paper-makers in England, or by coffee-planters and arrow-root growers in the West Indies. The fibre may be dried, by being hung over lines made of the same material. These, when dry, may be pressed and packed.

For carrying on the culture of the Plantain on an extensive scale, in the West Indies, it is stated that the materials will cost £2000, buildings £500, purchase of land £1500, working capital £1000=£5000. The estimated expense in cultivating one quarree or 5⅕ English acres, in Plantains, will be £30, as the work can be easily performed by one labourer in 300 days, at 2*s*. sterling per day. A quarree will produce 18 tons of mill-fibre, the cost of the preparation of which is as follows:

For workmen's wages, soda, lime, and fuel, at £3 per ton	£54
Freight to Europe, at £4 per ton	72
Manager	30
Duty, insurance, office fees, &c., at £1 per ton	18
	£174

Thus making the total expense of producing 18 tons of fibre £174, or £9 13*s.* 4*d.* per ton.

By another statement, derived from different data, but somewhat similar sources, it has been calculated that Plantain fibre, in a coarse state, might be laid down in England, at £10 6*s.* 8*d.* But some expense would be incurred in cleansing the fibre for finer purposes. In another account, also taken from West Indian information, it is stated that the cost of well-cleaned fibre would amount to £7 1*s.* 3*d.*, to which, of course, freight would have to be added; while half-stuff for paper-makers might, at the same time, be produced from the refuse at about half that sum.

As Plantain fibre has not yet, as far as we have heard, been systematically prepared as an article of commerce, these calculations of cost are somewhat conjectural. But they are interesting, as showing, from the experiments which had been made, that large quantities of a valuable product may be obtained at a comparatively cheap rate; and this, from what is now a complete refuse—that is, the stem and leaves; while the expenses of culture are paid for by the fruit. And the more so, as the data are West Indian, where the prices of material and the wages of labour are much higher than in India.

Specimens of Plantain fibre, and a barrel of it for experimental purposes, were sent by two Exhibitors from Demerara, also some from Porto Rico (*v.* 'Illust. Cat., p. 982); and it was stated that the fibre might be obtained in very large quantities from the Plantain cultivation of the former colony. It is calculated that upwards of 600 lb. weight of fibre might be produced annually from each acre of Plantains, after reaping the fruit crops. It is further stated, that "at present, the stems of the Plantain trees, when cut down, are allowed to rot on the ground. If a remunerative price could be realised for this fibre, a new branch of industry would be opened up to the colonists."

From India, unfortunately, we have no statements showing

the rates at which Plantain fibre, tow, and pulp, might be obtained as articles of commerce. Dr. Hunter, of Madras, has done much in showing the various purposes to which this valuable product might be applied; as he sent to the Exhibition of 1851 both the fibre and the tow in a well-cleaned state. The former about four feet in length, and also dyed of several colours, as well as twisted into fine cord and into rope. Some Plantain rope was, moreover, sent in a tarred state. A portion of the tow was sent in a state fit for packing and stuffing, and some converted into paper; of the latter, some was almost as thin as silver paper, and some of it seemingly as tough and tenacious as parchment, well fitted for packing paper, as apparently little affected by water. But in this country, some excellent letter paper has been made from the Plantain fibre. Besides the above, Plantain meal was sent by Professor Key from Madras, and preserved Plantains from Jessore. But dried Plantains seem already established as an article of commerce at Bombay, as we observe them among the exports for the year 1850-51, from thence to Cutch and Guzerat, to the extent of 267 cwt., valued at 1456 rupees. So that the various applications of which Plantain fruit and fibre are susceptible have been already made in India. It remains only to produce them as cheaply as the other products of the country.

Dr. Hunter, in his experiments, found that the fibre cost about three annas, or about sixpence, a pound—which is prohibitive as an article of export; but he states that if regular supplies of the fibre were required, the price might be reduced to two annas. He also mentions that, at Madras, the rate at which the stems were at first supplied was ten annas for one hundred trees; but this was raised to four rupees for the same number, when he began to make use of them. This is a sufficient proof that they are not very abundant there. But "in the vicinity of some of the Zillah (that is, of District) Jails, the Plantain is cultivated very extensively, but no use is made of the stems, which are allowed to rot on the surface of the ground." This is also the case in most parts of India.

On the opposite coast of Arracan, the Plantain is abundant. What seem to be the layers forming the stem of such a plant, and about seven feet in length, are sold there in a dried state, and called *Pa-tha-you Shaw;* some of it even twisted into a bast-rope, is sold for the same sum, that is, for one rupee the maund, or for about three shillings per cwt.

As the above Shaw or *bast* of an unknown plant is sold at so cheap a rate, as well as the other basts sent from Arracan to the Exhibition of 1851, even after some preparation, there is no reason why Plantain fibre might not be sent cheaply into market. I have no doubt that it would very soon command a price equal to its real value, as a material for paper-making, for cordage, or for textile fabrics. The fibre might be collected in situations where the plant is already cultivated, in gardens, or where it grows wild, and its stems not turned to any account. Or it might be cultivated in fields on its own account, either with or without other crops, such as Pan or *Piper Betle*, or Ginger, Turmeric, &c. The fruit in its fresh state, near towns, or in a preserved state, or converted into meal, ought to pay all the expenses of, and afford some profit on the culture. The stems and leaves would thus be obtained at a minimum of cost—that is, simply of carriage.

Indeed, if the crushing mill were not of too cumbrous a nature, it might be brought into the vicinity of the field, in the same way that the natives of India construct a sugar-mill and boiler in the immediate vicinity of where the Date tree is grown or the Sugar-cane cultivated. A mill, consisting of the rollers of a sugar-mill or an enlarged churka, with an Archimedean screw, or with cog-wheels, or with bands, to which motion is given by bullocks, as practised in various parts of India, would probably be sufficiently effective, and certainly economical. The separation of the different qualities of fibre, with the washing, combing or heckling, and drying, might at first all be performed by hand, where labour is so cheap. If all the fibrous matter, or the combings or tow only, should be required for conversion into half-stuff for paper-makers, nothing is more effective, and at the same time so economical, as the Dhenkee of India. To this attention has been recently called by Mr. Henley ('Journ. of Soc. of Arts,' vol. ii, p. 486), and which, as he describes, "resembles in principle our European tilt-hammer." "Its cost would be—erected in place—engineers, foundations, and all charges included— three shillings; and this charge supposes the more than usually heavy machine employed for paper-making!" "The total wages for the preparation of 20 to 30 lb." of suitable material, "would amount to sevenpence-halfpenny." Mr. Henley adds, that "in the event of employing such fibres as the Plantain leaf-stalk, a small pair of hard wood grooved rollers, such as they employ for squeezing sugar-cane, would be very useful. Their cost is two shillings."

Having, in my Lecture before the Society of Arts, recommended the Plantain as likely to yield an abundant supply of material for paper-making, Mr. Henley observes: "From extensive cultivation of the Banana or Plantain, which surrounds almost every house, it is probable this material would form one of the first objects of attention by paper-material collectors; but from its coarse, stringy nature, it would be cheaper in the state of fibre than as half-stuff. This plant offers great advantages for our views generally, for it is truly in the position of refuse, inasmuch as it has already paid the charges of its cultivation by its products in fruit. The interior of the plant, or true flower-stem, is eaten as a vegetable by the natives; the lower part being perfectly mild, whilst the upper extremity, near the bunch of fruit, pours out, on cutting it across, a limpid fluid, which is very acrid and deleterious, and is a true substantive olive dye on cotton cloth, as indelible as marking ink, for which it may be substituted." With regard to the price at which such materials could be obtained, Mr. Henley says: "I am of opinion that contracts could be made, according to the ordinary usages of the country, at the rate of from one rupee eight annas, or three shillings, to two rupees eight annas, or five shillings, per maund of 82 lb., deliverable at any central depôt within a radius of twenty miles. These prices are equal to from about £4 4*s*. to £7 a ton; and that, of these, the lowest-priced material could be landed in London, paying all charges, for £13 4*s*., and the more expensive, which would include articles equal to linen rags, at £16 5*s*."

Having already noticed the facility with which the species of Plantain may be cultivated in suitable climates, we may mention that we have lately tasted some excellent fruit of *Musa Cavendishii*, grown in a Fernery on Putney Heath. We have chiefly to warn cultivators against planting the Plantain too close together; for though this may produce fineness of fibre, it will also diminish strength, and want of free ventilation may produce disease. For separating the fibre, it may be a question whether smooth or grooved cylinders will be best for so fleshy and moist a substance, but it is very necessary to remember that the pulp or the fibre must be thoroughly dried, in order that it may not undergo decomposition when in transit in the hold of a ship.

Of the value of the Plantain fibre for paper-making, there can, I conceive, be no doubt. Some paper, though unbleached, but excellent as far as substance and tenacity are concerned, was sent from India by Dr. Hunter, in 1851. In the year 1846, Mr. May showed the author some beautiful specimens of note and letter paper made from Plantain fibre. He was at that time anxious to establish a manufactory for Plantain paper in Calcutta, but subsequently went to one of the British colonies in South America; and we have also noticed (p. 89) the fact of a gentleman having shown specimens of paper made from Plantain fibre in Demerara. Mr. Routledge subsequently made some excellent paper, both of a tough and of a fine quality, from the fibres of species of Musa—sheets of which he has presented to the author, who has lately seen specimens of similar paper in the hands of Mr. Sharp. Besides which, excellent paper has for some time been made from the refuse of or from worn-out Manilla rope. All which facts prove that an excellent material for paper-making may be had in inexhaustible supplies, whenever those chiefly interested choose to take the necessary measures for securing such a supply.

We may now therefore notice the other uses to which Plantain fibre can be applied.

Lieut.-Col. Whinyates, Principal Commissary of Ordnance, in a letter to the Secretary to the Military Board at Madras, states that the Plantain oakum or tow sent by Dr. Hunter is "undoubtedly of a very superior description, and admirably adapted for packing. From the soft, elastic character of the fibre, he also conceives that it would be a desirable substitute for coir in stuffing hospital beddings, &c. But he fears that the supply is too limited, and the cost all too high, being at that time (October 29th, 1850) about three annas the pound."

STATEMENT showing the comparative Strengths of the undermentioned Specimens of Rope, Cord, String, &c., made from the fibres of the Plantain, with Hempen Rope, as exemplified in a set of Experiments carried on at the Arsenal, Fort St. George, in July, 1850.

Number marked on label.	LABELLED.	Arsenal Number.	Description.	Circumference.	Length of Rope, &c., used.	Weight required to break the Rope, &c.	Weight required to break: After immersion in water 24 hours, dried in the shade, and tested 7 days after.	After being immersed in water 10 days, and dried in the sun.	Manilla Rope of same circumference.	English Hemp Rope of same circumference.	Weight of one Fathom of each description: Plantain.	Manilla.	Europe.
				In.	Fms.	lb.	lb.	lb.	lb.	lb.	oz.	oz.	oz.
1	Rope and String made from the fibres of the Plantain. Mr. Lima. Porto Novo.	1	Line	0¾	2	248	—	—	—	—	2 1-16	—	—
		2	String	0¼	1	54½	—	—	—	—	0 4-16	—	—
2	Rope and Line made from the fibres of the Plantain, by the prisoners of the House of Correction.	3	Line	1	2	288	—	—	—	—	2 7-16	—	—
		4	ditto	0¾	2	190	—	—	—	—	1 12-16	—	—
		5	String	0½	1	114	—	—	Bengal log line 137	—	0 9-16	—	—
3	Rope made from the fibres of the Plantain, in the House of Industry. Fibres prepared in the House of Corr., Madras.	6	Rope	3¼	2	2330	2387	2050	4669	3885	19 9-16	28 11-16	39
		7	ditto	1½	2	638	—	—	869	—	6	5	—
		8	ditto	1½	2	694	—	—	869	—	5 13-16	5	—
		9	ditto	1⅜	2	624	—	—	—	Ratline 638	4 5-16	—	5 1-16
4	Rope made from the fibres of the Plantain, by a pauper in the Monegar Choultry, Madras.	10	Line	1	1¾	323	—	—	—	—	2 10-16	—	—
		11	ditto	1	1	330	—	—	—	—	3	—	—
		12	ditto	0¾	2	183	—	—	—	—	1 8-16	—	—
		13	ditto	0¾	0¾	362	—	—	—	—	1 9-16	—	—
5	Rope and String made from the fibres of the Plantain, by five Europeans in her Majesty's Jail.	14	Rope	1¾	2	1240	1266	762	1490	1184	7 9-16	9 8-16	13
		15	ditto	1⅜	2	974	—	—	—	—	5 8-16	—	—
		16	String	0½	1	185	—	—	Bengal log line 137	—	1 4-16	—	—
		17	ditto	0¼	1	38	—	—	—	—	0 5-32	—	—
6	Ditto, ditto, by the same prisoners, from fibres of the Plantain prepared in the House of Correction.	18	Rope	2	2	1490	—	—	—	—	11	—	—
		19	ditto	1¾	2	1322	—	—	1490	1184	8 6-16	9½	13
		20	ditto	1¼	2	806	—	—	757	Ratline 638	5	3¼	5 1-16
		21	String	0¼	1	43½	—	—	—	—	0 3-16	—	—

With respect to the strength of Plantain fibre, I may state, that in some experiments which I have had made on Plantain fibre, some from Madras bore a weight of 190 lb., but the specimen from Singapore bore not less than 390 lb., while a salvage of Petersburgh Hemp, of the same length and weight, broke with 160 lb. A twelve-thread rope of Plantain fibre made in India broke with 864 lb., when a similar rope made of Pine-apple fibre broke with 924 lb. Even from these experiments, it is evident that Plantain fibre possesses sufficient tenacity to be applicable to many, at least, of the ordinary purposes of cordage, as is very clearly shown by the experiments detailed in the annexed tabular statement. But it is probable that the plants grown in a moister climate than that of Madras will possess a greater degree of strength. The outer fibres may also be converted into a useful kind of coarse canvass, as has been done by Dr. Hunter; and the more delicate inner fibres most probably into finer fabrics, as is the case with those of the Abaca or *Musa textilis;* when equal care has been taken in the preparation and separation of the fibres, and there is some experience in weaving them.

Having seen the rate at which such materials may be imported, both from the East and the West Indies, it is desirable to have some idea of the prices which are likely to be realised for Plantain fibre or pulp, when introduced into the markets of Europe. Manilla Hemp, which has long been in demand both in America and in Europe, had a nett average price, for the ten years previous to 1852, of £32 per ton. In part of the years 1844 and 1845, it sank as low as £22 to £25; and the consumption increased so much, that the price rose, in 1852, to £44 and £50 for the average kinds; but, independently of what was used for cordage and coarse purposes, there was a considerable consumption of the fine, white qualities, for which horse-hair had originally been used. In the recent rise which took place (April, 1854), Manilla Hemp was quoted at from 70*s*. to 76*s*. per cwt. Though common Plantain fibre is not possessed of the strength of Manilla Hemp, yet it is fitted for many of the ordinary purposes of cordage and canvass, and some of the fine kinds for textile fabrics of fine quality and lustre. In the communication from Demerara, already quoted, it is stated that "in 1846, a gentleman (probably Mr. May) visited this colony, and exhibited several specimens of cloth of a beautiful silky texture, and specimens of paper of superior quality, manufactured from the fibre of Plantains grown in the Jardin des Plantes." There is no doubt that some of the more delicate fibres of the interior might be used for such purposes; and for these, a high price would, no doubt, be realised; and for the coarser, outer fibres, which are fit for cordage, at least £30, some say £35, a ton; while some of the superior tow would be a good substitute for horse-hair, for stuffing beds, &c.; and the different qualities of half-stuff producible from the combings, &c., of different parts of the plant, would produce half-stuff, at least equal in value to the rags which sell in ordinary times from 16*s*. to 20*s*. a cwt. But when its qualities are better known, it probably would sell at still higher rates, as there would be no labour in sorting, and no loss of material in cleaning. Mr. Betts was induced, in India, to attempt the preparation of the fibre, from seeing a remark in the 'London Price Current,' of Dec., 1839, that considerable supplies of a new sort of Hemp from the stalk of the Plantain tree had realised from 6*d*. to 8*d*. per lb.; and the Society of Arts were induced, as long since as the year 1762, from the apparent importance of the subject, to offer a premium for the production of this fibre (*v*. 'Jury Report,' p. 102).

Therefore, even with the least sanguine expectations, and on the most moderate computations, there is every prospect of a certainty of demand, accompanied by remunerative prices. With this in view, we may conclude our observations on this subject, which may appear to occupy too much space, and to have been treated of too much in detail. But if properly considered, it cannot but appear of vast importance to the natives of tropical countries, and to planters and colonists abroad, to utilise so valuable and abundant a product, which is now allowed to run to waste, and of which, if they increase the cultivation, they will at once attain the twofold object of multiplying the supply of food for the body, at the same time that they are increasing materials for diffusing information for the mind.

THE PALMS (*Palmaceæ*).

The Palms, so conspicuous in tropical countries for their lofty pillar-like stems, surmounted by apparently inaccessible fruit or gigantic foliage, are no less remarkable for the many useful purposes they are calculated to fulfil. The fruit of some is edible, of others abounding in oil, the sap of a few forms a pleasant beverage, and may by evaporation yield sugar or be fermented into a spirit. The stems of some species are gorged with farinaceous matter, which may be separated as a starch-like powder or granulated into sago. The broad leaves, from their great size and hard surface, are useful for thatching the cottages of the poor, or for making umbrellas for the rich. The narrow-leaved kinds are plaited into mats and baskets, or smoothed so as to be fit for writing on; while the leaves of several, when in a young and tender state, are eaten, both raw and in a cooked state, and are hence called Cabbage Palms. Some abound in strong unyielding fibre, while others form wood which is applicable to all the purposes of timber. Hence, several are valuable articles of culture in the countries where they are indigenous, or where the soil and climate are suitable for their growth—as, for instance, the Date Palm in Arabia and Africa, the Oil Palm in the West of Africa, the Cocoa-nut in India and its Islands, together with the Betle-nut, Palmyra, and Talipat Palms; while the Sago, the Ejoo, and the Betle-nut Palms flourish in the moist warm climates of the Malayan Peninsula and of the Indian Archipelago.

The Palms abound chiefly in the tropical parts of South America, as well as of the Old World; but a few species extend to rather high latitudes, as an Areca to lat. 38° S. in New Zealand, and a Sabal (Chamærops, *Auct.*) to lat. 40° N. in North America; while the Dwarf Palm, a native of the North of Africa, is now at home in the South of Europe. There even the Date Palm is grown in a few sheltered situations; though it is in the hot and dry soil of Arabia and Africa that it attains the greatest perfection, and furnishes a principal part of the diet of its inhabitants, as well as an article of commerce. *Phœnix sylvestris*, a variety or species of the same genus, is common in most parts of India. A Chamærops is found in Nepal, and one on the Khasya Hills, at elevations of from 5000 to 8000 feet; while *C. Ritchiana* is found in the Khybur Pass, and probably all along the mountainous range from Affghanistan to Sindh. But it is in far southern latitudes and in a different climate that the Cocoa- and the Betle-nut Palms are objects of extensive culture; as well as the Sago Palms, of which the Ejoo or Gomuto of the Malays is one (the *Arenga saccharifera* of botanists), abounding in sap, which can be used as palm wine or converted into sugar; yielding at all times strong and durable fibre. The older trees when cut down yield sago, as do *Sagus Rumphii* and *S. lævis*, especially abundant in and near Sumatra. The latter is remarkable among Palms for throwing up young plants around it in the same manner as the Plantain. Both kinds of Sago tree are strongly recommended for cultivation—the Arenga on low coasts near the sea, but the species of Sagus even on the edges of the marshes which abound in such situations.

It is no doubt to some one of these Sago trees that Sir John Maundeville alludes, when he says: "In that land grow trees that bear meal, of which men make bread, white and of good savour; and it seemeth as it were of wheat, but it is not quite of such savour. And there are other trees that bear good and sweet honey; and others that bear poison.—And if you like to hear how the meal comes out of the trees, men hew the trees with an hatchet, all about the foot, till the bark be separated in many parts; and then comes out a thick liquor, which they receive in vessels, and dry it in the sun, and then carry it to a mill to grind, and it becomes fair and white meal; and the honey and the wine, and the poison, are drawn out of other trees in the same manner, and put in vessels to keep." ('The Book of Sir J. Maundeville,' chap. xviii.) But we have only to notice such Palms as are useful for their fibres.

The species of CALAMUS, or those yielding the different kinds of Cane, have little of the appearance of Palms, as they are usually remarkable for their weak and trailing stems, which often extend to a great length, and ascend the loftiest trees. It is these long stems, which, when divested of their sheathing leaves, form the canes of commerce—some so much admired as sticks; others for their flexibility, conjoined with tenacity.

These, when their smooth and shining dense outsides are separated in strips, are universally employed for *caning* the bottoms of chairs, of couches, and for other articles. Some are occasionally twisted into ropes, in the localities where they are indigenous; but they are more generally employed as sticks, and for mat-making and cane-work, as their great strength allows of such narrow strips being employed, as to allow of large spaces being left, and thus enables strength to be combined with lightness and free ventilation.

The species of Calamus abound in the Islands of the Indian Archipelago, as well as in the Malayan Peninsula. A few species are found within the Madras territories, but in India they chiefly abound in the forests of the districts of Chittagong, Silhet, and Assam, whence they extend along the foot of the Himalayas as far north as the Deyra Doon, where a species is found which the late Mr. Griffith has named *C. Royleanus*, and applied the name of *C. Roxburghii* to the plant which Dr. Roxburgh called *C. Rotang*, common in Bengal and on the Coromandel Coast. Both are called *bet*, and used for all the ordinary purposes of cane; as are *C. tenuis* of Assam, *gracilis*, *extensus*, and others. *C. Scipionum* of Loureiro, Mr. Griffith considered to be the species which yields the well-known Malacca Cane, but the plant does not appear about Malacca. He was, however, informed that the canes are imported from Siak, on the opposite coast of Sumatra.

The extensive uses to which Canes are applied, both in their entire and split state, are well known. They are abundant in all the moist tropical parts of the East, both on the continent and in islands. In Java, the cane is cut into fine slips, which are platted into excellent mats, or made into strong, and, at the same time, neat baskets. In Japan, all sorts of basket-work are made of split cane, and even cabinets with drawers. Cane is also platted or twisted into cordage, and slender fibres are made to answer the ordinary purposes of twine. It is stated that in China, as also in "Java and Sumatra, and indeed throughout the Eastern islands, vessels are furnished with cables formed of cane twisted or platted. This sort of cable was very extensively manufactured at Malacca." The species employed for this purpose is probably the *Calamus rudentum* of Loureiro, which this author describes as being twisted into ropes in these Eastern regions, and employed, among other things, for dragging great weights, and for binding untamed elephants. So Dampier says: "Here we made two new cables of rattans, each of them four inches about. Our captain bought the rattans, and hired a Chinese to work them, who was very expert in making such wooden cables. These cables I found serviceable enough after, in mooring the vessel with either of them; for when I carried out the anchor, the cable being thrown out after me, swam like cork in the sea, so that I could see when it was tight; which we cannot so well discern in our hemp cables, whose weight sinks them down—nor can we carry them out but by placing two or three boats at some distance asunder, to buoy up the cable, while the long boat rows out the anchor." The tow-ropes mentioned by Marco Polo as used by the Chinese for tracking their vessels on their numerous rivers and canals, seem also to have been made of cane—and not of bamboo, as sometimes stated—as they were split in their whole length of about thirty feet, and then twisted together into strong ropes some hundred feet in length.

Mr. G. Bennett says, in his 'Wanderings,' ii, p. 121, that he "remarked some Chinese one morning near Macao, engaged in making some very durable ropes from rattan. The rattans were split longitudinally, soaked, and attached to a wheel, which one person was keeping in motion, whilst another was binding the split rattans together, adding others to the length from a quantity he carried around his waist, until the required length of the rope was completed."

Though apparently insignificant, Canes yet form a considerable article of commerce, inasmuch as in some years between four and five millions of them have been exported from the territories under the government of the East India Company.

Though not employed for their fibres, yet as connected with the different kinds of the genus Calamus, we may mention the different Canes which are imported. Most of them are produced by species of Calamus. For the commercial names of these we are indebted to Mr. W. Sangster. The walking sticks called "Penang Lawyers" are the stems of a small Palm called *Licuala acutifida*, as also mentioned at p. 96.

The Ground Rattan is distinguished by its straight head, and straight and stiff character altogether, as well as by its pale colour; though some are at least an inch in diameter, and others not half that thickness. Some are distinguished by a hard, and others by a soft bark. It is not known whether the slender are of the same species as the thicker kinds, growing in different situations, or from roots of different ages, but *Rhapis flabelliformis* is said to yield the Ground Rattan.

The Malacca Cane is supposed to be produced by *Calamus Scipionum,* but said to be imported from Siak, on the coast of Sumatra. Some of these are simply mottled or clouded, others of a brown colour, in consequence, it is said, of their having been smoked. The more slender specimens of these, with the longest internodes, are those most highly valued.

The most common kind of Cane, that employed for caning chairs, &c., is known in common by the name of Rattan Cane. This must be yielded by a variety of the long trailing species which abound wherever the genus is found. The most northern, named *Calamus Royleanus,* no doubt yields the Rattans collected in the Deyra Doon, while *C. Roxburghii* no doubt yields those collected in more southern latitudes. But it is probable that a variety of species yield the thin Rattans of different localities, and some of which have already been mentioned.

Another kind of Rattan is called Dragon Cane. This is thicker than the last, both light and dark coloured, with long internodes and a hard bark, less flexible than the common Rattans, but strong, springy, and much valued. A variety, with soft bark, is called Manilla Dragon Cane.

Other kinds of Canes, imported from China, are known, one with stiff stems and large knots by the name of *Jambee,* and one as *Whanghee.* This has a pale, hard bark, and flexible stems, with internodes of about an inch and a half or two inches, and a number of little holes at the knots.

Some which are occasionally called Canes, are produced by species of Bambusa, Saccharum, and other grasses.

Calamus Draco, a native of Sumatra and the Malay Islands, yields, as a natural secretion of its fruit, the best D'jurnang or Dragon's blood, which has been an article of commerce from the earliest times, and still continues in demand.

The CHAMÆROPS, called *Palmetto,* is among those best known in Europe. *C. Ritchiana,* called *Maizurrye* in Pushtoo, and

Pfees in Sindhee, is a most useful plant. Of it are made sandals, baskets, mats, &c., and its moonyah or fibre makes twine and ropes in Sindh. It is of extensive use in Affghanistan for making cordage; in the same way that the Hemp Palm, also a species of Chamærops, was found by Mr. Fortune to be employed in Northern China; and as *Chamærops humilis*, or Palmetto, is in the North of Africa and South of Europe, for making baskets, brooms, mats, and cordage. Indeed, paper and pasteboard are made of its fibres by the French in Algeria.

The true DATE TREE (*Phœnix dactylifera*), the Palm tree of Scripture, flourishes in comparatively high latitudes, and is well known to afford the principal article of food to the natives of Arabia and of the North of Africa; while the leaves are employed in making mats, baskets, &c.; and at Cairo cordage is made of fibres obtained from the footstalks of the leaves. Though the tree grows well in India, it does not there produce any edible dates; but *Phœnix sylvestris*, the *Khujjoor* of India, which closely resembles the former in character, is found in every part of that country, as near Madras, to its north in Mysore, in Bengal and the North-West provinces up into the Punjab. This tree is especially valued in many places, as its sap or Palm juice (*tari*) is either drank fresh from the tree, or fermented for distillation, when it yields a common kind of spirit or *aruk*. In Bengal it is valuable as yielding a considerable quantity of the sugar produced in that province, and known as Date sugar. Each tree, "on an average, yields 180 pints of juice, of which, every twelve pints are boiled down to one of *goor* or *jaguri*, and four of goor yield one of good powder sugar; so that the average produce of each tree is about seven or eight pounds of sugar annually." (Roxburgh.)

The leaves are very generally employed for making mats and baskets, and also bags in Bengal. The footstalks of the leaves are beaten and twisted into ropes, which are employed for drawing water from the wells in Bellary and other places. One species of *Phœnix* (*P. paludosa*), the *Hintal* of Bengal, abounds in the Soonderbunds, while another, *P. farinifera*, common on dry, barren, sandy lands on the coast, and on the hilly country between the Ganges and Cape Comorin. Its stem abounds in farinaceous matter, which the natives make use of as food in times of scarcity. The leaflets are wrought into mats for sleeping on. The common footstalks of the leaves are split into three or four, and made into baskets of various kinds.

The leaves of many of these Palms are employed for thatching, for making chattahs or umbrellas, punkahs, and hats. Thus, those of *Licuala peltata*, the *Chattah-pat* of Assam, are in universal demand in that valley. Scarcely a single ploughman, cow-keeper or cooly, but has his Jhapee or Chattah made of Chattah-pat.[1] (Jenkins.) But the leaves of this Palm are coarser than those of another, the *Toko-pat* of the Assamese, which has been named, in honour of the zealous Commissioner of Assam, *Livistona Jenkinsiana,* by the late Mr. Griffith. Col. Jenkins says of this species: "This Palm is an indispensable accompaniment of every native gentleman's house, but in some parts it is rare, and the trees are then of great value. The leaves are in universal use throughout Assam, for covering the tops of doolees (palkees), and the roofs of khel boats; also, for making the peculiar hats, or rather umbrella-hats (jhapees) of the Assamese. For all these purposes the leaves are admirably adapted, from their lightness, toughness and durability."

The PALMIRA tree of Europeans (*Borassus flabelliformis*), and the *Tar* of the natives of India, is to be seen in almost all parts of India, and occasionally as far as 30° N. lat. It is stated by Dr. Roxburgh to be, next to *Caryota urens*, the largest Palm on the Madras coast, and that it seems to thrive equally well in all soils and situations. The seeds, when young, are eaten by the natives, being jelly-like and palatable. The tree, during the first part of the season, yields a pretty large quantity of toddy (palm wine). This is either drank fresh drawn from the tree, or boiled down into a coarse kind of rob called jaggery, or it is fermented for distillation. The wood, near the circumference of old trees, is very hard, black, heavy, and durable. By the natives the leaves are universally used for writing upon with an iron style. They are also employed for thatching houses, for making small baskets, mats,

[1] The stems of *Licuala acutifida* afford the well-known walking sticks known by the name of "Penang Lawyers." (Griffith.)

&c., and some also formed into large fans, called vissaries. The fibres of the leaves (*Palmyra nar*) are employed on the Madras side for making twine and small rope. They are about two feet in length, strong, wiry, and not unlike those of Esparto (p. 31). Near the base of the leaves there is also found a fine down, which is used for straining liquids through, and also for stopping bleeding from wounds.

Among other Palms which are valued for different products and employed to supply the place of cordage plants, we may instance the species of CORYPHA. Of these, *C. Gebanga* has its young leaves plaited into baskets and bags, affording much employment to the people in Java. The leaves are also employed for thatching, and for making broad-brimmed hats. So, *C. Talliera*, the *Tara* of Bengal and the *Talipat* of the Peninsula, is much employed for making leaf hats and leaf umbrellas. The leaves, moreover, when smoothed, are much used for writing on, and also for tying the rafters of their houses, as they are strong and durable. Thus, also, *C. umbraculifera*, the *Codda-panna* of Madras and the *Talipat* of Ceylon, and very like the former, is common in Ceylon, and found also on the Malabar coast. Of this the leaf, being dried, is very strong and limber—and, according to Knox, "most wonderfully made for men's convenience to carry along with them; for though this leaf be thus broad [enough to cover fifteen or twenty men] when it is open, yet it will fold close like a lady's fan, and then it is no bigger than a man's arm; it is wonderfully light." "This tree is within, a pith only; they beat it in mortars to flour, and bake cakes of it, which taste much like to white bread; it serves them instead of corn before their harvest is ripe." (Knox's 'Ceylon.')

CARYOTA *urens* is another of those Palms which are common to India and Ceylon. In Malabar it is called *Evim-pannah*, and *Jeroogoo* in Telinga. Dr. Roxburgh describes it as highly valuable to the natives of the country where it grows in plenty. During the hot season, a single tree will yield at the rate of one hundred pints of toddy or palm wine in the twenty-four hours. The pith, or farinaceous part, is equal to the best sago. The natives make it into bread, and boil it into thick gruel.

It is the *Kittul* of the Cingalese; of which, according to Knox, "the inside is nothing but a pith, as the former. It yieldeth a sort of liquor, which they call *telligee*: it is rarely sweet and pleasing to the palate, and as wholesome but no stronger than water." It "bears a leaf like to that of a betel-nut tree, which is fastened to a skin as the betel-nut leaves are, only this skin is hard and stubborn, like a piece of board; the skin is all full of strings as strong as wire; they use them to make ropes withal." In a recent account of the 'Vegetable Products of Ceylon,' by Mr. Ondatjee, of which the author has been good enough to send me a copy, it is said that the *black fibre* from the leaf-stalks of the *Caryota urens* (*kittul*) is manufactured into rope, which is of great strength and durability, being used for tying wild elephants. The Rodyahs, or outcasts among the Kandyans, make this rope, generally with considerable skill, as it is both regular and compact. There is also a woolly material found at the base of the leaves, which is stated to be sometimes used for caulking ships.

EJOO OR GOMUTO FIBRE (*Arenga saccharifera*, Labil.; *Saguerus Rumphii*).

Malay—Ejoo, Sejee. *Sumatra*—Anou.

The *Ejoo* or *Gomuto* fibre, so well known in Eastern commerce and as used in Eastern shipping, is hardly known in the Western world. It is, however, occasionally heard of by the name of "vegetable bristles." Though a portion of the fibres may be likened to stiff bristles, the greater part is more like black horse-hair. This is celebrated, in the countries where it is produced, both for its strength and for its imperishable nature, even when exposed to wet. It is supposed to be the same as the *Cabo negro* of the Spaniards of Manilla. The tree yielding it was described and figured by Rumphius ('Herb. Amb.,' i, p. 57, t. 13) under the name of Gomuto, or *Saguerus*; but the latter name being too similar to that of the true Sago tree, has been changed to *Arenga*, from the native name *Areng*, under which it was described by Labillardiere. The specific name has been given from the large quantity of sugar procurable from its sap by cutting the spadices of the male flowers.

We thus observe that the tree is valuable for several very distinct, and all very useful products. It is described by Marsden, in his 'Sumatra,' under the name of *Anou,* as a Palm of "much importance, as the natives procure from it *sago* (but there is also another sago tree, more productive); *toddy,* or palm wine, of the first quality; *sugar,* or jaggary; and *ejoo.*" Dr. Roxburgh, writing in the year 1799, says of it: "I cannot avoid recommending to every one who possesses lands, particularly such as are low and near the coasts of India, to extend the cultivation thereof as much as possible. The palm wine itself, and the sugar it yields, the black fibres for cables and cordage, and the pith for sago, independently of many other uses, are objects of very great importance, particularly to the first maritime power in the world, which is in a great measure dependent on foreign states for hemp."

This Palm is to be found in all parts, from the Gulf of Bengal to all the Asiatic islands on its eastward, especially in low moist situations and along the banks of rivers.

Dr. Roxburgh describes the trees (in 1810) which had been introduced into the Botanic Garden at Calcutta about twenty-four years before, as from twenty to thirty feet in height, exclusive of foliage or fronds, which rise from fifteen to twenty feet higher. These fronds or leaves are pinnate, and from fifteen to twenty-five feet long. The trunk is straight, at first covered entirely with the sheaths of the fronds or leaves, and the black horsehair-like fibres, called by the Malays *Ejoo,* which issue in great abundance from the margins of these sheaths. As the tree advances in age and size, these drop off, leaving an elegant, columnar, naked trunk. He further states that he had observed that each of the well-grown thriving trees produces about six leaves annually, and that each leaf yields about three quarters of a pound weight of these fibres, and, therefore, each tree about four pounds and a half. But some luxuriant trees yield at least one pound of fibre from each leaf.

As these black fibres issue from the sides of the sheaths, they necessarily surround the stem, and may be cut off without injury to the tree. Even in commercial specimens, some may be seen covered both on the upper and lower surface with dense cellular membrane, having between them a mass of these black fibres. These are supported by thicker or whalebone-like fibres, which are attached to the thinner fibres by cellular tissue. These stiff fibres are employed in Sumatra as styles for writing with on the leaves of other Palms, &c., as mentioned both by Marsden and Bennett.

These fibres are further described as stronger, more durable, but less pliant and elastic than those of the *Coir;* but they resist decay, and are therefore more fit for cables and standing rigging, but less fit for running rigging. "The native shipping of all kinds are entirely equipped with the cordage of the *Gomuto,* and the largest European shipping in the Indies find the advantage of using cables of it. It undergoes no preparation but that of spinning and twisting,—no material similar to our tar or pitch, indispensable to the preservation of hempen cordage, being necessary with a substance that, in a remarkable degree, possesses the quality of resisting alternations of heat and moisture. The best *Gomuto* is the produce of the islands farthest east, as Amboyna and the other Spice Islands. That of Java has a coarse ligneous fibre; the produce of Matura is better. Gomuto is generally sold in twisted shreds or yarns, often as low as a Spanish dollar a picul, and seldom above two; which last price is no more than one sixth part of the price of Russia hemp in the London market. Were European ingenuity applied to the improvement of this material, there can be little doubt but it might be rendered more extensively useful."

Milburn, again, in his 'Oriental Commerce,' mentions the Ejoo as of all vegetable substances the least subject to decay, and that it is manufactured into cables, and the small cordage of most of the Malay vessels made of it: "it is equally elastic with coir, but much more serviceable, and floats on the surface of the water." These fibres are universally employed, in the countries where the trees are indigenous, for making cordage for their nets and seines, as well as for the rigging of their vessels, as also cables. These are described by all as remarkable for their tenacity and durability, and as not undergoing any change by exposure to wet, not even when stowed away in a wet state. In some experiments made by Dr. Roxburgh, some thickish cord bore 96 lb., and some smaller 79 lb.; while coir of the same size bore only 87 lb. and 60 lb. respectively. Besides the above horsehair-like fibres, there is at the base of the leaves a fine woolly material (baree), much employed in caulking ships, as stuffing for cushions, and as tinder. Ejoo was sent to the Exhibition of 1851, *via* Singapore, from Malacca, as separated from stiff fibres, and as prepared for manufacture or export, and prepared as sinnet, or coarse line for making ropes or cables. The portion belonging to each leaf having apparently been cut off close to the sheath, and each measuring about three feet in breadth and two feet in length. The bundles of the coarse and fine fibres are about six feet in length, and about twelve inches in diameter, neatly tied up with split cane. Interspersed among the coarser, there are some finer fibres, something like black wool. The sinnet is coarse, but strong, and broke with a weight of 85 lb., when coir of about the same size broke with 75 lb.; but the comparison is not very exact.

Mr. Kyd, the celebrated ship-builder of Calcutta, possessed a cable made of the Ejoo fibre, which he had had for four years exposed to all weathers, and which raised the bow anchor of a merchant ship of 500 tons, buried in the sands of the Hoogly; in two previous attempts at which, three Russian hempen cables had given way.

Besides making strong and durable cordage, the Ejoo fibre is no doubt applicable to a variety of purposes for which horsehair and bristles are now employed.

Cocoa-nut Tree and Fibre (*Coir; Cocos nucifera*).

Bengalee—Narikel. *Hindee*—Naryul. *Tam.*—Tenga.

The Cocoa-nut, little if at all known to the Ancients, was particularly noticed by the Arabs, being by them called *Jouz-hindee* or Indian nut; but at much earlier periods, in Sanscrit works, by the name of Nari- and Nali-kera. It is, no doubt, the "great nut of India," which Sir John Maundeville mentions among the trees of that country, as producing nuts as large as men's heads. In the East, where it is indigenous, it must from the earliest times have attracted the attention of the inhabitants. But it would be impossible now to distinguish the trees which have been introduced from those which are now growing apparently wild, on the various tropical coasts and islands where they are found in such vast abundance. As, for instance, in the Maldive and the Laccadive Islands; also, on the Malabar coast and in Ceylon, as well as on the eastern side of the Bay of Bengal, whence it ascends both the Burrampooter and Ganges Rivers to considerable distances. Likewise, in most of the islands of the great Archipelago forming the *India aquosa* of old authors, from the Sunda Isles to Molucca, and in those of the Pacific Ocean. It is, moreover, cultivated in various tropical parts of the New World. The Cocoa-nut (*Cocos nucifera*) and the Oil Palm (*Elæis guineensis*) have been remarked by a distinguished botanist, Mr. Brown, as the only two of their group (*Cocoinæ*) found in the Old World.

The Cocoa-nut Palm is one of the great ornaments of the shores of tropical countries. The cylindrical stems, with a diameter of about two feet, attain an elevation of from sixty to one hundred feet, and are surmounted with their crowns of numerous, wavy, and which from their appearance may almost be said to be feathery leaves. These are by botanists often called fronds, and by travellers their footstalks are often called branches. They are gigantic in size, being about twenty feet in length, with a strong, tough stalk, which forms the midrib, and has a number of narrow and long leaflets ranged along the two sides. The fruit is borne in bunches, of which there are from eight to twelve, each bearing, on trees growing in favorable situations, from five to fifteen nuts, so that each tree may produce from eighty to one hundred nuts annually. Mr. Bennett has well observed that the tough and thick (and it may be added, light) covering of the nut protects the germ while it floats even on salt water, and it is thus borne to barren spots, where it germinates, and causes even the smallest islets, just appearing above water, to become covered with clumps of Cocoanuts, as the fruit falling springs up and forms young trees around the original tree. Thus the Cocoa-nut is found on barren, uninhabited islands, as well as in populous districts; and though it attains the greatest perfection on the coast, it may yet be seen at considerable distances in the interior, and even at some elevation, as 800 feet in Ceylon. The Singalese have a saying, that Cocoa-nut trees only flourish where you can walk and talk among them. This evidently means that the trees must not be planted too close together; nor should any undershrubs be allowed to grow about their roots.

The Laccadive Islands are famed for the good quality of the

coir which is made there and exported to the Malabar coast. The Cocoa-nut tree is almost the sole object of culture and the chief means of subsistence, each person consuming about four nuts per diem. The principal inhabitants generally own considerable numbers of trees, and the custom prevails of marking trees with certain house marks, in the same way that sheep are marked in other countries. Taxes are levied on these trees, according to immemorial usage; and mortgages are secured on them at the rate of one rupee per tree of good quality.

The soil and climate of these islands is so well adapted to the Cocoa-nut, that they require to be looked after only for the first year; after which they are transplanted, and watered for a few weeks, until they take root, when they are left entirely to themselves, and come into bearing at periods varying from eight to twenty years, and will continue to bear for seventy or eighty years. In the island of Kiltan, it is said that a nut buried with a knife will grow, requires no attention, and comes into bearing early. The tree is not so large and strong as that of the coast, and the nut about two thirds of the size only, and rounder in shape. The husk is smaller and less woody, and the fibre finer and more delicate, but stronger than that of the coast nut. The nut is also said to be more compact and oily, and to keep better than the coast nut, although, for the sake of the coir, the nut is cut before being quite ripe. Many of the trees are cut for their sap, called *neera*, which the islanders drink in its unfermented state. The juice is drawn frequently, and fermentation checked by the addition of lime or chunam. "They are still so strict in the abstinence from all fermented liquors, that the manufacture of toddy would not be tolerated in the islands." (Robinson on 'Laccadives,' 1846.) Of the extent of the cultivation, we are informed that in the islands under British protection—that is, in Amendeevy, Kadamat, Kiltan, and Chetlat, containing in 1844 a total population of 3609—there were 122,153 Cocoa-nut trees. Of these, 8129 were chouk or unproductive, 45,070 young trees and plants, and 69,254 were fully productive.

Of the abundance of the Cocoa-nut tree on the Malabar coast, we may form an idea from the description of the chief town, Cannanore; as the topes or clumps of Cocoa-nut are said "to be seen between the officers' houses, surrounding the cantonments in every direction, and extending in the distance as far as the eye can reach; and the cantonment may be said to be imbedded in a forest of these trees." But it is abundant everywhere, and in many places forms a belt along the whole coast.

The majority of the houses on the Malabar coast are roofed with Cadjan—that is, with the dried leaves of the Cocoa-nut—which resist the rain better than tiles; but the roofs should be fresh thatched before the accession of the rainy season.

The average produce of Cocoa-nuts in the whole of Malabar is estimated at from 300 to 400 millions annually, which are valued at half a million of rupees; but in addition to this, from 20,000 to 25,000 candies of Copra (or the dried kernels) are exported, valued at 400,000 rupees.

The Cocoa-nut flourishes on the coasts of the southern provinces of the Indian peninsula, and succeeds on many parts of the western coast of the Bay of Bengal, as well as in the southern parts of that province. It also succeeds well on the eastern coasts of that bay, though the cultivation has not been carried on in the former Burmese territories to the extent of which the coasts are susceptible, nor even to the degree which the people require for their own consumption, as considerable quantities have long been imported from the Nicobar Islands. The trees are said to begin to produce fruit in the eighth, and to be in full bearing in the twelfth year after planting, and yield from eighty to a hundred nuts annually. But this is probably above the average.

Mr. Baumgarten, in a paper on the agriculture of Malacca ('Journ. Indian Archipelago,' iii, p. 710), while considering what kinds of cultivation are most inviting, states that those of an indigenous kind claim a preference, such as the Cocoa-nut, Betel-nut, Sago, and Kabong,[1] with the usual variety of fruit trees found in the Dusans of Malacca. He further states, that "supposing a planter purposes opening a Cocoa-nut plantation, he should choose a gently sloping or level surface, with a portion of swampy land in its vicinity for a paddy-field for food for the labourers." "The Malays," he says, "bestow

[1] All these are Palms; and of them, *Cocos nucifera* and *Areca Catechu* are no doubt the first two. The Sago tree is probably *Sagus lævis*, and the Kabong, *Arenga saccharifera*.

little care on their Cocoa-nut gardens. The Cocoa-nut there begins to bear at the end of the seventh year, but full crops cannot be expected until the ninth year. During this interval the utmost average quantity that can be expected will not exceed twenty-five nuts annually. But the fruit-bearing power of the trees may be considerably improved by extracting toddy from the blossom-shoots for the manufacture of jaggery, during the first two years of its productiveness; after which it may be discontinued. The subsequent annual produce may be safely reckoned at fifty nuts per annum; and forty may be considered the average number obtained from trees that are crowded to within fifteen feet of each other. The Cocoa-nuts sell for about eleven dollars per thousand." Mr. Baumgarten also recommends, that during the first four or five years, Millets, Chillies, Kechong (pulse), Sweet Potatoes, Yams, and Pumpkins, be cultivated in the intervals of the Cocoa-nut plantation.

Dr. Buchanan, in his journey across Mysore and down to the Malabar coast, in 1800–3, observes that in some places he found the green Cocoa-nuts sold for making ropes, at the rate of 2000 for about 8*d.*; but the husk of the ripe Cocoa-nut was not fit for the purpose (i, 156). These are commonly burnt for fuel (ii, 50). The green husks of the nuts which have been cut for their juice are steeped in water for six months. They then beat them on a stone with a stick, and rub off with their hands the rest of the adhering substance. The fibres, or Coir, are then fit to be twisted into yarns. In South Malabar (ii, 401), he says, a little bad Coir is made from the husks of the nuts that are used green in the country; a few of the nuts are exported with the husk on, but in general they are sent to the north inclosed in shell only.

USES OF THE COCOA-NUT TREE.

The Cocoa-nut tree is valued not only as applicable to many of the same purposes as other Palm trees, but for the sap procured by cutting the spathes of the flower-stalks, which is either drank in its fresh state, boiled down to a coarse sugar or jaggery, or allowed to ferment into spirit and vinegar. The milk of the nuts also forms a wholesome drink, while the kernel is used as an article of diet or in cookery in its fresh state, or dried and exported by the name Copra. In both states it is well known to abound in oil, which is used in the East for anointing the body, for the lamp, and for culinary purposes, and is now exported in such enormous quantities to Europe. The nut, besides, yields large quantities of a fibre which is to be more especially the object of our attention.

That the Cocoa-nut is one of the most valuable trees of tropical regions has long been known. It is therefore well worthy of cultivation in such situations as are suitable to it; as it abounds in products useful as articles of diet, as well as for commerce and manufactures. The celebrated Rumphius has given a very elaborate account of the Cocoa-nut Palm, and of its uses, under the name of *Palma indica major*, or Calappa, in his 'Herb. Amboin.,' i, pp. 1—25. Mr. G. Bennett, in his 'Wanderings,' has also given a very interesting account of it (vol. ii, p. 295); as also Mr. Robinson, of the Madras Civil Service, in his 'Report on the Laccadive Islands,'[1] published in the 'Madras Literary and Scientific Journal.' From these sources we condense the following notice of the useful products of this "Prince of Palms."

The Cocoa-nut, valued as it is in its ripe state, is probably, in the countries where it is indigenous, most used as an article of diet in its young or green state. It then affords both solid food and a pleasant drink, because it contains an abundance of the fluid, which Mr. G. Bennett says is beautifully clear, and has a sweetness, with a slight degree of astringency, which renders it a very agreeable beverage.[2] This he always found cooling and refreshing in all his excursions in intertropical countries. The pulp of the young nut is delicate, easily removed with a spoon, and may very well be named a vegetable blancmange. The ripe fruit is also eaten, but it is more frequently employed in cookery; the grated kernel being placed in a cloth, water is poured on it, a white juice is extracted by pressure, which, Mr. Bennett says, "may with propriety be

[1] See also the 'Wernerian Trans.,' vol. v, for a full account of the uses of this tree; as also Mr. Marshall, in his 'Natural and Economical History of the Cocoa-nut,' 1832.

[2] Mr. Bennett mentions that in Ceylon, house-plasterers use the water of the green Cocoa-nut as an ingredient in their white-washes, made of pure lime. It is a general practice of the natives of India to add some vegetable matter to their cements.

termed 'Cocoa-nut milk.' It is used either with or without the grated kernel in their various curries and mulligatawnies." Besides these edible parts, the heart, or the very young leaves of this Palm, as well as of some others, is called the *cabbage*, and, according to all accounts, forms "an excellent vegetable, either cooked or dressed in stews, hashes, or ragouts."

The beverage known to Europeans as toddy or palm wine, is obtained from the flower-spathes, before the flowers have yet expanded. These are themselves astringent, and used medicinally. To procure the toddy, the spathe is first tied with the young leaves, and is then cut a little transversely from the top, and beaten either with the handle of the toddy-knife or with a piece of hard wood. After some days, an earthen chatty or vessel, or a calabash, is hung to the spathe, so as to receive the toddy as it exudes. This is collected every morning and evening; the spathe being cut a little every day.

If this palm wine is drawn early in the morning, it forms a pleasant drink. But fermentation takes place in the liquor a few hours after it has been collected, and it is then used by the bakers as yeast. The fermented liquor or toddy is much drank by the natives; at other times the spirit is distilled from it, and forms one of the kinds of arrack or *aruk*, that is, spirit. One hundred gallons of toddy produce by distillation, it is said, twenty-five of aruk. Or it may be allowed to undergo the acetous fermentation and produce very good vinegar. Or, instead of being allowed to ferment, the toddy may be made to yield *jaggery* or sugar. For this purpose, a supply of sweet toddy is procured mornings and evenings, particular care being taken that the vessels employed have been well cleaned and dried. Eight gallons of sweet toddy, boiled over a slow fire, yield two gallons of a lusciously sweet liquid, which is called *jaggery-* or *sugar-water;* which quantity being again boiled, the coarse brown sugar called jaggery is produced. The lumps of this are separately tied up in dried banana leaves.

Cocoa-nut oil is one of the best-known products of this Palm, from its extensive employment in Europe, especially for making the excellent candles known as Stearine. In the East, it is employed as a lamp-oil, and for anointing the body, especially after it has been rendered fragrant by mixture with such aromatic oils as those of sandal wood and of jessamine.

The oil is obtained by first removing the kernel from the shell, which is boiled in water for a short period; it is then pounded in a large mortar, taken out, and pressed. The milk, as it is called, is then boiled over a slow fire, when the oil floats on the top, which being skimmed off, is afterwards boiled by itself. Two quarts of oil, it is said, may be procured from fourteen or fifteen Cocoa-nuts.

"The Malabar method of extracting the oil, is by dividing the kernel into two equal parts, which are ranged on shelves made of laths of the Areca Palm or of split bamboo, spaces being left between each lath of half an inch in width; under them a charcoal fire is then made, and kept up for about two or three days, in order to dry them. After this process they are exposed to the sun on mats, and when thoroughly dried (then called Koppera or Copra), are placed in an oil-press, or siccour." These form articles of export to Bombay and elsewhere.

Cocoa-nut oil is liquid at the ordinary temperature of the countries where it is produced, but becomes solid at lower temperatures, as about 70°, and has a specific gravity of ·892. It is one of the fixed or fatty oils, of which such large quantities are now imported into this country, and, like them, consists of both solid and fluid constituents; the latter, or Oleine, being separated by pressure from the solid parts called Stearine. The solid fat of the Cocoa-nut is by others distinguished by the name of Cocein, which has been so largely employed in making Stearine candles, but which, from the chemical changes taking place in the process, are now called Stearic, and which are made in such enormous quantities and of such excellent quality under Mr. G. Wilson's intelligent superintendence at Belmont, Vauxhall. In consequence of this increased demand, and the facilities afforded by the establishment of a Government steam-engine at Colombo for separating the oil with greater facility, as well as to the duty having been taken off, we may account for the great increase in the importation of this oil.

Cocoa-nut oil was sent to the Exhibition of 1851, from different parts of the Madras territories, and of very fine quality, by Messrs. Sainte, of Cossipore—for these a Prize Medal was awarded. The refuse or oil-cake is stated to be excellent food for fattening pigs and poultry.

The imports, which were in 1838, 32,666 cwt., had risen to 85,463 cwt. in 1848, and have since continued to increase.

	Cwt.		Cwt.
1848 .	85,463	1851 .	55,915
1849 .	64,452	1852 .	101,863
1850 .	98,039	1853 .	164,196

How large a proportion of this is brought from India, will appear from the following analysis of the quanties:

	Imported into United Kingdom in 1850. Cwt.
Cocoa-nut Oil imported from British Possessions in India .	85,096
" " " in Australia .	6,315
" " other parts . . .	6,628
	98,039

Cocoa-nuts, from the quantity of fibre on their exterior and oil in their interior, are necessarily well suited for burning. Hence they are sometimes fixed on stakes, and used to illuminate roads, &c. The shell itself, when burnt, yields an excellent kind of charcoal. In their entire state they are used for a variety of purposes, such as hooqas, vessels to hold water, cups to drink out of; and with handles fixed into them, they serve as ladles and spoons. We sometimes see them brought home as curiosities, highly polished on the outside; sometimes scraped so thin as to be semitransparent; at other times, stained black, elaborately carved, and mounted in silver.

Besides these various products, the wood of the Cocoa-nut tree is used for various purposes, as among the Singalese, when it has become old and the tree has ceased to bear, for making small boats, frames for houses, rafters, &c.; also for spear-handles, furniture, and fancy articles of different kinds. It is also exported to European markets, where it is known by the name of *Porcupine wood.*

The Singalese split the fronds in halves, and plait the leaflets neatly, so as to make excellent baskets, and, under the name of *cadjans*, they form the usual covering of their huts, as well as of the bungalows of Europeans; and are exported to northern parts, where the Cocoa-nut does not flourish so well: 149,500 were imported into Bombay in the year 1850-51. The dried fronds are sometimes used as torches or for fuel; their midribs, tied together, are sometimes used as brooms for the decks of ships, as the fibres of the stalk are woody, brittle, and difficult to clean.

The leaves are also in other places plaited into mats and screens, and also made into baskets; and combs are said by Mr. Bennett to be made of the midrib of the leaflets in the Friendly Islands. In the Laccadive Islands mats are made of the Cocoa-nut leaf, cut out of the heart of the tree just before the unfolding of the leaf, though this involves the loss of the bunch of fruit which comes out with each leaf. It is probable that the leaves of the *chouk* or unproductive trees are chiefly employed. These mats are, however, of fine quality, and much esteemed when exported. In these islands they are employed for the sails of the smaller boats.

Though the Cocoa-nut is best known, for the fibrous covering of its nuts which is so well known under the name of Coir, it also produces a downy fibre which is used to stop bleeding from wounds. This is altogether of a more delicate nature, and forms a kind of network, which is beautifully white, and even transparent, when young. It is thus seen at the bases of the young fronds; but as these attain maturity, this natural matting becomes coarser, tough, and of a brownish colour. It may be stripped off the tree in large pieces, which are used both in India and Ceylon as strainers for palm wine or cocoa-nut oil, or for straining sago or arrow-root. Mr. Ellis describes it as "consisting of long and tough fibres which regularly diverge from both sides of the petiole of the leaf. Sometimes there appear to be two layers of fibres, which cross each other, and the whole is cemented with a still finer, fibrous, and adhesive substance: the singular manner in which the fibres are attached to each other, causes this curious substance, woven in the loom of nature, to present to the eye a remarkable resemblance to cloth spun and woven by human ingenuity" (vol. i, p. 53). This is very similar to the arrangement of the Ejoo fibre, which has been already described, but in which both coarse and fine fibres are intermixed.

The husk or rind of the Cocoa is thick and full of fibres, which in their separated state are so well known by the names of Coir or Khair. In order to remove this husk, an iron spike, or sharp piece of hard wood, is fixed in the ground. The nut is then forced upon the point, which passes through the fibres, and thereby separates the rind from the shell. In this manner, Mr. Marshall says, a man can clear 1000 nuts daily. The husk, cut transversely, is frequently used for polishing furniture, scrubbing floors, and as a substitute for brushes and brooms.

Mr. Robinson describes the method of making Coir in the Laccadives, as follows: "As the husk gets hard and woody if the fruit is allowed to become quite ripe, the proper time for cutting it is about the tenth month. If cut before this, the Coir is weak; if later, it becomes coarse and hard, and more difficult to twist, and requires to be longer in the soaking pit, and thus becomes darker in colour. When cut, the husk is severed from the nut and thrown into soaking pits. These, in some of the islands, are merely holes in the sand, just within the influence of the salt water. Here they lie buried for a year, and are kept down by heaps of stones thrown over them to protect them from the ripple. In others, the soaking pits are fresh-water tanks behind the crest of coral. In these, the water not being changed becomes foul and dark coloured, which affects the colour of the Coir. When thoroughly soaked the fibrous parts are easily separated from the woody by beating. If taken out of the pits too early, it is difficult to free the Coir from impurities. If left in too long, the fibre is weakened, as is said to be the case also with that soaked in fresh water." These different modes are also practised in Ceylon. "At Calpentyra and the Akkara-pattoo, the natives separate the Coir by burying the husks along the border of the extensive salt-water lake, and when, after six months or more, they are dug out very clean, the fibres easily separate from the cellular tissue of the husk. This mode of preparing the fibre prevents the offensive smell emanated by macerating the husk, so common along the road from Colomba to Matura." (Ondatjee.)

The Coir from the islands of Kadamat, Kiltan, and Chetlat, in the Laccadives, is said to be of the best description. The manufacture into cordage of the Coir is entirely in the hands of the women of the Laccadives. When soaked sufficiently long, it is taken out of the pit and beaten with a heavy mallet. Subsequently, it is said to be rubbed with the hands until all the interstitial cellular substance is separated from the fibrous portion. "When quite clean it is arranged into a loose roving, preparatory to being twisted, which is done between the palms of the hands in a very ingenious way, so as to produce a yarn of two strands at once. No mechanical aid, even of the rudest description, has yet found its way into these islands." (Robinson.)

It is curious that in these islands, Coir is one of the chief commodities of barter for the necessaries of life, as rice, salt, tobacco, &c. The Coir is made up for their petty traffic in short *kuts* of a fixed length and weight, and at the end of the year these are collected and made up into lengths of 70 to 75 fathoms, as received by the Government.

Mr. Robinson, in his 'Report on the Laccadives,' states that the difference in the quantity of Coir manufactured from a coast nut and from an island nut is very considerable. We may premise that forty Cocoa-nuts are said to yield 6 lb. of Coir in Ceylon. Mr. Robinson says: "Three large coast nuts will yield 1 lb. of Coir, measuring twenty-two fathoms; whereas, ten small, fine island nuts go to about 1 lb. of Coir—but this will measure thirty-five fathoms: 2 lb. of such yarn, measuring from seventy to seventy-five fathoms, are made up into sooties, of which there are fourteen to a bundle, averaging about a maund of 28 lb. A Mangalore candy of 560 lb. will thus be the produce of 5600 nuts, and should contain about 20,000 fathoms of yarn. The actual price of Coir received by the islanders, is about thirteen rupees per candy. The value of the Coir produce of a tree is calculated to be from two to two and a half annas; and that of the produce of one hundred trees from fourteen to fifteen rupees. "The average value of the total raw produce of a tree bearing fruit, would then be seven annas to half a rupee; and that of a plot of one hundred trees, forty-five rupees." For the nuts which they export to the Malabar coast, they get from seven to ten rupees per thousand, or rather 1100, as ten per cent. is always allowed for luck in these sales. The islanders export from 300,000 to 400,000 nuts annually. The natives bring their Coir to the coast, in March and April, which is then received into the Government Godowns. Until the year 1820, all Coir was paid for at the rate of twenty-one rupees fourteen annas per Mangalore candy, or twenty-five rupees per Calicut candy of 640 lb. After that year, the Coir was divided into three classes. Since then, the average price paid for a Mangalore candy of Ameendevy and Kadamat Coir, has been twenty rupees and two annas (or twenty-three rupees per Calicut candy of 640 lb). But for the Kiltan and Chetlat Coir, which are the best, an average of twenty rupees twelve annas and seven pie, or twenty-three rupees twelve annas per Calicut candy, is paid. Up to A.D. 1825-26, the Bombay and Bengal Governments took almost the whole of the Coir brought from these islands, and credited the Mangalore collectorate with twenty-five rupees per candy. The price has since fallen very much during the last twenty years. It has been frequently below the price paid to the islanders, and at best, has never yielded above twelve to twenty per cent. profit. The average imports of Coir have been from five hundred to six hundred candies. (Robinson.)

Coir, besides its principal use as cordage, is much used in India in place of hair for stuffing mattresses, and is certainly preferable to those stuffed with ox- and cow-hair, which, I am informed, are still sent out to India. It is also employed for stuffing cushions for couches, and saddles.

Dampier also mentions that the Spaniards in the South Seas make oakum to caulk their ships, from the husk of the Cocoa-nut, "which is more serviceable than that made of hemp; and they say it will never rot." He adds: "I have been told by Capt. Knox, who wrote the relation of Ceylon, that in some places of India they make a sort of coarse cloth of this husk of the Cocoa-nut, which is used for sails. I myself have seen coarse sail-cloth made of such a kind of substance." ('A Voyage round the World.') But this seems to be made from the fibrous substance found at the bottom of the leaves; for in Knox's 'Ceylon,' Suppl., p. 250, it is stated: "The filaments at the bottom of the stem may be manufactured into a coarse cloth called *gunny*, which is used for bags and similar purposes."

From the details which we have given respecting the preparation, and other points connected with Coir, it is evidently a substance of considerable value; and though there is some difficulty both in separating and in twisting this fibre, it seems long to have been applied to useful purposes—as cordage for the boats and shipping of the East. Some of the boats even, in Ceylon and on the Coromandel coast, are composed of planks sown together with Coir yarn. So Sir J. Maundeville: "In that island are ships without nails or bands, on account of the rocks of adamants (loadstones), &c." Though imported from the islands in the form of sinnet, it may be manufactured into cordage of any size and cables of various bulk. A quantity of hawsers and cables are now annually exported from Ceylon.

The character of Coir has long been established in the East, and is now well known in Europe as one of the best materials for cables, on account as well of its lightness as its elasticity combined with considerable strength. These are further valuable as being durable, and little affected even when wetted with salt water.

Numerous instances have been related of ships furnished with cables of this light, buoyant, and elastic material, riding out a storm in security, while stronger-made, though less elastic ropes of other vessels have snapped in two, and even when chain cables have given way. Indeed, until chain cables were so largely introduced, most of the ships navigating the Indian seas were furnished with Coir cables. Mr. H. Dalrymple, Master-Attendant, &c., at Madras, states in one of his reports: "Cordage from good Coir is extensively used by vessels of all descriptions in India. In vessels of 600 tons it is commonly used for lower rigging. The yarns being tarred previous to its being laid up in Europe, are preferred for lanyards to the lower rigging."

Though rough to handle, and not so neat-looking as hemp cordage for rigging, it is yet, when properly made, sufficiently pliable, and being elastic, is well suited for running rigging where lightness is an advantage, as for the more lofty sails and sheets; but from its elasticity it is not considered so well adapted for standing rigging.

Dr. Roxburgh, in his experiments, found that tan was not applicable, and it is sometimes stated that it is not capable of taking tar; but even in Dr. Roxburgh's time, tar had been successfully used in the Coir cables made at Calcutta. Mr. Hornby already mentioned, states, that he could make from the Cocoa-nut fibre (Coir), rope of every size up to a 14-inch cable; indeed that such had been made by the prisoners, and was then under trial by the Government Marine authorities. Some beautiful specimens of 8-inch rope were sent by Messrs. Harton, of Calcutta, to the Exhibition of 1851, in the form both of cold and of warm register rigging. The latter is well covered with tar.

The comparative strength of Coir cordage is well known, but we may, nevertheless, mention, that in some experiments made by Dr. Wight, Coir cordage broke with 224 lb., when *Hibiscus cannabinus* bore only 190 lb., but the Moorva, 316 lb.

It having been inferred, a few years ago, that instead of sending Russian Hemp and Europe-made cordage to Bombay, it would be practicable to make good cordage and cables there, as had long been the case at Calcutta. It was observed, in reply, that a good manufactory of Coir rope could no doubt be established there; as when a Mr. Rennie had his manufactory at Bancoot, several of the country ships used Coir for standing rigging. Also, that with good materials and machinery he manufactured cordage which superseded some of the imports from Europe; with the exception of buntlines and leechlines, which chafe against the sails, and for which, therefore, Coir will not answer. The largest ropes used there are for hawsers and for messengers: and of these, Coir hawsers are much employed in the port of Bombay. As it may be interesting to know the kinds of cordage chiefly employed in the East, as well as its weight and cost, we subjoin the following

STATEMENT SHOWING THE COST OF EVERY DESCRIPTION OF COIR CORDAGE USED BY THE GOVERNMENT VESSELS, INCLUDING THE CHARGES FOR MANUFACTURE, ETC.

	No.	Ms.	Sr.		Co. Rs.	As.	P.
Coir Cable of 14-inch .	1	44	15	at 6 1 11 per md.	271	9	1
Coir Hawser, 8-inch .	1	16	25	„	101	11	10
„ 7-inch .	1	12	30	„	78	0	5
„ 6-inch .	1	9	20	„	58	2	3
„ 5-inch .	1	5	32	„	35	7	11
Coir Rope of 4½-inch coil .	1	5	6	„	31	8	3
„ 4-inch coil .	1	3	35	„	23	11	5
„ 3½-inch coil .	1	2	37	„	17	14	5
„ 3-inch coil .	1	2	12	„	14	1	3
„ 2½-inch coil .	1	1	28	„	10	6	5
„ 1½-inch coil .	1	0	28	„	4	4	6
„ 1-inch coil .	1	0	20	„.	3	1	0

STATEMENT SHOWING THE VALUE AND WEIGHT OF A COIL OF COIR ROPE OF THE DIFFERENT DESCRIPTIONS MADE IN BOMBAY AND BENGAL.

Description.	Bengal.		Bombay.		Difference.
	Weight. cwt. qr. lb.	Value. Rs.	Weight. cwt. qr. lb.	Value. Rs.	Rs.
1 Coir Cable of 14 in.	32 2 4	—	32 1 7	—	—
" 8 in.	12 0 21	—	11 1 10	—	—
" 7 in.	9 1 10	—	10 1 9	—	—
" 6 in.	6 3 24	—	7 1 0	—	—
" 5 in.	4 0 27	—	4 0 0	—	—
1 coil Coir Rope, 4½ in.	3 3 2	—	3 2 16	—	—
" 4 in.	2 2 27	—	3 0 22	—	—
" 3½ in.	2 0 15	—	2 2 20	—	—
" 3 in.	1 2 20	—	2 0 0	—	—
" 2½ in.	1 0 27	—	1 1 25	—	—
" 1½ in.	0 2 1	—	0 2 20	—	—
" 1 in.	0 1 13	—	0 1 25	—	—
	76 3 7	649 14 9	79 1 14	592 13 3	57 1 6

Supposing 648 cwt. of the above kinds of cordage were required:

Value of this at the Bombay rates of 7 7 6 per cwt. .		Rs. 4839 12 0
Ditto at Bengal rates, viz., at 8 5 9 per cwt., is	Rs. 5416 14 0	
Freight to Bombay, say, at one rupee per cwt. .	648 0 0	
		6064 14 0
Difference in favour of Bombay Coir . .		Rs. 1225 2 0

In calculating the rate per cwt., the Bengal maund is estimated at 82 lb.; and in turning the maunds into English weight, fractional parts have been omitted.

As the authorities at Bombay complained that the market could not always be relied on, for meeting demands as they arose for good Coir cordage for the public service; and as each fresh demand was taken advantage of for raising the price or for trying to pass off inferior articles at a high rate: a rope-walk has been authorised (January, 1853) to be established at the Mazagon Dockyard, in order to enable the Indian Navy and Public Departments to be supplied with good Coir cordage. The Collector of Mangalore was to supply the Maldive, probably Laccadive Coir, at thirty rupees per candy, and three rupees for boat freight to Bombay.

The above account[1] of the uses of the Cocoa-nut Palm would be very incomplete if we omitted all notice of the various purposes to which Cocoa-nut fibre is applied in this country, and in which so much ingenuity is displayed. We therefore borrow the following contemporary account of the articles exhibited at the Great Exhibition of 1851.

"It is instructive to witness the many useful and ornamental purposes to which the vegetable fibre of the Cocoa-nut may be applied. Of the manufacture of the fibre which envelopes the shell of the nut, the principal exhibitors at the Crystal Palace are Messrs. Wildey and Co., of Holland Street, Blackfriars Road, and Mr. Treloar, of 42, Ludgate Hill. The first-named firm show specimens of Cocoa-nut fibre in various stages of preparation. Commencing with the husk, we have first the cleaned fibres, separated from the intervening vegetable substance; then, a selection and preparation by patented machinery of the fibre for making brushes and brooms—a substitute for bristles; and next we have the fibres still further cleaned, curled, and dyed to resemble horse-hair, such as upholsterers use for stuffing mattresses; and, lastly, follow samples of yarn and cordage of different kinds, together with matting, door-mats, and netting for sheep-folds.

"The articles exhibited by Mr. Treloar still further illustrate this novel and interesting manufacture. The stair-carpets and floor-mattings produced by this exhibitor consist of upwards of twenty different registered patterns, all of which are new, and one of which now covers the floors of the Symposium, at Gore House. The brushes comprise every kind; and, so far as it is possible to form an opinion from mere observation, they appear quite as well adapted for all ordinary purposes as the best bristle brush—while, no doubt, the difference in price

[1] The statement frequently made of the Cocoa-nut Palm growing only in the vicinity of the sea, in consequence of the presence of salt in the soil, has not been noticed; nor the common custom of placing some salt round a cocoa-nut, when it is planted and expected to germinate. The sea-coast is well known to be distinguished by its moist climate, as well as by the soil below the surface being moist. Both these afford facilities for the growth of the plant, while the salt which is often placed round the germinating nut is positively useful in preventing white ants from eating it up. In consequence of the injury these cause, it is considered preferable to transplant the young plants when they have put forth three or four leaves, and in rainy weather, *i.e.*, in May and June, keeping the plantation clear from weeds and white ants.

is considerable. It is not easy, one would suppose, to place much ornament about a door-mat, without interfering with its utility. But Mr. Treloar has succeeded in producing, from a variety of shades of colour, a very ornamental door-mat, having a crown worked in the centre. There are a great number of small articles, such as table-mats, fancy baskets, &c., all made of the same useful material. But the greatest novelties yet produced from Cocoa-nut fibre are the bonnets and hats shown by this exhibitor. These are of a bright cinnamon colour, and attract considerable notice on account of the ingenuity displayed in their fabrication." The Ejoo fibre might well be intermixed with that of the Cocoa-nut for some of the above purposes.

To give some idea of the importance of the Cocoa-nut Palm, we may conclude with the following table of the value of the Imports of Coir and Coir rope into the three Presidencies for three years; for which I am indebted to the tables of the Statistical Department of the India House.

Coir and Coir Rope imported into	In Year 1847-48.		In Year 1848-49.		In Year 1849-50.	
	Foreign.	India.	Foreign.	India.	Foreign.	India.
Calcutta . Rs.	27,438	85,780	21,615	55,999	21,673	65,261
Madras . .	45,987	15,598	57,323	17,309	44,711	23,900
Bombay . .	873	76,571	333	116,338	1,618	143,210

Subjoined is a tabular view of the Exports and Imports of the different products of the Cocoa-nut, for the year 1850-51, in order to show the extensive influence of the plant. This must not be estimated simply according to the value of money in Europe but in India, and the tree viewed as the source of employment and of comfort to great numbers of the people of the East. But it is obvious that these Exports and Imports give but a small idea of the usefulness of the plant to the people where it is indigenous, as they find a use for every part of it.

In the following table, a few trifling entries appear, and also some imports from places from whence we should not expect them; but this is owing to ships' stores being sometimes landed and sold, instead of being used on board of ship. In some cases the value only is given, but generally both quantity and value, in the official Reports published in India. It is from these that the following facts have been taken:

BENGAL PRESIDENCY.
From May 1st, 1850, to April 30th, 1851.

Imported into Calcutta.	Cocoa-nuts.	Shells.	Kernels.	Oil.	Coir and Coir Rope.
From United Kingdom .	—	—	—	—	515
„ North America .	—	—	—	—	192
„ Pegu . . .	—	Rs. 125	—	—	—
„ Penang . . .	Rs. 20	—	—	—	—
„ Ceylon . . .	12,116	1,676	—	—	449
„ Maldives . .	109,299	4,169	—	—	3,826
„ Coast of Coromandel	11,100	—	—	Mds. 33	—
„ Malabar . . .	16,996	—	Mds. 56,507	—	9,259
Total . .	—	—	Mds. 56,507	Mds. 33	14,241
Value . .	Rs. 149,646	Rs. 5,970	Rs. 176,398	Rs. 231	Rs. 56,542
Exports from Calcutta.					
To United Kingdom .	—	—	—	363	138
„ North America . .	—	—	—	—	638
„ Cape of Good Hope .	—	—	—	—	139
„ China	—	—	—	—	126
„ Mauritius . . .	—	—	—	201	193
„ New South Wales .	—	—	—	20	349
„ Pegu	—	—	—	382	1,076
„ Penang . . .	—	—	—	52	—
Total . .	—	—	—	Mds. 1,018	Mds. 2,654
Value . .	—	—	—	Rs. 6,891	Rs. 18,009

MADRAS PRESIDENCY.

Exports.	Cocoa-nuts.	Shells.	Kernels.	Oil.	Coir and Coir Rope.
From Rajahmundry.					
To Pegu	Rs. 10,140	—	—	Galls. 4,537	—
„ Mauritius . . .	—	—	—	420	—
„ Bengal . . .	—	—	—	2,009	—
From Malabar.					
To United Kingdom .	—	—	—	173,394	Cwt. 10,388
„ Arabian Gulf . .	—	—	Cwt. 82	686	3,761
„ Ceylon . . .	—	—	867	36,670	3,361
„ France . . .	—	—	—	11,663	667
„ Maldives . . .	—	—	—	510	15
„ Mauritius and Bourbon	—	—	—	116,715	881
„ Bengal . . .	—	—	914	—	3,418
„ Bombay . . .	—	—	108,701	251,402	74,735
„ Indian French Ports .	—	—	652	33,229	—
„ Goa	—	—	—	—	1,324
„ Malacca Straits . .	—	—	—	—	92
„ Travancore . .	—	—	—	24,883	17
From Canara.					
To Arabian & Persian Gulfs	—	—	—	—	1,038
„ Bengal . . .	—	—	—	—	4,500
„ Bombay . . .	—	—	—	—	5,091
Total	—	—	Cwt 111,216	Gls. 656,118	Cwt 109,288
Value . .	Rs. 10,140	—	Rs. 431,008	Rs. 144,952	Rs. 246,852

BOMBAY PRESIDENCY.

BOMBAY IMPORTS.	Cocoa-nuts.	Cadjans.	Kernels.	Oil.	Coir and Coir Rope.
From Ceylon	—	—	143	—	Cwt. 239
" Goa	3,822,220	—	86	—	53
" African Coast	694,830	—	—	—	—
" Arabian Gulf	—	—	142	—	—
" Malab. & Canara, Br.	19,243,154	—	88,225	102,875	61,273
" " Foreign	1,974,786	—	72,530	—	10,405
" Concan, British	969,415	149,500	3,024	1,234	5,934
" " Foreign	65,000	—	—	—	—
" Cutch	—	—	—	57	—
" Guzerat	—	—	—	164	8
" Sindh	—	—	—	469	—
" Aden	—	—	20	—	—
Total	26,670,105	149,500	164,223	Gls. 104,799	77,912
Value	Rs. 375,243	Rs. 2,990	Rs. 689,722	Rs. 76,417	Rs. 175,392
EXPORTS.					
To Arabian Gulf	—	—	—	—	141
" Goa	—	—	—	—	4
" Malabar	—	—	—	—	2
" Aden	—	—	—	—	117
" Concan	—	—	—	—	42
" " Foreign	—	—	—	—	5
" Guzerat	—	—	—	—	4,214
Total	—	—	—	—	5,705
Value	—	—	—	—	Rs. 19,653

The details of the foregoing tables do not yet give a complete view even of the external commerce of Cocoa-nut products, for the Imports and Exports *by land* from or into neighbouring districts or from and into Foreign States do not appear. And of those imported, the quantities retained for home consumption are not distinguished from those which are re-exported, and which, though they cannot be enumerated again in the grand total, yet contribute to the activity of commerce. We have, therefore, prepared the following table of the Re-Exports of Cocoa-nut products, from the same official Reports. Some discrepancies appear, as, for instance, no Cocoa-nuts are entered as exported from Malabar, Canara, or Goa; and yet, in the Bombay lists, they are stated to be largely imported from these very districts.

BENGAL PRESIDENCY.

Re-Exports.	Cocoa-nuts.	Kernels.	Oil.	Coir and Coir Rope.
From Calcutta.				
To United Kingdom	—	—	—	265
„ Penang	—	—	—	12
Total	—	—	—	Mds. 277
Value	—	—	—	Rs. 1161

MADRAS PRESIDENCY.

Re-Exports.	Cocoa-nuts.	Kernels.	Oil.	Coir and Coir Rope.
From Vizagapatam.				
To Bengal	664,455	—	—	—
From Malabar.				
To United Kingdom	—	—	19,999	Cwt. 5,193
„ Arabian Gulf	—	—	—	1,289
„ France	—	—	11,663	126
„ Ceylon	—	344	3,400	504
„ Mauritius and Bourbon	—	—	—	69
„ Bengal	—	411	—	4,302
„ Bombay	—	4,330	—	9,720
Total	664,455	Cwt. 5,085	Gals. 35,062	Cwt. 21,203
Value	Rs. 2681	Rs. 17,135	Rs. 7,545	Rs. 65,983

BOMBAY PRESIDENCY.

Re-Exports.	Cocoa-nuts.	Kernels.	Oil.	Coir and Coir Rope.
To United Kingdom	—	—	—	Cwt 37,467
„ Mauritius	—	—	—	461
„ African Coast	—	—	—	198
„ North America	—	—	—	871
„ Arabian and Persian Gulfs	—	Cwt. 108	—	803
„ Calcutta	26,300	12,434	—	449
„ Cutch	1,109,799	1,265	—	1,877
„ Soumeinaee	625	37	—	—
„ Goa	—	3	—	16
„ Malabar and Canara	—	—	—	107
„ Aden	—	—	—	4
„ Sindh	134,355	9,800	—	473
„ Concan, British	8,531,025	51,953	—	2,586
„ „ Foreign	—	149	—	32
„ Guzerat	12,685,658	19,319	—	8,435
„ „ Foreign	933,835	8	—	10
Total . . Mds.	23,421,597	Cwt. 95,079	—	Cwt. 53,789
Value	Rs. 373,743	Rs. 452,605	—	Rs. 180,010

In the Imports into Bombay from the African Coast, there appears an article entitled Cocoa-nut Jarry, of which 449, valued at 386 rupees, were imported; and there were re-exported, 280, valued at 170 rupees, to the Persian and Arabian Gulfs, and 2600, valued at 43 rupees, to Sindh. Here there is evident discrepency, but the total is made 2880, valued at 213 rupees.

In addition to these purely Indian exports and imports, it must be remembered that this Palm is extensively cultivated, and everywhere equally useful. The culture has greatly increased in Ceylon, as well as on the Malabar coast of India. The imports of Oil we here see have greatly increased, and amounted, in the year 1853, to 164,196 cwt.; and will probably continue to increase, as it will be long before there is a limit to the demand. Of Coir, about three millions of pounds used to be manufactured in Ceylon, when the Dutch held that colony. In the year 1838, there were imported into this country—of Coir rope and twine, 5842 cwt., and of Coir fit for making into mats, 167 tons 13 cwt.

Of the imports of Coir, &c., from Malabar and from Ceylon, we may form some idea, from the following note, from the best authority, that of the Messrs. Noble, who state respecting the "imports from Cochin of Coir yarn, rope, junk, and fibre into this country, that there exist no certain data in this article on which to form a correct judgment (a great portion being taken into the same ship, both at Cochin and Ceylon, as broken storeage, of which a very uncertain account is kept), a general idea can only be given of quantities, which are as under:

Coir Yarn . . .	about	1300	tons annually.
„ Rope	„	800	„
„ Junk	„	1000	„
„ Fibre	„	150	„

"From Ceylon we get rather over 2000 tons of yarn and about 900 tons of rope. Junk is now only a small article from this port. Of fibre we get about 260 tons to 300 tons."

Other useful Palms.

To the above list of useful Indian Palms, we might easily add some, such as *Zalacca macrostachya,* used for making baskets and for tying Nipa leaves (p. 36), as well as mention the native names of others employed for many of the same purposes as the foregoing. But these would in many instances prove to be the same plant under different names in different districts; showing the necessity of appending a correctly ascertained scientific name to any local one under which a traveller or planter may describe a useful plant or its product. For in this way only are others enabled to recognise it, and, therefore, in cases where an observer is himself unable to identify or to describe a natural product, it is of great advantage that he should send sufficient materials of a plant along with its products, to Societies or to qualified individuals, in order that these may identify and refer them to their proper plants.

We might also have mentioned many of the Palms of other countries, which are applied to various useful purposes on account of the fibrous materials with which their leaves abound. Thus the Chinese are said to make cables of Palm leaves. The *Areca vestiaria* is so called from clothing being made from its fibres, and *Rhapis cochinchinensis* is employed for thatching, &c. The Doum Palm of Egypt (*Hyphæne thebaica*) is, like the Date Palm, used for making utensils of various kinds, as are also various South American Palms; while, in North America, Palmetto thatch forms an article of export, and the leaves of *Lodoicea Seychellarum* (the Palm yielding the formerly much famed "Cocos de Mer" or "Double Cocoa-nut") are formed into baskets and flowers—for a specimen of which, in the Mauritius collection, a Prize Medal was awarded at the Exhibition of 1851.

The detailed accounts we have given of so many of the Palms prove incontestably the great value of these plants to the regions where they are indigenous—yielding flour and sugar, milk and honey-like fluids, demulcent drinks and fiery spirit, fibre for cordage and for clothing, leaves for thatching and for platting, as well as wood for a variety of purposes. There is little doubt that some may yield the fibre which so abounds in their leaves, sufficiently easily to be useful to the paper-maker.

GENERAL OBSERVATIONS ON THE FIBRE OF ENDOGENS.

In a previous observation, we have already stated that an arrangement of fibre-yielding plants, according to scientific principles, would be found to be one which was also practically useful. We have seen that the fibres of Endogens separated for economic purposes, are contained in the leaves of these plants; also, that these leaves are usually long and narrow, or, as botanists describe them, sword-shaped. Their veins, moreover, are parallel, and not reticulated; also, arranged longitudinally, as are likewise the woody fibres; and all so regularly, that if these leaves were to grow together round the central flower-stalk, they would form rings of woody and vascular tissue, much as we see in Exogens or, indeed, in the different species of Musa or Plantain, in which the rings seen on the transverse section of the so-called stem, are actually formed by the encircling of the flower- and fruit-stalk or core by the sheathing foot-stalks of the leaves.

Hence, to separate such fibres, simply scraping with a piece of wood, or beating between two stones, is sufficient. Therefore, passing them between rollers, such as those of the common cotton *churka* of India, if enlarged, or those of a sugar-mill, would not only be efficient, but economical. Whether these rollers should be plain or grooved, must be ascertained by experiment, and will depend, in some measure, upon the external hardness of the leaves, or their more or less fleshy nature; as this might soon fill up the grooves. Motion might be given to such cylinders, either by the Archimedean screw, cog-wheels, or by bands, moved by hand, or by bullock- or horse-power as practised in the cotton-cleaning machines and sugar-mills of different parts of India. Careful washing of the separated fibres is essential, in order to get rid of the adhering mucilaginous or other matter and the cellular texture, but the boiling in an alkaline ley may probably be dispensed with, as it does not seem to be practised in all places. But steeping in water, followed by fermentation and decomposition, is followed in some of these localities, and no doubt facilitates the separation of the fibre, at the expense, sometimes, of its strength, as well as of its colour. Careful drying cannot be omitted, as, if packed up in a moist state, fermentation followed by complete destruction would ensue.

The characteristic of these fibres generally, is that they are white in colour, of different degrees of fineness, and most of them capable of bearing a considerable strain, but liable to break at knots. They are, therefore, not suited to all the purposes of cordage, but admirably so to many, from strength and lightness, as well exemplified in the case of Manilla Hemp. There is, however, an unreasonable prejudice against white cordage, though its true nature can be better ascertained than when soaked with tar. From the experiments of Du Hamel and others, it appears that this substance, unless carefully washed, promotes the decomposition of vegetable fibre; and though it is undoubtedly useful at the surface when ropes are exposed to wet, there does not seem any advantage in its covering the interior. Many compositions could, no doubt, be devised, for covering the exterior, which would be efficacious in excluding wet.

These fibres, though well known to the natives of the countries where the plants are indigenous, have not attracted from others the attention which they deserve, especially as they are produced in abundance, and necessarily very cheaply, as most grow in a wild state, or from the refuse of cultivation that has already paid its expenses. Almost all, moreover, are produced on the sea-coast, or in moist climates traversed by navigable rivers, and therefore could cost little for carriage. All would be valuable as affording employment for the people, and material useful to them for a variety of purposes, if not for exportation.

Of these, we have shown that both Grasses and Sedges abound as well on the banks of the Indus as of the Ganges, and might be turned to useful account. The Pine-apple abounds in Assam and the Tenasserim provinces; and in the islands near Singapore nearly 2000 acres are covered with it, according to Mr. Logan,[1] who recommends their cultivation for the manufacture of Pina cloth. The Moorva and the True Aloes, as well as some of the so-called "Silk-grasses" of South America, and the inner fibres of the Plantain, resemble each

[1] 'Journ. of the Indian Archipelago,' vol. ii, p. 528.

other in fineness of fibre, and therefore of fitness for the manufacture of similar textile fabrics, which are esteemed, at least, by the people of the East, and worn by them. All may, moreover, be twisted into fine twine or cord, and the refuse form excellent materials for paper-making. The Pita or Agave, commonly called Aloe, as well as the Yucca, New Zealand Flax, Manilla Hemp, and the outer fibres of other Plantains, are coarse in texture, and fitted for cordage, at least for ordinary purposes. But if we take the Manilla Hemp as an example, or the French experiments on the Pita, or its employment for naval purposes in South America, we may consider it as fitted, with ordinary precaution, for most of the purposes of cordage, as well as from its lightness for upper rigging. In the experiments made at Madras, the Agave fibre grown there certainly did not stand the trial to which it was subjected. But, as we have stated in the article on the subject, the cause of this is not easy to determine, whether owing to natural weakness of the fibre, or to the high temperature of the water in which the ropes were exposed, producing fermentation and consequent decomposition. All of these, as well as the finer kinds, are well fitted for paper-making, and therefore cannot fail to be always in demand.

In cultivating any of these on account of their fibrous product, it is an important point to determine the proportion in which this is yielded by the several plants. In this, as might be expected, there is considerable discrepancy in the statements of different observers—some mentioning a few ounces, where others find pounds of fibre. By some, from one seventh to one tenth part of fibre has been obtained, but this will depend upon the greater or less dryness of the leaves operated upon. In the experiments upon New Zealand Flax, it was calculated that 16 cwt., or 1792 lb. of fibre might be obtained per acre. Dr. Roxburgh obtained two crops of 1613 lb., or 3226 lb., per acre of the Moorva fibre. In one statement respecting Plantain fibre, it is stated that 600 lb. of fibre may easily be obtained per acre in addition to the fruit, but others, calculating upon four or five pounds per plant, and only 450 plants to the acre, calculate that from 1800 lb. to 2550 lb., or about a ton an acre, might easily be obtained. Others, counting upon the suckers which are successively produced, calculate upon much higher returns, which, with good cultivation and manuring, may, no doubt, be realised. But, as there is danger in over-crowding, from the want of ventilation, and weakness of fibre from the thinness and delicacy of the plants which would be produced in a crowded plantation; it is safer to leave to practical experience, to ascertain the degree to which a plantation may be safely and profitably crowded.

It has also been shown that the expenses of producing fibrous material in suitable localities, and with appropriate means and machinery, ought not to exceed from £9 to £10; and that even from India, some of these fibrous productions can be landed in England for from £13 4*s*. to £16 8*s*. per ton, according to difference of quality. While we have been informed by competent judges, that most of the above fibres, but especially the Plantain and Pine-apple fibre, are worth about £30 to £35 per ton, if sent in sufficient quantities and in a proper state. The difference in value, therefore, would easily repay any extra trouble in preparing the fibres in a careful manner, especially if we consider how cheaply Jute is grown and prepared, as will be shown in the following pages.[1]

[1] Mr. Dickson (*v.* p. 133) is of opinion that, though many of the white fibres, as has already been noticed, pp. 125-6, are fit only for rope- and twine-makers, others are suited for textile purposes, as, for instance, the Pine-apple fibre; even "for the spinning of yarn for the fine cambric manufactures in Ireland."

The Author has also been informed by one of the best judges of the value of such fibres and of their tow, that he has understated the prices which might be obtained for them if sent in a clean state to market; but the Author has purposely done so, after careful inquiry, that the expectations of planters might not be raised above average prices, in order that they might confine the expenses of production within proper limits.

The Author has omitted to notice, under the head of Plantain products, a piece of cloth, five yards and a half in length and twenty-six inches in breadth, sent by the Singapore Committee to the Exhibition of 1851. It is described "as being manufactured by the Arafuras, or mountaineers of the remote Eastern island, said to be New Guinea, but more probably Ceram, where the aborigines are known to manufacture articles from native fibres;" and is compared with the cloth made by the Saccalaves of Madagascar, from the fibre of a succulent plant called the "Traveller's tree," probably a Musa. The above cloth is of whitey-brown colour, like holland. The fibres are not twisted, but the ends gummed together, as already related at p. 40. The cloth is striped across, or in the direction of the woof, with threads of cotton.

ON THE FIBRES OF EXOGENOUS PLANTS.

We have already noted the great differences in point of internal structure, between what botanists call Endogenous and Exogenous growth, a distinction which we have shown to be useful even for practical purposes. Exogenous plants may in general be at once known even by their leaves, of which the venation is reticulated or net-like, and not parallel as among the Endogens; and therefore the fibres, united to each other in meshes, cannot be separated from the leaves for economical purposes, but must be obtained from other parts of these plants, where the said fibres lie nearly parallel to each other, as, for instance, in the bark.

The peculiar structure of Exogens may also be seen on making a transverse section of the stems or branches, for instance, of the trees of European climates. There we may see rings of wood and layers of bark. But in annual stems, we see in the centre a circle of white cellular tissue, called pith, and round it a layer of wood-like matter, which in some plants is called *boon*, or *shove*. This is surrounded by layers of cellular tissue, which, examined longitudinally, form a tubular sheath, inclosing the other parts. It is in some plants composed of long and tough elongated cells or fibres, which are sometimes called *bast*, and is covered externally by a delicate skin or cuticle. It is these bast fibres which are separated from the Flax and Hemp plants, and familiarly known by these names.

If we proceed to examine the transverse section of an Exogenous branch or tree, we see a number of rings, proportioned to its age. In the centre we observe the pith, which is usually small when compared with the bulk of wood. There may also be observed a number of lines, usually lighter coloured, radiating from the centre towards the circumference. These are called medullary rays, and formed of cellular tissue like the pith. This is surrounded by a longitudinal canal, which is called the medullary sheath, and contains spiral vessels. Outside of this are the rings of wood, formed of vessels and of woody tissue; those near the centre, called the heartwood, are denser and more highly coloured than those which are more external. Of these, the youngest are known by the name of sap-wood, and are those most recently formed, as all additions of wood are on the outside of the growth of previous years, in these trees.

On the outside of the layers of wood, we find the part called bark, but composed also of a series of layers; of these the oldest are on the outside, and may in some trees be seen splitting and scaling off in a withered and dead state. The new layer of bark will, however, be found in the inside of all, and next to the young wood. The structure of this part can be best examined in the bark of a young shoot. It will be found to be composed of two layers of cells, which receive different names from botanists, having the delicate epidermis or cuticle on the outside; but in the inside of all, the layer consists of tough, elongated cells and vessels, and is called *liber* or *bast*. This part is very conspicuous in the Lime tree of Europe, which, by the stripping off of its bark, yields the bast of which Russia mats are made. In the East, species of Grewia, of Hibiscus, and of Mulberry, are equally remarkable for their bast.

Besides the above characteristics in the leaves, wood, and bark of Exogens, we may also observe distinctions in their seeds and flowers, by which they may also be readily distinguished. Thus, the seeds of Exogens contain two seed-lobes, which, in sprouting, become the two seed-leaves, as seen in the germinating of Peas, Beans, Cucumbers, &c.; while in Endogens only a single seed-leaf is seen, as in the sprouting of Wheat and Barley, Rice, or the Date tree. In the flowers, also, distinctive characters may be observed; but we shall direct attention only to those of the Exogens, in which we may see the flowers composed of stamens and pistils, surrounded on the outside by floral envelopes.

In some, these floral envelopes consist of two distinct kinds —the outer usually green and the inner variously coloured; both consisting sometimes of several pieces more or less united, as seen in the Flax plant, the Jute, the Hibiscus and Cotton plant, the Sunn, and many other fibre-yielding plants.

Or, these two layers may be composed of the several pieces of each, or of the sepals and petals, united together into a single piece, as seen in the Convolvulus, the Jessamine, and Vinca. The last contains tenacious fibre, is allied to the old genus Asclepias, which abounds in plants yielding strong fibre, as the *Asclepias gigantea*, &c.

Some plants have only a single floral covering, which may be green or otherwise coloured, as may be seen in the Hemp, the Nettle, China grass, and other fibre-yielding plants.

Plants belonging to this division of the Vegetable Kingdom are the best known on account of their fibres. Of these many are remarkable for their strength and useful properties.

Having lately had occasion to report on some Indian fibres, I was anxious to ascertain the comparative strength of several of those fibres, which were, upon the whole, but little known. I therefore had equal weights and equal lengths of several of these fibres taken, their ends tied and fixed in a vice, and then the number of pounds ascertained with which each broke. In these experiments:

Petersburgh clean Hemp	broke with	160 lb.
A fibre from Travancore, called Wuckoo	,,	175
Yercum fibre	,,	190
Jubbulpore Hemp	,,	190
China grass, from China	,,	250
Rheea fibre or China grass, from Assam	,,	320
Wild Rheea, also from Assam	,,	343

Hemp from Kote Kangra, in the Himalayas, bore 400 lb. without breaking.

Though we hope to be able to show convincingly, that many of these Indian fibres are possessed of all the good qualities required of such substances, I know that objections are made to most of them. To some, that they are coarse; to others, that they are not strong enough, or that they break at knots; also, that they are incapable of fine subdivision on the hackle, or that they do not spin well, or have little twisting property on the spindle; but I suspect that the greatest of all objections is that modifications of machinery are sometimes required for new fibres. With regard to the alleged coarseness, and that they are not capable of fine subdivision; this is, in most cases, merely a question of preparation, which might be carried to a greater extent in India, or in this country, before attempting to spin them. I gave several of these fibres to Mr. Dickson, of Deptford, and he returned them to me in a few days, in a state in which I was scarcely able to recognise them, from their soft and silky, hair-like appearance; and I have little doubt but that the progress of experiment will show that this change can be effected at a comparatively small cost. With respect to their breaking at knots, this appears to be the case only with the white fibres, of which we have just treated, and which in this respect are like New Zealand Flax and Manilla Hemp. Some of the same objections were made against the Jute, when first introduced; and many years elapsed before it came to be used as it now is, and considered indispensable to the manufacturers of some localities. For instance, about 15,000 tons are annually employed in Dundee alone. Jute is certainly characterised by fineness, silkiness, and facility of spinning; but it is less strong than many other Indian fibres, which are possessed of similar properties with greater strength, as we hope to be able to show among the Mallow and other nearly allied tribes of plants. Among the Nettles, we hope to be able to prove that the combination of strength with fineness and capability of being spun, is as great in the Rheea fibre from Assam as in the China grass from China. When, at the end of last year, I was endeavouring to prove that many of these fibres were fit for all the purposes of rope-making, I was equally told that they were weak, or would not twist, or not take tar. I have since had some of them made into every variety of cordage, from fine whipcord to a five-inch rope, and I find that, in all cases, many of those of which I am now about to treat, exceed Russian Hemp in strength, and are therefore more than efficient substitutes.

Though some practical men have stated that these Indian fibres do not subdivide, and will not spin, others are of a contrary opinion; and though I shall have occasion to refer to each more particularly under its respective head, I may yet take the present opportunity of referring to the statements of Mr. Dickson, published in the 'Journal of the Society of Arts.' In the then expected deficiency of Russian Hemp and Flax, and looking to the sources whence consumers might obtain substitutes for them, he observes: "From the experiments I have made on all kinds of fibre, I fearlessly assert that they can have a cheaper and better supply of fine and coarse fibre from India, for rope-makers and fine spinners, than it is possible for them to get from any other country, and the samples in the Society's rooms are a proof" (referring to his own and the East India House specimens then displayed there). "Dr. Royle gave a very correct account of the superiority in the strength of the Himalayan Hemp compared with that of Russia; but that is not the only advantage to be gained by the importers and consumers of Hemp." "I have made the Himalayan Hemp so soft, fine, and white, that it will not only take the place of Petersburgh Flax—now £60 per ton, the best of which can only make 40*s*. warp yarn—but it can be used in place of Dutch Flax, at £80 per ton; and I speak from twenty years' practical knowledge, when I say it is capable of being spun into 60*s*. warp yarn."

"The Rheea fibre, or Assam grass, when so prepared by the machines and liquid, is a finer, and, consequently, more valuable fibre. It is equal in strength and fineness to China grass, at £100 per ton." "The Yercum, which very much resembles Belgian Flax, is also well calculated for prime warp yarns, and worth £100 per ton." The Wuckoo nar, Mr. Dickson places near this in another statement. "The Neilgherry Nettle is a most extraordinary plant; it is almost all fine fibre, and the tow is very much like the fine wool of sheep, and no doubt will be largely used by wool-spinners." "The Madras Hemp, and Bombay and Sunn Hemps, will at all times command a market, when *properly cleaned out*, at £45 to £50 per ton, for twines or common purposes."

In another published statement (Flax Works, Grove Street, Deptford, April, 1854), Mr. Dickson says of—

"Madras Hemp, valued when imported at £24 per ton:

	cwt.	qr.	lb.	cwt.	qr.	lb.
Madras Hemp				2	3	3
Produced by the machines:						
Clean, long fibre, good, valued at £45 per ton	1	1	7½			
Clean tow, valued at £30 per ton .	1	1	9			
Waste	0	0	14½	2	3	3

Cost of preparation . 6*s*. 1½*d*.

"This Hemp, when prepared with the patent liquid, became soft, white, and so fine when hackled, as to bear the closest comparison with Flax at £80 per ton. It is better than any Russian Flax for fine spinning."

Practical men alone can judge of practical questions, when they have made careful experiments on new products, and have laid aside all prejudices in favour of old ones. The Author can only vouch, as he has already done, that he was surprised with the improved appearance and fineness of many of the coarse-looking Indian fibres; though he ought not to have been so, from what he had previously seen of some of these fibres. This more especially, as there is no rational reason why the varied soil and climate of India should not produce as finely divisible fibres as any produced in the short, but warm and dry summers of Russia. These fibres would, moreover, look as well in the market, if the natives of India would take the same trouble with their preparation as is done in Europe with Flax and Hemp.

This appears a favorable opportunity for calling attention to the little justice which the natives of India do to the products of their own country; for most of their fibres, like their cotton, come to market intermixed with much dust; some, moreover, almost in the state of bast, upon which freight and charges have to be paid before they can be used either for cordage or for textile purposes. Manufacturers, therefore, give a lower price for them than would be the case if they reached this country in a clean and workable state.

A considerable loss is likewise sustained, by what is very unusual, that is, the *extra* care bestowed on some of these fibres in different parts of India. Some are twisted into rope-like bundles; others are plaited into the form of Chinese pigtails, or tied together with knots at the ends. In this case, these ends must at once be cut off, and the fibres thus much shortened, before they can be used. When twisted or plaited, boys and girls are obliged to be employed in untwisting and opening them out, in order to bring them to a state from which they have been needlessly removed. All that is necessary is that the fibres should be tied in convenient-sized bundles; and retained in the state in which they are removed from the plant, and that in which they must be when undergoing the different processes of preparation, that is, nearly parallel to each other. They may then be simply tied together near the thicker end, so as to form what are called ***heads:*** or they may be similarly tied in two or three places, if it is thought desirable to do so, with long fibres. Such fastenings can most easily be cut across with a knife, and with the least possible expenditure of time and labour; so as to expose the fibres in a state in which they can be immediately made use of. Besides this mode of tying up the bundles of fibres, which would, in fact, save much of the time and labour now injuriously expended, it would be desirable if the natives could be induced, generally, to pay more attention to the preparation of these fibres, especially in not macerating the plants longer than absolutely necessary for the purpose of separation, as already referred to at p. 29. The benefits of such care would soon be apparent in the increased demand and improved prices for Indian fibres, not only in this country but in other parts of the world.

FLAX, LINSEED (*Linum usitatissimum, Linaceæ*).

Sans.—Atasee. *Hind.*—Atees, Ulsee. *Beng.*—Mushina. *Persian*—Kutan.

The Flax plant is one of those which was cultivated by the earliest of the civilised nations of antiquity, and has continued to be so to the present time, and is becoming every day of still greater importance. We may see from the paintings in the tombs of Egypt, that it was early cultivated in that country; and we can also prove that it was so, from a microscopic examination of mummy-cloth. We read in the book of 'Exodus'[1]

[1] The word Pishtah undoubtedly refers to the Flax plant, of which the preparation for its fibre is so clearly represented in the Grotto of El Kab. The words *bad, butz,* and *shesh,* which occur so frequently in the Scriptures, are supposed to indicate different kinds of Linen. But it has been doubted whether, in a language like the Hebrew, it is probable that so many names are applied to the produce of one plant, or whether it is not more probable that they refer to the products of different plants. The Author has ventured to think that Linen, Cotton, and Hemp were all known; and are mentioned—Cotton (Karpas), in Esther i, 6. *Bad* is very similar to the Sanscrit *pat. Shesh* differs only in the aspirate from *husheesh,* which is one of the Arabic names of the Hemp; as the Author has pointed out in the respective articles in Kitto's 'Cyclopædia of Biblical Literature.'

of the flax and the barley being smitten by the plague of hail in Egypt, and in 'Joshua' of the spies, who had been sent to report on the state of Jericho, being hid with stalks of flax. From many other passages, we know that the spinning and weaving of Flax were common occupations of the people in Palestine. Subsequently, it was much cultivated both by Greeks and Romans. In India, Flax has also been cultivated from very early times, but strange to say, for its seed only, and not on account of the fibre; which everywhere else is the principal object of attention. This is probably owing to India possessing, as one of its indigenous products, the Cotton plant, which requires only the bursting of its fruit to display an elegant and easily spun material, which can be obtained from the Flax only after considerable labour.

We have lately seen how important the Cocoa-nut Palm, one of the princes of the vegetable kingdom, is, not only to the countries where it is produced, but also to those into which its products are introduced. The Flax plant, on the contrary, is one of the humblest of those which are cultivated, and yet it is hardly less important, though not particularly useful as an article of diet. Its slender stem, narrow leaves, and beautiful blue flowers, give it an elegant appearance. Its smooth and shining seeds have their external coating formed of much condensed mucilage, while the white kernel is gorged with oil, especially valued for its drying properties; and the refuse or oil-cake affords a nutritious diet for cattle. The fibre or Flax separated from the stem may be made use of for cordage, for coarse fabrics, or for the finest cambrics and lawns. Hence it is a principal object of attention in Russia and Poland, a highly successful culture in Belgium, carried on also in Germany, France, and Italy, the object of frequent legislative enactment in England, and of recent most successful cultivation in Ireland. Hence, also, it was re-established by the late Pasha in Egypt. It has been frequently recommended for culture in India on account of its fibre, as it already is in almost every part of that country for its seed.

Upon consideration, it will no doubt appear remarkable that this small annual plant should be profitably cultivated over so great an extent of the globe, and in apparently so great a diversity of climate. But the fact is that the winters of these southern latitudes enjoy a temperature which nearly approaches that of the summers of more northern countries. Therefore, in Egypt and India, Linseed is sown in autumn, and the stalks harvested in early spring, even before the seeds have begun to be sown in the more northern places where it is cultivated. This winter cultivation of southern latitudes has probably given origin to the autumnal sowings of European latitudes. But this lowering of temperature is not all that the plant requires for the production of fine flax, as we shall immediately more particularly inquire. But the natives of India, who are more ingenious in their devices and more successful in their agriculture than is generally allowed, have adopted methods of culture, such as thin sowing, though intermixed with, or in drills as an edging to, other crops, which ensures them an abundant crop of the produce they desire—that is, the seed—which is large and plump; while the stems remain short, branch much, flower freely, and become loaded with bolls filled with the seeds, which abound both in mucilage and in oil.

But before proceeding to a description of the plant, the modes of culture, or the preparation of the fibre, we may briefly notice the importance of these products to the countries producing or importing them, and how beneficial they may probably become to other countries which possess a suitable soil and climate, and no more profitable object of culture or of export.

Several able writers, as Messrs. M'Adam, Nichols, and Wilson, having, within the last few years, drawn attention to the importance of the culture of Flax, we may make use of the facts which they have collected, and apply them to India. Mr. M'Culloch has observed with regard to this country, that "the legislature has paid more attention to framing laws regarding the husbandry of Flax than to any other branch of rural economy;" but not with much success, "as the culture of Flax is, on the whole, found to be less profitable than the culture of corn." It has, moreover, always "been considered one of the most severe crops." This, however, we shall see is not necessarily the case, according to the improved methods of culture and of preparation of fibre. But even in the present day, £1000 per annum has been granted since 1847 to the Royal Flax Improvement Society, for the culture of Flax in Ireland, according to the Act 10 and 11 Victoria, cap. 115; and with considerable advantage, as the culture of Flax has greatly increased. The quality of the Flax has also been so greatly improved, that the Jury of Class IV of the Exhibition of 1851, stated—"The entire collection shown by the Royal Society for Improving and Promoting the Growth of Flax in Ireland is so highly valuable, and so clearly illustrates the great advances which have been made and the important service which this Society has rendered to the country, that they determined to mark their high appreciation of their labours by recommending them to have one of the Council Medals."

But, notwithstanding the endeavours of successive governments, the supply of home-grown Flax has never reached the extent required by our manufacturers. At present, it is considered that the consumption is equal to 150,000 tons. About 70,000 tons were, for several years, annually imported; or more precisely, in the year 1831, 46,820 tons: in the year 1843, about 72,000 tons were imported; but in 1853 no less than 94,000 tons, or an increase of about 31 per cent. in the last decennial period. If the 150,000 tons be valued at an average of forty, or, according to others, at fifty pounds a ton, the amount is enormous. To this must be added "£1,500,000, the value of 650,000 quarters of linseed, used as seed and for crushing purposes; and about £500,000, the cost of 70,000 tons of oil-cake, which we annually import, in addition to that made at home, for feeding purposes. The quantity of Flax fibre necessary to supply the demand of the United Kingdom would consume the produce of 500,000 acres; while in Ireland, during the past year, only 136,000 were cultivated, and, probably, not a fourth of that quantity in the rest of the kingdom." (Wilson.) The seed is imported from India, Egypt, Russia, Sicily, Prussia, and Holland; and the oil-cake from France, Germany, and the United States.

Mr. Fane is of opinion that—"Under proper arrangements, the whole might be home-grown. If all were, the money result would be enormous, because every ton of fibre involves the growth of eight tons of flax straw—eight tons of straw being required to produce one of fibre; and every ton of straw involves the production of six bushels of seed, worth at least 6*s*. 6*d*. a bushel. These would give the following money result:

1,200,000 tons of straw, producing six bushels of seed to each ton, at 6*s*. 6*d*. a bushel, would give . .	£2,340,000
150,000 tons of fibre, at £50 a ton, would give . .	7,500,000
	£9,840,000."

Without advocating, or considering it desirable, that all the increasing quantities of Flax required by our manufacturers should be, or can be grown in this country, we may take advantage of the information collected as applicable to other countries. It has, indeed, been objected, by Mr. H. S. Thompson, that if forty stone of Flax (value 7*s*. 6*d*. per stone) is the average produce of a reasonably well cultivated acre of Flax, 70,000 tons of imported Flax would require 280,000 acres of land for its cultivation, which is "clean and in good tilth," *i.e.*, "precisely in the state in which it is best fitted for producing corn," and "on an average at least four quarters." "The 280,000 acres required to produce the Flax now imported, would therefore produce, if cropped with wheat, 1,120,000 quarters, worth (at 7*s*. per bushel) £3,136,000; which approaches tolerably near to the estimate given by Mr. Nichols of the value of the imported Flax, viz., £3,490,000." But these objections are made to the occupation of good land in a country like England, where the whole quantity is but limited, and "where every acre of even moderate fertility has its work to do, and no new crop can be introduced without displacing an old one;" but do not apply, as stated, to countries like America and Australia, where there may be an unlimited extent of fertile but uncultivated land. Nor, indeed, to many parts of India, where more corn is grown than is required by the people, and for which they would gladly substitute some readily saleable or exportable product. Further—

"If we refer to the statistics of British and Irish exports, we find that in 1843 there were shipped from the United Kingdom, in round numbers, 91,000,000 yards of linen, and that the exports of 1853 reached nearly 130,000,000 yards; the total value of all kinds of linen and yarn exported in the former year being £3,702,052, and in the latter £5,910,355." ('Belfast Mercury.')

Though the culture of Flax is considered by some as not particularly eligible for the best-cultivated lands of England, it is yet, in other countries, accounted a most desirable object of attention, being in Belgium called "the Golden Crop," and in Ireland "the Rent-paying Crop." In Russia, it is one of the principal objects of culture, and has been much extended by the continual advances of English capital; while in Egypt, the culture was re-established by the vigorous but despotic policy of the late Mehemet Ali. In India, it is to be hoped that the ryots may be induced to cultivate it in suitable localities, on account of the fibre, as they already do for the sake of the seed. In such situations, it will, no doubt, be an eligible crop, as land is cheap and labour almost everywhere abundant. Mr. Nichols says—"The quantity of Flax which ought to be cultivated in any locality, must, in some measure, be governed by the quantity of labour there obtainable. One acre in a hundred, and one in fifty, have each been named as a suitable proportion to be applied for the growth of Flax. In former times the farmer was by law required to cultivate one acre with Flax, out of every sixty acres occupied." And he further observes: "If the quantity of Flax grown be limited by the labour which can be obtained, so may the amount of obtainable labour be said to indicate the extent to which culture ought to be carried in any locality. It is calculated that an acre of good Flax, as it stands in the field, containing, say about fifty stone of fibre, will afford employment for from twelve to fourteen weeks to a man skilled in the several processes of its preparation." But it is not to men only that the Flax affords employment, but also to women and to children; as it is skill rather than strength that is required for many of the operations. Hence, its introduction is very desirable in suitable localities, where population is abundant.

Success in culture will, therefore, depend on many considerations; as it is necessary to have a suitable soil and favorable climate; also, a sufficient population, with facilities for the sale and the transit of the produce. At present, Flax is produced over a very wide area, and there seems no sufficient reason why this may not be still further extended.

The principal sorts of Flax which are imported into this country are Russian, Prussian, Egyptian, Dutch, Belgian, and French. Of these the first three are, speaking generally, coarser in nature than the last three. The proportion per cent.

of the (say) 80,000 tons imported from different countries may be judged of by the following table, as given in the Jury Report of Class IV, p. 96, calculated on the average imports of 1840, 1844, and 1849. The details are given in the successive editions of M'Culloch's 'Commercial Dictionary,' and will be given for one year at the conclusion of this article.

	1840.	1844.	1849.
Russia . .	69	70	74
Prussia . .	11	10	10
Holland . .	9	8	6·5
Belgium . .	6·5	7	4
France . .	3·5	3·5	1·5
Other Countries .	1·5	1·5	4·5

The increase under the last head, in this table, is chiefly due to the importation of Flax from Egypt. Some is also imported from Italy, Sicily, and Turkey. Much Flax is grown in Ireland, and also in the West and North of England.

Though all the above countries produce some coarse Flax, it is chiefly from Russia, Prussia, and Egypt that this kind is imported, and is that which is chiefly required in increasing quantities. In a letter with which I have been favoured from Mr. J. M'Adam, he observes—"It is certain that all hot countries, or those which, like Russia, have a short, warm summer, cannot furnish fine Flax fibre; but it is precisely coarse fibre that is now so much wanted. The bulk of fine Flax used in the linen manufacture is trifling compared with the coarse. A Belfast or Leeds mill of 5000 spindles will consume only 200 to 250 tons of Flax annually; while one of the same size, at Dundee or Kirkaldy, will consume 1000 to 1200 tons. Belgium, Holland, France, and Ireland can supply all the world with fine fibre; but Russia and Egypt cannot keep pace with the demand for coarse." The quality of the latter has, however, greatly improved of late years. "Fifteen years ago, Egyptian Flax was selling at Belfast for £24 a ton, and, in some cases, as low as £18. It now readily brings £30 to £40 on an average, and since the war has run up to £56." The above average prices ought to pay for its growth in India, considering that Jute is grown and prepared there, and sold at still lower prices.

In order to succeed in the culture in new situations, it is necessary to know what is considered requisite in the situations where the cultivation is successful. We shall, therefore, first consider the nature of the plant, and then its culture in Europe, and, subsequently, the attempts which have already been made in India to produce Flax. From these, and the extended information which we now possess, we shall draw our conclusions respecting eventual success, either in the old or in new localities, of the wide-spread territories of India.

THE FLAX PLANT AND ITS PRODUCTS.

The Flax plant belongs to the natural family of Linaceæ, so named from the botanical name (Linum) of the genus to which it belongs. The species are found chiefly in temperate parts of the world, with a few in tropical regions; most are remarkable for the tenacity of the fibre of their inner bark. The native country of the Flax plant is unknown; but as it was cultivated by the earliest civilised nations, it is probably a native of oriental regions, from which it has travelled southwards into India and northwards into Europe.

Description of plant.—It is an annual, with long and slender but fibrous roots, which penetrate to a considerable distance into the soil, where this is loose and friable. The stem is smooth, simple, and erect; branched, or, as usually cultivated, branching only towards the top; from one and a half to three feet in height. It consists of a pith and woody part, with the layer of bast fibres covered with cuticle on the outside.

The leaves are alternate, sessile, linear-lanceolate, and smooth. The flowers, of a blue colour, are arranged in a corymbose panicle. The sepals or green outer leaflets of the flower are five in number, ovate acute, slightly ciliated, nearly equal to the capsule in length. The petals, blue in colour and five in number, are obscurely crenate, comparatively large, and deciduous. The stamens are equal in number to the petals and alternate with them, having their filaments united together near their bases into a kind of ring. The ovary, or young seed-vessel, is divided into five cells, and is surmounted by five stigmata. Capsule, or *boll*, roundish, but rather pointed at the apex, divided into five perfect cells, each of which is again subdivided by an imperfect partition, thus forming ten divisions, each of them containing a single seed. These seeds are oval in shape, flattened or plump, smooth and shining, of a brownish colour externally, but sometimes white; always white internally: the seed-coat mucilaginous, and the kernel of the seed oily and farinaceous.

Besides other species of the same genus, such as *L. perenne*, which affords a strong though coarse fibre, and one difficult to separate from the woody matter, there are some varieties of the true Flax plant known; but these are much fewer than is the case with most other long-cultivated plants. Dr. Lindley, as already quoted by Mr. J. Wilson, in his paper on 'Flax; its Treatment, Agricultural and Technical' (in 'Journ. Royal Agric. Soc.,' vol. xiv, p. 188, 1853), describes two different forms:

1. The *Linum humile* or *crepitans* (the Springlein or Klanglein of the Germans), a plant somewhat shorter and more inclined to branch than the other, and possessing larger capsules, twice as long as the calyx, which burst with considerable elasticity when ripe; its seeds, too, are both larger and of a paler colour.

2. The *Linum usitatissimum* or true winter flax (Winterlein of the Germans), which has smaller capsules, scarcely larger than the calyx, not bursting with elasticity, but firmly retaining their seeds, which are of a dark brown colour.

Mr. Wilson adds, that "in Austria and North Europe, where the winters are severe, and the snow lies too long on the ground to admit of early tillage in the spring, the Winterlein is extensively used, and sown in the autumn; the summer season being too short and too hot to admit of the successful cultivation of the Springlein. With us the custom is to sow in the spring, though, no doubt, in some of our northern districts, where the ground cannot be got ready sufficiently early in the spring, Flax could be advantageously cultivated if sown in the previous autumn."

The Indian plant, called *ulsee* or *tesee*, may be considered a variety which has acquired certain characters from the peculiarities of soil, of climate, and of long and peculiar culture. It is always short, probably not more than eighteen inches in height, much branched, loaded with bolls, which are filled with large, ovoid, plump seed. That this retains its character even in other situations, appears from a fact, of which I have been informed by Mr. M'Adam, the able secretary of the Society for the Promotion of the Growth of Flax in Ireland. The Society having imported some seed for experiment from India, found that the plant did not grow beyond fourteen or eighteen inches.

But that it is also ready to change its habit, is evident from facts to be detailed respecting the experiments which have been made in India. I have also been informed that in a recent experiment made by Mr. Burn, in Sindh, with thick sowing and irrigation, it grew at once to upwards of two feet. I have no doubt that, with a repetition of the process of thick sowing for a few times, the Indian seed would produce plants with tall, straight, and little-branched stems, each with but comparatively few bolls and seeds.

A perfectly white variety of Linseed is common in the Saugur and Nerbuddah territories, which was brought to the notice of the Agricultural Society of India by Col. Ousley. Seeds sent by him were distributed to different parts of the country by the Society. Mr. Finch, of Tirhoot, after two years, returned five maunds; and stated that three fourths of his crop were destroyed by caterpillars, while the common Linseed grown in the vicinity of the white, was left untouched by them.

The useful products of the Flax plant consist of the seeds and of the fibre or Flax. Linseed, or the seeds of the Flax plant, are oval, pointed in shape, compressed with a sharp margin; brownish coloured, smooth, and shining on the outside, but white internally, and without odour. The outside has a bland, mucilaginous taste, in consequence of the skin of the seed being covered with condensed mucus. The white part, or almond of the seed, has an oily taste, from containing fixed oil, which is separated by expression.

These seeds, analysed by Meyer, consist, in one hundred parts, of 15·12 mucilage (nitrogenous mucilage with acetic acid and salts, according to some), chiefly in the seed-coat, 11·26 fatty oil in the nucleus. In the *husk*, emulsin 44·38, besides wax 0·14, acrid soft resin 2·48, starch with salts 1·48. In the *nucleus*, besides the oil, gum 6·15, albumen 2·78, gluten 2·93, also resinous colouring matter 0·55, yellow extractive with tannin and salts (nitre and the chlorides of potassium and calcium) 1·91, sweet extractive with malic acid and some salts 10·88.

The condensed mucus which abounds in the testa of the seed is readily acted on by hot water, and a viscid mucilaginous fluid is formed, in which are two distinct substances; one completely soluble in water, analogous to common gum, called

Arabine by chemists; the other portion is merely suspended, and is considered to be analogous to the Bassorine, found chiefly in Gum Bussora, and in Cherry-tree Gum. Alcohol produces a white flaky, and acetate of lead, a dense precipitate in mucilage of Linseed.

Linseed oil, which we have seen is contained in the kernel of the seeds, is obtained by expression, and may be either cold-drawn, or, as usually obtained, after the seeds have been subjected to a heat of 200°. The former, as in the case of cold-drawn castor oil, is paler, with less colour and taste than Linseed oil prepared with the aid of heat. This is of a deep yellow or brownish colour, of a disagreeable smell and taste, specific gravity 0·932, soluble in alcohol and ether; differing from many other fatty oils, especially in its property of drying into a hard, transparent varnish—a peculiarity which is increased by boiling the oil, either alone, or with some of the preparations of lead.

"The yield of oil from a bushel of East Indian seed is 14¾ lb. to 16 lb.; of Egyptian, 15 lb; of Sicilian, 14½ lb. to 15½ lb.; of Russian, 11 lb. to 13 lb.; of English or Irish, 10¾ lb. to 12 lb."

Linseed oil, according to Sace, is composed of Margarine and Oleine in nearly equal proportions. But the oleic acid of Linseed differs from that of other fatty bodies. The anhydrous acid is composed of carbon 46, hydrogen 38, oxygen 5. The Margaric acid is as usual composed of carbon 34, hydrogen 33, oxygen 3. The Glycerine obtainable from Linseed oil in large quantities, is also similar to that procured from other fats.

Linseed, after having had the oil expressed from them, are in the form of a flat mass, commonly called *oil-cake*. This being reduced to coarse powder, forms the Linseed meal which is so commonly employed for making poultices, though these are also formed of the simply powdered seeds. Here it is evident, from the internal oleaginous and external mucilaginous parts being all ground together, and their properties elicited by hot water, an admirable mixture is produced for making a readily made emollient poultice. From the chemical composition, it is also evident how nourishing the Linseed is likely to be, and, indeed, from experience, is well known to be, for fattening cattle.

10

CHEMICAL CONSTITUENTS OF THE FLAX PLANT.

In addition to the composition of the seed, it is interesting to know that of the plant in general. This we are now able to do in a very satisfactory manner, from Dr. Hodges' 'Lecture on the Composition of the Flax Plant,' and his paper read before the British Association, at Belfast, 23d September, 1852. In this he communicated the history of a crop grown by himself for experimental purposes, and the progress of which he was able carefully to watch, from the sowing of the seed to its conversion into dressed Flax for the market. From this we obtain the following information:

July 28th.—One plant of Flax, in seed, was taken—height above ground, 31 inches, root, 5½ inches long; length from surface of field to first branch, 24 inches. About 5 inches of the lower end of stem had become yellow. The weight of entire plant was 71·1 grains. It was cut into three portions, which were separately incinerated, with the following results:

"1. Root and lower part of stem weighed, dried, 6·60 grains, gave 0·094 ash=1·424 per cent.

"2. Capsules and branches, dry, weighed 9·47, gave ·293 ash=3·094 per cent.

"3. Middle portion, dry, weighed 5·55, gave ·143 ash. Ash in dry stem, 2·622 per cent.

"August 10th.—One plant taken—entire length with root, 37 inches; length from surface of soil to branches, 29 inches; stem of a light straw colour; leaves withered on 10 inches of stem; capsules 10 in number—seeds green; weight of entire plant, 71 grains; branches and capsules, 31·8 grains; water in plant, 45·335 grains; solid matter in do., 25·665; inorganic matter in do., 1·006 grains.

PER-CENTAGE COMPOSITION.

		dry.
Water	63·852	
Organic matters	34·732	96·08
Ash	1·416	3·92
Total	100·000	100·00

"August 25th.—The pulling of the crop was begun. A plant was taken and examined; weight of entire plant, 62·40 grains; weight of capsules, 22·50.

PER-CENTAGE COMPOSITION OF STEM.

	In Fresh Plant.	Dry.
Water	56·64	—
Organic matters	41·97	96·89
Ash	1·39	3·11
Total	100·00	100·00

"Water in straw of plants as sent to the steeping works, after 14 days' exposure to the air in stooks, 12·2 per cent; water in air-dried capsules, 11·84 per cent; weight of the air-dried Flax, with bolls produced on the experimental field, 7·770 lb.

COMPOSITION OF THE CROP.

"One hundred parts of the ash of the dry straw and capsules had respectively the following composition:

	Ash of Straw.	Of Capsules.
Potash	20·32	16·38
Soda	2·07	6·25
Chloride of Sodium	9·27	12·98
Lime	19·88	13·95
Magnesia	4·05	3·91
Oxide of Iron	2·83	0·38
Sulphuric Acid	7·13	14·51
Phosphoric Acid	10·24	23·26
Carbonic Acid	10·72	6·37
Silica	12·80	0·67
Total	99·31	99·66

"The proportion of nitrogen contained in the straw and capsules were ascertained to be as follows, per cent.:

1. In the straw, dried at 212°	0·53
2. In the capsules or bolls, ditto	1·26

"The general results of the examination of a specimen of Flax straw taken from the experimental crop, are as follow: The presence of a volatile oil having been indicated, a quantity of the stems of the plant carefully deprived of the seed capsules was distilled with water containing common salt; and from the distillate, which was without action on litmus, I obtained an oil of a yellow colour. Five pounds of the stems afforded about ten grains of this oil, which had an agreeable, penetrating odour, and the distillate of the stems suggested the peculiar smell which is remarked on entering a room where Flax is stored. The solutions obtained on examination were found to contain wax; traces of chlorophylle; a peculiar green resin; a bright brown gum resin, which presented some of the characters of the principle which Pagenstecher termed *linen*, but could not be identified with it; a modification of tannic acid which afforded a grey precipitate with perchloride of iron, but was not affected by solutions of isinglass or tartar emetic; gum, not affected by solution of borax or basic silicate of potash; a brown colouring matter; albumen; casein; starch; pectin; cellulose; and salts."

The result of Dr. Hodges' experiments has been further placed in a very clear light by Mr. Wilson. The object of these was to ascertain the relative proportions of the produce of Flax, and also the distribution of inorganic matter in them. The Flax employed had been steeped in the ordinary way, and was found to contain 1·73 per cent. of ash. Of this, air-dried straw, 4000 lb. weight, were taken, which produced:

Of dressed fibre	500 lb.
,, fine tow	132 ,,
,, coarse tow	192 ,,
Of fibre in all	824 lb.

These products contained:

In the dressed Flax	4·48 lb.	of ash.
„ fine tow	. 2·08	„
„ coarse tow	. 2·56	„
Or, in the whole of the fibre	9·12 lb.	of inorganic matter.

So that 59·08 lb., which the crop had withdrawn from the soil, remained in the useless portion, while only 9·12 lb. were carried off in 824 lb. of the dressed fibre and tow.

Analyses of the Flax plant and of the soils in which it is grown were first carefully made by Sir R. Kane, and afterwards by Dr. Hodges and others. They have been repeated by Messrs. Mayer and Brazier, in the Laboratory of the Royal College of Chemistry.[1] The localities from which the latter obtained their specimens of Flax, by the aid of Mr. A. Marshall, of Leeds, were Esthonia or Estland, Livonia or Lievland, Courland, and Lithuania. The first of these districts, with the second and third mentioned, are situated on the eastern shores of the Baltic; the fourth, Lithuania, is the only inland country.

From their analyses, the following comparative table was made, from which it will be readily seen, in what points the ashes of these different specimens agree in composition.

	Lievland.	Courland.	Lithuanian.	Estland.
	I.	II.	III.	IV.
Potash	43·42	37·44	36·61	25·70
Soda	—	3·74	3·06	8·37
Lime	21·35	25·39	24·09	26·41
Magnesia	7·79	7·71	7·45	11·74
Sesquioxide of Iron	1·15	1·13	1·04	1·02
Manganese	—	trace.	—	—
Chloride of Sodium	—	1·94	3·75	1·67
„ of Potassium	1·31	—	—	—
Phosphoric Acid	10·94	8·31	14·30	15·47
Sulphuric Acid	5·66	5·89	3·65	4·64
Silicic Acid	8·38	8·45	6·05	4·98
	100·00	100·00	100·00	100·00

"We also append, in a tabular form, the results of Sir R. Kane's analyses of this plant, taken from his paper, read before the Royal Dublin Society, on the 6th of April, 1847.

"To facilitate comparison, we have re-calculated these analyses after deducting the carbonic acid.

[1] Mr. Mayer is now Professor of Chemistry at Madras.

	A	B	C	D	E	F	G
	Courtrai District.		Antwerp District.				
	Heestelt.	Escamaffles.	Hamme Zog.	Not named.	District in Holland.	Dublin.	Armagh.
Potash	9·69	30·62	26·67	28·62	21·35	11·78	6·60
Soda	24·16	none.	16·88	0·48	12·65	11·82	6·61
Lime . , . . .	19·37	22·04	22·15	21·19	21·30	14·85	23·67
Magnesia	4·34	4·45	4·70	4·05	3·50	9·38	4·22
Sesquioxide of Iron .	5·66	2·03	1·31	2·53	2·74	,, ,,	14·10
Alumina . . .	0·56	0·58	0·86	,, ,,	1·67	7·32	,, ,,
Manganese . . .	trace.	trace.	trace.	,, ,,	,, ,,	,, ,,	1·12
Sulphuric Acid . .	7·93	8·33	8·18	13·43	11·22	3·19	9·30
Phosphoric Acid . .	14·10	15·78	10·66	12·19	12·82	13·05	7·29
Silicic Acid . . .	3·85	4·54	3·20	3·36	6·18	25·71	0·94
Chloride of Sodium .	10·34	11·63	5·49	14·15	6·57	2·90	26·15
	100·00	100·00	100·00	100·00	100·00	100·00	100·00

"On comparing the results of our analyses with those of Sir Robert Kane, we find at once that the general features of both are identical, although, as might be expected, discrepancies present themselves respecting the individual constituents. In the ashes, both of the Belgian and of the Russian specimens, we meet with a very large amount of alkali (nearly 40 per cent.): the quantity, too, of phosphoric acid is very considerable (from 10 to 15 per cent.) Our analyses then furnish a further proof that Flax must be classed among the most exhausting crops, for, the amount of valuable mineral substances which we remove from the soil in this plant considerably exceeds the quantity which is generally extracted from it in the form of wheat or corn.

"From a statement of Mr. M'Adam,[1] it appears that one rood of land yields about 12·7 cwt. of recently pulled Flax plant. If we take this number as the basis of calculation, and the average per centage of ash at 3·53 lb., of alkalies at 39·58 lb., and of phosphoric acid at 12·51 lb., we find that a Flax crop removes from a rood of land not less than 12·21 lb. of alkalies, and 5·94 lb. of phosphoric acid. On the other hand, we have learnt from the researches of Mr. Way,[2] that a rood of land, which has served for the cultivation of wheat, loses (an average taken from a great number of analyses) about 7·5 lb. of alkali and 6·9 lb. of phosphoric acid. These figures show that the amount of phosphoric acid in the Flax crop closely approaches that of the wheat, whilst the latter extracts only about half the quantity of alkali which we find in the former. Hence, it would appear, that a Flax crop is at least as exhausting as a crop of wheat.

"There is, however, one striking point of dissimilarity between the cultivation of wheat and that of Flax, and we are indebted to Sir Robert Kane for having for the first time brought this point under the notice of the farmer in a forcible manner, viz.: that while the mineral ingredients which we remove from our fields in wheat, or cerealia in general, become constituents of food, and enter in this manner into a circulation, from which, even under very favorable circumstances, they return to the soil only after the lapse of some time; the woody fibre of Flax, as a necessary preliminary

1 'Royal Agricultural Journal,' vol. viii, p. 361.
2 'Royal Agricultural Journal,' vol. vii, p. 593.

to its being used by man, is separated to a considerable extent from those very mineral substances which are so essential for its successful growth. This mineral matter, when economised in a proper manner by the farmer, may be returned to his field to keep up the equilibrium of its fertility.

"The vegetation of the Flax plant resembles in this respect the growth of the sugar-cane, from the culture of which, we expect a material consisting entirely of atmospheric constituents. The inorganic substances taken up by the plant are only instruments used in its production, which should be as carefully preserved as tools in a manufactory, and will then do further duty in promoting the elaboration of future crops."

Messrs. Mayer and Brazier then directed their attention to the soils upon which the different specimens of Flax had been grown, samples of which, through the kindness of Mr. Marshall, had likewise been forwarded to Dr. Hoffman. These soils all gave a brownish colour to boiling water, owing to a portion of the organic matter being soluble in that menstruum.

From their various analyses, Messrs. Mayer and Brazier obtain, by calculation, the following amounts of constituents of 100 parts in the soils:

	Lievland.	Courland.	Lithuania.	Estland.
Potash	0·5011	0·3241	0·5466	0·3726
Soda	—	0·1320	0·0452	0·0480
Lime	0·3751	0·7816	0·4980	0·7955
Magnesia	0·2006	0·1304	0·1805	0·3619
Alumina	1·1919	1·8731	2·1418	2·0102
Sexquioxide of Iron	1·8076	2·3767	3·1900	2·0206
Manganese	trace.	trace.	trace.	trace.
Chloride of Sodium	0·0455	0·0247	0·0421	0·0790
Sulphuric Acid	0·1539	0·0880	0·1206	0·1618
Phosphoric Acid	0·1399	0·0538	0·0805	0·1597
Organic matter	4·7176	4·0300	4·3442	4·8630
Insoluble residue after deducting organic matter	91·0634	88·4872	88·4724	88·2364
	100·1966	99·3016	99·6619	99·1087

The insoluble residue constituting the greater portion of the soil, was fused with carbonate of potash. Upon calculation, they yielded the following results per cent:

	Lievland.	Courland.	Lithuania.	Estland.
Lime	traces.	1·8727	0·8778	2·0120
Alumina	11·6270	6·1145	2·2452	5·7549
Sesquioxide of Iron	tracės.	traces.	traces.	traces.
Phosphoric Acid	traces.	traces.	none.	traces.
Silicic Acid	79·3424	81·5000	85·0938	80·5676
	90·9694	92·6224	88·2168	88·3345

In all the four soils, they found, comparatively speaking, considerable quantities of alkali, especially potash, and also of phosphoric acid. They closely resemble the Belgian soils analysed by Sir Robert Kane, as may be seen from the tables which they borrow from Sir Robert's paper.

	Heestert.	Escamaffles.	Hamme Zog.	Not named.	Holland.
Potassa	0·160	0·123	0·068	0·151	0·583
Soda	0·298	0·146	0·110	0·206	0·306
Lime	0·357	0·227	0·481	0·366	3·043
Magnesia	0·202	0·153	0·140	0·142	0·105
Alumina	2·102	1·383	0·125	0·988	5·626
Sexquioxide of Iron	3·298	1·663	1·202	1·543	6·047
Manganese	trace.	trace.	a trace.	no trace.	trace.
Chloride of Sodium	0·017	0·030	0·067	0·009	0·023
Sulphuric Acid	0·025	0·017	0·013	0·026	0·023
Phosphoric Acid	0·121	0·152	0·064	0·193	0·159
Organic matter not driven off at 100° per cent.	3·123	2·361	4·209	3·672	5·841
Clay	14·920	9·280	5·760	4·400	17·080
Sand	75·080	84·065	86·797	88·385	60·947
	99·703	99·600	99·975	100·081	99·783

In conclusion, the authors express their warmest thanks to Dr. Hofmann for his instruction and valuable advice during the prosecution of these analyses. (*v.* the details in the 'Proceedings' of Chemical Society.)

That we may have a complete view of what is required in soils for the successful culture of Flax, we adduce Sir R. Kane's analyses of three Irish soils and one Belgian, from the report of the Flax Improvement Society of Ireland. The Irish soils, as described by Mr. M'Adam, were from the counties of Londonderry and Tyrone, and were considered very good for Flax. The Belgian was from Duffel, in the province of Antwerp, and may be taken as representing a third-rate class of Flax soil in that country, requiring much manure, but producing good crops. The large proportion of sand and the little moisture in this last, deserve notice :

	Irish, No. 1.	Irish, No. 2.	Irish, No. 3.	Belgian.
Silica and Siliceous Sand	73·72	69·41	64·93	92·78
Oxide of Iron	5·51	5·29	5·64	0·66
Alumina	6·65	5·70	8·97	1·11
Basic Phosphate of Iron	0·06	0·25	0·31	0·21
Carbonate of Lime	1·00	0·53	1·67	0·35
Magnesia, Alkalies, and Sulphuric and Muriatic Acids	0·32	0·25	0·45	0·12
Organic matters, with Nitrogen	4·86	6·67	9·41	2·74
Water	7·57	11·48	8·62	2·03
	99·78	99·78	100·00	100·00

CULTURE OF FLAX.

The importance of Flax culture being admitted, we may devote a few words to the objections which are usually alleged against it. These chiefly consist of the opinions entertained respecting the exhausting nature of a Flax crop. This is certainly true, where everything is taken from the soil and nothing returned to it; but the elementary principles of which both cotton and fibre, as well as sugar, consist, are now known to be obtained almost entirely from the atmosphere. Therefore, by taking away only the cotton, the flax, or the sugar, and returning all the other parts of the plant to the soil, these products will impoverish the soil as little as it is possible for any culture to do. This, as far as Flax is concerned, may be effected by some of the improved methods of preparing the fibre, and by feeding cattle on the oil-cake of the seeds, and thus returning all the other constituents which had been taken from the soil. Mr. Nichols observes that "every farmer will be enabled, by applying the seed of his Flax crop to that purpose, to obtain a supply of the richest manure, which, with the offal separated from the fibre in course of preparation, will serve to renovate the soil and secure its undiminished fertility." This we find fully proved by the foregoing and other analyses of the different parts of the plant, and of the soil in which it has been grown, as well as of the products obtained in the improved steeping and preparation of the fibre.

The analyses of Mayer and Brazier correspond closely with those made by Sir R. Kane, of specimens of Belgian Flax; and their conclusions also coincide with his: that, while the mineral ingredients which we remove from our fields in Wheat, become constituents of food, the woody fibre of Flax is separated from those very mineral substances which are so essential for its successful growth; and they forcibly observe that "the inorganic substances taken up by the plant, are only instruments in the production of Flax, which should be as carefully preserved as tools in a manufactory, and will then do further duty in promoting the elaboration of future crops."

Climate.—One of the most important considerations in attempting the culture of Flax in new situations or countries is that of climate, though one that is very frequently neglected. On this subject, Mr. M'Adam has made some very just observations, which we shall afterwards have occasion to refer to. He observes that though the climate of the British Isles is well adapted to the growth of this plant, those districts which possess the most equable temperature will be found the most suitable. A regular supply of genial moisture in spring, without an excess of wet in autumn, is most favorable. Our climate is better adapted to Flax, in some respects, than that of Belgium, since the severe droughts which frequently occur there in spring often destroy the crop. If, after springing to the height of two or three inches, a long continuance of drought should occur, with a hot sun, the heat parches up the earth, as the delicate leaves of the plant are unable to exclude the scorching rays from the surface soil, and the roots have not penetrated sufficiently deep to secure a supply of moisture. "Flax is then in the most critical state; the plant droops, turns a whitish yellow, and, if the drought continue long, dies on arid tracts of land. In such a case Flax may be beneficially watered; and a regular water-cart will go over an acre a day."

When the plant acquires a sufficient height to thoroughly cover the ground, dry weather becomes comparatively harmless; but occasional gentle showers are very needful to produce a regular and vigorous growth. "In fact, a slow, steady growth, from the germinating of the seed to the maturity of the plant, is requisite for the quality and yield of fibre. Hence it is found that in countries approaching the northern limits of the temperate zone, the short, hot summers induce too rapid growth, and, although the quantity of fibre produced is pretty large, it is never of a fine reed. This is strongly exemplified by Russia, as, out of an export frequently reaching 40,000 to 50,000 tons per annum, none sells higher than £48; whereas, in Belgium and Holland, the price often reaches £150 and £180 per ton." The best samples of British Flax sell for £65 to £70 per ton, or even £85 per ton.

"For the same reason, insular climates or long lines of coast, whose position insures a more equable temperature and continued supply of moisture from spring till autumn, are found to produce the best Flax. In such the plant springs up to a height of thirty or forty inches, in a straight, slender stem, with few or no branches, and only two or three seed-vessels to each stalk." Thick sowing produces the same effect.

So, also, Mr. Nichol: "Flax will bear a good deal of moisture, and, in fact, thrives best in a moist climate. Hence the peculiar suitableness of England for its growth; our climate being generally more humid than that of the Continent, especially in the Western counties. Indeed, long-continued drought is the chief enemy the flax-grower has to dread." (p. 447.)

The hot summers of Russia and Egypt cause a dryness and brittleness of fibre, and prevent its retaining that elasticity, pliancy, and oiliness which characterise the Flaxes of Belgium, Holland, and Ireland.

"In Egypt, though the plant attains great luxuriance in the rich alluvial soil of the Nile, yet the fibre does not attain fineness and softness, and, notwithstanding the efforts made to improve the culture and preparation, its value has not exceeded £44 per ton." .

Culture.—In connection with the climate we may notice peculiarities of culture in different countries.

"In Flanders a great variety of crops are raised; the farms being for the most part small—the majority varying from eight or ten to twenty and thirty acres." (p. 448.) "Every Belgian farmer, whether large or small, grows Flax sufficient to keep himself and his people employed when not at work on the land."

The cultivation of Flax in Flanders is conducted with the greatest care. The ground is well ploughed, rolled, enriched with liquid manure, harrowed, and when the seed is sown again harrowed in with a light harrow, and the surface rolled. The fields when thus accurately prepared display an extreme degree of neatness and smoothness. The liquid manure is prepared with considerable care. It consists of the urine of cattle in which rape-cake has been dissolved, and in which the cleansings of privies from the neighbouring towns and villages have been mixed; and is collected in subterranean vaults of brick work. About 2800 gallons (beer measure) are allowed to the English acre.

In Russia the Flax is cultivated with less care, and without any manure in the Ukraine. The time of sowing is from the 25th of May to the 10th of June, and that of reaping, from the end of August to the end of September. The Flax is about four months in a state of vegetation.

The directions for culture which, however, are most desirable for us to notice, are those which have been drawn up with so much care for the guidance of cultivators in Ireland. We, therefore, reprint, in full, the—

DIRECTIONS FOR THE PROPER MANAGEMENT OF THE FLAX CROP, COMPILED BY THE COMMITTEE OF THE ROYAL SOCIETY FOR THE PROMOTION AND IMPROVEMENT OF THE GROWTH OF FLAX IN IRELAND.

The following directions have been carefully arranged from the mass of information obtained by the Society and their agriculturists, during their ten years' experience in the improved system of management:

Soil and Rotation.—By attention and careful cultivation, good Flax may be grown on various soils; but some are much better adapted for it than others. The best is a sound, dry, deep loam, with a clay subsoil. It is very desirable that the land should be properly drained and subsoiled; as, when it is saturated with either underground or surface water, good Flax cannot be expected.

Without method there cannot be success. Different soils require a difference of rotation. In the best soils of Flanders, Flax is grown in the third year of a seven-course rotation, or the fifth year of a ten-course rotation.

It is not considered generally advisable to grow Flax more frequently than once in ten years; not because it exhausts the land more than any other crops, but because good *Flax* cannot be had, at short intervals, on the same soil.[1] In Belgium it invariably follows a corn crop—generally oats; and in this country, where oats is such a usual crop, the same system might be profitably pursued: but it must be understood, that it is only after oats following a green crop or old lea, and never after two or three succeeding crops of oats—which bad practice still prevails in some districts. It is a very general error among farmers, to consider it necessary that Flax

[1] The following rotation, which would bring Flax once in ten years, has been proposed:—First year, potatoes; second, barley, laid down with grasses; third year, cut for soiling; fourth year, pasture; fifth year, flax; or the one half might be better in flax, the other in oats, so that, with the return of the rotation, which would be in five years, the flax could be put on the ground which, in the last rotatory course, was under corn, throwing a range of ten years between the flax crops coming into the same ground.

A gentleman of much practical knowledge recommends the following as being the most profitable:—1. Oats after the grass and clover. 2. Flax pulled in August; then ploughed and harrowed in with two cwt. guano and two cwt. gypsum; then sown with rape. 3. Potatoes or turnips, well manured. 4. Wheat, sown in spring, with clover and ryegrass. 5. Hay and clover. 6. Grazing. 7. Oats. 8. Flax and winter vetches; guano, as before mentioned. 9. Turnips, well manured. 10. Barley, sown with ryegrass and clover. 11. Clover and hay. 12. Grazing. 13. Oats. should follow a potato crop. Except on very poor soils, a better crop will be produced after grain, and the double benefit of the grain and Flax secured. If old lea be broken up, and potatoes planted, followed by a grain crop, a very fine crop of Flax may be obtained in the ensuing year.

Preparation of the Soil.—One of the points of the greatest importance in the culture of Flax, is by thorough-draining, and by careful and repeated cleansing of the land from weeds, to place it in the finest, deepest, and cleanest state. This will make room for the roots to penetrate, which they will often do to a depth equal to one half the length of the stem above ground. (Sometimes twenty to thirty inches.)

After wheat, one ploughing may be sufficient, on light friable loam, but two are better; and, on stiff soils, three are advisable—one immediately after harvest, across the ridges, and two in spring, so as to be ready for sowing in the first or second week of April. Much will, of course, depend on the nature of the soil, and the knowledge and experience of the farmer. The land should be so drained and subsoiled, that it can be sown in flats, which will give more evenly and much better crops. Subsoiling should not be done at a less interval than two years prior to the Flax crop. This gives the land time to consolidate. But, until the system of thorough-draining be general, it will be necessary, after oats, to plough early in autumn, to the depth of six or eight inches. Throw the land into ridges, that it may receive the frost and air; and make surface drains to carry off the rains of winter. Plough again in spring, three or four inches deep, so as to preserve the winter surface for the roots of the Flax. The spring ploughing should be given some time before sowing, to allow any seeds of weeds in the land to vegetate, and the harrowing in of the Flax seed will kill them, and save a great deal of after weeding. Following the last harrowing, it is necessary to roll, to give an even surface and consolidate the land, breaking this up again with a short-toothed or seed harrow, before sowing, which should be up and down, not across the ridges or anglewise.

Seed.—The seed best adapted for the generality of soils is Riga, although Dutch has been used in many districts of country, for a series of years, with perfect success. American seed does not generally suit well, as it is apt to produce a coarse, branchy stem. If used, it should be on deep, loamy soils. In buying seed, select it plump, shining, and heavy, and of the best brands, from a respectable merchant. Sift it clear of all the seeds of weeds, which will save a great deal of after trouble, when the crop is growing. This may be done by fanners, and through a wire sieve, twelve bars to the inch. Home-saved seed has produced such excellent crops, of late, that it is strongly recommended that every farmer should only sow, each year, as much foreign seed as would produce a sufficient quantity for his Flax crop of the following season.[1] The thinner portion of the crop would be the best for this purpose, as, when Flax grows thin, it produces much seed. This plan, besides the saving effected in the price of foreign sowing seed, would effectually secure the farmer from any danger of loss from fraudulently made up seed. It will be best, in most cases, to use the seed which is saved from this, in the following year, for feeding, or to sell it for the oil mills, although it often produces good crops.

Sowing.—The proportion of seed may be stated at three and a half imperial bushels to the Irish or plantation acre; and so on, in proportion to the Scotch or Cunningham, and the English or statute acre. It is better to sow too thick than too thin; as, with thick sowing the stem grows tall and straight, with only one or two seed-capsules at the top, and the fibre is found greatly superior, in fineness and length, to that produced from thin sown Flax, which grows coarse, and branches out, produces much seed, but a very

[1] The produce of seed averages about twelve bushels the statute acre, so that the seed saved off one statute acre would sow about five.

inferior quality of fibre. The ground being pulverized and well cleaned, roll and sow. If it has been laid off without ridges, it should be marked off in divisions, eight to ten feet broad, in order to give an equable supply of seed. After sowing, cover it with a seed harrow, going twice over it—once up and down, and once across or anglewise—as this makes it more equally spread, and avoids the small drills made by the teeth of the harrow. Finish with the roller, which will leave the seed covered about an inch—the proper depth. The ridges should be very little raised in the centre, when the ground is ready for the seed, otherwise the crop will not ripen evenly; and, when land is properly drained, there should be no ridges. The sowing of clover and grass seeds along with the Flax is not advised, when it can be conveniently avoided, as these plants always injure the root ends of the Flax. But carrots may be sown, in suitable soils, in drills, so that the person pulling the Flax may step over the rows, which may be afterwards hoed and cleaned, and should have some liquid manure. A stolen crop of rape or winter vetches, or of turnips of the stone or Norfolk globe varieties, may be taken, after the Flax is pulled. Rolling the ground after sowing is very advisable, care being taken not to roll when the ground is so wet that the earth adheres to the roller.

Manure for the Flax Crop.—Recent chemical investigations have shown that the fibre of Flax does abstract from the soil certain matters, although not in so large a proportion as several other commonly cultivated crops. To supply to the soil all the matters which the entire plant requires, so as to leave the land in the same state of fertility as before, the following compound has been proposed as a manure, which may be sown broadcast on the land, prior to the last harrowing before sowing the Flax seed:

FOR A STATUTE ACRE OF LAND.		*s.*	*d.*
Muriate of Potash, 30 lb.,	cost about	2	6
Chloride of Sodium (common salt), 28 lb.,	"	0	3
Burned Gypsum, powdered, 34 lb.,	"	0	6
Bone Dust, 54 lb.,	"	3	3
Sulphate of Magnesia (Epsom salts), 56 lb.,	"	4	0
		10	6

[Oil-cake of rape, cameline, and colza, applied either dry or with urine, are also recommended as manures.]

Weeding.—If care has been paid to cleaning the seed and the soil, few weeds will appear; but if there be any, they must be carefully pulled. It is done in Belgium by women and children, who, with coarse cloths round their knees, creep along on all-fours. This injures the young plant less than walking over it (which, if done, should be by persons whose shoes are not filled with nails). They should work, also, facing the wind, so that the plants laid flat by the pressure may be blown up again, or thus be assisted to regain their upright position. The tender plant, pressed one way, soon recovers; but if twisted or flattened by careless weeders, it seldom rises again.

Pulling.—The time when Flax should be pulled is a point of much nicety to determine. The fibre is in the best state before the seed is quite ripe. If pulled too soon, although the fibre is fine, the great waste in scutching and hackling renders it unprofitable; and, if pulled too late, the additional weight does not compensate for the coarseness of the fibre. It may be stated, that the best time for pulling is, when the seeds are beginning to change from a green to a pale brown colour, and the stalk to become yellow for about two thirds of its height from the ground. When any of the crop is lying, and suffering from wet, it should be pulled as soon as possible, and kept by itself. So long as the ground is undrained, and imperfectly levelled before sowing, the Flax will be found of different lengths. In such cases, pull each length separately, and steep in separate pools, or keep it separate in the same pool. Where there is much second growth, the Flax should be caught by the puller just underneath the bolls, which will leave the short stalks behind. If the latter be few, it is best not to pull them at all, as the loss from mixture and discoloration by weeds would counterbalance the profit. If the ground has been thorough-drained, and laid out evenly, the Flax will be all of the same length. It is most essential to take time and care to keep the Flax even, like a brush, at the root ends. This increases the value to the spinner, and, of course, to the grower, who will be amply repaid, by an additional price, for his extra trouble. Let the handfuls of pulled Flax be laid across each other diagonally, to be ready for the—

Rippling, which should be carried on at the same time, and in the same field, with the pulling. If the only advantage to be derived from rippling was the comparative ease with which rippled Flax is handled, the practice ought always to be adopted; but, besides this, the seed is a most valuable part of the crop; being worth, if sold for the oil mill, £3 per acre, and if used for feeding stock of all kinds, at least £4 per acre. The apparatus is very simple. The ripple consists of a row of iron teeth screwed into a block of wood. This can be procured in Belfast, or may be made by any handy blacksmith. It is to be taken to the field, where the Flax is being pulled, and screwed down to the centre of a nine-feet plank, resting on two stools. The ripplers may either stand or sit astride at opposite ends. They should be at such a distance from the comb, as to permit of their striking it properly and alternately. A winnowing sheet must be placed under them, to receive the bolls as they are rippled off; and then they are ready to receive the Flax just pulled, the handfuls being placed diagonally, and bound up in a sheaf. The sheaf is laid down at the right hand of the rippler, and untied. He takes a handful with one hand, about six inches from the root; and a little nearer the top, with the other. He spreads the top of the handful like a fan, draws the one half of it through the comb, and the other half past the side; and, by half a turn of the wrist, the same operation is repeated with the rest of the bunch. Some, however, prefer rippling without turning the hand, giving the Flax one or two pulls through, according to the quantity of bolls. The Flax can often be rippled, without being passed more than once through the comb. He then lays the handfuls down at his left side, *each handful* crossing the other, when the sheaf shall be carefully tied up and removed. The object of crossing the handfuls so carefully, after rippling, when tying up the beets for the steep, is, that they will part freely from each other, when they are taken to spread out on the grass, and not interlock, and be put out of their even order, as would otherwise be the case. If the weather be dry, the bolls should be kept in the field, spread on winnow-cloths, or other contrivance for drying, and, if turned from time to time, they will win. Passing the bolls first through a coarse riddle, and afterwards through fanners, to remove straws and leaves, will facilitate the drying. If the weather be moist, they should be taken in-doors, and spread out thinly and evenly on a barn floor or on a loft, leaving windows and doors open, to allow a thorough current of air, and turned twice a day. When nearly dry, they may be taken to a corn kiln (taking care not to raise it above summer heat), and carefully turned, until no moisture remains. By the above plan of *slow* drying, the seed has time to imbibe all the juices that remain in the husk, and to become perfectly ripe. If it be taken at once from the field, and dried *hurriedly* on the kiln, these juices will be burned up, and the seed will become shrivelled and parched, little nutritious matter remaining. In fine seasons, the bolls should always be dried in the open air, the seed thrashed out, and the heaviest and plumpest used for sowing or crushing.

The light seeds and chaff form most wholesome and nutritious feeding for cattle. Flax ought not to be allowed to stand in the field, if possible, even the second day; it should be rippled as soon as pulled, and carried to the water as soon as possible, that it may not harden.

Though immediate rippling is thus recommended as the general practice, it may not be convenient in all situations to adopt it. We, therefore, add directions for *stooking* from other authors.

"Flax is always pulled up by the roots: these handfuls are usually laid across each other, and subsequently bound up into small sheaves; these are set up in circular stooks, the butts of each being spread out as much as possible, to allow the air to have free access to them: there they remain until sufficiently dried; they are then either stacked in the field or at the homestead, or the seed is separated at once, and then merely the stem or straw stacked." (Wilson.) "The drying must be sufficient to prevent their heating. They must then be tied up in small sheaves or beets, and then carted home." (Nichol.)

"Many different modes, both of stacking and separating the seeds, exist: probably, the cheapest and most efficient is to pass the straw through plain rollers, which crush the capsule and let the straw pass through uninjured." (Wilson.) "The seed is separated from the capsule, or 'boll,' by winnowing, and the straw remains to be stacked in the usual way." (Nichol.)

Under favorable circumstances we may expect an average crop to produce from 30 cwt. to 40 cwt. of straw, and 12 to 16 bushels of seed, to the acre.

GENERAL OBSERVATIONS ON CULTURE OF FLAX.

From these various details respecting the culture of Flax in the localities where it succeeds best or is most extensively cultivated, we become acquainted with the points requiring most attention. We learn that though one of the crops occupying a shorter time than most others, it is, like these, liable to failure, and from causes often beyond our control. Of these, the most important appears to be climate; as, of this, the temperature should be moderate, and the moisture, though not excessive, yet abundant and continuous, except at the period of gathering the crop. We also learn that though sandy loams and alluvial soils appear best suited to its cultivation, which water may permeate and the roots spread through it in every direction; yet the soil ought to be able to retain moisture sufficiently to benefit the plant, and not let it run off at once, as some open soils do. Manure in many soils is useful; but in others, or when a large quantity is applied, the Flax is apt to grow coarse. Then it will not yield a fine fibre, and is apt to be lost from the weakness of the stem. Hence, it seems to succeed best after a corn crop which has been manured, or on recently turned-up ground. The soil requires to be well tilled, and brought to a level, in order that the Flax plants may all grow of the same length. In Great Britain and Ireland draining is most important, but in India, facilities for irrigation will be not less so. It ought to be freed from weeds as much as possible; and there is no fear of the land becoming exhausted, if the modern methods of culture and of preparation are adopted.

In selecting seed, considerable care is necessary, though, perhaps, too much importance is attached to foreign seed.[1] The interchange of seed is useful for all crops, and, therefore, is no doubt beneficial for Flax; but it is a question whether it should be carried to the extreme extent of always using foreign seed, or limited to only using it occasionally. Some prefer Riga seed; others, that which has been obtained as the first crop from such seed. Dutch seed is preferred by others, especially for heavy soils. American seed is not generally approved of in this country; but it has succeeded well in India.

Excellent crops have been grown in Ireland, from seed saved from the Russian; and it is recommended by Mr. M'Adam and others, that enough of the foreign seed should be produced annually, to raise seed for sowing the crop of the following year. In Norfolk and Essex, Flax has been grown year after year from seed produced in the country, and good crops have continued to be obtained. Mr. Nichol says that the seed may be either home-grown or foreign—Flax equally good being raised from both; but an occasional use of Dutch, Belgian, or Riga is recommended as affording the completest change; but that the seed "grown in England appears to be the best, both from its great weight and freedom from weeds."

Early sowing is especially recommended, and Mr. Wilson considers that even autumn sowing might be suitable in some localities; but the time of sowing must, of course, depend entirely on the season which is to follow for the growth of the crop; and must be very different in Egypt from what it is in

[1] Riga seed is imported in barrels, containing 3½ bushels, and covered with a coarse linen bag. The barrels are branded in Russia by officers named *brackers*, who classify the seed, as it arrives from the interior, under the terms "sowing seed," "rejected sowing seed," and "crushing seed." But, notwithstanding this, Riga seed usually contains from 15 to 20 per cent. of the seeds of weeds, and therefore requires to be carefully sifted. Dutch seed is seldom adulterated. It comes in old wine-hogsheads, containing 7 bushels each.

Riga seed varies in price from 7*s.* to 16*s.* per bushel; and Dutch from 7*s.* to 13*s.* 6*d.* per bushel. (M'Adam.)

Ireland. By sowing early, that is, in the latter end of March or the beginning of April, the crop might be gathered in before the regular corn harvest in England. But another advantage is, that early sowing is followed by slow and steady growth, which is indispensable for obtaining a fine fibre. Later in the season, vegetation is more rapid, the fibre grows more quickly, and has not time to fine and mellow. The fineness of fibre, however, depends also upon the proportion of seed which is employed. From two to three bushels per acre—the latter for fine fibre, and the former for medium quality of fibre; therefore, $2\frac{1}{2}$ bushels, or about 130 lb. of clean seed is a fair average to the English or statute acre; but if the crop of seed is the principal object, then six pecks per acre is sufficient.

The time of pulling is, of course, a subject of the greatest importance, as, if pulled too early the fibre will be flimsy, and if too late, it will be coarse. If the object is to obtain very fine fibre, then the crop is pulled before the seed is quite ripe, and the seed should then be taken off by rippling. As long as the seed is in the husk it continues to ripen; but if good seed is required for future sowings, it should be grown for this purpose, and allowed to ripen fully. In the directions of the Irish Flax Improvement Society, it is strongly recommended to separate the seeds immediately from the stems, and thus to preserve a portion of the crop, which, in many places, is now unnecessarily wasted. According to ancient custom, the plants should then be steeped for a longer or shorter period, but often the former, to the manifest detriment of the fibre. This may all be avoided, either by stacking the dried Flax stems until some convenient time, or adopting some of the improved methods for separating the fibre.

With a few observations on the proportions of the different parts of the crop obtainable per acre, and the probable profits of the culture, we may proceed to apply the information which we have collected to India, and ascertain what are the prospects of success in the different parts of that wide-spread territory.

PROFITS OF THE CULTURE OF FLAX IN GREAT BRITAIN.

Mr. Nichols gives an estimate of the value to the grower of an acre of Flax; observing that, "although any such estimate must at best be uncertain, depending as it does upon variable contingencies, it may nevertheless not be without its use in this place.

"The produce of Flax per acre, under a good system of cultivation, is generally found to be from 40 to 50 stone—although 60 stone is not unfrequently obtained; and this quantity has, in several instances, been grown in Norfolk within the last few years. Forty stone per acre may, therefore, I think, be assumed as a safe average. The price for Flax of average quality may fairly be taken at 7*s*. 6*d*. per stone of 14 lb.; but that of the finer qualities is much higher. The general yield of seed per acre is from 16 to 24 bushels, but it sometimes rises to 30 bushels—and 20 bushels may, therefore, be taken as a moderate average. The price of Linseed varies from 8*s*. to 10*s*. per bushel for the finest sorts for sowing, to 6*s*. and 7*s*. for the common kind, such as is used for crushing and cattle feeding; 7*s*. per bushel may, therefore, be assumed as a fair average. Against these estimations must be placed the rent of the land, and the charge of cultivation and preparing the fibre for market. The amount for an acre of Flax will then stand as follows:

	£	*s*.	*d*.		£	*s*.	*d*.
Rent, rates, and taxes . .	1	10	0	40 stone of flax, at 7*s*. 6*d*. .	15	0	0
2½ bushels of seed, at 9*s*. .	1	2	6	20 bushels of seed, at 7*s*. .	7	0	0
Tillage	1	0	0	Chaff, refuse, flax, and tow .		10	0
Pulling, steeping, &c. . .	1	10	0		22	10	0
Beetling 20 bushels of seed, at 1*s*., and re-tying the flax	1	0	0	Deduct outlay . .	10	2	6
Breaking and scutching 40 st., at 2*s*. per stone . .	4	0	0	Leaving a balance in favour of the grower, of . .	£12	7	6
	£10	2	6				

"Making every allowance," Mr. Nichols concludes, "for unfavorable seasons, and the other contingencies to which Flax growing, in common with all other agricultural operations, is subject, a profit of £10 or £12 per acre may, I think, be reasonably expected by the grower of Flax, provided he attends properly to the business, and makes the most of the fibre and the seed."

Mr. Nichols, however, refers also to an account published by Mr. S. Druce, of Ensham, near Oxford, who gives £8 as the rate of profit. But, as Mr. Nichols observes, he only obtained 23 stone per acre; and his Flax was evidently of inferior quality, as it sold for only about 5*s*. per stone.

According to some accounts, about 800 lb. per acre is sometimes obtained in Great Britain. In the United States, 400 lb. of good clear Flax, and 8 or 10 bushels of seed, are considered a medium crop.

Mr. M'Adam has given two estimates: No. 1 being for an acre, sown thinly, with a view to having a large produce of seed, which necessitates a coarser description of fibre; and No. 2 being sown more thickly, producing less seed, but a finer fibre. The expenses of the culture and preparation of both are about £9. The first (No. 1) is expected to yield 38 stone of Flax (16 lb. each), at 6*s*. 6*d*.; 18 bushels of seed, at 6*s*. 6*d*.; and 50 bushels of husks, at 4*d*.; yielding a profit of £10. No. 2 is expected to yield 30 stone of Flax, at 9*s*. 6*d*.; 10 bushels of seed, at 6*s*. 6*d*.; husks, 8*s*.; yielding a profit of £8 14*s*. 6*d*.: but the value of the Flax may reach as high as 15*s*., or even 20*s*. Mr. M'Adam observes that "the profits are usually pretty equal, whether the Flax be grown primarily for seed or for fibre; the greater produce in the first case of seed, and the higher value of the dressed Flax in the second, maintain a just equilibrium."

REPORT ON THE CULTURE OF FLAX IN INDIA.

"India having, at least, for centuries grown the Flax plant, on account of the oil yielded by its seeds (Linseed), the country has very naturally been looked to as a source of Flax fibre; the supply of which is so greatly diminished by the war with Russia.[1] The Belfast Chamber observe, that "as India annually exports nearly 100,000 quarters of seed to Great Britain and Ireland, it has been calculated that the plants

[1] The following formed the substance of a Report prepared by the Author, in August, 1854, and is printed nearly as it was written.

which produced this quantity of seed would yield, annually, at least 12,000 tons of fibre—value, say £500,000; all of which now goes to waste." Besides the above quantity of seed, much is also exported to North America and to other countries, and much is consumed in the country in the form of oil, while the cake is in some places employed in feeding their cattle. There can be no doubt, therefore, that the question is one of considerable importance, not only to this country, which requires such immense quantities of Flax fibre, but to India, which produces such enormous heaps of seeds, and is supposed to waste so much of valuable exportable material. But it does not follow that the production of fibre is in proportion to that of seed. Indeed, we have often to check vegetation, in order to favour the production of flowers and fruit; while an undue growth of the parts of vegetation, that is, of the stem, branches, and leaves, is often obtained at the expense of the parts of fructification.

The subject, however, has not escaped notice.

The earliest attempt to produce Flax in India seems to have been made by Dr. Roxburgh about the beginning of this century, as at that time, the East India Company having established a Hemp farm in the neighbourhood of Calcutta, he made many experiments on the substitutes for Hemp and Flax. He also cultivated Hemp and Flax in the Company's farm at Reshera, in the neighbourhood of Calcutta.

Of Flax, he says, it is very generally cultivated during the cold season in the interior parts of Bengal and Behar. "Samples of the Flax have frequently been procured by the Board of Trade, and sent to England to the Honorable Court of Directors, so that it is from home we may expect to learn its properties. If the Flax has been found good, large quantities may be reared at a small expense, as the seed alone which the crop yields must be more than equal to the charges to render it profitable to the farmer." ('Obs. on Subs. for Hemp and Flax,' p. 17.)

The Author, as long since as the year 1834, stated in his 'Illustrations of Himalayan Botany:' "In India the Flax is cultivated only on account of its seed, of which the mucilage is valued as a demulcent in medicine, and the oil in the arts; but the plant, which in other countries is most valued, is there thrown away; and others, such as *Hibiscus cannabinus* and *Crotolaria juncea*, are cultivated almost in the same field, for the very products which this would yield. It seems, therefore, worthy of experiment whether a valuable product might not be added to the agriculturist's profits, without much additional expense."

And again, in the year 1840, the Author called attention to this subject, in his 'Essay on the Productive Resources of India.'

In the year 1839, moreover, a Company was established, by the influence of Mr. A. Rogers, at one time one of the Sheriffs of London, expressly for the growth of Flax in India. Money was subscribed; a Belgian cultivator and a Belgian preparer of Flax were sent out to Bengal, with both Riga and Dutch seed, and all the tools which are employed in the culture and preparation of Flax in Europe. A pamphlet, moreover, was published, in which full directions were given for the culture and preparation of Flax, and illustrated with figures of the various tools employed for this purpose. The subject was warmly taken up by the Agricultural Society of India, and a small committee appointed of members who took a special interest in the subject.

The directions of the Irish Flax Society were printed in their 'Proceedings,' as well as those of Mr. Andrews from the 'Northern Whig.' Translations of plain directions were made into the vernacular languages, which, as well as models of the tools, were distributed. The Gold Medal of the Society was offered for the production of a large quantity of Flax, and smaller prizes for the natives. Experiments were made by several members of the Society, in different parts of the Bengal Presidency, as well as by the Belgian Farmers.

Specimens of the Flax produced having been sent to Calcutta, comparisons were instituted between the samples produced by different individuals, and those from European and from indigenous seed. Mr. Deneef, the Belgian farmer, pronounced the samples worth from £44 to £60 a ton; and some that was produced from country seed and heckled, was thought worth £66 a ton. Some of the specimens sent to Liverpool, were valued at from £30 to £45; and those which were forwarded to me by the Secretary of the Agricultural Society, were pronounced by Mr. Hutchinson, of Mark Lane, to be worth from £40 to £45 a ton. The experiments were made chiefly near Burdwan, Monghyr, and Shahabad; but the best native seed was obtained from the northern station of Saharunpore, and a white Linseed from the Saugur and Nerbuddah territories. A little Flax was also produced by Mr. Williams, at Jubbulpore, under the direction of Mr. Macleod.

Mr. Leyburn gave as the result of his experiments near Shahabad, that the expenses of culture of a bigah of land, and the preparation of the fibre, amounted to Rs. 25 1a. 3p.; and the profits to Rs. 27 1a. 5p., supposing the four maunds of Flax produced to be worth £35 a ton.

In consequence of a communication which had been received from the Honorable Court of Directors, Sir T. H. Maddock, at that time Secretary to the Government of India, addressed a letter to the Agricultural-Horticultural Society. In this the Society was requested, in order to assist the Government in determining on the measures proper to be adopted for improving the cultivation of Flax, to supply such accurate, detailed information as they may possess, or as they may be able to obtain.

The Society accordingly prepared a report which contained everything that was known at that time on the subject of the cultivation of Flax in India. This was forwarded to the Government, and also published in their 'Proceedings' for Nov., 1841. In this report, the Society took a very favorable view of the probabilities of the profitable culture of Flax in India.

The Revenue Secretary to the Indian Government, on this, wrote (November 22d, 1841) to the Agricultural Society, that—"The cultivation of Flax can no longer be considered a doubtful experiment, since it appears from your report to have proved in many instances successful; and where successful, to be very fairly profitable. His Lordship in Council is therefore much inclined to doubt whether any bounty or reward from Government is necessary, or would be justifiable."

Notwithstanding this favorable inference, the Flax Company did not go on with the cultivation; the various individuals who had taken up the culture did not proceed with their experiments, the several medals offered by the Agricultural Society seem never to have been claimed, and there are no appearances of the culture of Flax on account of its fibre in any of the places where the experiments were made. It is probable, therefore, that the success which appeared sufficient when the experiment was of the nature of garden culture, was not realised when on a greater scale.

M. de Verinne, indeed, states that the experiment in the season of 1840-41 was a complete failure at Bullea, owing to too little seed having been sown, to the unusually dry weather at the late sowings, and to the improper time (the hot winds) in which the Flax was cleaned.

Mr. Wallace, who had carried on the cultivation for three or four years at Monghyr, writes on the 8th July, 1841: "The crop has been in a great measure a failure this year. About one eighth the produce that a favorable season would yield." But in the year 1844, he again forwarded samples to the Agricultural Society, which were improved in cleanness and were also softer than the produce of former years, from the same cultivation. These were portions of several tons that had been grown at Monghyr, and which he intended shipping to Dundee, the port to which his last batch was sent. But Mr. Wallace added, with regret, that after several years' labour, with a view to establish Flax cultivation at Monghyr, and after having taught the art of dressing the article to many parties, the speculation must be abandoned unless the Government gave some encouragement. He therefore requested the assistance of the Society in bringing the subject to the notice of the authorities. It is stated at a subsequent meeting, that the Committee of the Society, after being furnished with further details respecting the cultivation, did not feel inclined to refer the subject to the Government. But neither the details referred to, nor the reasons of the Committee for their decision are given, and, therefore, we are unable to ascertain the real causes of failure after several years' trial.

Mr. Henley, an intelligent merchant from Calcutta, to whose observations I have already referred at p. 36, having made some careful experiments on the culture of Flax, has favoured me with the following account:

"I have paid much attention to the fibres during my residence near Calcutta, and, not wishing to conclude from hearsay only, generally cultivated most things myself, having a large piece of ground available. I sent up to Baugulpore (an excellent *Flax seed* district), and obtained a considerable quantity of native-grown Flax straw, after the removal of the seed. I had it collected from various fields, so as to obtain an average. This material was in every instance too *bushy* for the proper production of fibre, and the yield was very trifling, and in fact worthless for manufacturing purposes. The bushiness arose from the practice of the natives, who grow several plants, as you are aware, at once, in the same field. The Flax plants were consequently planted too far apart for fibre-yielding purposes.

Not yet fully satisfied on the question, I took a patch of land (three cottahs), the best I could pick out, fine, friable loam, fit for anything—it had been a cauliflower bed, and was therefore deeply spade-cultivated and highly manured—its last crop, cauliflowers, having nothing prejudicial to a Flax crop. I began very early in the season, had it turned up and laid for a fallow; two months after, again pulverized and weeded; and again—four times in all; with the addition of a large supply of fine old cow-dung. I had it now sown in the proper season, with the best Flax seed, very thickly planted, so as to draw it up as free as possible from lateral branches. Everything promised well. The field grew beautifully, and soon attained a height of three feet. I began to collect the crop, first, as soon as the flower had completed its growth and the seed-vessels began to form; secondly, as soon as the seed-vessels had fully formed, and were filled with green, but immature seeds; and lastly, after the seed was fully ripe. I took great pains in water-retting the samples—generally removing them from the water rather underdone, for fear of occasioning weakness in the fibre from over-retting.

In every instance, the quantity of fibre was small and weak, and very inferior to the samples of Flax deposited at the Agricultural Society's Museum, obtained from Jubbulpore, and other upper-country districts. No Indian Flax, however, which I have seen, equals in nerve and general good qualities those of European growths."

As the above is no doubt a correct account of what occurs with the Flax plant in the moist climate of Bengal, of which the effects may perhaps have been aggravated by too great richness of soil; it might be inferred, that a different result would take place in the drier climate of the upper or North-West provinces of India. This is certainly the case, but though the product is different, it is not, from the shortness and brittle nature of the fibre, more suitable for the ordinary purposes of Flax.

Mr. Hamilton, of Mirzapore, one of the up-country stations alluded to, "sent some bales of the stalks to Calcutta, for the inspection of the Belgians, and was told that the shortness of the stalks would prevent their manipulation."

It is evident, therefore, that there is some difficulty in producing good Flax in India. This difficulty is, no doubt, the climate; while the native methods of culture are the most unsuited to the production of good fibre. Mr. M'Adam, Secretary to the Royal Flax Improvement Society, has, in his Prize Essay on 'The Cultivation of Flax,' well observed "that a slow, steady growth is requisite for the quality and yield of fibre; also a temperate climate, that between the parallels of 48° and 55° being the best; and a continued supply of moisture from spring till autumn." He also observes that "the hot summers of Russia and of Egypt cause a dryness and brittleness of fibre, and prevent its retaining that elasticity, pliancy, and oiliness which characterise the Flaxes of Belgium, Holland, and Ireland."

But considered generally, it is not to be expected that a plant which attains perfection in Belgium, and is so successfully cultivated in the vicinity of Belfast, would succeed well in the hot and moist, but sometimes dry climate of Bengal. In fact, if the Flax was not one of those plants which, like the cereal grains and pulses, can be grown in the cold-weather months of India, it could not be cultivated there at all. But with this culture, we have the anomaly, of the seeds being sown in autumn,[1] when the climate is still hot and the ground moist, and the plant has to grow while the temperature is daily becoming lower and the soil drier—no irrigation being usually employed with these winter crops, though dew begins to fall as soon as the ground becomes cooled at night. In some places, the crop attains perfection in about ninety days, is collected in January, the coldest month; in others, not until February or March, when the rapid rise of temperature is favorable to the ripening of seeds, but not to the production of fibre.

Of all parts of India there are none that appear to me better suited to the growth of Flax than the Saugur and Nerbuddah territories, as the soil is rich and prolific, and the climate a medium between the extreme moisture of Bengal and the dryness of the North-West provinces. The Wheat of this district is considered superior to any seen in the English market, with the exception of what comes from Australia. The Gram (*Cicer arietinum*) and the Linseed are also of finer quality than any produced elsewhere in India; while the suitableness of the climate for the production of good fibre is proved by the length

[1] In Egypt, also, the seeds are sown about the middle of November, in the plains which have been inundated by the Nile, and plucked in about 110 days.

and strength of the Jubbulpore Hemp, as grown by Mr. Williams; as well as by the specimens of Flax which he has likewise grown.

The Indian method of culture is certainly not suited to the production of fibre, but the seeds abound in oil. "The yield of oil from a bushel of Indian seed is from 14¾ lb. to 16 lb.; of English or Irish, 10¾ lb. to 12 lb." Therefore, it is evident that the Indian ryut succeeds in his object, as well as the Irish farmer, who grows the Flax plant for its fibre, but neglects to gather the seed: though this is not only a saleable product, but one which abounds in nutritious matter for his cattle, and would further afford the means of fertilising his fields. As it has been found difficult to persuade the Irish farmer to gather the double crop, I believe it would be hopeless to induce the Indian ryut to change a culture which is suitable for his purposes, without the aid of successful example in his neighbourhood. You might make him grow less seed, but I much doubt whether we should get him to produce any useful fibre; and without his co-operation it would be impossible to attain any considerable success. Indeed, the Agricultural Society of India have given it as their opinion, in one of their resolutions,—"That the culture and preparation of Flax in India, so as to be able to compete with the Flax of Belgium or Russia, can only be effected by practical European growers instructing native cultivators in the art; and, further, that an entire change in the mode of cultivation, as well as in the preparation of the plant, is necessary to produce the article in a proper state."

It has, indeed, been made a question, whether a good supply of fibre and of seed can be procured from the same crops. One gentleman, in reply to my inquiry, informed me (London, 4th July) that "it has been found impossible to preserve both seed and fibre, *i.e.*, for the better qualities of each; and that the plan pursued is simply to gather before the seed ripens, when the delicacy and softness of fibre form the desideratum, but to leave the plant standing until the fibre is dried and greatly injured, in order to secure the superior seed fit for sowing;" and this is the result of information collected after a residence of many years in the interior of Russia. Another gentleman replies to the same inquiry, from Belfast, on the 8th July: "It is not only quite practicable to have good seed and good fibre at the same time, but it is the universal rule in all countries except Ireland, where we have only been able to get the more intelligent farmer to abandon the wasteful practice of steeping the Flax stems without removing the seed. The finest Flax in the world is grown in Belgium, yet the seed is saved from it."

But as there is no doubt, from the experiments of the Indian Flax Company, and from other more recent facts, such as the production of Flax as far south as on the Shevaroy Hills, at Jubbulpore, and near Lahore, that Flax can be produced in India, it seems desirable to ascertain whether it cannot, by careful culture and improved processes, be produced as a profitable crop in some parts of the country; because, as I have before said, "I cannot think that that which is done successfully in Egypt, is impossible in every part of India;" and there can be little doubt that, in some places, at least, coarse Flax could be produced, as well as some for the paper-makers.

I am informed that the Messrs. Hamilton, of Mirzapore, propose, this year, attempting the culture of Flax, in the tract of land of which they have a grant, in the Goruckpore district, and which I should consider a more favorable locality than any near Mirzapore. I would suggest, that Mr. Williams, at Jubbulpore, should be requested to make an experiment, to ascertain the quality of the Flax which may be produced in that locality, as well as the quantity obtainable per begah or acre; attempting at the same time to preserve the seed. Mr. Williams has already grown a little Flax, he is accustomed to the preparation of fibre, and the soil and climate are both, I conceive, more favorable than in most parts of India.

I would also recommend that Dr. Jameson, the Superintendent of the Botanic Garden at Saharunpore, should be directed to make a small experiment, both in the plains and in the hills, in order to ascertain the same kind of facts respecting the Flax plant when grown according to European methods for the sake of the fibre. The Agricultural Society of the Punjab are already attempting the culture, as the Secretary has addressed a letter to the Court, requesting an opinion respecting the quality of the Flax which they have already produced; but the specimens have not yet arrived. (Further information has, however, recently been received, and will be afterwards detailed.)

Though I am well aware that Government experiments are not likely to prove profitable where those undertaken by individuals have failed, especially as these had good scientific and practical advice, I am yet sanguine in thinking that experiments conducted in the localities I have indicated, would give information which would be practically of great value for extensive tracts of country. The people are acquainted with the culture and preparation of *Sunn* fibre, and might easily be instructed by the European gentlemen to whom I have alluded, in applying the instructions for the culture of Flax in the 'Proceedings of the Agricultural Society of India' for the years 1840 and 1841, including those prepared by M. Deneef, the Belgian farmer, after practical experience in India, published first in 1840, and then in 1842.

I have not thought it necessary to refer to the opinions respecting the exhausting nature of Flax as a crop. By the methods of steeping the stalks in steam and hot water, it has been ascertained that the time required for the separation of fibre can be very greatly reduced; while the steep-water, where no fermentation has taken place, has been proved to be useful as manure water for the soil. Feeding cattle, moreover, upon a portion of the seed, produces manure which is invaluable in restoring much of what has been taken from the soil. But as these methods are not applicable to the present state of the culture in India, I will only allude to the probability of some of the mechanical methods of separating the fibre from the green flax, as very likely to be of useful application."

Since, according to some accounts, considerable success attended the experimental culture of Flax in India, while others considered it a failure, it is desirable to ascertain the causes of this discrepancy, and to draw some conclusions which may be of use to other parts of India, if not to the places where the experiments were made. This we may probably effect, by analysing the statements of the different experimentalists.

Shahabad Experiments.

The cultivation of Flax in India in recent times seems to have begun at Shahabad, in 25° of north latitude, in the year 1837. In the 'Proc. of the Agri.-Hortic. Society,' there is a communication from Mr. G. Leyburn, of

Nunnoa Factory, giving an account of the sale in London, on 17th July, 1838, of some Flax grown by him. "The Flax, per Windsor, is landed sound. No. 1 sold for £28 per ton, and No. 2 for £14 per ton—nine months' credit. They are described as harsh, and without the softness characteristic of Russian Flax. Prices of the latter being lower than usual, P. T. R. selling here at this time at £40 per ton."

Mr. Leyburn states that he prepared his first sample of Flax in the common way, from plants which had borne seed. He sent them to Messrs. Truman and Cook, who reported that any quantity of a similar article would find a ready sale, at £35 a ton. In the following year, Mr. Leyburn entered on the cultivation rather extensively, and succeeded in producing an article of lengthened staple, and of a quality vieing with the Flax of Russia. A portion of the cultivation was carried on in the bed of the Soane River, and part in the uplands of the district: some of it was prepared before the seeds were ripe. He calculates the probable profits of the culture to be:

PER BEGAH:[1]	Rs.	A.	P.
Rent of land	1	8	0
Ploughing		8	0
Seed	1	8	0
Pulling, beating seed off, watering	5	9	3
Packing, cartage, preparation (nearly all hand-labour) .	16	0	0
	Rs. 25	1	3

Produce.	Rs.	A.	P.
Linseed, 5½ mds. . . .	5	8	0
Flax, 4 mds., at (say) £35 per ton	46	10	8
	52	2	8
Deduct expense of cultivation, as per contra . . .	25	1	3
Profit on one begah of land .	27	1	5

With a factory in full play and effective machinery, Mr. Leyburn considers that the manufacturing price of the article would be three to four rupees a maund, which is equal to about £9 or £12 a ton. But to give effect to the production of this article, the aid of European enterprise is necessary. (It is particularly deserving the attention of indigo-planters). He failed in overcoming the deep-rooted prejudices of the native cultivators, and could not induce them to enter on a cultivation which held out to them a prospect of more than ordinary profit for their labour.[2]

Experiments of the Flax Society.

We may now proceed to notice the efforts of the London Flax Experimental Society. Mr. Woollaston, in presenting, on their behalf, some specimens of Flax grown in Bengal, and prepared in Calcutta, observed that—

"The object of the Society is not at this time to produce a large quantity, but to ascertain how good a quality can be readily obtained, the growth of India, and such as shall readily compete with the Russian and Belgian Flax in the Home market.. This object has been already attained to a con-

[1] The begah of land in Shahabad is something more than the Bengal begah, which is 1600 square yards, or the third of an English acre.

[2] M. Bonnevie, indigo-planter at Rungpore, writes: "Having great difficulty to prevail on these ignorant cultivators to plant it—owing to a superstitious belief that the vengeance of an evil spirit will befall them for introducing the cultivation of a new article. Flax grows remarkably well here, and I have no doubt would succeed well in this district. The Zemindars now commence to show an inclination to improve agriculture in general."

siderable extent. These samples far surpass the Russian Flax," and he regretted that "the Government of India have not responded to the recommendation of the Horticultural Society in granting a bonus to the Experimental Society of 10,000 rupees, to further its objects."

"The seed received from England, Mr. Woollaston further remarks, has been distributed freely to all applicants who were desirous of trying the cultivation. The models of implements were sent out from Belgium, and facsimiles made for any person requiring them at the *bonâ fide* cost of the materials. Private profit or gain has never been allowed to interfere. Every kind of information, as far as possessed, has been freely imparted to all inquirers, and every endeavour made to excite an interest in the experiment.

"Its importance in a national point of view is incalculable. Both as developing the resources of India, in enabling England to supply herself from her own possessions in a most important raw material, and in no longer making her dependent, for what may well be considered necessaries, upon a foreign and rival power. These observations, Mr. Woollaston considers, will apply in a great measure to Hemp also, in the cultivation and manufacture of which, the Experimental Society are deeply interested. The successful introduction of these two staples into England, from this country, will not only prove a blessing of the largest degree to *India* generally, but be a severer blow to Russian aggrandisement and encroachment than the destruction of her fleets, or the annihilation of her armies."

The Agri.-Horticultural Society having recommended that the bonus of 10,000 rupees should be given for the furtherance of the objects of the Flax Society, Lord Auckland, who was at that time Governor-General of India and was as warmly interested as any one in the improvement of its resources, was also a political economist: the Secretary to Government was directed to reply:

"His Lordship cannot but regard with interest the public-spirited proceedings of the gentlemen who have come forward to promote the improvement of the cultivation of Flax in India, but it is only in very rare instances, and with the view of exciting a direct and general competition, that he would attempt by encouragement or bounty to influence the course of commercial and agricultural enterprise, and he does not feel that the case before him is one which would justify the special interference of the Government.

"*Fort William, July* 29, 1840."

Mr. Deneef, the Belgian farmer, and Mr. Bernard, the preparer of Flax who had been sent to India by the Society, were of great use in examining the soil and giving directions on the mode of culture best adapted to the country, as well as in reporting on the different samples of Flax which were grown in the country. Mr. Deneef's directions for the cultivation of Flax, drawn up after he had had practical experience in the country, remain as a valuable document for the guidance of others. These we, therefore, reprint from the 'Journal of the Agri-Horticultural Society' for the year 1842, p. 393.

PRACTICAL INFORMATION ON THE BEST MODE OF CULTIVATING FLAX IN BENGAL. BY MR. DENEEF, BELGIAN FARMER.

"In accordance with my promise, I send you as follows, a detailed report of my observations since my arrival in India, on the cultivation of the Flax plant.

I will not enter on an explanation of the mode adopted in the cultivation of this plant in Europe, because nothing is easier than to do so theoretically, but will content myself with informing you, from my own practical experiments, of the means at our disposal in this country, which can readily be made available for the production of Flax and its seed.

1. Such portions of land as are annually renewed by the overflowing of the Ganges, or which are fresh and rich, are the best adapted for the cultivation of Flax.

2. After the earth has been turned up twice or thrice with the Indian plough, it must be rolled; because without the aid of the roller the large clods cannot be reduced, and the land rendered fine enough to receive the seed. The employment of the roller, both before and after sowing, hardens the surface of the earth, by which the moisture of the soil is better preserved, and more sheltered from the heat of the sun. About and near Calcutta, where manure can be obtained in great abundance for the trouble of collecting it, Flax may be produced of as good a quality as in any part of Europe. Manure is the mainspring of cultivation. It would certainly be the better, if the earth be well manured, to sow first of all, either *Sunn* (Indian Hemp), or Hemp, or Rice, or any other rainy-season crop; and when this has been reaped, then to sow the Flax. The tillage of the land, by means of the spade (*kodalee*) used by the natives (a method which is far preferable to the labour of the plough), with a little manure and watering at proper seasons, will yield double the produce obtainable from land tilled without manure and irrigation.

The mode of forming beds of six feet in width with intervening furrows, in use in Zealand and in Belgium, is very inconvenient in India, because great care must be taken to preserve the moisture of the soil; and on the other part, for the purpose of weeding, they are unnecessary. When proper Linseed, freed from mustard seed is sown, I think that the Flax requires no weeding at all in India.

3. The proper time to sow the Flax in India is from the beginning of October until the 20th of November, according to the state of the soil. The culture must be performed, if possible, some time before the sowing. The Flax which I have sown in November, was generally much finer and much longer than that sown in the former month, which I attributed to the greater fall of dew during the time it was growing. The quantity of country seed required to the Bengal *beega* is twenty *seers*, but only fifteen *seers* of the foreign seed, because it is much smaller and produces larger stalks. The latter should be preferred; it is not only more productive in Flax, but, owing to the tenderness of its stalks, it can be dressed much more easily.

4. The Flax must be pulled up by the roots before it is ripe, and while the outer bark is in a state of fusibility. This is easily known, by the lower part of the stalks becoming yellow; the fusion or disappearing of the outer bark is effected during the steeping, which may be fixed, according to the temperature; say, in December at six days, in January five, in February four days, and less time during the hot season. The steeping is made a day after the pulling, when the seed is separated, and then the stalks are loosely

bound in small sheaves, in the same way as the *Sunn.* The Indians understand this business very well, but in taking the flax out of the water it should be handled softly and with great care, on account of the tenderness of its fibres. When it is newly taken out, it should be left on the side of the steeping pit for four hours, or until the draining of its water has ceased. It is then spread out with the root-ends even, turned once, and when dry it is fit for dressing or to be stapled.

5. To save the seed, the capsules, after they are separated from the stalks, should be put in heaps to ferment from twenty-four to thirty hours, and then dried slowly in the sun to acquire their ripeness.

6. When Flax is cultivated for the seed alone, the country Flax should be preferred. Six *seers* per *bega* are sufficient for the sowing. It should be sown very early in October, and taken up a little before perfect ripeness, by its roots, separately, when it is mixed with mustard seed; the Flax seed being intended for the purpose of drying oil, is greatly injured by being mixed with mustard seed, by which mixture its drying qualities are much deteriorated. With regard to the dressing of the raw material, most of the coolies are now acquainted with the process, and I have not therefore alluded to it. Should you desire any further information on the subject, I am ready to afford it."

Mr. Deneef, in reply to some queries circulated by the Agri.-Horticultural Society, observed that too dry or saline soils were injurious to the culture, but that his own had been a heavy clay soil; also, that the Bengal begah contained 14,400 square feet, or one third of an acre, and that he sowed of foreign seed, 28 lb.; of American, 36 lb.; but of plump Patna, or native seed, not less than 40 lb , on account of its larger size. That the foreign seed cost Rs.8 a maund of 82 lb., while the native then cost Rs.2 8.

The acclimated American seed he found to succeed well in India. But on a previous occasion (Feb. 10, 1841), he had observed of some samples grown at Entally, from acclimated English seed, from country seed, and some from Saharunpore seed, (from 30° of N. lat.,) that the sample from this last was very superior to the others. Of two samples from acclimated American seed, one grown in rather poor ground, the other in a rich soil—"The former," he observed, "is a most beautiful sample, containing great length of stalk with thinness; the other is of very little value, the goodness of the soil having caused the plant to become stunted and branchy."

Mr. Deneef further observed, that he obtained the longest and finest fibres in sowing from the 25th of October to the 15th of November: this he ascribes to the plant being covered every morning with a heavy dew; while that which he had sown in the beginning of October, in the same soil and the same seed, was much shorter in stalks, but much more productive in seed,—"the rain being very scarce from the first days of October until the end of December, in this part of India." (But the ground is still hot, and the temperature high at this period.) The begah will yield 100 lb. of seed from foreign seed, and about 12 per cent. more from native seed.

He concludes with an approximate account of the cost (amounting to £32) of raising a ton of Flax from Foreign seed, well dressed, and which would be worth £50 in the English market; stating that 80 lb. of Flax for a begah of land is a very small product. "When we shall be able to have the seed from our own product, Rs. 60 on that article will be saved." The account is as follows:

30 begahs' rent for six months—the other six months for other crops	Rs. 45
10 maunds of American or European seed, at Rs. 8 . .	80
6 begahs of superior (spade) cultivation, at Rs. 5 . . .	30
24 begahs, four necessary ploughings, each Rs. 3 . .	72
Sowing, malees, recolt, rippling, steeping, carrying, and petty expenses	48
28 maunds dressing, in a very clean way, at Rs. 3 8 . . .	98
Breaking of flax-tools	7
	Rs. 380

Return :—1 maund Flax.

19 to 20 maunds Seed.

7 to 9 Codilla.

Chittagong Flax.—One of the most southern districts in the Bengal Presidency, where Flax has been prepared, is that of Chittagong. A. Sconce, Esq., at that time Collector of Chittagong, forwarded, in March, 1843, some samples of Flax which he had grown there from acclimated Europe seed; that is, from seed re-produced for two or three years from imported seed, and sown there in the month of November. He suggested to the Society the awarding of small prizes to natives who cultivated the Flax on account of its fibre. His object being "to interest chiefly those who are familiar with the cultivation of Linseed (which is common enough for the purpose of extracting oil) and the country *Sunn*." He states that he had had an opportunity of observing in that season the very great difference between Flax grown from Europe and from country seed—the latter being softer and finer, but very much shorter, and very much weaker. If this is found to be the case by others, the length might probably be easily increased by cultivation. The samples examined by the Flax and Hemp Committee were reported on as follow :

Undressed Flax.—This sample contains more Tow than Flax ; it is badly prepared, dirty, and not adapted for the Home market ; but the

Dressed Flax—strong, clean, of very superior quality, but of short staple : if it were a little longer, say six inches, it would realise a very high price in the Home and Continental markets. Mr. Deneef said of it that the staple, though short, was most beautiful ; but the mode of preparation (having been hackled) is "too expensive to admit of its yielding a profitable return, even were it to sell at the value I affix to it, viz., £60 a ton."

Burdwan Flax.—Four samples of Flax grown at Burdwan were presented to the Agri-Horticultural Society, by Mr. J. Erskine, in July, 1844. Of these, Nos. 1, 3, and 4 were the produce of acclimated and up-country seed mixed together—sown in October and November, 1843, and reaped in February and March, 1844. No. 2 was the produce of up-country seed, sown on 15th October, and reaped on the 27th February. Mr. J. Law having examined these samples, considered them all as of a fair quality ; and judging from the prices of the different marks of the article then in Britain, valued Nos. 1 and 2 at £32, No. 3 at £34, and No. 4 at £30 per ton, landed in England.

Bullea Experiments.

Mr. de Verinne, Superintendent of Flax cultivation at Bullea (twelve miles below Benares), in reply to the queries, states, as already mentioned, Sept. 20, 1841, that the experiment of the previous season had been a complete failure. He sowed 130 Duncanee begahs, each containing 28,336 square feet, double of the Bengal begah. The soil was not manured, but ploughed seven and eight times. Somewhat sandy soils are the best. The hard soil which the natives select for growing Flax for the seed remains in clods, and cannot be pulverized. He first sowed one maund of seed (from the Chupra district) per begah. Mr. Bernard, one of the Belgian farmers, thought this too much; he reduced it to 20 seers, or 40 lb., which proved too little (and evidently so, as the same quantity is recommended by Mr. Deneef for the Bengal begah, which is only half the size). He began sowing on the 16th of October, and concluded by the end of the month; the plant was ready for steeping on the 10th of February. He recommends sowing in the beginning of October, as there is moisture enough at the surface of the ground to sow broadcast. Early sowings, also, will in general do away with the necessity for irrigation, which is otherwise indispensable, and expensive. (But is not the greater heat both of the soil and of the sun more injurious than the greater dryness of the soil late in the season, when dew falls?) He states, that from the 10th of September till the 20th of January, when the Flax was in seed, and had ceased growing, there was no rain. About fifty begahs were sown with drill-ploughs, because there was no moisture at the surface of the ground, but as Mr. Bernard disapproved of this mode, the rest was sown broadcast, when they were obliged to irrigate the land.

The plants having been pulled by the 10th of February, and the seeds taken off, the stems were steeped in (indigo) vats. The first vat was steeped nine days; the second and third, ten days; and the fourth and fifth, eleven days, the weather having got cooler from the fall of a shower of rain. Range of thermometer, 60 to 70°. The plant for steeping was not perfectly ripe, but the small plants were left to ripen their seed.

The crop was small, owing to the unfavorable season. Only 1 maund 25 seers of seed, and 70 lb. of Flax per begah, while the Duncanee begah ought to yield from 150 to 200 lb. of clean Flax.[1] The proportion of Flax to the Tow or Codilla, varies according to the weather in which the Flax is cleaned; if prepared in the dry weather or hot winds, or from April to the end of June, the proportion is one third Flax to two thirds Tow; if prepared in damp weather, or from July to October, it is half to half. With regard to the cost, M. de Verinne says: "Supposing the season to be an average one, and the produce of the begah to be 150 lb. of clean Flax, 100 begahs would give 6¾ tons, and the cost, according to the annexed estimate, being Rs. 2237, will show the cost per ton, landed in Calcutta, to be Rs. 331, or £33. In making up the estimate, I have calculated the expenses according to those of the experiment of last year. Only the produce has been valued at 150 lb. per begah," though 70 lb. only were obtained.

[1] With these Indian returns of the produce per begah (which is at Bullea two thirds of an acre), we may contrast a statement by Dr. Hodges: "From the returns of the Royal Flax Society, and from my own inquiries, I would estimate the average produce of a statute acre in the North of Ireland of air-dried Flax straw, with bolls, at two tons, which, by the seeding machine, are usually reduced to 3360 lb. By the various processes of the rural manufacturer, the amount of dressed Flax or fibre obtained averages from four to five cwt. per acre."

Estimate of the probable expense for the cultivation of 100 begahs of plant, the manufacture, and the despatch of the produce to Calcutta.

Land rent for 100 begahs, at Rs. 4 3	Rs. 450	0	0
Irrigating the lands, if there is no moisture at the surface, at R. 1 per begah	100	0	0
Six ploughings, at 4 annas each per begah	150	0	0
Chikorage, or cleaning the fields before sowing, at 8 annas per begah	50	0	0
150 maunds of seed, at R. 1 8 per maund	225	0	0
Plucking the plant, at R. 1 per begah	100	0	0
Weeding, at 8 annas per begah	50	0	0
Taking off the seed, at R. 1 per begah	100	0	0
Filling the vats, taking the plant out, spreading and turning it, &c., at 12 annas per begah	75	0	0
Breaking the Flax for cleaning, at R. 1 4 per begah	125	0	0
Cleaning the Flax, at 2 annas per pound	468	12	0
Gunny bags, for bales	20	0	0
Making up the bales	14	0	0
Boat-hire, at 8 annas per ton	50	0	0
Chaundar (person in charge of boat)	7	0	0
Carriage of the plant, at R. 1 per begah	100	0	0
Four Zilledars, for six months, to look over the cultivation, at Rs. 3 each per month	72	0	0
	2156	12	0
Exchange, at Rs. 3 12 per cent.	80	14	0
	Co.'s Rs. 2237	10	0

Monghyr Experiments.

The culture of Flax was commenced near Monghyr, on the Ganges River, in the year 1839; and specimens were presented to the Agri-Horticultural Society, in May, 1840, and again in the month of September in the same year.

The strength of this Flax, as ascertained by Professor O'Shaughnessy, of the Medical College, Calcutta, was as follows, and as compared with other kinds tried at the same time.

Monghyr, undressed	40,000
Archangel	43,000
Baltic, dressed	42,033
Ditto, undressed	19,075
Irish, dressed	17,075

Mr. Deneef considered it the best sample of India-grown Flax that he had seen.

The sentiments of some of the members of the Flax Committee were as follow:

Mr. Hodgkinson.—The samples of Flax are of middling quality; the fibre fine and strong, but deficient in cleanness and colour. The first defect arises from carelessness in scutching.

Mr. Willis.—The Baltic *rough Flax,* which of all the specimens it is the most legitimate for us to compare with the Monghyr *undressed one,* is superior to it in colour, lustre, mellowness, and cleanliness.

The *Monghyr undressed Flax,* not having undergone the degree of cleansing, and preparative manipulation which has been given to the *Baltic rough Flax*, being more ligneous, &c., is not exhibited with all the comparative advantage it otherwise would have shown.

The Monghyr *undressed* specimen seems to possess more *tow* in proportion than the rough Baltic one. Its length of fibre seems somewhat inferior to that of the Baltic one. Its strength of fibre seems good. But after all it seems so promising a production that I think the parties engaged in the experiment would do best to send home a good supply of it to the various markets of London, Liverpool, and Scotland, that they may derive the opinion of merchants, brokers, and manufacturers as their most true and unerring guide.

Mr. Wallace again submitted, in August, 1841, two samples of Monghyr-grown Flax, to show the improvement on last year's produce. He stated that they were average samples of thirty-four bales (nearly four tons) which had just been shipped by the *Mary Bannatyne*, for London.

No. 1.—Grown from country seed on a strong black soil, which had been inundated by the river, and retained its moisture through the season. The seed was sown on or about 10th November, 1840. Twenty seers of clean seed to a begah (the begah is rather larger than that of Bengal); the plant was allowed to ripen fully, and the seed come to full maturity. This was all saved by rippling combs, which separate it easily from the stalk. The soil received very little preparation; it was drilled with one plough, another plough following in the same track in which the seed was sown. The plant was pulled about the 20th March, and steeped for three days. The breaking or crushing of the plant was done by machinery; the scutching by hand. A man could clean of this quality of plant five seers a day. The outturn per begah was 9 stone, such as the muster, and 3½ maunds of seed.

No. 2.—Grown from country seed on a light sandy soil, also inundated by the river; was sown about 8th October, with the same sort of seed; the land was well prepared, having had three or four ploughings; the seed was sown broadcast 25 seers per begah; it was allowed to ripen fully; it was pulled 28th February, and steeped 4½ days. The outturn of this was about 1½ stone per begah, and one maund of seed—no rain having fallen from the time of sowing, seven eighths of the crop was lost; the dressing of this was similar to the other. A man could not scutch more than 2½ to 3 seers per day.

Mr. Wallace, in his reply to the queries of the Society, states that the begah at Monghyr contains 3600 square yards—three fourths of an acre, and that the inundated land is to be preferred. Alluvial land will yield a crop if not too sandy, but that the higher land is preferable if rain fall two months after sowing; that dry soil produces a good plant, but of very coarse quality. He sows at the latter end of September for *seed* only, but from 15th October and all November for fibre, to the extent of 60 lb. to the begah if sown broadcast, and 40 lb. if sown in drills.

The American and Europe seed, he states, produce double the quantity of fibre, half the quantity of tow, and of a finer quality, but only half as much seed as the native. Of this the price in the district was from R. 1 4 to R. 1 8. That he reaps from the 25th of February to the 10th of May. That the average crop is about 9 stone, or 126 lb. per begah; and that sixteen of these are required to produce a ton of Fax; with of tow, first quality 36 lb., and second quality 14 lb. per begah; while there is an average crop of 3½ maunds of seed. The time of steeping varies from two to three days in the hot months, to four and five days in February, October, and November, and to seven and eight days, in the cold months of December and January; and that one day more is to be added for dry plants of the preceding season; and that the cost of Flax laid down in Calcutta, per ton of 20 cwt., is from £12 to £15, all expenses included.

These expenses consist of rent of land, R. 1 8 to Rs. 2 per begah. If the ryut uses his land in the other months, then four annas less than the above rates. Coolies obtainable at 1½ annas per day for rippling, steeping, or carrying to the factory; or one rupee for fourteen bundles of 3½ cubits in girth, tightly compressed. It is steeped in a vat, and taken out when the fibre will separate easily from the wood, and then dried in the sun. It is crushed by being passed under large iron rollers, and then placed on the edge of a board, where the fibre is separated from the wood by striking it with a wooden sword. The expense is Rs. 3 per bazar maund, and the conveyance to Calcutta, Rs. 20 per 100 maunds. Notwithstanding the small cost (£12 to £15) for a ton of Flax laid down at Calcutta, which was pronounced of good quality, and probably similar to the other Indian Flaxes, which were valued in England at various prices, varying from £35 to £45; also stating that the amount realised on the sale of the seed is calculated to have more than covered the expenses of cultivation, rippling, and steeping (Report in 'Agric. Soc. Proc.,' Nov., 1841, pp. 38 and 95): the speculation did not succeed. For we find in the 'Proceedings' of the same Society for February, 1844, pp. 45 and 165, Mr. Wallace, intimating, in reference to his operations for several years past with a view to establish the cultivation of Flax at Monghyr, that he was afraid, from the serious drawbacks he had experienced, that he should be compelled to abandon the speculation unless some encouragement was afforded by Government. The Society having referred all the papers and samples of Flax received from Mr. Wallace to their Hemp and Flax Committee for report, it is stated that one of the members was in favour of an appeal to Government, while the other three were opposed to such a step; but as neither the facts nor reasons for either side are given, we are unable to draw any other general conclusions.

The foregoing rather detailed account of the experiments culture, preparation, and cost of Flax grown in different parts of India, may appear to the reader to have occupied more attention than their importance entitles them to. But without going through this labour, it would be impossible to draw any satisfactory conclusions for the prosecution of any future experiments in the same or in other parts of the country, if such should be thought necessary. But it is first desirable to know what was thought of these fibres when sent to the markets of this country. This we are fortunately able to do, from some of the results having been published, and from some of the specimens having been sent to the India House.

A detailed report is given from Liverpool of the first samples grown, and of which a report had also been made by Mr. Deneef. But he generally rated them higher than they were valued in this country, though we are unable to distinguish exactly the respective specimens in the two reports.

The Secretary next submitted an extract of a letter which he had been favoured with by Mr. Hodgkinson on some samples of Flax (similar to those so favorably reported on by the Flax Committee of the Society) forwarded by him to Liverpool. (*v.* 'Report' 1841, p. 41.)

The letter, which bears date January 30, 1841, is from Mr. Grey, and he says: "From what I can judge, and having shown them to a friend here who has probably as much through his hands as any other in Liverpool, a partner of William Jackson, Son, and Co.

"Mr. Murray seemed far from sanguine about them, but I trust they indicate the capability of producing an article of great importance and extent.

"1st. The best is a lot (country Flax, native seed, 26th May, 1840)—this may be worth £40 to £45 per ton here; it is finer, softer, and better than

"2d. The large parcel (country Flax, native seed, 27th May, 1840)—which has a fine broad fibre, and not much inferior; it is worth £40, if in quantity equal to sample.

"The lengths are too unequal, which makes it fall upon the hackle, and is a disadvantage. Of these two samples the fibre is by no means weaker than of many other such Flaxes, and probably when this is the case it arises from the preparation.

"3d. (Bengal, May, prepared by Belgians.) Dew-ripening weakens, I understand, the fibre, hurts the colour, and even prevents its bleaching as it ought to do, and for which such Flax would be used. Where water is obtainable for steeping, this method should not be resorted to.

"4th. (Indian Flax, No. 1, grown in the neighbourhood of Calcutta, worth at least £30 per ton.) This is better, but seems, if I mistake not, also to be dew-ripened. It is worth £35 here, however.

"5th. These from imported seed don't seem equal to the produce of native.

"6th. The heckled Bengal Flax, does not show to advantage, being imperfectly dressed, and happens to be of a dry, hard nature.

"7th. (Country Flax, native seed, 26th May, 1840.) This mark is similar to the first, but you will distinguish it, being darker coloured and harsher.

"The first is the best, I think, decidedly. Weakness of fibre is an insuperable fault where it exists, and it may be perhaps avoided by better preparation. The Belgians' is very weak, and some of the others.

"TOWS. One of these (Bengal Tow, native seed, 30th May, 1840), seemingly the clearing or last tow, is a very good thing, worth in Dundee £30 to £33, I should say; the others from firmer tools before this, £20. Another of same mark as first worth perhaps £16. These are of great consumption, as recommended before to your attention. Codillas from £12 @ 16 20 per ton would do well, and could be obtained from the waste in preparing the better Flax, observing always that the staple be good and the fibres strong, though they need not be of great length by any means. In Flax the longer the better, though not required beyond moderation, but the fibres should be *equal* and uniform, so as all to split and yield as much dressed as possible. These Flaxes on the whole resemble most the common Newry Flax, which costs £40 @ 50 per ton, wanting the natural sap, in which all these are deficient.

"The quality I think will not be of the best for some time, but much that would sell largely in Dundee or even Belfast might be obtained; in Dundee every thing is used, down to the coarsest; but Flax worth £40 to £60 per ton is most saleable, and to the most certain and best buyers. The Codillas and Tows there seems no doubt of, and Flax to bring from £30 to £45 per ton also."

The next report we have is on the samples of Flax grown in the following year.

Agricultural Society of India, 11*th Aug*., 1841.

1.—Four specimens of country-grown Flax, prepared in Calcutta.—*Presented by Mr. H. Woollaston on behalf of the "London Flax Experimental Society."*

No. 1.—Is a sample of Flax of last year's growth, from English seed, *not acclimated.* Six hundred pounds of this quality, Mr. Woollaston mentions, were forwarded to London by the *Bucephalus;* and by the last mail Mr. Rogers advises that it was valued at £50 per ton.

No. 2.—Is a sample from *acclimated* English seed, grown in Entally. The seed was sown last November, and the plant gathered in February, having been in the ground 85 or 90 days.

Mr. Woollaston states that this sample is considered much *superior* to No. 1, and that Mr: Deneef attributes its superiority, to the seed being acclimated, which renders the separation of the under-bark much easier, and leaves the Flax finer and softer. Mr. Deneef estimates its value compared with No. 1 at £56 per ton.

No. 3.—Is a sample from the same seed and growth as No. 2—but consists of *picked* portions of plant, so as to furnish a specimen of the degree of fineness that it is possible to produce. This sample is superior even to No. 2, and nearly equal to the best produced in Belgium; much surpassing the Belgian ordinary qualities. Mr. Deneef estimates its value at £60 the ton.

No. 4.—Is a sample of Flax from *country* seed grown and prepared at Bowsing Factory, district of Burdwan; estimated in London at £40 to £45 the ton.

Some specimens of the Flax grown this year having been sent to the India House, and having, in March, 1841, been examined by Mr. Hutchinson, of Mark Lane, he thought them very favorable specimens of so recent an experiment, as they seemed to be equivalent to Russian and Polish Flax, which was selling at that time for £40 a ton; and one of the specimens appeared of a quality which might sell for £45 a ton in the then state of the market.

Mr. Enderby, then of the rope-manufactory at Greenwich, thought yarn made of it very good, and that nothing could prevent both the Flax and Yarn proving valuable articles of commerce, if sent in quantities, and of uniform and sorted qualities. Messrs. Noble have recently informed the Author that they also had received specimens, and thought them equal to the middling and even better qualities of Russian Flax. There seems no doubt, from the concurrence of opinion, that the Flax produced in India was sufficiently good to stand favorable comparison with both Russian and Egyptian Flax, and was, therefore, of the kind which is much required, and which could be consumed here in the largest quantities. The question, therefore, is whether it can be produced at a cost so as to yield a profit to both planters and the merchants who would export from India to England.

OBSERVATIONS ON EXPERIMENTS.

On reviewing the accounts and the results of these experiments, it appears that, though abandoned too soon in some situations, they were carried on for a sufficiently long period in others to allow of reliable deductions being drawn from them, if full information on all points had been supplied. The soil does not seem to have been complained of; but though drainage is essential in many parts of Europe, the power of irrigating will be found most useful in the East. The climate is obviously very different from what the plant meets with in Ireland, as not a drop of rain seems to fall from the time of sowing to that of reaping the crop; but heavy dews compensate for this deficiency during a part of the season. But as this dryness of climate prevails over a great part of India during the season of cultivation—that is, from the end of the rainy season to the beginning of the hot weather—it is evident that irrigation is necessary for such cultivation, and must not be too expensive. Perhaps the double monsoon of the Madras Presidency might in some localities afford a suitable climate, if the temperature is not too high. A perfectly appropriate climate may no doubt be obtained at different elevations on the Himalayas, and in some of the mountainous ranges of the South of India; but European superintendence may not be available and the expenses of transit be too great. The Saugur and Nerbuddah territories appear favorable, from their more moderate climate; while some of the districts of the North-West, of Sindh, and the Punjab, may be found suitable, from the command of irrigation and the prevalence of a moderate temperature.

The proportion of seed required having been ascertained by Mr. Deneef, we cannot but observe the unexpected results obtained from the sowing of some native seed—the Flax produced from Saharunpore seed having been considered to be of excellent quality, and, in Liverpool, to be the best of all the specimens sent. American seed was found to be suitable to the country;

but it is remarked that when sown in a rich, it did not do so well, as when sown in a poorer soil. The whole question of what is the best seed for the untried soils and climates of new countries is one of considerable difficulty. It does not follow that seed from a rich soil and the most careful cultivation is necessarily the best for transference to a poorer soil and drier climate; indeed, the converse would, in many cases, appear to be the more suitable course. But even in the case of Wheats, some from Australia and from the Nerbuddah, pronounced the finest in the English market, have never produced good crops in this country, notwithstanding the most careful attention. Indeed, the most advisable course appears to be to grow the best native seed, and as thickly sown as is found to be suitable, for the express purpose of changing the branching nature of the plant, and then making an exchange with the seed of other districts following the same course; in order to insure that interchange of seeds which is so beneficial for all kinds of crops, and is conspicuous in India in the indigo crops of Bengal being grown from the seeds of the North-West. In the directions for culture in Europe, we have seen that early sowing is necessary to produce good fibre, and late sowing for seed; but in India the reverse course is to be followed, for early sowing, in consequence of the high temperature, induces rapid but, from the dryness of the climate, stunted growth, with an abundant production of seed; while later in the autumn the temperature is lower, the growth is slower, but the dews being heavy, there is greater moisture, and this, with the slower growth, produces finer fibre. The early sowing is preferred by some, in order to save the expense of irrigation, but this must sometimes be with the sacrifice of the quality of fibre.

With respect to the cost at which Flax can be produced in India, we find Mr. Leyburn stating that he gets four maunds of Flax, or 328 lb., from about one third of an acre of land, at a cost of £2 10*s*., or for about £17 a ton; and that this sold for £28 a ton in London; but we do not find that he proceeded with the cultivation. Mr. Deneef calculated the cost of Flax produced by him to be £32 a ton, with a profit of £8, which would afterwards amount to £14. Mr. de Verinne calculated the cost would be £31 a ton, with an average crop; though he did not get half the quantity. The cost of both is evidently too high, unless the finer qualities of Flax are produced. Mr. Wallace who continued the longest, and produced Flax at the cheapest rate—that is, from £12 to £15—ought to have succeeded, as he states that the expenses of cultivation were paid for by the seed. But we find him, as we have already stated, representing to the Agricultural Society that he should be unable to go on with the culture, from the discouragements he had met with, unless assisted by the Government. Though the difficulties are not specified, they must have been greater than appear from the published accounts, and therefore the facilities and the profit are not so great as they appeared to the Agri-Horticultural Society,—who thus unintentionally induced the Government of Lord Auckland to consider that public aid was not necessary.

It is very evident that such experiments can only be made under the superintendence of Europeans, when, if successful, they may be adopted by natives. In repeating the experiments in more favorable situations, it would seem very desirable at first to ascertain as accurately as possible the quantity of produce of ordinary quality obtainable per acre, with good cultivation in a favorable locality, on an average of years, and then to endeavour to improve the quality. The profits of the two kinds of cultivation and preparation are not very dissimilar (*v.* p. 163) in Europe. Though manufacturers may require more of the coarser qualities of Flax, planters will of course grow that for which they can get the best prices; though it will be safest at first to reckon only on getting the prices of Russian or Egyptian Flax.

We may proceed now to inquire where else Flax may be cultivated in India.

CULTURE IN SAUGUR AND NERBUDDAH TERRITORY.

The foregoing experiments were made almost entirely in the provinces of Bengal and Behar; but it has been mentioned that the central province of the Saugur and Nerbuddah territories seems well adapted for the culture of Flax, from the nature of the soil and climate. Here, indeed, some Flax has already been grown by Mr. Williams, of which I have been favoured with a small specimen, and from whom we shall have further samples as well as information. This being the result of a first experiment, on a small scale, is not, perhaps, calculated to give a fair idea of what is practicable, particularly as we are without any information respecting the mode of culture, or the kind or quality of seed which was employed. But Mr. M'Leod, now Commissioner in the Punjab, mentions in one of his reports, that the growth is very luxuriant there. The Flax is comparatively short, light coloured, and rather dry, and more like Egyptian than any other kind of Flax.

It might be objected to the growth of Flax so far in the interior, that land-carriage for so great a distance would be an insuperable obstacle. But, as Mr. Williams finds it suit his purpose to send his now-famed Jubbulpore Hemp even to Calcutta, there seems no reason why Flax should not be equally able to bear the expenses of culture and of transit. In this direction, there is, moreover, an excellent road, described by the Cotton Committee of the Agri-Horticultural Society, 8th January, 1840. "From Jubbulpore to Mirzapore, on the banks of the Ganges, the great cotton-mart of the North-West provinces, a bridged and metalled road of 239 miles in length, equal to any in England, has been made by Government; at all the stations, the means of transport, and on the river, boats of every description, abound." This road is regularly kept up, and a toll levied at the base of the ghauts. The native princes have, however, without contributing to its expenses, diminished its utility by levying extra duties on the goods passing through their territories. (*v.* 'Journ. Agric. Soc.,' vol. viii, p. 115.[1]) There is a prospect, however, of these being remodelled. The most important consideration, nevertheless, is that of climate. According to the concurrent testimony of different observers, as reported in the Author's work, on 'The Culture and Commerce of Cotton in India,' p. 311, &c., deficiency of moisture is seldom complained of; and there will, probably, be seldom any excess in the season when the Flax would be cultivated—that is, in the cold-weather months. Hence the chief difficulty in India will be diminished, if not entirely escaped.

[1] See also a letter by Montague Gore, Esq., to the same effect, in 'The Times,' in the summer of 1853.

CULTURE IN THE MADRAS PRESIDENCY.

Though not within the limits of the Bengal Presidency, we may here most appropriately mention that good Flax has been produced still further south, where elevation produces lowness of temperature accompanied with moisture of the atmosphere, as on the Shevaroy Hills and on the Neilgherries. Dr. Cleghorn, Secretary of the Agri-Horticultural Society of Madras, is well qualified to give the best advice on localities where experiments may most fitly be tried; and Professor Mayer is there, to give the benefit of his chemical investigation of the Flax plant and soil. Mr. M'Ivor, in charge of the Public Garden at Ootacamund, is well situated for making experiments on the growth of Flax in the cool and moist climate of the Neilgherries, if the culture should in other respects appear desirable.

Linseed has long been cultivated in the Madras Presidency, though not to any great extent. Dr. Ainslie mentions the seed under the name of *Aliverei*, and states that in the southern parts of the Peninsula, the Mootchie men and oil painters make use of Linseed oil. But we now find Linseed among the Exports: in the year 1850-51, there were exported 801 cwt. of Linseed from Fort St. George, nearly all to the United Kingdom.

CULTURE IN BOMBAY PRESIDENCY.

In the Bombay Presidency, Linseed is also cultivated, as in all other parts of India, and has of late years been exported in considerable quantities. We observe that in the year 1850-51, 59,076 cwt., and in 1852-53, 162,015 cwt. = Rs. 486,046 in value, were imported into Bombay from the Concan; and that there were exported to the United Kingdom, in 1850-51, 50,102 cwt., valued at Rs. 170,112, and in 1852-53, 114,309 cwt. = Rs. 342,926 in value. We do not observe that any attempts have been made to grow Flax. It is probable that the low country along the coast may be too hot, and the country above the ghauts too dry; but of this those who are located in these parts can most correctly judge, if it should be thought desirable to make the attempt. Col. Sykes describes Linseed as generally cultivated in the Dukhun.

The export of Linseed from Bombay is now estimated at an annual value of about four lacs of rupees, although five years ago it did not exceed one lac. This the Chamber of Commerce ascribes to the improvements on the Thulghaut road, and to the consequent reduced cost of conveyance in carts instead of on bullocks.

PROPOSED CULTURE IN BUNDLECUND.

An article has lately appeared in the 'Benares Recorder' (15th July, 1854), proposing the culture of Flax and of Hemp in Bundlecund; observing that "with less capital than what English merchants now expend in Russia, India can produce Flax which will not be inferior in fibre or colour to the Riga Flax. In Bundlecund the soil is almost free and unoccupied; and the land rent is also so low, that failure in the cultivation of either of these two products—Flax and Hemp—would be impossible. There are numerous hill streams with clear water, over the whole country, that would admirably serve the purpose of steeping." But the great uncertainty is the climate, which, like the parts of the Gangetic valley which have been alluded to, is very dry during the season of cultivation. But it is certainly worthy of inquiry, by those favorably situated for the purpose, whether, by irrigation, or by the aid of the dew which undoubtedly falls in the cold weather, this dryness might not be sufficiently obviated to allow of the production of good Flax.

CULTURE IN THE NORTHERN DOAB.

The most northern station from which any Flax was sent during the experiments of the Flax Society was Allygurh, in 27° and 28° of north latitude. Mr. J. Saunders, on the 26th July ('Proceedings,' p. 100) wrote that he had sent a sample of the Flax which he had grown on the banks of the Kote Nuddee. But he described it as prepared with very clumsy tools, and cost him about four rupees a maund for merely breaking; as to scutching, it has had none.

The finest seed was, however, obtained from Saharunpore, in 30° of north latitude—a locality with which the Author is well acquainted, but where no Flax is produced, and where the soil and climate are dry during the cold-weather months and season of cultivation; that is, from October to March, with the exception of some rain at Christmas time, often called the *chota bursaut*. The district has, however, enjoyed the advantage of canal irrigation for more than twenty years, under the superintendence of Sir Proby Cautley, greatly to the benefit of the country and people. This would give great facilities for Flax cultivation, and would not be expensive.

The experimental culture which has been sanctioned to be made by Dr. Jameson in the Botanic Garden at Saharunpore, as well as in the Himalayas, will no doubt be carried on with his characteristic energy. The experiment will be useful from the information which it will undoubtedly afford for comparison with those which have been made in Bengal and Behar, as Saharunpore is situated near the north-western extremity of the Gangetic valley, and the temperature is such that there is every prospect of the plant being slow in growth, and that, with the aid of canal irrigation, the growth will be such as to insure sufficient length of fibre. Of the temperature in the cold-weather months we may judge from the following, deduced from the Author's observations while he was Superintendent of the Botanic Garden; from which it will be seen that November would be the fittest month for sowing, and the crop could be gathered in February or March, before the heat becomes great.

Mean Temperature.[1]

Oct.	Nov.	Dec.	Jan.	Feb.	March.	April.
74	64	55	52	55	67	78

In the Himalayas the season of cultivation is the same as in Europe; for there, as here, the winter months are too cold for the growth of plants—but the spring and summer temperature is exactly suited to the growth of an annual like the Flax plant.

Mean Temperature.

March.	April.	May.	June.	July.	August.	Sept.	Oct.	Nov.
53	59	66	67	67	66	64	57	50

As far as temperature is concerned, there is evidently a long period for cultivation, and different months might be selected

[1] See the Author's Report on the Botanic Garden at Saharunpore, 'Journ. of the Asiatic Society,' vol. i.

for the purpose. But there is a great difference in the moisture of the different months, as the rains come on in the middle of June, and are excessive for three months. But it would be interesting to ascertain the effects of such moisture on the growth of a fibre like that of Flax. It is probable that the plant would require to be supported, to prevent its being laid.

CULTURE OF FLAX IN THE PUNJAB.

The Punjab, so recently acquired, is already as settled as any of the older provinces, in consequence chiefly of the energy and intelligence of the Service being applied to devising methods of Government suitable to the people and country, instead of attempting to introduce English institutions among foreigners who are unable to appreciate or to take advantage of them. In the Punjab, we see some of those who were fighting against us, now employed in the far East with our own troops; but many being necessarily left without employment, are ready to take to or return to agricultural pursuits. The vigorous measures which have been adopted, while they give security and freedom of communication, will also greatly facilitate agricultural pursuits; especially as some of the public works in course of execution are canals of irrigation.

There, the Kote Kangra valley teems with Chinese Tea shrubs, the first of which were planted in the year 1848, that is, immediately after the conquest of these hills by Lord Hardinge; and the Tea which has been prepared from these plants is considered to be of the first class of China Teas, by such excellent judges as the Messrs. Thompson. The culture of Silk has lately been introduced by the Agri-Horticultural Society of the Punjab—the first specimens having been sent to Calcutta and to this country, were considered to be naturally of good quality, but very indifferently reeled. Mr. W. H. de Verinne having been sent up by the Government with an establishment of silk-winders and -reelers from Morshedabad, and some samples of silk of their winding having been sent to Calcutta and to the India House, the former was pronounced by Mr. E. Kilburn, on 1st September, as "requiring only a little more attention to rank with the product of the best Bengal Filatures," and which would have been worth in

May about Rs. 12 8 per Factory seer. The specimens sent to the India House were submitted to the Messrs. Durant, who gave a most carefully drawn up report, and pronounced them excellent specimens of Bengal Silk, but requiring a little more care; and worth from 14*s.* to 15*s.* a pound in London. Vigorous measures have in consequence been adopted for the prosecution of the culture by plantations of different kinds of Mulberry, besides the kind which is already common in the country, which, in the opinion of Mr. de Verinne, is almost equal to the Bengal Mulberry. It is probable that some difficulties may be experienced from the dryness of the climate in the plains of the Punjab; but there can be none in the hilly districts, where the Tea plant is flourishing. Some of the native Wools also having been highly approved of, twenty-five Merino Rams have been imported by the Government from Australia, for the further improvement of the breed of Sheep.

That some parts of the district are well adapted for the production of fibres, is evident from the Kote Kangra Hemp, to be afterwards described, proving one of the strongest of known fibres. The Agri-Horticultural Society of the Punjab, therefore, have begun their experimental cultures in a very favorable locality, from the great variety of soil and of climate within the command of their members. If the Geography of Plants and of Animals is attended to, as well as the Principles of Culture in new situations, little doubt need be entertained respecting the success of the above cultures as well as of Flax.

Though Linseed is so extensively produced throughout India, we hear nowhere of the fibre being valued and separated. But when we get to the confines of cotton-producing districts—that is, into the Punjab—we find that some Flax, prepared by the natives on their own account, is separated in the neighbourhood of Lahore. For we are told that the stalks of the Linseed plant yield a fibre, which is made into twine, and used for the network of their charpaes or native beds. This information was elicited in consequence of inquiries originated by Mr. Frere, the distinguished Commissioner of Sindh from his desire to promote the culture of Linseed in the province under his charge. The fibre, however, of the Linseed plant is separated in still more northern parts, as some seed of Bokhara Flax sown in England was found to be that of the common Flax.

The inquiries made respecting the growth of Linseed in the Punjab elicited the following facts:

On the Cis-Sutlej it is stated that three seers to a begah are sown broadcast when alone, or in drills; probably as an edging to other crops. Three maunds of Linseed considered a good crop. The stalks and husks considered refuse and useless. The seed sells for 18 seers for the rupee to oilmen. A maund of seed yields of oil 10½ seers; of oil-cake 29½ seers. The oil sells for 5 and 5½, and the oil-cake at 60 to 66 seers for the rupee.

In the Jalindhur Doab, Linseed is cultivated, especially in the Khadir or inundated land of the Beas and Sutlej Rivers; but plants always small; seed sells for 20 to 30 seers for a rupee. It is also cultivated in the Sheerwul, or tract of country in which the soil is firm and covered by a deposit from the rains, with the subsoil always moist—ripens before barley, and generally before wheat.

Linseed is also cultivated in the rich loamy soils of the Kangra district skirting the Himalayas, but chiefly in the eastern parts, on account of the seed, which sells for 20 to 100 seers for the rupee—Flax itself burnt.

In the Punjab, sown with barley and mussoor (or lentils) in Katick (Oct. and Nov.), and is ripe in Cheyt (March and April); usually sown intermixed with the above crops, or in separate patches. Never irrigated, but grown along the Sutlej, in Khadir land, or that which is inundated during the rainy season, but never manured.

In the Lahore division, it is grown chiefly about Sealkote and Deenanuggur, and is the only part where the fibre seems to be made use of, as it is stated that the stalks yield a fibre which is made into twine, and used chiefly for the network of their charpaes or native beds. The price of the seed is about Rs. 2 8 per maund. Few localities are stated to be well suited to it, and the seed was in little demand. Twine made of the fibre was sent, but no notice seems to have been taken of its quality.

From the above details of cultivation, it is evident that though Linseed is very generally known, it is nowhere extensively cultivated, as is evident from the price of the seed, which is dear in comparison with that of Wheat. Some of the uses are well known; for instance, the oil is used as a drying oil, and the bruised seed, mixed with flour, is described by Major Edwardes as given as a strengthening food for cattle, and the oil-cake is no doubt employed for the same purpose; while the fibre is sufficiently valued to be separated in some, though burnt in most other places. It would seem much in favour of the production of good fibre that the growth is much slower than in the southern provinces of Bengal.

The Society began some experiments on the culture of Flax, in the cold weather of 1853, with seed obtained from Saharunpore; that is, the same place from which the best seed was obtained in the experiments in Bengal and Behar, and which produced such good Flax. (*v.* p.p. 176 and 182.) The samples were prepared under the superintendence of Corporal Keenan, of H.M.'s 10th Regiment. Of the opinion formed of these samples when sent to Calcutta, Mr. Wood, Secretary of the Chamber of Commerce, writes: "7th June, 1854. The general opinion regarding the Flax is very favorable. It is considered the finest that has been ever grown in the country; and that the cultivation of it might be encouraged." Some of the special reports are as follow:

Mr. Stalkartt writes:—"This Flax is decidedly the best specimen of this country's growth, and I should say a good merchantable article. It is very difficult to give a thorough report upon it, as we have none from Europe to compare it with. From the test it did not appear very strong, and from its smell I should say that oil had been used in the preparation; perhaps with an improved method it would have greater strength, as oil, generally speaking, deteriorates greatly the strength of Hemp and Flax. I would like to see it in greater bulk; a handful is not a fair sample."

Report from Mr. Haworth.—"Although I am not a member of the Flax and Hemp Committee, I am glad to have had the opportunity of examining the sample forwarded to the Society by Mr. Cope. On the whole, I think, its preparation does great credit to Corporal Keenan; any shortcoming is owing to the finer heckles not being ready. I think the length of fibre is good; the colour of the greater part is bright and healthy—that portion shows good strength; there is, however, a small part of the sample of a dark dull colour, which, I think, is caused by over-retting, and that portion of the sample is, as might be expected, weaker than the rest. If the natives of this country could produce such Flax as this specimen under notice, from the immense fields now grown in Bengal for seed only, what an enormous amount would be added to the value of our exports."

Mr. Stalkartt is a rope-maker, of the firm of Messrs. Harton and Co., of Calcutta, and wished ten maunds to be sent to him by the quickest transit—bullock-train and steam-boat—in order to see what he could do with it in his own business. He wished also for "a couple of maunds of the tow," as he thought "it might be useful for the railway." Mr. Stalkartt's remark about oil being used in the preparation, is referred to by the Secretary of the Society, and contradicted, "as no oil was used." It is probably an accidental testimony to the softness of the fibre, which, in most of the Flaxes from warm countries, is found to be dry and hard.

The Sub-Committee appointed by the Society to draw up a proposition for Flax arrangements, submitted the following—

Suggestions regarding the improvement in, and increase of, the cultivation of Flax, or Linseed plant, for the sake of its fibre.

1st.—It is to be made generally known that a premium, of Rs. 500, has been sanctioned by the Supreme Government of India, to be given for the largest area of land that may be appropriated, in the Punjab and the Cis- and Trans-Sutlej States, to the culture of Flax, during the season of 1854-55, being not less than 25 acres in any one village.

2d.—A second premium, of Rs. 350, has been similarly authorised, for the next largest area so cultivated, being not less than 20 acres, in any one village, and—

3d.—A third premium, of Rs. 200, is to be granted for the third largest piece, being not less than 15 acres in any one village; that is to say, the Government will award the first premium to any one land-holder, or village community of land-holders, who may, in his or their own village, cultivate, for the production of Flax fibre, ground aggregating, in the whole, 25 acres, or as much upwards as the owners may choose.

Moreover, the Government of India have sanctioned the purchase, on behalf of the Society, of the entire crop of merchantable Flax, including the fibre, if of the required length, that may be produced in the Punjab, and to pay for it at the current market rate of the Flax seed, with 25 per cent. added for the fibre.

It is to be a condition that not less than sixty Company's seers of Flax seed, be sown on each begah, cultivated with a view to competition; and that the growers be informed that Government is prepared to purchase the whole of the seed, and likewise the fibre, if of the proper quality, on the terms above stated, but that the authorities be instructed not to purchase such produce unless it measure, in the stem, three and a half feet in length or more; that it be well dried, and the seed just on the point of ripening, but not so ripe as to allow of its falling out of the pod by the way.

The directions for cultivation are as follow: If the following instructions are strictly attended to, there is no doubt that the Flax will all be of the required length of staple. Not less than sixty seers of Flax must be sown, broadcast, that is with the hand, on each begah, as the thicker it is sown the longer will be the plant, and the more free it will be from branches, which are very injurious. The land must be thoroughly freed from weeds by repeated ploughings, previous to sowing; it must be well manured with the richest manure procurable, such as is given to land for tobacco; be smoothed, and divided into beds as for wheat. The seed must be sown between the 1st and 15th November, but not later. The Flax land must be watered as frequently as wheat-land; and the fields must be kept perfectly free from weeds until the Flax is six or seven inches high. After that, no more weeding will be required. The land selected should be light loamy soil; Khadir land is the best. When the seed begins to show signs of ripening, the Flax must be pulled gently by the root, and laid on the ground to dry in rows. When thoroughly dry, it must be tied up in bundles as large as a man can conveniently span with both hands, and it can thus be easily measured. The seed can be stripped off (rippled) on arrival of the consignment at Lahore, and the final price be arranged according to the current rate of Linseed in the Lahore market. That is, if the successful, or any other, competitor (all Flax will be bought that is of the required length, whether a premium have been awarded for it or not), who may deliver Flax, yielding 125 maunds of Linseed, will, if, as at present, the nerik be Rs. 2 8 a maund, receive Rs. 312 8 for the seed, and 25 per cent., or Rs. 78 2, additional, as compensation for the fibre, or Rs. 390 10 in all.

It is to be understood that successful competitors are to be paid for their crop as well as others; but that no cultivators are bound to sell, should they wish to dispose of their crop in any other manner.

It might be explained to the ryuts, that those who are not successful in growing Flax of the required length, will find a ready market for the seed in Mooltan, whence it will be conveyed to Sindh for export to England.

It is further strongly recommended, as a new feature in the proposed measures, for improving the cultivation of this important staple, that the Society be authorised to hire, on behalf of Government, from 30 to 40 begahs of land, in the immediate vicinity of their garden, for the cultivation of Flax, during the coming season, so as to admit of a comparison being drawn between the Flax grown by the zumeendars and the plant reared under probably more favorable circumstances. The seed required for each begah, the purchase of which, it is hoped, the Government will also sanction, will be one maund and a half (at a cost of about Rs. 4), and the land is obtainable at Rs. 20 per begah; for which sum the cultivators undertake to perform all agricultural operations, such as ploughing, watering, weeding, sowing, and reaping, *for one year*—a plan by which the grower can ascertain the expenses of his crop to a rupee. It is strongly recommended to the Meeting that, in confident anticipation of the sanction of the authorities to this measure, which anticipation they venture to rest on the past liberality of Government, and the great importance of the subject, and also on account of the advanced state of the season, the Secretary be, at once, empowered to make arrangements for obtaining land.

The vigorous proceedings of the Agri-Horticultural Society of the Punjab, and the ready patronage of the Government, including the purchase of the produce, ought to produce some decisive results, if the soil and climate are found to be favorable; and of this there can be little doubt, from Flax having been produced there last year, and from the description given of it by the members of the Hemp and Flax Committee of Calcutta. The specimens stated to have been forwarded to the India House have not been received. But while the best method of culture will be ascertained by the Society in their own cultivation, it is to be feared that the length of stem required (three feet six inches) will exclude much of what may be grown by the ryuts. The extension of the culture will no doubt reduce the price of the seed, and enable it to be sold at such rates as to allow of its becoming an article of export to Europe.

The Society having included in these recommendations an application for some tons of the best Linseed (mentioning especially the Belgian) as well as some tools, to be sent them, this was approved of, and forwarded by the Indian Government, in August, 1854; but as it was obviously too late for any large quantity of seed to be sent in time for the sowings of this year, small quantities were sent out by the overland route for the sake of comparison with the native seed, and also some tools as specimens. But as it is extremely doubtful what kind of seed will answer best in the soil and climate of the Punjab, it has been thought preferable to send the seeds of different kinds—as Riga, Dutch, American, English, and Irish.

CULTURE OF FLAX IN SINDH.

The province of Sindh, about 360 miles in length, extending from 23° 37′ to 28° 32′ N., consists of a delta of extensive alluvial tracts, intersected by numerous canals and water-courses, which enable cultivation to be carried on by irrigation; thus making up for the deficiency of rain. Though the temperature of a great part of the year is high, it is probable that that of the cold-weather months may be sufficiently low to allow of the successful cultivation of Flax and Linseed, at the same time with the Wheat, Barley, and Oil-seeds which form the Rubbee or cold-weather crops of Sindh, as of most parts of India.

Indeed, Mr. Frere, the enlightened Commissioner of Sindh, wrote to the Board of Administration of the Punjab, to have inquiries made throughout that territory on the extent and nature of the Linseed cultivation therein—the result of which inquiry has been given in the preceding pages.

A commercial gentleman, to whom were referred the specimens of the Punjab Linseed, and the prices at which it was sold, observes "that there, as in Sindh, the culture of it is altogether upon so limited a scale as barely to supply local wants, and judging from the Rs. 2½ per maund quoted as its sale price in Lahore, which, with cost of carriage to Kurrachee, 800 to 1000 miles, would stand in higher than the ruling rates in Bombay." "The quality of the Linseed" he considered "good, and such as would command the highest prices in Mark Lane, which average about 48*s*. per quarter."

Upon this, Mr. Frere justly remarks that "the present prices of an article, which is at present grown in small quantities merely for local consumption, afford no means of judging of the price at which it can be profitably grown in large quantities for exportation; and looking at the way in which it usually flourishes in wheat-land in India, and at the present prices of wheat, I feel little doubt but that it can be grown very cheaply in many parts of the Punjab and Sindh. The facilities which exist for water-carriage down the Indus will render its transport cheap; while great and constant demand exists for it in Bombay.

"I think, therefore, that it is an article to which attention may be profitably directed in any district where it is desirable to discover articles of produce adapted for exportation."

The Bombay Chamber of Commerce observe: "Linseed of the quality described as the growth of the Punjab would, under all ordinary circumstances, command a ready sale in this market, at from Rs. 3 4 to Rs. 3 8 per cwt. of 112 lb.; and during the greater part of the past year the price has been as high as Rs. 3 12."

The Author has been favoured with a letter (dated 19th August, 1854) from Mr. Frere, in which he states that—"For the last two seasons attempts have been made, with very satisfactory results, to introduce the culture of Linseed into Sindh. It grows well in the ordinary wheat-lands, and under every disadvantage, there has been no failure traceable to soil or climate. I have no doubt but that, in a few years, it will become one of the staple articles of export."

He also states that attention has begun to be directed to the fibre, and that Mr. Harvey, who was in early life practically engaged in Flax farming in Ireland, and who has now been some years resident in Sindh, has commenced some experiments, and hopes to be able this season to send to this country some specimens of Flax grown in Sindh. In a previous page it was mentioned that Mr. Burn, who had been some years in Sindh, had seen some thick-sown Flax growing there luxuriantly, and which he had no doubt would produce Flax, though it had only been cultivated on account of the seed.

Some Europe seed, for the sake of comparison with the native seed, and some heckles, which Mr. Harvey wished for, have been, at Mr. Frere's request, forwarded, by order of the Court of Directors, by the overland route to Kurrachee. There seems no doubt of success to at least the same extent as in Egypt, if the culture is persevered in until the proper methods of cultivation and of preparation have been carefully ascertained.

SEPARATION AND PREPARATION OF FLAX FIBRE.

We have already seen that the stem of the Flax plant consists of a central wood-like part, called shove or boon, and of the tough fibres called bast or harl covered by cuticle, all cemented together by gummy and azotized compounds. These parts are so closely adherent to each other, and the fibres to one another and to the cellular tissue, that they are with difficulty separated from each other, and the fibres obtained for economic use. But it may be observed that if green vegetable matter be exposed to the continued influence of wet or of drought, disunion of the adherent parts takes place; and that they may then be readily separated from each other. The same effect takes place if some of the constituent parts are dissolved out by the agency of a chemical solvent, or water at different temperatures, the rest being set free, the fibres may then be easily separated. All these methods have been and are employed for the separation of Flax fibre in different localities. These are fully detailed in various works, as well as in the papers of the authors we have referred to, in the 'Journal of the Royal Agricultural Society of England.' The directions of the Royal Flax Society are full and detailed, and include most of the essentials given in Mr. MacAdam's Prize Essay.

The oldest method, probably, is that called *Dew-retting*, when the Flax straw or stems are spread out on the grass, and exposed to the action of the atmosphere, combined with that of dews or rain, or, in the absence of these, they are carefully watered. This, though an effectual, is an uncertain, and also a very tedious process, requiring from three weeks to a month for its completion. Archangel Flax is thus prepared. Mr. MacAdam informs us that it is practised among the Walloons, and also in the United States of America, and that Flax thus prepared requires a shorter time for bleaching.

The most generally adopted plan is that of *steeping* the Flax stems, either in slow currents of water (and that of the River Lys is particularly celebrated) or in pits or pools of water. The action of water is useful, partly, by giving origin to fermentation, which loosens the adherence of the constituents, or, at certain temperatures, by dissolving some of the constituents and setting free the others. Both methods are practised in India, in different parts; but the steeping so as to produce fermentation is that generally adopted, and, according to Mr. Deneef, well understood by the natives of India—who, indeed, must have long, as they now largely practise the art, from the quantities of Jute and of Sunn which they prepare by this method. Though not applicable in all points, especially in the time required, from the difference of temperature, the instructions of the Royal Flax Society are so full, that we reprint them here, for comparison with the other directions.

Watering.—This process requires the greatest care and attention. River water is the best. If spring water has to be used, let the pond be filled some weeks, or months, if possible, before the Flax is put in, that the sun and air may soften the water. That containing iron or other mineral substances should never be used. If river water can be had, it need not be let into the pond sooner than the day before the Flax is to be steeped. The best size of a steep-pool is 12 to 18 feet broad, and 3¼ to 4 feet deep. Place the Flax loosely in the pool, in one layer, somewhat sloped, and in regular rows, with the root end underneath; the tie of each row of sheaves to reach the roots of the previous one; cover with moss sods, or tough old lea sods, cut thin, laid perfectly close, the sheer of each fitted to the other. Before putting on the sods, a layer of rushes or ragweeds is recommended to be placed on the Flax, especially in new ponds (or packed in crates which are weighted down). As sods are not always at hand, a light covering of straw may do, with stones laid on it, so as to keep the Flax just under the water; and as the fermentation proceeds, additional weights should be laid on—to be removed as soon as the fermentation ceases, so as not to sink the Flax too much in the pool. Thus covered, it never sinks to the bottom, nor is affected by air or light. A small stream of water, allowed to run through a pool, has been found to improve its colour. In this case, if the pools are in a line, the stream should be conducted along the one side, and run into each pool separately, and the water of each pool run off, along the opposite side, in a similar manner. It will be sufficiently steeped, in an average time, from eight to fourteen days, according to the heat of the weather and the nature of the water. Every grower should learn to know when the Flax has had enough of the water, as a few hours too much may injure it. It is, however, much more frequently *under*-watered than *over*-watered. The best test is the following: Try some stalks of average thickness, by breaking the *shove*, or woody part, in two places, about six or eight inches apart, at the middle of the stalk; catch the broken bit of wood, and if it *will pull freely out, downwards, for that length, without breaking or tearing the fibre, and with none of the fibre adhering to it*, it is ready to take out. Make this trial every six hours after fermentation subsides, for sometimes the change is rapid. Never lift the Flax roughly from the pool, with forks or grapes, but have it carefully handed out on the bank, by men standing in the water. It is advantageous to let the Flax drain twelve to twenty-four hours, after being taken from the pool, by placing the bundles on their root ends, close together, or on the flat, with the slope; but the heaps should not be too large, otherwise the Flax will be injured by heating.

Spreading.—Select, when possible, clean, short, thick pasture ground for this operation; and mow down and remove any weeds that rise above the surface of the sward. Lay the Flax evenly on the grass, and spread thin and very equally. If the directions under the head of rippling have been attended to, the handfuls will come readily asunder, without entangling. Turn it two or three times while on the grass (with a rod about eight feet in length, and an inch and a half in diameter), that it may not become of different shades, by the unequal action of the sun, which is often the case, through inattention to this point. Turn it when there is a prospect of rain, that the Flax may be beaten down a little, and thus prevented from being blown away.

Lifting.—Six to eight days if the weather be showery, or ten to twelve if it be dry, should be sufficient on the grass. A good test of its being ready to lift is to rub a few stalks from the top to the bottom; and, when the wood breaks easily, and separates from the fibre, leaving it sound, it has had enough of the grass. Also, when a large proportion of the stalks are perceived to form *a bow and string*, from the fibre contracting and separating from the woody stalk. But, the most certain way is, to prove a small quantity with the handbreak or in a flax-mill. In lifting, keep the lengths straight and the ends even, otherwise great loss will occur in the rolling and scutching. Tie it up in small bundles; and, if not taken soon to be scutched, it will be much improved by being put up in small stacks, loosely built, with stones or brambles in the bottom, to keep it dry, and allow a free circulation of air. Stacks built on pillars would be the best.

Drying, by fire, is *always most pernicious*. If properly steeped and grassed, no such drying is necessary; but, to make it ready for breaking and scutching, exposure to the sun is sufficient. In some districts, it is put to dry *on kilns*, in a damp state, and is absolutely burned before it is dry, and the rich oily property of the Flax is always greatly impaired. On this point, the Society can scarcely speak too strongly, as the Flax is either destroyed, or rendered not worth one half of what it would be, if properly dried.

As success in the above processes depends in a great measure upon the quality, as well as on the temperature of the water, and this being frequently cold in northern latitudes, led to the invention by Schenck, in 1846, of his patented process in which the requisite degree of temperature could be obtained, and, of course, maintained, as well as increased. This, though apparently a new process, has long been adopted in the East; as the natives of Sumatra, and likewise of the district of Rungpore, have employed warm water, as well as some chemicals, for the separation of the fibre of different plants, as we shall see under the head of Sunn and of Nettles.

In *Schenck's process* the temperature of the steep-water is kept at 80° to 90°, but may be increased to that which is favorable to the process of fermentation—for the effects depend upon the destructive power of fermentation quite as much as in the old process. A great saving of time is effected—as not more than seventy-two hours is required for the fine, and about ninety-six hours for the coarse qualities; and a more uniform fibre is, moreover, produced.

A disadvantage of this process, in comparison with some others, is that, during the process of fermentation, the same kind of gaseous exhalations are given off as in the ordinary method. These gases have been stated "by chemists to consist chiefly of carbonic acid and hydrogen, in nearly equal parts." Dr. Hodges has clearly shown that the fermentation is of a peculiar character, traces only of acetic acid being found, while butyric acid is generated in large quantities.

Other objections have been stated—such as that the fibre was weakened when over-heated; and another, that a most offensive matter adhered to the straw, and that, in the process of scutching, the scutchers could not bear the smell of the irritant dust which flew off. With regard to other objections—such as that the yield of fibre would be less, that it would be weakened, and that the linen made from it would not bleach properly—a Committee of the Royal Irish Flax Improvement Society, after carefully conducted experiments, reported, first, that the uniformity of temperature had the effect of increasing the yield of fibre. With regard to the weakening of the fibre, the Committee ascertained that the Flax steeped in the ordinary way spun to 96 lea yarn, and that by Schenck's system to 101 lea yarn. In the second, the cold-steeped gave 60 lea and the hot-steeped 70. The third objection was submitted to an extensive bleaching firm, whose evidence in favour of the hot-water process was very decided. The heated water of the ordinary Indian tulaos, at some seasons of the year, will be sufficient for this purpose, and will not be injurious to the fibre, if it is otherwise good. The process only requires to be more narrowly watched than in Europe.

But we observe in the 'Journ. of the Chemico-Agricul. Society of Ulster,' for January, 1853, it said, that—"In Ireland, great expectations were entertained that by the plans for this purpose, which were introduced by the late Mr. Schenck, the preparation of Flax for the spinner would be made entirely a factory operation." "In Ireland, however, the establishments erected under Schenck's patent, have not, generally, given satisfaction." "In England and Scotland, we are aware that the system has been more successfully carried out;" but "Schenck's process, which is, in fact, merely the ordinary method of the farmer, regulated and accelerated, was, however, adopted by many persons but imperfectly acquainted with the various requisites for success." But Mr. MacAdam, at the late meeting of the Royal Flax Improvement Society, November, 1854, seems to consider it still as the best method.

Having, at pp. 146-7, given Professor Hodges's analysis of the Flax plant, we will here subjoin his further observations on his experimental crop, and his analysis of the steep-water. He first observes that the crop, having been air-dried, was removed to the steeping works at Cregagh.

It was there placed in stacks, and after some time prepared for steeping. The first operation for this purpose is the removal of the valuable bolls or capsules. This, in these establishments, where the cost of labour is carefully considered, is usually most expeditiously and perfectly effected, by means of a machine composed of two cast-iron rollers, to which motion is communicated by a belt from the steam-engine. Between these the Flax is passed and the capsules bruised, so that the seed can be readily shaken out. Having been deprived of its bolls, by this machine, it was found that the 7770 lb. (*v.* p. 146) of Flax were reduced to 52 cwt., or 5824 lb.

Of the portions of the plant removed by the seeding machine, 910 lb. consisted of clean seed, 1036 lb. of husks, leaves, and sand. The loss experienced by the Flax in steeping was 13 cwt. From the 52 cwt. of seeded straw, the produce of the experimental crop, there remained 6 cwt. 1 qr. 2 lb. of marketable fibre.

The taste of the steep-water, at first, is rather agreeably acid, but followed by the peculiar plant-like taste of the Flax. By the addition to the liquid of carbonate of lime, its acidity is destroyed. Contrary to what has been stated, in some reports on this subject, the liquid, I found, at the conclusion of the process, yields merely a trace of acetic acid, and in numerous experiments, no trace of the evolution of sulphuretted hydrogen could be detected at any stage of the fermentation. When the Flax is allowed to remain in the vats after the usual time, a new series of changes, and a fresh and rapid extrication of gas, take place. I have made, during the last three years, numerous experiments, with respect to the composition of the steep-water, from several establishments, and, also, from the common steep-pools, which afforded me some interesting results, and satisfied me that the fermentation which is induced by steeping Flax in water resembles the so-called butyric acid fermentation; merely traces of acetic acid, and invariably large quantities of butyric acid having been detected in every case. In fact, the fragrant butyric ether, so extensively employed in the preparation of pine-apple rum, and in flavouring confectionery, might readily be obtained, in large quantities, from the stinking waters of the Flax pool.

To ascertain exactly the effect produced by steeping, and the composition of the steep-water, I obtained from the works at Cregagh, a sample of Flax straw unsteeped, a portion of steeped straw taken from the same lot, and a gallon of the steep-water taken from the vat immediately after the removal of the Flax. The composition of the ash obtained by burning the extract of the steep-water, and the samples of the straw, is given in the table. The spring water employed at the works is moderately hard, indicating, on Dr.

Clarke's scale, 8 degrees. It was not considered necessary to deduct the ingredients supplied in it, as these would add but little to its fertilising value. An imperial gallon of the liquid of the vat was found to contain in grains and tenths—

Organic matters	136·7
Inorganic matters	131·4
Total solid matters	268·1 grains.

Composition of the Ash of the Flax Straw before and after Steeping, and of the Inorganic Matters of the Steep Water.

100 parts of each respectively contained—

	Unsteeped Flax.	Steeped Flax.	Ash of the Steep-water.
Potash	13·88	11·40	19·31
Soda	5·33	4·17	—
Chloride of Potassium	—	—	3·83
Chloride of Sodium	6·47	3·28	21·24
Lime	18 86	17·69	8·23
Magnesia	4·10	5·50	10·18
Oxide of Iron	5·40	5·76	2·02
Sulphuric Acid	11·16	4·07	6·10
Phosphoric Acid	9·63	11·87	3·77
Carbonic Acid	10·37	20·06	23·30
Silica	15·23	15·78	1·12
Sand	—	—	0·60
	100·43	99·58	99·77
Ash per cent. in the Straw	3·89	2·59	—

100 grains of the dried extract of the steep-water contained 1·56 nitrogen, =1·89 grains of ammonia: therefore, an imperial gallon would be capable of supplying five grains, and a vat, containing 3000 gallons of water, 2 1-10 lb., worth about 1*s.* 2*d.* to the farmer; while the same amount of liquid, placed on his field, would convey to them about the same amount of phosphoric acid.

By the kindness of the proprietors of the Steeping Works, at Cregagh, who have liberally given me an opportunity of inspecting the books of their establishment, I am enabled to give the following statement of the changes which 100 tons of Flax undergo when treated by Schenck's process.

100 tons of air-dried Flax straw yield—

	Tons.
1. *By Seeding*—33 tons of seed and husks, leaving of seeded Flax .	67·00
2. *By Steeping*—67 tons of seeded Flax yield of steeped straw .	39·50
3. *By Scutching*—39½ tons of steeped straw yield of dressed Flax .	5·90
" " of tow and pluckings .	1·47

Watt's Patent Process.—The advantages of Schenck's method of preparation, are sufficiently considerable to ensure its adoption at once in an uncertain climate like that of the British Isles. But it was yet to be proved whether the process of fermentation was essential to the separation of the fibre; and whether, if it was got rid of, we might not obtain an equally good fibre, avoid the noxious exhalations, and even utilise the products of the steep-water, which had previously always been a nuisance. All this has been done by Watt's method of preparing Flax, and which I had the advantage, in September, 1852, of viewing, through the kindness of Dr. Hodges, before all the works at Messrs. Leadbetter's were quite completed; but even in this state, the Author saw enough to be at a loss whether most to admire, the skill with which the principles of science had been brought to bear on the perfecting of a practical art, or the success with which mechanical contrivances had been applied to the completeness of every part of the process. We subjoin the following account from the 'Journal of the Chemico-Agricultural Society of Ulster,' for January, 1853. To this, we have added Dr. Hodges's analysis of the steep-water, obtained by this patent process.

"At the meeting of the British Association of Science in this town, in September, the details of a new and totally different process for the separation of the Flax fibre was, by permission of the patentee, Mr. Watt, first made known to the public, by Dr. Hodges, and excited much interest. Since that time, trials of the new process have been made on a most extensive scale, at works erected for the purpose in Belfast. As various imperfect accounts of Mr. Watt's process have been published, the following account of the apparatus, and operations connected with it, will be interesting to our readers.

"In Mr. Watt's process the solution of the cementing matters of the Flax straw, and the separation of the fibre, is effected, not by the ordinary methods of fermentation, but by exposing the straw to the action of steam, in a chamber of peculiar construction, and afterwards subjecting it to pressure, applied by means of heavy metal rollers. The first operation consists in placing the seeded Flax in a chamber, formed of plates of cast iron.

"The chamber used measures about twelve feet in length, and is about six feet broad and six feet in depth, and contains about fifteen cwt. of Flax. On the top is a tank for containing water, also of cast iron, about eighteen inches deep, the bottom of which forms the roof of the chamber, and through which passes a tube, furnished with a valve. There are two doors in the ends of the chambers, through which passes a tube, furnished with a valve. There are two doors in the ends of the chamber, through which the Flax is introduced, and these, when the steam is admitted, are secured by screws. A false bottom, formed of perforated iron plates, such as are used in malt-kilns, is raised about six inches from the bottom of the chamber; and, resting on this, there is an upright throw-pipe, the use of which we shall presently describe. The chamber being filled with Flax, and the doors secured, steam is admitted, and when the straw has been thoroughly saturated with moisture and softened, a weight is placed upon the valve on the top, so as to confine the steam, which, as it strikes against the cold bottom of the water-tank forming the roof of the chamber, is condensed, and made to descend in streams of distilled water, which dissolve the soluble matters of the softened straw, washing them into the lower part of the chamber. The liquid, as it accumulates, is conveyed into a reservoir, and employed as food for cattle. The analysis of this liquid is given at p. 208. Towards the conclusion of the process, when nearly all the soluble matters have been removed, the liquid is allowed to collect until it rises above the false bottom, and, by placing a weight upon the safety-valve in the roof, the pressure of the confined steam causes it to ascend in the throw-pipes, by which it is discharged in showers over the straw. The throw-pipes, it may be mentioned, are not essential, and in some of the vats they are not used. In their stead, a square iron reservoir is placed on the top of the chamber, and communicating with it by a pipe with a stop-cock, into which the liquid accumulated in the chamber is pumped, and discharged occasionally over the straw.

"In from twelve to eighteen hours, the steaming process is completed, and the straw, when withdrawn from the chamber, is immediately subjected in small parcels to the successive action of two pair of heavy iron rollers, by which it is pressed into flat tape-like bands, and deprived of nearly all the moisture contained in it; the longitudinal pressure also removes a considerable portion of the epidermis, or outer envelope, and facilitates the removal of the woody matter in scutching. Each pair of rollers used exerts a pressure equal to 10 cwt.

"The after-treatment of the pressed straw does not present

any remarkable difference from the system pursued in the hot-water steeping establishments. The straw is secured between rods, and suspended in a drying chamber, heated by the waste steam of the engine. The arrangements for this purpose at the Bedford Street works of Messrs. Leadbetter consist of rooms with floors formed of spars. Below this flooring passes a pipe conveying steam, by which the air admitted by openings at the bottom of the chambers is heated, and made to ascend through the Flax. The circulation of the air is ingeniously effected by a series of revolving beaters kept in action below the steam-pipe."

The following extract from the Report of a Committee of the Royal Flax Society gives the results of an experiment made at Messrs. Leadbetter's works:

In this experimental trial, a quantity of Flax straw, of ordinary quality, was taken from the bulk of the stock at the works, weighing $13\frac{3}{4}$ cwt. with the seed on. After the removal of the seed, which, on being cleaned thoroughly from the chaff, measured $3\frac{3}{4}$ imperial bushels, the straw was reduced in weight to 10 cwt. 1 qr. 2 lb. It was then placed in the vat, where it was subjected to the steaming process for about eleven hours. After steeping, wet-rolling, and drying, it weighed 7 cwt. 0 qr. 11 lb.; and on being scutched, the yield was 187 lb. of Flax; and of scutching tow, 12 lb. $6\frac{1}{2}$ oz. fine, 35 lb. 3 oz. coarse. The yield of fibre, in the state of good Flax, was, therefore, at the rate of $13\frac{1}{2}$ lb. from the cwt. of straw with seed on; 18 lb. from the cwt. of straw without seed; $26\frac{1}{4}$ lb. from the cwt. of steeped and dried straw.

The time occupied in actual labour, in the processes from the seeding of the Flax to the commencement of the scutching, was $13\frac{1}{4}$ hours, to which, if eleven hours be added for the time the Flax was in the vat, twenty-four hours would be the time required up to this point. The scutching, by four stands, occupied six hours sixteen minutes. But, in this statement, the time required for drying is not included, as owing to some derangement in the apparatus, no certain estimate could be made of the actual time required in that process. It would appear, however, that about thirty-six hours would include the time necessary, in a well-organized establishment, to convert Flax-straw into fibre, for the spinner.

The cost of all these operations, in this experiment, leaving out the drying, for the reasons noted, appeared to be under £10 per ton of clean fibre, for labour, exclusive of general expenses.

A portion of the fibre was sent to two spinning mills to be hackled, and to have a value put upon it. The valuation of the samples varied from £56 to £70 per ton, according to the quality of the stricks of fibre sent, and the yield on the hackle was considered quite satisfactory.

Appended to this report is a note of the time occupied in the different processes during the experiment, and of the number of persons employed in each.

It is to be hoped that so promising a plan may, on more extended experience, be found fully to warrant the high anticipation formed from what is already known concerning it. (Signed on behalf of the Committee,)

RICHARD NIVEN, Chairman.

Belfast, 3d Nov., 1852.

Appendix.

Note of the time occupied, and of the number of persons employed in each of the processes witnessed by the Committee, on the experimental trial of Mr. Watt's system of preparing Flax fibre :

	No. of Persons employed.		Time occupied.	
	Men.	Women & Boys.	Hours.	Minutes.
Seeding	4	8	1	15
Placing in vat . .	3	4	0	15
Cleaning seed . . .	1	0	3	0
Taking out of vat . .	2	3	0	30
Wet-rolling and putting in drying room	1	16	2	20
Rolling for scutching . .	0	11	1	8
Striking for ditto . .	0	7	4	47
Total . .	11	49	13	15
Scutching . . .	4	0	6	16

Analysis of the Liquid obtained in Watt's Patent Flax Process.

At a meeting of the Chemico-Agricultural Society of Ulster, Dr. Hodges gave an analysis of the liquid obtained in Watt's Patent Flax Process, and an account of the new process of preparing Flax, patented by Messrs. Watt and Leadbetter, which, he said, offered the only practical method of economising the matters which are separated from the Flax plant in its preparation for the manufacturer, which had hitherto been proposed. The liquid which remains in the flax-vats employed in the new process possessed none of the disagreeable qualities of the ordinary steep waters. It was free from smell, and in taste and colour somewhat resembled an infusion of senna leaves. It was, in fact, a strong tea, containing, unchanged by fermentation or putrefaction, the soluble matters of the stem of the Flax plant. It was, at the present time, advantageously used at Messrs. Leadbetter's works in feeding pigs. As it was desirable to ascertain the exact composition of this liquid and its nutritive value, he had procured a sample of it from the Bedford Street works, and had it submitted to chemical examination. The following were the results: One gallon evaporated to dryness gave—

Of Organic matters . . .	353·97 grains.
„ Earthy and Saline matters . . .	161·49 „
Total amount of solid matter .	515·46 grains.

The organic matter afforded on analysis 14·79 grains of nitrogen.

The earthy and saline matters were found to possess the following composition :

Composition of the Ash of the Steep-water of Flax.

	Per cent.	In a gallon
Potash	27·17	44·63 grains.
Soda	3·18	5·12 „
Chloride of Sodium . .	21·58	34·61 „
Lime	5·91	9 49 „
Magnesia	4·60	7·40 „
Oxide of Iron . . .	0·83	1·33 „
Sulphuric Acid . . .	15·64	25·11 „
Phosphoric Acid . . .	5·66	9·01 „
Carbonic Acid . . .	12·43	19·96 „
Silica	3·00	4·83 „
	100·00	161·49 grains.

Dr. Hodges stated that the Flax liquid possessed considerable feeding qualities; and Mr. Leadbetter in reply to his inquiry said that it had not been found to exhibit any purgative effect—the pigs at his works received it mixed with turnips and the husks of the Flax, and were in a thriving fattening condition.

The vat liquid, Dr. Hodges observed, could be drawn off in a more concentrated form than the sample examined, and it would be easy for the manufacturer, by employing a hydrometer, to supply it of uniform strength.

Composition of the Ash of Flax Shoves.

The shoves, or refuse woody matters, which are separated in scutching Flax, are at present employed in the steeping works as fuel. Dr. Hodges, in the course of the extended investigation of the Flax plant, in which he is at present engaged, found that the ash which remains on the incineration of these matters had the following composition, and might, therefore, advantageously be economised for use as manure. 100 parts of ash afford:

Potash	7·73
Soda	5·91
Chloride of Sodium	1·78
Lime	20·15
Magnesia	5·46
Oxide of Iron	5·60
Sulphuric Acid	6·50
Phosphoric Acid	10·43
Carbonic Acid	20·10
Silica	16·00
	99·66

1000 lb. of shoves yield, on combustion, 19½ lb. of ash.

Upon this, Professor Wilson remarks: "Here then we have a process which presents the following advantages over the ordinary methods: 1st. Great saving in time. 2d. Economy of fibre. 3d. Avoidance of any nuisance, and beneficial application of waste products." All proving that a great advance had been made in principles in this process.

As closely connected with Watt's, we subjoin Professor Wilson's account of another process. "No sooner, however, had the spinners given their testimony in favour of Watt's fibre, than another process was patented by Buchanan, which appears to be an improved application of the same principle as Watt's—for the solvent power is clearly not due to the steam, as made use of by him, but to the hot water occasioned by its condensation. In this, the steeping is effected by *repeated immersions* in a tank of heated water, arrangements being made by which the temperature is never allowed to exceed a certain degree—a point of great importance, both as regards the abstraction of the azotised extractive matter, and also the quantity of fibre produced. It is well known that albuminous solutions, containing even a very small proportion of albumen (1 in 1000), coagulate at a temperature of 180°, and then became insoluble; and it is always considered that fibre is more or less injured if exposed beyond a certain temperature. These two important points have been taken advantage of in Buchanan's process: the temperature of the steep-liquor is kept between 150° and 180°, and the operation, both as regards time and produce, more satisfactorily performed. The process is quite *automaton*—thus saving labour and the risks consequent upon carelessness; and the mechanical arrangements by which it is effected are very simple and inexpensive."[1] So far as the experiments have gone, it has been found that by ten immersions, the whole of the colouring matter of the Flax has been removed. By this process, the Author concludes we have all the advantages obtained by water; economy of products, increased economy of time—only four hours being required instead of twelve; and, in addition, great economy of labour. Another great improvement is claimed by Buchanan —his method of drying the steeped shove preparatory to scutching. The process in Watt's method is also very perfect, but Professor Wilson had been unable to obtain, at the time he wrote (16th May, 1853), any results of the working of the process on a commercial scale.

Mr. C. Fane, referring to the difficulties experienced in the fermentative processes, has given a graphic account of another method by which the fibre of the Flax, as no doubt of other plants, may easily be separated. Subjecting the wet fibres to heavy pressure is now adopted in most of the improved processes.

"At this juncture, an English gentleman, a Mr. Pownall, in endeavouring to work out Mr. Claussen's idea of obtaining from Flax a fibre that would spin on cotton-machinery, made a most valuable discovery, as to the preparing Flax for the common linen purposes, which was this, that if the Flax straw, when taken out of the water in which it had been steeped and fermented, were *instantly, and before drying,* subjected to *severe pressure* and a *stream of cold water,* the pressure would press

[1] Professor Wilson's paper in 'Journ. of Agric. Soc.,' vol. xiv, p. 204.

out, and the water would wash away almost all the gluten remaining in the plant not removed by the fermentation.

"It is impossible to over-estimate the value of this discovery. The grand difficulty in the management of the Flax plant had always been the difficulty of hitting the happy mean between *over*-fermenting and *under*-fermenting the straw. If the straw were not fermented enough, the gluten was not sufficiently discharged, and then the woody parts of the plant stuck to the fibre so strongly, that nothing short of violent blows of the scutching instrument would remove it, and violent blows broke much of the fibre into short lengths, called tow, of little or no value. On the other hand, if the straw were fermented too much, then the gluten was, indeed, sufficiently discharged, and moderate blows sufficed to remove the woody matter; but in that case the fibre was weakened, and the blows, moderate as they were, again broke the fibre into tow. In either case the yield of valuable fibre was unsatisfactory, and the reed and quality deteriorated, and it was only in those cases where the exercise of the greatest care and judgment had enabled the steeper to trim most happily between fermenting *too much* and fermenting *too little*, that a satisfactory yield of fibre was obtained. Mr. Pownall's discovery at once triumphed over this hitherto almost insuperable difficulty, because it enabled him to stop short in the process of fermentation before he arrived at the *point of danger*, and yet remove the gluten even more effectually than *excessive* fermentation had previously done; from which there resulted the following advantages:

"1st. The squeezing and washing so completely cleansed the fermented straw, that the objection to Schenck's hot-water system, arising from the putrid matter re-adhering to the straw, and flying off from the straw in dust in scutching, at once disappeared; and hence the mills erected for hot-water steeping resumed work, and no impediment now exists to steeping being carried on *all the year round*.

"2d. Fermentation need never be carried beyond the perfectly safe point, and hence the fibre is not weakened.

"3d. The woody matter is easily removed by moderate blows of the scutching instrument, because the sticky matter no longer impedes the operation, and hence the yield of fibre is much greater.

"4th. The fibre obtained is of a singularly soft and pliable character, and is much preferred by the spinner.

"5th. The subsequent process of bleaching is greatly facilitated, because it is the gluten which remains in the fibre which resists the action of bleaching ingredients, and under Mr. Pownall's process the gluten is effectually removed.

"The use is spreading more and more every day, and the results are universally acknowledged as most satisfactory. The process adds from £10 to £30 to the value of the ton of Flax, according as the raw material is of inferior or superior quality; and the expense is the merest trifle."

These methods of preparing the fibre from Flax stems which have been dried and stacked, afford considerable advantages, as the seed becomes more ripe, and the farmer can choose a leisure time for the preparation of his Flax—or, better, he may confine his attention to growing the Flax, and then send it for careful preparation to the factory or rettory.

Steeping green.[1]—With the above methods of separating Flax which has been stacked, we may contrast that of steeping the stems when green, and of which Professor Wilson says, that "when the quantity is small and can be worked up at once, would appear to be the most advantageous." M. Dufermont, cultivateur à Hem (departement du Nord), found that when the Flax was used green, the steeping only required from six to seven days; and that six days' grassing gave the Flax a finer colour than could be obtained by any other means. It was dried and ready for scutching in three weeks; whereas the ordinary time in the district averaged from a year to a year and a half. He found also that it yielded 5 per cent. more fibre, which was worth fully 10 per cent. more money in the market. The Flax was pulled before it was quite ripe, the seed-bolls removed by rippling, and the straw immediately placed in the pits. The seed, however, was reduced about two francs per hectolitre in value. The details of the experiments he gives thus:

[1] The steeping of Hemp when in a green state, was strongly recommended by the Abbé Brulles; and the natives of India insist upon its being the best mode for *Sunn*, q. v.

FIRST EXPERIMENT.

	Value.	Original value.	Dried.	Steeped and dried.	Scutch'd	Value per kilom.	Value of Seed.	Gross value.
	Francs.	Kilogs.	Kilogs.	Kilogs.	Kilogs.	Francs.	Francs.	Francs.
Green Flax .	222	4·030	—	826	191	1·70	27	357·70
Dried do. .	222	4·030	1·142	178	178	1·55	31	305·90
Difference .	—	—	—	—	—	—	—	51·80
SECOND EXPERIMENT.								
Green Flax . .	6·05	100	—	26·000	6·350	1·90	—	12·06
			Grmmes.					
Dried do. . .	6·05	100	30·250	22·500	5·500	1·65	—	9·07
Difference . .	—	—	—	—	—	—	—	2·99

The practice of steeping green is carried on to a large extent in the Waes district in Belgium.

CHEMICAL PROCESSES.

The action of water and the production of fermentation may truly be considered chemical operations, but the term is usually applied to other processes in which the action of soap, of acids, or of caustic or of carbonated alkalies, or of some salts, is employed to effect the separation of the fibres from each other, as well as from the cellular tissue and accompanying glutinous secretions. The natives of India have long been in the habit of bleaching their muslins by boiling them in a ley of carbonate of soda, and then washing them in a weak solution of citric acid obtained from the juice of limes or of lemons. So in other parts they boil the bast of certain plants in a ley of wood-ashes, in order to facilitate the separation of the fibres (see Nettles). Some of the chemical methods which have been invented in Europe are similar to these.

In the 'Jury Report' of Class IV, by Professor E. Solly, for the Exhibition of 1851, we have an account of the old German process, called "Molkenrost," sometimes used in preparing the finer sorts of Flax. This was steeped for four or five days in a warm mixture of milk and water, and thus the desired degree of fermentation in the Flax stems was produced. This is distinct from the more modern process in which linen was boiled by the Dutch in a weak alkaline ley, and subsequently treated with sour buttermilk, of which no doubt the lactic acid was useful in removing the alkali, as well as in dissolving some of the impurities of the fibre, and thus was nearly identical with the Indian process of bleaching. Subsequently, salt of sorrel (that is, an oxalate of potash, or the same salt which is so abundant in the leaves of the *Gram Cicer arietinum*,) and sulphuric and muriatic acids were employed, but were found to be too costly. The careful experiments of Hermbstaedt at the beginning of this century threw much light on the chemical principles involved in, and on the influence of temperature on the separation of the fibre of Flax.

These chemical processes have again attracted much attention, since the process patented by M. Claussen has shown how much the nature and appearance of fibre may be changed by the action of such agents. But this, like many other inventions, has many points of similarity with what had been done long before without attracting much attention. Of it we have the following account in the above 'Jury Report,' p. 97: "This process (patented August, 1850) consists essentially in boiling the cut and crushed stems of the Flax, Hemp, or other plant, in a dilute solution of caustic soda, containing about one two-thousandth part of alkali. The fibrous matter is then removed, and plunged into a bath of dilute sulphuric acid, consisting of one five-hundredth part of acid, in which it is boiled for about an hour. It is next transferred into a solution, containing about ten per cent. of carbonate of soda; and, lastly, when it has remained in the latter for an hour, it is plunged into a weak solution of sulphuric acid, consisting of one part of acid to two hundred or five hundred parts of water; in this it is left for about half an hour, and the process is completed. The effect of these several processes is 'to divide and split up' the fibre in a most remarkable manner, so as completely to alter its character. Flax thus treated is converted into a substance very nearly resembling cotton."

The idea of modifying the fibre of Flax and Hemp, so as to convert it into a kind of cotton, is by no means new. In 1747, it was proposed to convert Flax into cotton by boiling it in a solution of caustic potash, and subsequently washing it with soap. In 1775, considerable quantities of refuse Flax and Hemp were converted into Flax cotton by Lady Moira, with the aid of T. B. Bailey, of Hope, near Manchester. It appears that the fibre was boiled in an alkaline ley, or a solution of kelp, containing carbonate of soda, and subsequently scoured. The result of this was, that "the fibres seem to be set at liberty from each other," after which it may be "carded on cotton-cards." It appears that at this time "Flax cotton" was made and sold at threepence a pound. Some of it was spun into cloth for gowns, and also for waistcoats; but her Ladyship complains that the spinners were hostile to the discovery, for fear of its injuring the cotton trade, and the poor of the North of Ireland, to whom it was supposed it would be beneficial, were indifferent about the merits of the invention. Specimens of the Flax cotton and of the fabrics woven from it are still preserved in the Museum of the Society of Arts.

Several attempts were subsequently made in Germany to convert, with the action of alkaline solutions, Flax into a fibre resembling cotton, which could be used, either alone or together with cotton, in the manufacture of cotton goods, But there, as in Ireland, the manufacturers probably set themselves against the introduction of Flax cotton, and the work-people determined not to use the new material. The matter was subsequently investigated by Berthollet, by Gay-Lussac, and by Giobert, who employed alternately steepings in hot solutions of soap, alkali, and sulphuric or muriatic acid; and Berthollet observes that equally fine cotton is obtained from the commonest refuse tow as from the best Flax. (*v.* 'Jury Report,' p. 98.) More recently, in 1842, M. Rouchon, of l'Ecole Polytechnique, at Paris, has devised a method for preparing Flax by means of immersion in a weak acid solution for a short period, and then placing it in a mass kept moist by occasional waterings. These are repeated daily until the desired effect is produced. The Flax is kept tied up in small bundles, and a man and a boy could attend to two tons per day. (Wilson.)

As carbonate of soda is very abundant and cheap in most parts of India, as well as the vegetable acids, and as the natives are in the habit of employing both in one of their processes for bleaching muslins, they could easily be induced to apply this method to the improved preparation of Flax or of any other fibre.

MECHANICAL PROCESSES BY HAND.

In the preceding account, some processes have necessarily been hinted at and supposed to have been performed, because without them Flax could not have been prepared for sale. But these have not yet been noticed in detail. As they require tools for their due performance, and these cannot be well understood from mere description, we annex some woodcuts, for the use of which the Author is indebted to his publisher, Mr. G. Smith. They are the same which were used in the pamphlet published by the Indian Flax Society, and which was compiled from the then best authorities. Many improved methods of preparing Flax have since then been discovered, and are now employed in Europe, and will, no doubt, be found useful in an extended state of the culture in India. But at present the simplest tools are the most suitable, such as those formerly very generally employed, and still used in many places in this country, and such as are required for cleaning by hand instead of by machinery.

Of these we add, first, a figure of the instrument used for separating or rippling seed,—a process which is recommended to be performed by the farmer.

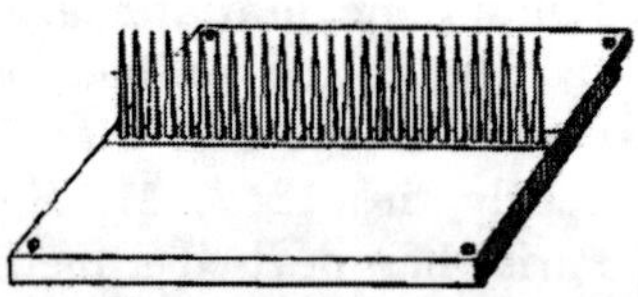

The ripple has already been described at p. 158.

The best ripples are made of half-inch square rods of iron, placed with the angles of iron next to the ripplers, 3-16ths of an inch asunder at the bottom, half an inch at the top, and 18 inches long, to allow a sufficient spring, and save much breaking of Flax. The points should begin to taper 3 inches from the top.

But in the Courtrai system the crop is stooked and ricked

in the field, and afterwards stacked or conveyed to the factory or rettory.

The Courtrai System.—This is the mode in which Flax should be saved for steeping on Schenck's or Watt's patent systems. It requires to be very carefully done, as inattention will reduce the value of the straw, and yield inferior fibre. The Flax stems should be put together in bunches, about one half larger than a man can grasp in one hand, spread a little, and laid on the ground in rows after each puller; the bunches laid with tops and roots alternately, which prevents the seed-bolls from sticking to each other in lifting. It should be stooked as soon after pulling as possible, and never allowed to remain overnight unstooked, except in settled weather. The stooking should go on at the same time as the pulling, as, if Flax is allowed to get rain while on the ground, its colour is injured.—It is then ricked, and allowed to stand in the field until the seed is dry enough for stacking.—The rick, if properly built, will stand secure for months. It can be stacked at leisure, or put in a barn, the seed taken off during the winter, and the Flax steeped in the following May; or it may be kept stacked, without receiving any injury, for two or three years, or even longer.

If the capsules or bolls are brittle, or the stems have been stacked according to the Courtrai system, the seed is beaten out with a small wooden stick shaped like a cricket bat; a bundle of Flax is laid on a board, and the bolls are broken with the bat and fall on the cloth below; or they are separated by thrashing with a stick, the foot being kept on the root end of the Flax to prevent its turning about. In some factories or rettories, the stems are passed between plain rollers, by which means the bolls are crushed, and the seed falls out, as mentioned at p. 159.

"*Breaking* is simply crushing the bark and breaking the wood-like part of the stalk into fragments, in order to facilitate the separation of the fibre; this is performed in various ways.

"In order to give the boon such a degree of brittleness as to make it part readily from the fibre, whereby this process is rendered easy, the Flax should be well dried in the sun.

"*Primitive mode of breaking.*—The woody part and bark are broken by twisting a bundle of stalks as it is passed along between the hands, taking care not to ravel or entangle the fibre. The fragments of the stalk, &c., are then shaken, scutched or beaten off by a wooden knife

eight or ten inches broad. The fibre thus cleared is the undressed Flax of commerce, worth 6*d.* to 8*d.* per lb., or 6 to 8 annas per seer.

"Another simple mode of breaking is by taking a handful of stalks in one hand, laying them upon a table or block, beating them with a wooden mallet or bat; afterwards drawing them forcibly over the edge of the table with both hands, and scutching, in order to free them from the fragments and stalks.

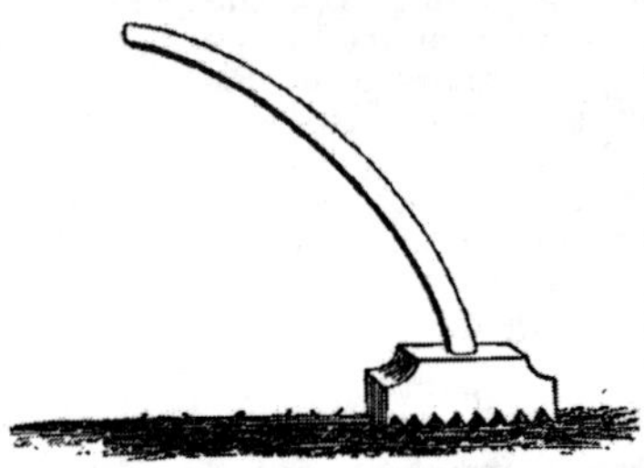

"Another method. The *Bott-hammer* is a wooden block (something of the size and shape of a denkee), having on its under face, channels or flutings, five or six deep lines, and it is fixed to a long bent helve or handle. In using it, a bundle of the dried Flax stalks is spread evenly upon the floor, then powerfully beaten with the hammer, first at the roots, next at the points, and lastly in the middle. When the upper surface has been well beat in this way, it is turned over, that the under surface may get its turn. The Flax is then removed, and well shaken to free it from the boon.

"By the hammer the whole wood is never separated from the textile fibres, but a certain quantity of chaffy stuff adheres to them, which is removed by another operation. This consists either in rubbing or shaking. The rubbing is much practised in Westphalia, and the neighbouring districts."

The common brake consists of four wooden swords fixed in a frame, and another frame with three swords, which play in the interstices of the first, by means of a joint at one end. The Flax is taken in the left hand, and placed between the two frames, and the upper frame is pushed down briskly upon it. It breaks the Flax in four places, and by moving the left hand, and rapidly repeating the strokes with the right, the whole handful is soon broken. An improved form of brake is worked by a treadle, and motion given it with the left foot.

"*Scutching-block which may be used with either of the methods of breaking.*—Fig. 4 represents a board set upright in a block of wood so as to stand steady, in which is a horizontal slit about three feet from the ground, the edge of which is thin.

The broken Flax held in handfuls in the left hand is inserted in this slit, so as to project to the right, and a flat wooden sword, eight or ten inches broad, generally of shape of fig. D;

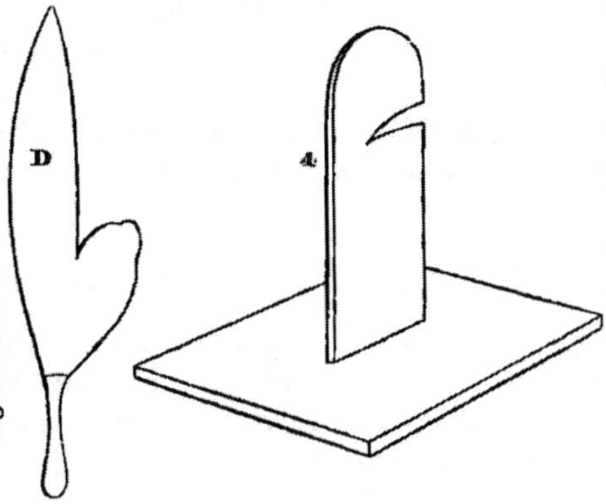

Fig. D. Flat sword or scutcher.

Upright board to clear the Flax of the wood.

the breadth of this knife is important; when too narrow it easily causes the Flax to twist round it, and thereby tears a portion of the fibres. With this knife the Flax is repeatedly struck, parallel to the board (and close to the slit), with perpendicular blows, to scrape off its wooden asperities. The part which lies in the slit is continually changed by a motion of the left hand.

"In flax-mills, the operation of breaking is performed by passing the stems between three fluted cylinders, one of which is made to revolve by horse or water power, and carries the other two round. That of scutching is accomplished in the same mill, by means of four arms projecting from a horizontal axle, so as to strike the stalk or boon in a slanting direction, until the useless parts are beaten away. The operation of these mills was at first much objected to, on the ground that they destroy much of the fibre before the woody part is all separated; but their mode of action has been greatly improved, and such mills are now very generally established in Ireland."

So great is the importance of properly made scutch-mills, that the Royal Irish Society have always made the state of the machinery employed for scutching Flax a principal object of attention. In the year 1852 an Act was passed by Parliament, extending the provisions of the Land Improvement Act to buildings for scutch-mills. Several have been reported on by the above Society, and a section of one is given in Mr. MacAdam's paper in 'Journ. Agric. Soc.,' vol. viii, p. 304. Messrs. MacAdam have lately invented a scutching mill which has the great advantage of being able to do without skilled labour.

These processes probably form the best introduction to the mechanical methods of separating the fibre.

MECHANICAL PROCESSES BY MACHINERY.

We have already observed that the intimate union between the constituent parts of plants may be dissolved by the action of water, by the fermentative process, or by chemical reagents, as well as in many instances by the mere absence of moisture. Thus we may see the union of the leaves with the parent plant ceasing on the approach of winter; or, more to the point, we may see the cuticle of the Birch bark peeling off, as well as the bark of other trees; or, if we take a cut branch of the Linden or Lime tree, some time after it has been cut, we may see the layers of bark separating from the branch and from each other. The herbaceous parts of leaves may also be reduced to powder, when the fibrous parts still remain; or we may take the dried bark of some fibre-yielding plant, and observe that, by rubbing it between the hands, the cuticle may become separated from the fibres, and these from each other. All facts proving that the fibres of plants may be separated, in some instances at least, by simple drying and by mechanical means. Several machines have of late years been invented for this purpose with more or less success. It is generally considered that such processes are fitted only for such fibres as are required for coarse purposes, such as for rope-making and coarse canvass. But the Author has seen some specimens lately, which seem to prove that such methods are capable of greater perfection than is supposed. They will be of certain advantage where nature has produced a good fibre, and the carelessness of man is liable to destroy its structure by over-retting, or any other inattention.

The first of these patents was taken out by Mr. James Lee

for his method of separating the fibre by mechanical means, and without the aid of water-retting. His discovery was thought of such importance, that Parliament granted him the peculiar privilege, that the time for the specification of his patent should be extended from six months to seven years. The Irish Linen Board expended a large sum in introducing the method into the Flax districts, and Mr. Wilson informs us that one of the machines is still preserved in the White Linen Hall at Belfast. Before the time, however, for specification arrived, Messrs. Hill and Bundy took out a patent for their machine for breaking and preparing raw Flax and Hemp.[1]

In this machine the frame is made either of wood or metal, which supports two conical rollers. These revolve independently of each other in proper brass bearings, a third conical roller being similarly supported under the top piece of the machine. All these rollers are *frustra* of cones made of cast iron. Whatever form of teeth be adopted, they must be so shaped and disposed with regard to each other, as to have considerable play between them, in order to admit the quantity of Flax stem which is intended to be broken and prepared. The upper piece of the machine, which carries the upper conical roller, is attached to the main frame by a moveable joint at its upper end, and is connected near its other

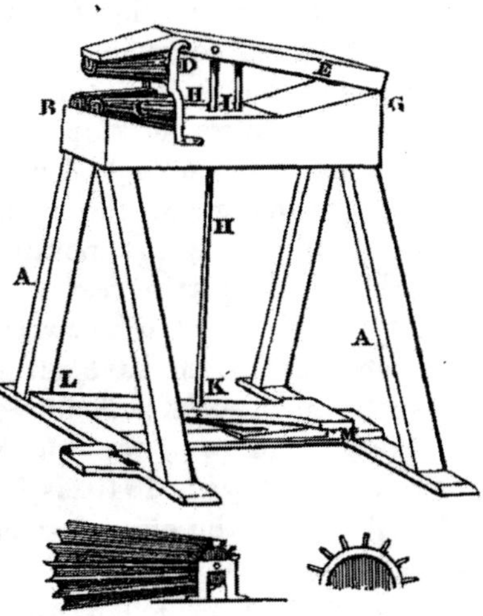

[1] Several of these machines appear by the following extract from a despatch, to have been sent to India by the Court of Directors: "A principle has lately been discovered for producing the fibre of Hemp, Sunn, Caloee, and other similar plants, in a most improved state, without steeping or dew-retting. We have judged it advisable to send you several of the machines, with some printed directions to assist in the use of them; and as very little tuition is necessary, so we have judged it proper only to have two men instructed in its operations, who belong to the ship in which they came, and who will attend to instruct those you may appoint to be taught." (Public Department, May 8th, 1816.)

end with an iron rod, which is attached below to a treadle with a spring, to which motion is given with the foot, while the Flax is held by the hands between the cones. The operation may be commenced and continued for some time with the larger part of the rollers, and finished with their smaller ends: this forming one of the advantages of using conical rollers.

If it is intended that the Flax shall be bleached before it is spun, then recourse is had to certain trays in which are contained the water or other fluid used for bleaching the Flax or Hemp. Then each small parcel is worked separately, while wet, through a machine, similar to that in which the Flax has been broken; but here the rollers should be cylindrical and made entirely of wood, with metal axles, and the teeth, which will be parallel, should be similar in form to those in the lower right hand section (p. 221). This operation will loosen the gluten and colouring matter, for the rinsing and wringing which must follow, and which is preceded by soaking the Flax in a weak solution of soap.

The above machine and process, though not now in use, are interesting, as among those which were the earliest employed, and as indicating the points which require to be attended to; though, in getting rid of one set of difficulties, others are encountered. But the powers and mechanical contrivances of the later inventions have surmounted many difficulties as well as given much greater facilities.

Another process, for which a Mr. Olcott obtained two patents in the year 1840, is interesting, as showing the power of rollers and the cleansing effects of water. This invention consists in taking the sun- or kiln-dried Flax in the stem, spreading it out upon a wide feeding cloth, from whence it passes through a series of long fluted wooden rollers, say thirty sets, that is, sixty altogether, viz., thirty upper and thirty lower rollers, which so crush and break the stalk, that most of the wood drops from the fibre, and renders the process of cleaning it easy.

The Flax, when separated from the wood, is twisted into a rope; the rope should be rove about the thickness of a stout man's arm. This rope is then passed through another series of fluted rollers about six inches wide, and made either of wood or metal; the ends are twisted together, and an endless rope thus made. The rollers, a series of twenty or thirty sets, are then put in motion, and a stream of water set flowing over them. The rope passing through in an endless round, the remaining particles of wood, or shoves, as they are technically called, are rapidly separated from the fibre, the gluten and colouring matter washed out, and the fibre itself reduced and divided into smaller and finer fibres. After the process has been continued a few hours, the rope is withdrawn, much diminished in size, and quite white. On untwisting it, when dried, the product is "Flax cotton." This article is much more beautiful than the finest cotton: it is almost as soft as silk, and exceedingly glossy, but when closely examined, presents many imperfections.

In the year 1851, Mr. T. Routledge completed a machine, consisting chiefly of peculiarly formed rollers, under which were passed the leaves of the Agave, Plantain, New Zealand Flax, &c. —that is, of all such plants as are arranged under the class of Endogens—then washing and separating the fibre. The machine was capable of turning out two or three tons of fibre per diem; and trials were made with it at Messrs. Pontifex and Co.'s.

Mr. Dickson, of the Flax Works at Grove Street, Deptford, has for some years been engaged in perfecting a machine which will break, scutch, and heckle Flax, as it is taken from the field, without being retted or steeped by any process; and if the Flax be afterwards boiled in his patent flax-steep, it will not only remain strong, but become white.

By this the expense of separating the fibre by hand is saved: this amounts to from 2*s*. to 2*s*. 4*d*. per stone of 16 lb., on an article the average price of which is from 8*s*. to 9*s*. per stone. It also supersedes the necessity of employing skilled hands, called scutchers, at 2*s*. 6*d*. or 3*s*. per day.

In a recent statement, Mr. Dickson observes that "his machines produce in one day out of one ton of green Flax stalks, 920 lb. of fibre; that is, 5¾ lb. out of 14 lb. of stalks. This, when prepared by his liquid, has produced 2 lb. 6 oz. of very fine fibre, or in all 515 lb. of fibre fit for spinners' use." Mr. Dickson further contrasts his process with that of others, stating that, from many experiments caused to be made by that most important and useful body, the Belfast Flax Society, and who recommend Schenck's process, it appears that Mr. Andrews, a gentleman of great practical knowledge in Flax culture, seems to be only able to obtain 9 lb. of Flax, and 15 oz. of Tow, out of 100 lb. of Flax stalks. Mr. MacAdam, the Society's Secretary, says that improvements have now been made, which enable parties working on Schenck's system, to produce 14 lb. out of 112 lb. of Flax stalks; but by a much more profitable process (that of Watt's), where 10 cwt. 1 qr. 21 lb. of stalks had been operated on, the result was 234 lb. of Flax and Tow; while his own process, Mr. Dickson states, produces 268 lb. of marketable fibre. Mr. Warner, of Trimmingham, the advocate of hand-scutching, commonly obtains 20 stone of scutched Flax out of one ton of stalks, at a cost of 2*s.* per stone.

The correctness of these conclusions, and the carrying them out on a large scale, are of course dependent upon a variety of circumstances. The Author can only vouch, as he has already done at p. 134, for the greatly improved appearance of some of the Indian fibres which have been subjected to Mr. Dickson's treatment, and he has been assured by good practical judges, that some of them might, in the state to which they have been brought, be at once used for many of the purposes of Flax. He therefore believes that much practical good will arise out of the mechanical method of separating the fibres of Exogens when in a dry state, and of those of Endogens when still moist and green.

The Author has lately had an opportunity of seeing some specimens of Flax from Northumberland, and of Hemp from Italy, prepared by Mr. Dickson, with his machines and liquid, and without steeping. One half of each specimen is in the dried state of the stems, so as to give every facility for comparison. These clearly prove the practicability of this method, and therefore of the preparation of fibre, for many purposes at least, without any steeping.

The Author has also seen some specimens of Indian fibre beautifully prepared by Mr. W. Gardiner.

At the meeting of the Royal Agricultural Society held at Lincoln this year (July, 1854), a machine, manufactured by Messrs. Ransome, was exhibited and worked by Mr. E. Davy, of Crediton, in which Flax fibre was separated from the cuticle and boon by mechanical means, and without any steeping, This was favorably mentioned in 'The Times' (July 20th, 1854), and the instrument was afterwards sent to Leeds for trial, though the Author has not seen any subsequent account of its performances.

The Author further observes it stated in the annual report for this year of the Royal Society for the Promotion and Improvement of the growth of Flax in Ireland, under the head of "Unsteeped Flax fibre," that "the plan of preparing the fibre without steeping has, on former occasions, been alluded to. It is now being carried out practically, on a very large scale, by Mr. Roche, M.P. for County Cork; and the fibre is stated to find a ready market in England, for certain coarse purposes. The price obtained is considerably under that of steeped Flax, but, as the expense of steeping is avoided, it is stated to be sufficiently remunerative." (Belfast, 24th Nov., 1854.)

Heckling.—Among the operations which have been incidentally mentioned, but not described, is that of *heckling*, also called *hackling*. This, however, is more a spinner's than a planter's business, though the latter do sometimes like to send their produce in the best state to market, as noticed even in some of the communications from India. It is, at all events, useful to know the degree of subdivision of which a fibre is susceptible. In this process, the fibres are not only split into their finest fibrils, but are also cleaned, and arranged parallel to each other; while those which are too short for spinning are separated, and form the finer kinds of tow. The *heckle* is a sort of comb, with several rows of teeth fixed into round or oblong blocks of wood; the whole resembling the *hand cards* formerly used for carding cotton, and for which the jaw-bone of the *boalee* fish is a substitute in carding cotton for the Dacca muslins. The teeth of the heckle are of iron or steel, differing in length according to their fineness, beautifully polished, tapering, and having the points exceedingly sharp. Heckles of different degrees of delicacy are employed in bringing fibre to the required extent of fineness.

Mr. Tomlinson has given the following clear account of the process: "In heckling Flax, only one card or heckle is used at a time. The workman with one hand seizes a strick or lock of Flax by the middle, throws it upon the points of the coarse heckle, and draws it towards him; at the same time with the other hand spreading the Flax, and preventing it from sinking too deeply among the teeth. By this operation, the Flax is divided into two parts; viz., the short fibres forming *tow,* which remains between the points of the heckle, and is from time to time removed; and the long fibres, called *line,* which remains in the hand of the heckler. One half of the length of the strick being properly heckled, the other half is turned round and prepared in a similar way. The process is then repeated upon the fine heckle, and continued until the required fibre is produced. It is calculated that 100 pounds of well-cleaned Flax will yield from forty-five to sixty pounds of line; the remainder consisting of tow, boony particles, and dust. Considerable force and dexterity are required to heckle well, for in the hands of an unskilful operative, the best Flax, instead of being separated into fine, delicate, parallel lines, will nearly all be converted into tow, which is much less valuable than line; but a good heckler throws the Flax more or less deep among the teeth, according to circumstances, feeling the amount of resistance required, and drawing it with the proper degree of force and velocity.

"To assist the heckler in splitting the filaments, the Flax is sometimes, between the first and second heckling, folded up into a bundle, and beaten upon a block with a wooden mallet, after which it is well rubbed with the hands.. A similar object is gained by bruising it upon a smooth board with a stiff brush, and also by boiling it with potash ley.

"Machines have been contrived for the purpose of superseding heckling by hand, and in all of them the Flax is not drawn through them as in working by hand; but, on the contrary, the sharp points or heckles are moved through the Flax, properly secured."

It has been already mentioned, that applications had been made, both from Sindh and from the Punjab, for some heckles. A few of them have been forwarded by the overland route, also breaks and scutchers, of the excellent manufacture of Mr. Perry, of Hunslet Old Mill, Leeds.

In connection with the foregoing process of heckling, may be mentioned that of dividing the Flax into lengths, as Mr. Tomlinson saw practised in the extensive mills of Messrs. Marshall, of Leeds. "The length of the Flax varies from twenty-six to thirty, or thirty-six inches; the part nearest the root is coarse and strong, the middle part fine and strong, and the upper part still finer, but not so strong. The Flax is therefore divided into three lengths, and the parts from the bottom, middle, and top being collected into separate heaps, or stricks, as they are called, several qualities of thread are afterwards formed from them. Sometimes, however, the whole length of the Flax is divided into four or five parts, which are called middles, ends, and middle and end middles."

This process it is especially desirable to notice, as showing the great importance of having the Flax of uniform quality.

EXPORTS OF LINSEED FROM INDIA.

The large exports of Linseed from India have frequently been mentioned. It is desirable, therefore, to give some of the details. By these we may observe, that though comparatively a recent trade, the article is already known to other countries besides England. The first Export of Linseed was made from Calcutta by Mr. Hodgkinson,

In the year	1832,	to the extent of	10 bushels, and increased
"	1833	"	2,163 maunds.
"	1834	"	2,826 "
"	1837	"	32,327 "
"	1839	"	167,601 "
"	1850	"	765,496 "

As the details of this export may be interesting, we subjoin the following table of the Imports of Linseed and Linseed Oil nto, and Exports from, the three Presidencies :

LINSEED OIL IMPORTED (1850-51) INTO	Calcutta.	Fort St. George	Bombay.
From United Kingdom	Rs. 7,984	—	—
" Amsterdam	805	—	—
LINSEED IMPORTED— From Concan	—	—	Cwt. 59,076
Value	Rs. 8,789	—	Rs. 201,035

Linseed Exported (1850-51) from	Calcutta.	Fort St. George	Bombay.
To United Kingdom	Ms.298,005	Cwt. 797	Cwt. 50,102
,, North America	421,407	—	—
,, France	44,986	—	—
,, Guam	56	—	—
,, Rotterdam	500	—	—
,, Mauritius	60	—	—
,, New South Wales	74	—	—
,, Trieste	384	—	—
,, Penang	24	—	—
,, Ceylon	—	4	—
,, Concan	—	—	10
Total	Ms. 765,496	Cwt. 801	Cwt. 50,112
Value	Rs1,530,902	Rs. 2271	Rs. 170,539

But the commerce of Linseed has since then much increased; amounting in 1852-3, for Bombay, of Linseed imported to 162,015 cwt., and of exported to 114,309 cwt.

Quality of Linseed Oil of India.—It may appear remarkable that Linseed Oil should be imported into Calcutta, when so much Linseed is exported for the express purpose of yielding its oil. This is in consequence of the Linseed Oil of India being considered as not possessed of the full drying properties of the oil prepared in Europe. But there is no doubt, this is owing entirely to the Indian Linseed being expressed before the Mustard seed has been separated, with which it is commonly mixed, in consequence of the two plants being often grown together. Mr. Bowen informed the Author that, when connected with one of the lighthouses in India, he had at one time under his charge some plate glass. This he made use of to separate the two seeds, by placing it on a slope: the round seeds of the Mustard rolled off, while the Linseed merely slipped down. These, when expressed, yielded as good drying oil as any he ever obtained from Europe. The same fact is confirmed by the following statements.

In a report from Mr. W. Ewin, Branch Pilot, to Capt. W. Hope, Master-Attendant at Calcutta, he acknowledges the receipt of five gallons of Linseed Oil, made at the Gloucester Mills, situated below Calcutta.

"I beg leave to say I painted my boat inside green with the above oil, without the assistance of turpentine, and it dried within the space of twenty-four hours; and do not hesitate to say if the above oil agreeable to the muster be given, that it is equal to the Linseed Oil received from the Honorable Company's Marine Yard, said to be Europe.

"Sandheads, H.C.P.V. *Sea Horse*, 2d January, 1837."

So Mr. W. Clark, commanding H.C.F.S.V. *Hope*, writes, 14th Dec., 1836:

"I have to report, for the information of the Master-Attendant, in reply to his letter (No. 39) of the 7th ult., that I have painted the *Hope*, outside, with the Gloucester Mill oil on one side, and that supplied by the Naval Store Keeper on the other,—both laid on at the same time; and of the two I must give the preference to the former, in drying and bearing a better gloss."

IMPORTS OF FLAX, TOW, AND LINSEED INTO GREAT BRITAIN.

In the following table we may see the immense quantities of Flax and of Linseed which are imported into Great Britain.

Account of the quantities of Flax, Tow, and Linseed, imported into the United Kingdom during the year 1851, *distinguishing the countries whence they were imported, and the quantities brought from each.* (*M'Culloch's 'Com. Dict.'*)

	Flax & Tow.	Linseed.
	Cwt.	Cwts.
Russia	818,676	417,950
Prussia	135,825	58,179
Hanseatic Towns	14,925	2,352
Holland	83,121	14,779
Belgium	79,973	55
France	3,802	36
Italy and the Italian Islands	1,885	1,667
Egypt	48,038	36,410
British Territories in the East Indies	48	93,814
United States of America	6	1,152
Other parts	7,885	4,077
Total	1,194,184	630,471

In reference to the expected deficiency of Flax during the year 1854, it has been observed, in the Report of the Irish Society: "So far, however, events have turned out differently from what was anticipated, the permitted import of Russian produce, through the ports of Prussia, having secured even a larger supply than usual of Flax, the quantity received, during the year ended the 5th of October last, being 86,837 tons from all countries, against 74,418 in the same period of 1852-53."

With regard to the cultivation in Ireland, the same Society observes:

From the returns which had been obtained, by order of the Lord-Lieutenant, it appears that the entire area under Flax in Ireland, in the present year, has been 150,972 acres, against 174,579 acres, in 1853. There has thus been a diminution, on the year, of 23,607 acres, or about 14 per cent.

The average annual growth from 1847 to 1853 inclusive, was 101,939, so that the crop of 1854 is about 50 per cent. above the average of the previous seven years.—From the very indifferent yield of the crop of 1853, there is reason to believe that the quantity of marketable fibre this year will be equal to that of the previous crop; and its value may be roughly estimated at about two millions sterling.

So late as 1850, the export of Irish Flax and Tow was but 3166 tons. Of the crop of 1853, the large amount of 7486 tons of Flax and 2763 of Tow—in all 10,249 tons, value £505,989—were shipped from Ireland to England, Scotland, and France.

A very important consideration is the price at which Flax sells. In the year 1840, fine French Flax sold for £90, and ordinary at £80 a ton; Flemish at £80; Friezland at £60; and varieties of Riga at about £48 a ton; at the same time that Jute was selling for £15. At present (Dec., 1854) the prices of Riga Flax vary, according to different marks, from £39 to £48; St. Petersburgh, 12 heads, £51; 9 heads, £45 10*s.*; 6 heads, £40 10*s.*; Archangel crown, from £54 to £59; and the cheaper kinds of Russian and Memel, from £31 to £45; Jute being at the same time sold at Dundee for from £19 10*s.* to £23 10*s.* Egyptian Flax sells for from £33 to £44. The seed is generally sold by the bushel, which weighs from 52 lb. to 54 lb., usually sent from Odessa in bulk, from Italy in sacks; the Riga and Dutch in barrels.

The marks by which several of these Flaxes are distinguished in M'Culloch's 'Dictionary,' are thus explained:

The best Marienburg is called simply Marienburg (M) or Marienburg clean; the second quality, cut (G M); and the third, Risten Dreyband (R D). Of the three other provinces, the first quality bears the name of *rakitzer*; as Druania rakitzer (D R), Thiesenhausen rakitzer (T R), and Lithuania rakitzer (L R). The cut Flax of these three provinces is the second quality, and to the third quality belong the *badstub* and badstub cut (B and B G), the paternoster (P N), and hafs three band (H D). Badstub and paternoster are the refuse of the rakitzer Flax, and the three band again the refuse of the former sorts, and consequently very ordinary. The Revel and Pernau consist of Marienburg, cut, risten, hafs three band, and three band. The Liebau and Memel growths are distinguished by the denomination of four and three band. These two sorts, as well as the Oberland Flax, come from Könisberg, Elbing, &c., and are little esteemed in the British markets.

In the imports of Flax, the terms *Codilla* and *Tow* are very often used as synonymous, but Codilla forms the first workings in the dressing of Flax, and is longer than Tow; it is more or less dirty, and in consequence sometimes cheaper than Tow. The fixed charges on twelve-head Flax at St Petersburg, are 73 roub. 63 cop.; on nine-head Flax, 80 roub. 50 cop.; and on six-head Flax, 91 roub. 61 cop. The charges on Flax in England, taking the price at £45 per ton, are £6 13*s*. 8*d*. (*v*. M'Culloch's 'Com. Dict.')

Since the foregoing parts of this article have been printed, the Author has received a letter from Lahore, dated 21st Oct., 1854, stating that they were led to believe, from various letters, that the production of Flax in the Punjab this year would be "considerable, and that we may look forward to a yield of from 200 to 300 tons of Flax, besides a large quantity of seed."

Dr. Jameson, to whom one of the Flax experiments has been assigned (*v*. p. 190), and whose opinion, from his extensive experience in the culture of Tea and knowledge of the country, is particularly valuable, wrote to the Author from the Himalayas, 6th Nov., 1854, to the following effect: "For some years I have been cultivating Flax on a small scale, from seed procured from Russia, and its fibre has been pronounced by parties in Calcutta, of a very superior description. I have already made arrangements to grow it more extensively this season, in two or three different situations. There is nothing to prevent this country supplying both Flax and Hemp on a vast scale. It possesses immense advantages in abundance of land and cheap labour. In the Punjab thousands of acres are available; and from the means of producing both Hemp and Flax cheap, this part of India will always be able to compete with other countries."

CONCLUSION.

The account of Flax has extended to a much greater length than is perhaps suited to the nature of the work. This is owing, partly to our having taken the opportunity of treating rather fully of the different points connected with the culture and preparation of this fibre, and partly to our having treated in detail of the attempts which have been already made to cultivate Flax in India. This we have done, in order to ascertain, if possible, the causes of failure, or rather of the want of commercial success; while the examination of the various questions connected with the analyses of soils, of the Flax and its products, as well as of steep-water, and the various methods which are now adopted for separating this fibre, cannot fail to suggest to cultivators in the East some methods of improving their own practice. Having already made some observations (*v*. p. 185) on the results of their experiments, we need now only observe that the chief want, seems to have been that of moisture during the season of cultivation. Therefore, we cannot but think, that when this deficiency is supplied, either by canal irrigation, or by the nature of the climate, as in the present experiments (*v*. pp. 188—195), that success will attend the efforts, and that the example will be useful to other districts. Considering the prices at which Indian-grown Flax formerly sold for in England, and the cost of growing such fibres as Jute and Sunn, which have long been sold at from £15 to £20, it appears quite possible to grow Flax as a profitable crop, especially as it is said that in some situations even the seed pays for the expenses of cultivation. But in case the fibre should not be good enough as Flax, some would be available as tow, and some for paper-makers, especially if reduced to the state of half-stuff by the use of the Indian dhenkee. The extra labour required for the preparation of the fibre can certainly be supplied as cheaply and as profitably in India as in any other country of the world. But if any difficulty is experienced, it would be easy for planters to induce native cultivators to grow the Flax in any particular manner and to sell it at certain rates, as they now do the Indigo plant. This the European now manufactures into Indigo of such excellent quality, as to hold the first place in all markets. Much of the same success might attend the culture of Flax if the climate were equally suitable; but it is yet sufficiently favorable in many parts to admit of at least as much success as has been attained in Egypt. It is only requisite that Rettories according to some one of the improved methods should be established in a few central situations, to which the ryuts could bring the results of their cheap agricultural labours, and where a due subdivision of labour and manufacturing cheapness could be substituted for a mixed system, suited only to early states of society.

LINDEN, JUTE, &c., of the family of *Tiliaceæ*.

The *Tiliaceæ* or Linden tribe are so named from the well-known European tree—a favorite in parks and public walks, and the source of an extensive commerce, inasmuch as the mats which are imported in such enormous quantities, are formed of the bark of this tree. But in the same family with the Linden tree, botanists place also the genus *Corchorus*, species of which yield the now well-known Jute of India, as well as the genera *Grewia* and *Triumfetta*, both of which contain species remarkable for the tenacity of their bark. The Tiliaceæ are also remarkable for mucilaginous properties. The leaves of many are edible, and the fruit of some afford pleasantly tasted acid berries.

LIME or LINDEN TREE (*Tilia europæa*), and RUSSIA MATS.

The Lime tree abounds in the forests of Europe, but especially in those of Russia; and is esteemed for its sweet-scented flowers. The wood of the tree is white and light, and employed for making furniture, for turning, and for carved works. The bark of these trees when steeped in water soon separates into thin layers, which are employed for making a coarse kind of rope, for making matted shoes much worn by the Russian peasantry, and also for making the mats which are so largely exported from Russia, and which are so extensively used in this country for packing furniture, as well as for gardening purposes, and for covering the floor. A Linden shoot growing in moist situations, is stated by Mr. Tooke as not fit for peeling, for the purpose of being platted into shoes, in less time than three years. To every pair of shoes, from two to four young Linden stems are requisite; and though these grow faster as they are cut, yet the consumption is enormous, and the destruction of the Linden tree is in consequence immense. For the better, larger kind of mats, trees of from eight to sixteen years are cut down when full of sap, and the bark is immediately separated both from the tree and the branches. It is first cut longitudinally, then raised with an instrument made of bone, and then torn off with the hand. When the bark has been removed, it is stretched on the ground to dry, two or three strips being laid one over the other, and kept straight by being tied down to long poles. They are employed for making ropes in some parts of England, and for well-ropes in France. When required for use, they are steeped in water, and the cortical layers readily separate from each other. The best of these layers are those which are in the interior, while the coarser layers are on the outside.

The manufacture of mats is nearly confined to Russia and to some parts of Sweden. Trees of from six inches to one foot in diameter are selected in the woods, and in the beginning of summer the bark is stripped from the trees in lengths of from six feet to eight feet. These are afterwards steeped in water, till the bark separates freely into layers; it is then taken out and separated into ribands or strands, which are hung up in the shade—generally in the wood where the trees grew from which they were taken; and in the course of the summer they are manufactured into mats. The fishermen of Sweden make fishing nets out of the fibres of the inner bark.

The trees from which the bark is taken are cut down in the summer, and, properly cut, are burnt in heaps into charcoal.

The sap is drawn off, and, when evaporated, yields sugar. The honey of the flowers is much sought after by bees.

The Lime tree is principally produced in the government of Vialka, Kostroma, and those immediately contiguous; and in the months of May and June—the period when the bark is most easily detached from the stem—the villages in the governments in question are almost deserted, the whole population being then in the woods employed in stripping the trees. The academician Köppen, who has carefully investigated this curious subject, estimates the average annual production of mats in European Russia, as follows:

Government of Vialka	6,000,000	pieces
" Kostroma	4,000,000	"
" Kasan	1,000,000	"
" Nijni Novgorod	1,000,000	"
" Vologda, Tamboff, Simbirsk, and Penza	2,000,000	"
Total	14,000,000	"

Köppen further estimates that about a fourth part of this

vast quantity, or $3\frac{1}{2}$ millions, are exported, the rest being consumed at home.

Archangel is the principal port for the shipment of mats, and it appears that on an average of the years 1851 and 1852, the export of mats from that port amounted to 615,360 pieces a year. Large quantities are also shipped from Petersburgh, Riga, and other ports. (M'Culloch's 'Com. Dict.')

The extent of the Imports of Russia Mats into this country may be judged of by the following statement furnished to the Author by Messrs. Wrench:

Year	Mats	Year	Mats
1832	840,000	1847	520,359
1840	817,772	1848	397,553
1841	508,485	1849	576,565
1842	532,401	1850	359,223
1843	861,565	1851	734,659
1844	449,817	1852	333,008
1845	634,041	1853	657,040
1846	898,619		

The price in Jan., 1834, was £4 10*s.* per 100, the duty included; in 1848, 95s. to 100*s.*; and in 1849, under 80*s.* In 1850, 90*s.*; 1851, 87*s.* 6*d.*; 1852, 85*s.* to 100*s.*; and in 1853, 120*s.* per 100.

Indian Substitutes for Russian Bast.

As stated above, botanists place in the same family of plants the European Tilia and the species of the Indian Grewia, from resemblance in points of structure. So, if we inquire into the uses of these plants, we shall find, that as Lime leaves used to be, and still are, employed in some parts of Europe, both in a green and dry state, as fodder for cattle, so in the Himalayas, cattle are fed with leaves of *Grewia didyma*, and some are stacked for winter use, for cattle, sheep, and goats; as the Author, when travelling there observed. As the inner bark of the Linden yields bast for mats, so is the inner bark of *Grewia oppositifolia*, called *bihul*, employed in the same mountains for making ropes.

The inner bark of many trees is employed in other parts of India for the same purposes, though it is not easy to identify the plants, from only local names being usually given by travellers. Thus, in the following account given by Capt. Biddulph in a letter to the Agri-Horticultural Society of India, in the year 1843, he states that, near Darjeeling, "the Lepchas make rope from the fibre of the Kullyhain, and stout bowstrings and sewing thread from the fibre of the Ruffickee tree." "Nothing can be more simple," Capt. Biddulph states, "than their mode of manufacture: the bark is torn off the Kullyhain when from five to fifteen years' growth; the inner bark or fibre is then detached, as shown in the specimen, washed for a few minutes in water, and when dry, pared or pulled into narrow strips, and twisted by the hand into rope of any thickness. The bark of the Ruffickee is taken off the plant when five or six feet high, and treated in the same manner as the former, except that the outer bark only requires to be scraped off with a knife. All the Lepcha fishing nets are made from the Ruffickee, and are remarkably light and strong."

Among the Mallow tribe (or *Malvaceæ*), and some allied families, as we shall afterwards see, there are several other instances of the same kind. To the Great Exhibition of 1851, specimens of several kinds of Bast were sent, both from Assam and from Arracan. Of these, the specimens sent from the latter were so promising, that the Author was induced to send them for examination and trial to the Horticultural Society's Garden at Chiswick; and as the opinion formed respecting them was favorable, he included the information in the following report:

"Having been lately much engaged in examining and showing to practical men the various fibres which were sent to the Great Exhibition of 1851, as well as those which have recently arrived from Assam, I was induced to turn my attention *to the subject of Bast*. Of this, large quantities are imported into this country, in the form of mats, from Russia, chiefly for the use of gardeners, who use them for covering pits and frames, or protecting plants, and afterwards, when pulled to pieces, for tying up plants and vegetables. The mats are also extensively used for packing cabinet-work and furniture in general.

"The subject may appear trifling, but it is calculated that

about 3,500,000 mats are exported from Russia, and about 500,000 to 800,000 are annually imported into this country. They are made of the bark of the Lime or Linden tree, which, when stripped off, is also made into shoes, cordage, sacks for corn, &c. The Linden tree is not found in India; but there are many which belong to the same family of plants found there, some of which probably yield similar products, possibly one or two of those to which I now wish to draw attention.

"Among the raw products sent from the province of Arracan, there were six kinds of Bast (which there seems to be called *Shaw*), with specimens of rope made with them. They were named—1, Theng-ban shaw; 2, Pa-tha-you shaw; 3, Shaw-phyoo; 4, Ngán-tsoung shaw; 5, Shaw-nee; 6, Eee-gywot shaw. Observing that some of these, from their strength, flexibility, and softness, were well calculated to answer the purposes of the Bast in ordinary use, I sent some specimens to Dr. Lindley, and requested him to have their useful properties ascertained in the Horticultural Society's Garden at Chiswick. As he informed me that both the Superintendents, Messrs. Thompson and Gordon, reported very favorably of them, I requested the latter to give me a detailed report, including all such information as would be useful to merchants in Arracan. The kinds sent to him were No. 2, Pa-tha-you shaw; 3, Shaw-phyoo; and one marked *Sanseviera zeylanica*, was probably a specimen from Cuttack.

"Though well aware that the freight must always operate against a bulky article of low price brought from so great a distance, yet there are occasions when, from a stoppage of, or a deficient supply from, ordinary sources, a rise of price ensues, which might be taken advantage of at a place on the coast like Akyab. I would, therefore, beg to suggest that the accompanying report should be sent to India for the information of the merchants in Arracan, or for publication in the journals in India. At all events, a knowledge of the good qualities of these Indian Basts might lead to their employment in India, and to their export to less distant countries than England. As it is possible that merchants in Arracan might wish to make mats in imitation of the Russian, I would suggest that a piece of one of these might be sent there; as by this the thickness of the transverse and the pliability of the longitudinal pieces of the Bast of which they are composed might easily be imitated.

"East India House, Jan. 16, 1854."

Report upon new kinds of Bast-matting from India.

"Hort. Soc. Gardens, Chiswick,
January 11, 1854.

"Sir,—The three pieces of Indian Bast sent appear all the same, at least I cannot detect any difference in their qualities or appearance; and I think, when it is made into mats, will prove an excellent substitute for Russian mats. It is very strong, is in broad strands, very pliable and tough when wetted, easily divided into small portions for the purpose of tying, &c., and is entirely free from knotty places; and when worked into mats in the Russian way, will be an excellent winter covering for pits and frames. The material, also, seems more firm and tough, and, I have no doubt, will last at least twice as long (in wear) as the best Russian mats; and, if sold at a less price, will in time supersede them.

"The price of Russian mats is now from £7 10*s*. to £8 per 100, wholesale; and from 2*s*. to 2*s*. 6*d*. each, retail.

"A full-sized Russian mat weighs about 5 lb. when new and quite dry, is 7 feet long and 4 feet broad, and is made with the rougher and worst strands worked crossways, and the thinner and longer strands longways in the mats.

"In making mats, it should be observed never to have any of them under the regular size, for small mats (either shorter or narrower) greatly detract from the value of full-sized ones when mixed with them.

"I remain, sir, your obedient servant,

"George Gordon.

"To Dr. Royle, &c. &c."

The appearance of these basts may be thus described. All were sent in the state of bast, and twisted into rope, from Akyab in Arracan. The price of all stated to be one rupee a maund, or about 3*s*. a cwt.

1. *Theng-ban shaw.*—Coarse-looking, and of a reddish-brown colour, but divisible into a number of very thin layers, with a good deal of flexibility, and some toughness. A portion twisted into rope.

2. *Pa-tha-you shaw.*—Strips seven feet in length, and fine in texture, light-coloured, formed of several easily divisible layers; the outer layers rather dense and compact, and the inner cancellar. A Musæ species (?).

3. *Shaw-phyoo.*—Long, thin, smooth layers, light-coloured, tough, and flexible; easily divisible into still finer layers.

4. *Ngan-tsoung shaw.*—Fibres and rope sent, but mislaid.

5. *Shaw-nee.*—Of a reddish-brown colour, rough and coarse, but twisted into rope.

6. *Eee-gywot shaw.*—Strips five to six feet in length, composed of several layers; of which one side is smooth and compact, but the layers on the other side thin but cancellar, all having a considerable degree of toughness.

Mr. Ripley, in 'Journ. Agri-Hortic. Soc.,' viii, p. 147, describes three barks under the names *Shaw-ne, Shaw-phrus*, and *Batharan shaw*. These may be Nos. 5, 3, and 2. But the spelling differs much. He also mentions several useful Rattans at Akyab.

There are no doubt a great variety of other basts, which might easily be procured from trees in Assam, Arracan, and all along the Malayan Peninsula, as well as on the Malabar Coast. In an account by Mr. Fenwick of the vegetable products of the Tenasserim he mentions a bast rope of considerable strength, and also that plantains and pine-apples are very abundant there. All the above places are on the sea-coast, or accessible by river. But Akyab, where so many are already produced, seems the most favorable situation for their export to Europe, if it should be found desirable. It is probable that several might be much improved by a little steeping in water, as practised with the Russian bast.

Some of those sent to the Exhibition of 1851, and of which the plants are unknown, may here be mentioned.

Patoo or *Asta* is a bast from Beerbhoom, is like the Putwa from Bhagulpore, and will be noticed with it.

Chehoor, a pale, brownish-coloured cordage from Beerbhoom, coarse, and of moderate strength.

Bark string, made by Hill tribes of Rajmahl, of useful size and strength.

Bark rope, with the coarse but strong fibre of which it is made: also from Rajmahl.

Several Bark cloths from the Islands, &c., will be mentioned with the Paper Mulberry, formerly *Morus*, now *Broussonetia papyrifera*.

There is a remarkable cord without name, which seems to be formed of a salvage of fibre, with a yellowish bark folded or laid round it, and of these, two threads so made up are twisted into a cord.

A bark like some sent as that of *Odina Wodier*, is full of fibrous material.

One of the best of the basts, and seemingly as like one of those from Arracan, was sent from Assam; the strips are from six to seven and eight feet in length, consisting of several layers, easily separable, tough, flexible, and strong. They have the number on them of the box in which was conveyed, and in which were contained Pine-apple fibre; but their appearance is totally different.

Several of the basts of different plants which are used by the natives, and of which the names have been ascertained, will be mentioned under the heads of *Hibiscus arboreus*, or *tiliaceus*, *Sterculia villosa* and *guttata*, *Bauhinia racemosa* and *scandens*, *Celtis orientalis*, *Antiaris Saccada*. Capt. Thompson reports upon a bast rope made by the Munnee-poorees, and on another from Singapore. ('Journ. Agri-Hortic. Soc.,' viii, p. 45.)

JUTE, JEW'S MALLOW (*Corchorus olitorius* and *capsularis*, *Tiliaceæ*).

Sans., *Putta*; Beng., *Pat*; fibre, *Jute*; cloth, *tat*, *chotee*, *megila*.

The name Jute is now so familiarly known, and this fibre is so extensively employed in some of our manufactures, that one is apt to think that it must have long been established as an article of commerce. This is far from being the case, for we find no notice of it even in comparatively recent dictionaries of commerce; and it is not above fifteen years since that it has come to be much employed in the manufactures of this country, though it has long been so employed in India, and its fibres much used for making both cordage and cloth.

Under the name of Jute, however, the fibre of two very distinct plants is included, though no recent accounts have been published by any of the present growers of Jute. Both plants are common in almost every part of India; the leaves of both are used as pot-herbs, and the stems of both yield fibre, and are cultivated on both these accounts; and both are placed by botanists in the genus Corchorus, which is so named from the *Korkhoros* of the Greeks, which also was a pot-herb, and, indeed, is by many supposed to have been one of the very plants which we have now to describe. This is the species called *Corchorus olitorius*, which is still cultivated in the neighbourhood of Aleppo, and is described by travellers in the East as eaten for a pot-herb in Egypt and Arabia, as well as in Palestine. Rauwolf saw the Jews about Aleppo using the leaves as a pot-herb; hence the old name of "Olus judaicum" in old authors; which by the French is translated Mauve de Juif, and by us "Jew's Mallow." It is supposed to be the plant alluded to in 'Job,' xxx, 4.[1] It is the same plant which, small and herbaceous in the dry soil of Syria, grows to a height of four or five feet in the North of India; but in the hot, moist climate of Bengal, attains a size that allows fibres of twelve feet in length to be separated from it.

The other plant, which we suppose also yields some of the Jute of commerce, is *Corchorus capsularis*, easily distinguished from the other by the form of its seed-vessels being globular instead of elongated and cylindrical. It is also more remarkable for an east and west, than for a north and south distribution. We have stated that it is to be found in most parts of India, and likewise in Ceylon. It is curious that Rumphius, in his 'Herb. Amboinense,' v. 212, t. 78, describes it under the name of Ganja (but this may be pronounced Gania), which is that applied in India to the true Hemp. By Malays it is called *Rami Tsjina*, that is, Chinese Rami; a name which we shall find is also applied by them to other fibre-yielding plants, as to the true Hemp, according to Rumphius, and also to the *Urtica nivea*, as we shall see under the head of China-grass. It is no doubt cultivated in China, where Roxburgh states it is called *Oi moa*.

This so-called Chinese Hemp—but a true Corchorus—was at one time supposed to be superior to the true Hemp, and attempts were made to introduce it into England; the account of which is detailed in the 'Phil. Trans.,' vol. lxxii. It is there stated, that seeds sown in England produced plants fourteen feet high, and nearly seven inches in circumference, though few produced mature seeds. But some, however, which came to maturity in the second season produced a crop

[1] 'Malluach,' in Kitto's 'Cyclopædia of Biblical Literature.'

16

of good Hemp, greater by one third than was ever known to be obtained in England. We may easily believe, therefore, that this may grow to a great height in the congenial climate of Bengal.

As both these plants seem to yield the fibre called Jute, we may describe both, before proceeding to treat of their culture or the mode adopted by the natives of India for separating their fibre.

Corchorus olitorius, Pot-herb, or Jew's Mallow, as seen in the Mediterranean region, is an herbaceous annual plant, only a foot or two, but in India of several feet in height, and erect in habit. The stem is smooth, cylindrical, and more or less branched. The leaves are of a lively green colour and smooth, alternate, on footstalks, oval or ovo-lanceolate in shape, with the margin dentate, and with the two lower dentilures terminated by a slender filament. The stipules are simple, awl-shaped, and reddish coloured at their base. The peduncles or flower-stalks are one- to two-flowered. The flowers are small, having the calyx consisting of five pieces or sepals, and the corolla of five yellow petals. Stamens numerous. Torus, or nectary cup-shaped, with glands at the base of the petals. Ovary solitary, ripening into a long, nearly cylindrical capsule, ten-ribbed, six to eight times longer than it is broad, five-celled, and formed of five valves, with five terminal points. Seeds numerous, with nearly perfect transverse partitions between them.

This is called *Putta* in Sanscrit, and *Pat* in Bengalee; flowers in the rainy season, and fructifies in October and November. Cloth made of it is called *Tat*, the fibre *Jute*.

Dr. Roxburgh states that there is a reddish variety of this, which the natives call *Bun Pat*, that is, Wild Pat.

Corchorus capsularis, or Capsular Corchorus, is also an annual, with a straight, smooth, and cylindrical, afterwards branched stem, from four and five to eight and ten feet in height. The leaves have long footstalks, and are oval, acuminate, thin, and of a light green; serrated at their margins, with the two lower serratures terminating in narrow filaments. The flowers are small, yellow, and like those of the other species in the number of their parts. The capsules are short and globose, wrinkled and muricated, with five cells, and composed of five valves; seeds few in each cell, and without transverse partitions. It flowers in the rainy season, and the fruit is ripe in September and October.

This is the *Ghi-nalita pat* of the Bengalese, and its fibre sometimes called *Nalta jute*. It is called *isbund* in North-West India. It has been called Chinese Hemp (*Rami tsjina*) by the Malays, and its fibre *China pat* by Roxburgh. The kind called *Teetah* pat is said to be a variety of this species.

It is cultivated both in Bengal and in China, on account of its fibre, which is separated by maceration, and used as cordage, both for agricultural purposes and for river navigation, as well as for making paper. It is also employed for making the coarse kind of cloth called Megila in Bengal; and another kind called *tat* or *choti*, whence, probably, has been derived the name *Jute*. This kind of cloth is now well known by the name *gunny*, and used for making *gunny bags*; a name derived either from the Ganja or Gania of Rumphius, or from *goni*, a name of *Crotalaria juncea* on the Madras side, (Buchanan); there the name Jute is in some places applied to its fibre, and also to that of *Hibiscus cannabinus*.

There are several other species of Corchorus common as weeds in every part of India, but all may easily be distinguished from the last by the roundish form of its capsules. The Author has found species at as great an elevation as 5000 feet in the Himalayas, but only in the rainy season.

Dr. Buchanan found both the above species cultivated in the districts of Dinajpore, Rungpore, and Purneya. In the last he was informed, that the Corchorus which is used for cordage is the species called by botanists *olitorius*, while that used as a pot-herb is the *capsularis*; just the reverse of what is the case in some other places, showing the probability of both species being cultivated for their fibres.

The fibre is long, soft, and silky, and well fitted for many of the purposes to which Flax is applied, as it is divisible into very fine fibrils, which, like those of the other species, are easily spun. It is possessed also of some strength and durability, even after 116 days' maceration, as in Dr. Roxburgh's experiments. Under the microscope, the fibres of the two species seem exactly alike.

It is generally stated that the fibres of Jute, or of those employed in making gunny bags, cannot be bleached. This is incorrect; they may not be bleached by ordinary methods. Indeed, a paper-maker mentioned to the Author, having discovered Jute in some rope, because it would not bleach. But the late Col. Calvert brought several specimens of beautifully bleached Jute to the India House, as well as some furniture damask made of it; and we observe that Mr. Rogers presented some of his bleached specimens to the Agri-Horticultural Society, in May, 1846.

Dr. Roxburgh has described the species *C. olitorius* as the Pat of the Bengalese, and as partially grown for the leaves and tender shoots, which are used by the natives—both Hindoos and Mussulmans—as an article of food. When wild it shoots out many lateral branches, which renders it a difficult matter to separate the fibres from the woody parts. In preparing the filaments, the plant requires much longer steeping in water than Hemp—a fortnight or three weeks being scarcely sufficient for its proper maceration. (*v.* p. 248.) He called attention to it as a substitute for Flax, from the length and fineness of its fibre.

The gunny bags, in which sugar and similar commodities are brought to this country from India, are made of this material. These are now sent to America for packing their cotton. Though only made known in the beginning of the century, it is now imported in immense quantities, and used for a variety of purposes, as it spins so easily, and being cheap, is therefore used for mixing. It used to be employed for mixing with Codilla; this is now used for mixing with Jute.

A description of the cultivation and manufacture of Jute was given by Baboo Ram Comul Sen (in 'Trans. Agri-Hortic. Soc.,' vol. ii, p. 91), where he mentions that the principal places where it is cultivated are Malda, Purnea, Natore, Rungpore, and Dacca—where both land and labour are cheap. He mentions four kinds—*Pat, Tasa, Mestah,* and *Coshta*—but without describing them; and quotes Roxburgh's descriptions of *C. olitorius, C. capsularis,* and *C. fuscus.*

Other names are given in other districts, as at Jungypore: 1, *Ghore Sun*; 2, *Puut*; 3, *Cooch-murda Paut*; 4, *Amleeah Paut.* The first and fourth may be Crotalaria and Hibiscus, and the second and third species of Corchorus. These may also be included under the names of *Amrah Sun, Chunduna Sun,* and *Putooa Sun.* Some Jute sent to the Exhibition of 1851, from Rungpore, was distinguished by the names of Suffed (white) Hemanty Pat; 2, Lal (red) Hemanty Pat; and 3, Lal Petrie Pat.

Culture.—The seeds are sown in April or May, when there is a sufficient quantity of rain to moisten the ground, which is generally low, and harrowed in the same manner as paddy (rice) land (in any land that will produce summer rice, which requires to be well ploughed and smoothed). The field is weeded after the plants are a foot and half high. When it has flowered, which happens about July and August (to 14th

Sept.,—B.), it is cut. The plants are three to twelve feet high, and the circumference of the stalk is about one inch. As the seed is not ripe when the plants are cut, some of them are left, to allow the seeds to come to maturity.

After the plants are cut down close to the roots, their tops are clipped off, and fifty to a hundred are tied together; ten to fifteen of these bundles are laid in a shallow tank or reservoir of water, like rafts, over which a quantity of turf and clods of earth are laid to make them sink under the surface of the water; it is allowed to remain there for eight or ten days, during which the cultivator daily visits it, in order to see that it is properly laid, and the trunks are not unduly rotted. When the bark separates, and the stalk and fibres become soft, the weight upon the raft is removed, and the stalks are unbundled. The dresser descends into the water knee-deep, and takes up five to eight sticks at a time. He breaks off two feet of them at the bottom; the bark, which is become soft like thread, is held in both hands, and the stalks are taken off. The fibres thus separated (and by mere washing are brought to the state of separated fibres,—B.), are dressed, and exposed to the sun, by hanging the bundles of fibres over bamboos to dry; they are afterwards partially cleaned, and finally made up into bundles of from one to two maunds for the market.

After the Pat has been removed, the fields of which the soil and elevation are suitable grow a winter crop of tobacco or mustard seed. The produce is differently stated to be from 400 lb. to 700 lb. per acre. The harvest price, according to Dr. Buchanan, was, in his time, about 12½ annas per 100 lb. Mr. Henley informs the Author that "Jute used to be sold some years ago for R. 1 8 for the bazar maund; but the demand in this country had had the effect of raising the price of Jute to double its old Indian value. At present, any fine, long, silky Jute is eagerly bought up at Rs. 2 8; still for inferior Jute I should say, dealing face to face with the village dulals, the price would not exceed R. 1 8 per bazar maund."

The culture of Jute has of late years been greatly improved in many places, as may be seen in much of that sent to market, and of which we have an instance in the sample of Jute presented for report by Mr. P. Carter of Bhojepore Factory to the Agri-Horticultural Society. This having been submitted to the members of the Flax Committee, the following favorable opinion has been expressed on it:

Mr. Hodgkinson.—This is the finest specimen of Jute I have ever seen—being bright, clean, strong, and of excellent staple; the root ends particularly well freed of the hard woody bark which characterises bazar Jute, and deteriorates its value.

I should say that £16 to £17 could be obtained for Jute of similar quality at home, being fully £2 per ton more than the ordinary descriptions now fetch.

Mr. Fergusson.—It is very good Jute, worth £3 to £4 per ton more than what is generally shipped.

Dr. Buchanan and Ram Comul Sen describe the Pat as spun by two kinds of spindles, the Takur and Dhara. A bunch of the raw material is hung up in every farmer's house, or to the protruding stick of a thatched roof, and every one who has leisure, forms with one or other of these spindles, some coarse packthread (sutoli), of which ropes are twisted for the use of the farm. The Dhara is a reel, on which a thread when sufficiently twisted, is wound up. The Takur is a kind of spindle which is turned upon the thigh or the sole of the foot. Ghurghurea is a third kind of spinning machine. It is only the lower Hindu castes, called Rajbongsi, Konget, and Polya, that form this packthread for being woven into sackcloth, and spin a finer thread from which the cloth called Megili, or Megila, is woven. By far the greater part of the cloth that is used dyed, receives the colour in the state of thread.

The coarse cloth, called Megili, is woven by the women of the lower class of people. Most families have a loom, and the people, especially the women in the afternoons, work a little occasionally, and this serves to clothe the family. The pieces consist of three or four narrow cloths sewed together, some four or five cubits long, and from two to three cubits wide, and are worth from two to eight annas each. Some have red and black borders. It is said to be more durable than cloth made of cotton.

CHATEE, OR JUTE CLOTH FOR GUNNY BAGS.

The kind of cloth called *chatee* is made from the same material, and is made of three different kinds, and always woven in pieces from three quarters to one cubit wide, of which two or three are sewn together into one piece before it is sold. The first kind, intended for bedding, is from four to five cubits long, and from two and a quarter to three cubits wide, and sells at about 8 rupees per 100 pieces. Secondly, that intended for covering bales of cloth is of the same dimensions, but is thicker than the former kind. The 100 pieces cost from 6 to 10 rupees. Thirdly, that intended for making rice- and sugar-bags is four cubits long, and one and a half or one and a quarter cubit wide, and ten bags cost 4 or 5 rupees. These are sewed or doubled and made into bags. The value of the manufacture in the Dinajepore district amounted to 160,000 rupees. (Buchanan.)

The principal places where Chatees are manufactured are Malda, Purnea, Natore, Rungpore, and Dacca; where the cultivation of Jute is extensive, and the price of labour and land very cheap. Ram Comul Sen says, "If the labour of spinning the Jute and weaving Chatee, are to be done according to the rules of labour at Calcutta, the price of gunny would be more than double that for which it is sold."

The greater part is cultivated by those who use or manufacture it; for almost all the small Hindu farmers weave cloth of this material, and every farmer requires some for the use of his farm.

On all the eastern frontier a great proportion of the women are clothed in the coarse cloth made of the Corchorus, which also gives them much employment. The value of the material consumed in those days was about 70,000 rupees. In the cold weather the poor cover themselves by night, and often by day with a sackcloth rug; and the rich usually put one under their bedding. Some is required for the packing of tobacco and for some grains, but much even in those days was exported to Calcutta, Patna, and other places. In the north-west part of Bengal a great proportion of the people used to be clothed with Megili or Pata. Specimens of this Pat clothing were sent to the Exhibition of 1851.

Since the foregoing remarks were written, indeed, since they have been in type, the Author has been favoured with the accompanying remarks from Mr. Henley, who has already been mentioned at pp. 36 and 168, and whom he had asked for some recent information respecting the culture and preparation of Jute.

The plant in question is by far the most extensively cultivated of all the fibrous family throughout the delta of Bengal. Its easy culture, rapid growth, and comparatively large produce present advantages not to be overlooked by that eminently practical and economical people, the natives of Bengal. Had it combined along with these advantages, the qualities of strength and durability, it would probably have superseded all other fibrous materials; but, rapid in its growth, it is again remarkably rapid in its decay—being in fact the most perishable of fibres. It is generally grown as an after-crop, during the rainy season, on high land, or land not subject to submersion, like rice land. A hot and moderately rainy season suits it best; excessive rains or bad drainage injure and deteriorate it. In this point of view it is a precarious and delicate crop; otherwise it presents the advantage of affording a more valuable return from land at that season, than any other crop which the cultivator can employ. It is sown broadcast, requires careful weeding when young, but soon acquires strength enough to keep off all intruders. The young leaves are eaten by the natives as a sort of spinach; they have, however, a coarse, weedy flavour, little suited to our European palates. No plant is more grateful for good cultivation than the one in question, in a good, loamy soil, well manured, or which has been well manured under a former crop. It attains a height of ten or twelve feet, with stems of three quarters of an inch in diameter. A poor crop, or one which had suffered from excessive rains, would have a height of only from three to six feet.

The crop being ripe, the stems are cut down close to the roots, made up into bundles, and laid to steep in some neighbouring ditch, where lumps of mud are placed on them to keep them submerged. Here they are carefully watched from day to day, the operator trying the bark with his nail, until he finds the decomposition arrived at the proper point. In preparing Jute intended for export, he will push the water-retting process to its utmost limits, short of actually destroying the fibre by excessive putrefaction. This is done in order to obtain that thoroughly detached silky character of fibre, according to which it is valued in the export market. Such Jute has always suffered more or less in strength.—Jute or Paut prepared for native consumption is much more durable than that prepared for export. It is likewise cheaper, as the yield per acre is much larger. It is much darker coloured, and not so clean. The natives are very particular in the selection of Jute for such purposes as pack-saddle bags for their transport oxen; or for their store-grain bags—great packages of six or eight feet diameter, erected on bamboo stages, and looking like our European brewery tuns. There are also a multitude of manufactures in this fibre, many of them possessed of considerable strength, some again of very fine texture.

To return to our water-retting process. The proper point being attained, the native operator, standing up to his middle in water, takes as many of the sticks in his hands as he can grasp, and removing a small portion of the bark from the ends next the roots, and grasping them together, he strips off the whole with a little management, from end to end, without breaking either stem or fibre. Having prepared a certain quantity into this half state, he next proceeds to wash off: this is done by taking a large handful; swinging it round his head he dashes it repeatedly against the surface of the water, drawing it through towards him, so as to wash off the impurities; then, with a dexterous throw he fans it out on the surface of the water, and carefully picks off all remaining black spots. It is now wrung out so as to remove as much water as possible, and then hung up on lines prepared on the spot, to dry in the sun.

Jute is never so beautiful as at the first moment of its preparation; for such is its proneness to decay—a true eremacausis of Liebig—that it changes colour from day to day, gradually descending from the beautiful pearly white, through shades of fawn colour and brown, with proportionate loss of strength. These changes, also, are occasioned or accelerated by causes which hardly affect other fibres; hence, one of the difficulties of bleaching, and the tendency to become brown, of all fabrics consisting of this material. That portion of the hank of fibre next the root, or where it has been held in the hand, being always more or less contaminated with bark and impurities, is cut off for about nine inches. These ends are sold to the paper-makers, and for mixing and making up various thick, coarse fabrics, of which whole cargoes, amounting to tens of thousands of pieces, are now annually taken off by the Americans from Calcutta, for cotton bagging and similar purposes, forming an entirely new trade.[1]

But the great trade and principal employ of Jute is for the manufacture of Gunny chuts or chuttees, *i.e.*, lengths suitable for making bags. This industry forms the grand domestic manufacture of all the populous eastern districts of Lower Bengal. It pervades all classes, and penetrates into every household. Men, women, and children find occupation therein. Boatmen in their spare moments, husbandmen, palankeen-carriers, and domestic servants; everybody in fact, being Hindoos—for Mussulmans spin cotton only—pass their leisure moments, distaff in hand, spinning Gunny twist. Its preparation, together with the weaving into lengths, forms the never-failing resource of that most humble, patient, and despised of created beings—the Hindoo widow—saved by law from the pile, but condemned by opinion and custom for the remainder of her days, literally to sackcloth and ashes, and the lowest domestic drudgery in the very household where once, perhaps, her will was law. This manufacture spares her from being a charge on her family—she can always earn her bread.—Amongst these causes will be discerned the very low prices at which Gunny manufactures are produced in Bengal, and which have attracted the demand of the whole commercial world. There is, perhaps, no other article so universally diffused over the globe as the Indian Gunny bag. All the finer and long-stapled Jute is reserved for the export trade, in which it bears a comparatively high price. The short staple serves for the local manufactures, and it may be remarked, that a given weight of Gunny bags may be purchased at about the same price as a similar weight of raw material—leaving no apparent margin for spinning and weaving.

The stems or stalks of the Jute crop are of almost equal value with the fibrous portion. They are beautiful white and straight stems, of a light, brittle wood, somewhat like willow switches, and have a multitude of uses amongst the natives, such as for the manufacture of charcoal for gunpowder and fireworks, for the formation of fences and enclosures, for pea and similar cultivation, and for the construction of those acres of basket-work which the traveller may remark near every native village. These are the enclosures in which the betel-pepper vine is cultivated, the leaf of which is

[1] The manufacture of Jute whiskey from these ends was tried experimentally, by subjecting them to the process of conversion into sugar with sulphuric acid, and afterwards fermenting. The produce had much resemblance to grain whiskey.

universally consumed by the million—peer or peasant. These stems have another extensive employ which cannot be passed unnoticed—that of furnishing a peculiar quality of fuel suited to the native process of careening boats on the banks of the rivers. Great flaming fires may be observed at night under the bottoms and sides of the native craft; men running to and fro with bundles of flaming faggots, applying them assiduously, as if they were occupied in trying to burn the craft. Looking at the structures themselves, built up of mats and thatch, and appearing like slovenly, ill-conditioned hay stacks, that an accidental spark would ignite, it appears surprising that such a determined effort should not produce that result. The only object, however, is to effect the destruction of the myriads of worms or teredæ, who, if not destroyed, would in a very short time have eaten up the whole fabric.

Bengal Jute has now attained such an important position in the commerce of the world, that any suggestion for its improved production merits attention; and there can be no doubt but that the application to it of the process of preparing the fibre without water-retting, would effect the most signal improvement in its qualities. Such could never make it equal to Flax or Hemp; but the method would increase the qualities of strength and durability, and fit it for all purposes in which moisture took no part, for to this agent it is peculiarly obnoxious. In reference to this point it may be worth noticing, that in cases in which it is desirable to ascertain the amount of Jute adulteration in such fabrics as sail-cloth (in which it appears to me to be a highly criminal fraud), a very good test may be found in high-pressure steam. A piece of such sail-cloth, kept for four hours in steam of 30 lb. pressure, lost on simple washing thereafter, 22 per cent.—the decomposed Jute actually washing out, and with little injury to the remaining fabric.

Besides being used in India and exported to England, it is sent to America, and will probably be required on the Continent; but it is necessary for the people, if they wish to retain or extend their trade, to keep up the quality of their produce, which is complained of in the following extract from a letter from America to the Author:

"The article of Gunny bagging for cotton is imported largely into this country from India; in fact, is superseding all other descriptions of cloth for that purpose. I have been asked several times what it is made of, and where manufactured. On both points I am ignorant, and should be much obliged if you will give me the information. It is superior to and liked better than any other bagging; but the manufacturers are already commencing to make it inferior, by mixing ordinary (Indian) Hemp or tow with it. They will spoil their market unless they desist from such practices, for the planters will not use an inferior, if they can procure a good article." (Georgia, 15th April, 1853.)

Some of the Jute lately imported has been twelve feet in length, in bales of about 4 cwt., bound round with Gunny cloth. The exports of Jute have already been alluded to when referring to the great increase which has taken place in this trade. Many other Indian fibres are possessed of equally good properties in some respects, and of very superior ones in others, and which require only to be known to be very generally appreciated in Europe.

JUTE, GUNNY CLOTH, AND GUNNY BAGS EXPORTED FROM CALCUTTA, IN THE YEAR 1850-51.

Exports.	Jute.	Gunnies and Gunny Cloth.
To United Kingdom	Ms.768,945	Nos. 69,636
,, France	13,931	—
,, Hamburgh	128	2,180
,, North America	9,242	2,290,427
,, Coast of Coromandel	598	1,955,150
,, Malabar	—	2,054,075
,, Penang and Singapore	—	1,043,600
,, Ceylon	—	357,290
,, New South Wales	54	32,125
,, Trieste	401	—
,, Java	—	242,550
,, Pegu	—	672,950
,, Mauritius	—	213,980
,, Cape of Good Hope	—	82,750
,, Guam	—	15,000
,, Arabian and Persian Gulfs	—	4,000
Total	Mds. 793,299	9,035,713
Value	Rs. 1,970,715	Rs. 2,159,782

The following statement shows the proportion of Gunnies and of Gunny Cloth; and also that a decrease took place in the former, and an increase in the latter in the two years given:

Exports from Calcutta.	1849-50.	1850-51.
Gunnies	12,961,441	8,759,185
Gunny Cloth	238,039	276,528
Total	13,199,480	9,035,713
Value	Rs. 2,683,551	2,159,782

Besides these there were exported from the Madras Presidency 58,950 gunny bags; but there is reason to believe that these are made of *Sunn*, or *Crotalaria juncea.*

Bombay being in a small island, cannot export any of its own growth; but as Gunny cloth is much required for packing cotton, it is imported in large quantities, as 167,820 pieces, valued at Rs. 397,097 (but in 1849, to the value of Rs. 548,384), from the United Kingdom, Ceylon, East Coast of Africa, and Soumeeanee, but chiefly from Calcutta; also from Cutch, Malabar, and Canara, Aden, Sindh, Concan, and Guzerat. But we also find the places mentioned after Calcutta as those to which Gunny cloth was exported, but not in any quantity, except 296,757 pieces to the Concan—the whole export for that year amounting to 391,279 pieces, and the re-exports to 3,403,453, valued at Rs. 468,177, therefore greatly exceeding the imports, and hence probably including some brought by the Causeway.

Indian Hemps, or those so called, as Sunn, &c.

In various notices of Indian fibres we frequently meet with the word *Sunn*, as indicating a particular kind of Indian fibre. Sometimes we find it called *Indian Hemp*, and we may often see *Hemp* enumerated as one of the exports from India. At other times we may see either the same or another fibre mentioned by the name of *Brown Hemp*. Now these various names are sometimes applied to the fibre of one or of two different plants, or they may be employed to distinguish the fibre of three distinct plants, all of which are grown for their fibres, and have been, and might be exported from India, though only two of them are now usually to be found among the exports from that country. Hence, to avoid ambiguity, it is necessary to notice the plants to which these several names are correctly applicable.

The true Hemp (*Cannabis sativa*) is everywhere cultivated by the natives in the plains of India, not on account of its fibres, but for the intoxicating property of its leaves and their secretions. In the Himalayas, however, the fibre is separated for economic purposes, and was exported from India to England during the last war, but we believe it has not been so for many years.

The fibre of the *Sunn* or *Taag* (*Crotalaria juncea*) is often called Indian Hemp, but incorrectly. It is the kind most generally cultivated all over India on account of its fibre, and is that usually mentioned in the exports from Calcutta under the name of Hemp, but also as Sunn. The plant may be distinguished by its flowers being of a bright yellow colour, and of the form of the Pea and of the Laburnum, while the leaves are entire and lanceolate.

The *Ambaree* (*Hibiscus cannabinus*), *Mesta paut* of Bengal, and *Palungoo* of Madras, is also very generally cultivated all over India, and exported of very good quality from the west side of that country. Its leaves are both entire and lobed, its flowers are large, and in shape resemble those of the Mallow, the Hollyhock, and the Cotton plant, of a sulphur-yellow colour with a dark brown centre. The fibre of this plant is, like that of Jute, sometimes called *paut*, and also *Indian Hemp*. It is often confounded with that of the Sunn, as it is one of the kinds of Brown Hemp of Bombay, though the two plants differ much from each other.

In the exports from the different Presidencies of India, it is very difficult to distinguish these two different kinds of fibre, inasmuch as the same name, Hemp, is applied to the exports from all the three Presidencies; but we believe, speaking generally, that the *Sunn* (*Crotalaria juncea*) is chiefly exported from all the three Presidencies, and one kind of Brown Hemp (*Hibiscus cannabinus*), along with the other kind, *Taag*, from Bombay.

OF MALVACEOUS AND OTHER FIBRE-YIELDING PLANTS.

As many plants have flowers and seed-vessels which closely resemble the Mallow, they have been united by botanists into a natural family of plants, which they have called *Malvaceæ*, or Mallow-worts. Some other families, such as the *Tiliaceæ* just described, and the *Sterculiaceæ* and *Byttneriaceæ*, to be immediately noticed, having also a considerable resemblance to each other and to the *Malvaceæ*, have been further grouped into a larger class which has been called *Malvales*. These groupings are interesting to us, inasmuch as they bring together, though in these different families, a number of plants which resemble each other in properties; for the greater number of the species not only abound in mucilage, but their barks in fibres which are manufactured into cordage. Of these, numerous instances will be mentioned in the following pages, but still more will probably remain to be enumerated and reported on by subsequent observers; and, therefore, colonists in tropical countries may search among these for fibre-yielding plants with considerable certainty of finding many possessed of very valuable properties.

The family of Malvaceæ or Mallow-worts is extremely numerous in species, which abound chiefly in tropical parts of the world in the form of trees and shrubs, though species, as the Mallow and Marsh Mallow, do extend to temperate climates. The known fibre-yielding plants belong to the genera *Malva*, *Hibiscus*, *Sida*, *Althæa*, *Lavatera*, *Urena*, &c.; besides *Gossypium*, the genus yielding Cotton. Of these we shall find many employed in different countries for yielding fibre for cordage and for other purposes.

AMBAREE, OR HEMP-LIKE HIBISCUS (*Hibiscus cannabinus*, *Malvaceæ*).

Ambaree in Western India; *Palungoo*, Madras; *Pooley Numajee*, Coimbatore; *Gongkura* of the Telingas; *Maesta paut* of the Bengalese; *Sunnee* at Saharunpore; *Wilaitee* (or foreign) *Sunn* at Muttra; *Deckanee Hemp* of Bombay.

From the variety of synonyms which we have given of this plant, it is evident that it must be generally known all over India; but from its having several distinct names of its own on the west, we should infer that it was a native of that side of India, or of the southern part of the Peninsula, as on the Bengal side its names are modifications of those of some of the other fibres. In Bombay, besides *ambaree*, its fibre is sometimes called Deckanee Hemp, to distinguish it from the *taag* or Conkunee Hemp (*Crotalaria juncea*). But it is very generally cultivated by the natives, though not in large quantities.

This plant, found as yet only in a state of cultivation, is a herbaceous annual of about three months' duration. The stem is straight and simple, of from three to seven feet in height, with here and there a few inoffensive prickles, otherwise smooth. The leaves are spreading, alternate, with long, slightly prickly footstalks; all are smooth, with their margins serrated; but the lower leaves are heart-shaped; those about the middle of the plant three-, four-, or five-lobed, with lanceolate acute lobes; while the leaves at the top are simply linear-lanceolate. Stipules awl-shaped. The flowers are solitary, with short peduncles in the axils of the leaves; very large; of a pale sulphur colour, with a deep purple centre. Of the double calyx, the outer is seven- to eight-leaved, each subulate, spreading, and inserted near the base of the inner calyx. This is five-cleft, divisions sharp-pointed, bristly, and glandular near the margins, and with a large gland on the middle of each division. The stamens numerous, with their filaments united into a hollow column. Anthers one-celled, bursting by a transverse chink. Styles equal in number to the ovaries, and rising through the staminal columns. Carpels joined into a five-celled, five-valved capsule, with few seeds in each cell.

Dr. Roxburgh says of this plant, in his 'Coromandel Plants,' vol. ii, p. 48, tab. 190, where a beautiful plate is given:

"It is much cultivated by the natives. Its leaves are in general used as an esculent vegetable, and taste something like sorrel. The bark is replete with strong and tolerably soft fibres, and is employed as a substitute for Hemp, to which it is much inferior both in strength and durability.

"The usual time of cultivation is the cold season, though it will thrive pretty well at all times of the year, if it has sufficient moisture. A rich loose soil suits it best. The seeds are sown about as thick as Hemp, but generally mixed with some sort of small or dry grain, rendering it necessary to be sown very thin, that the other crop (which is one of those grains that does not grow nearly so high) may not be too much shaded. It requires about three months from the time it is sown, before it is fit to be pulled up for watering, which operation, with the subsequent dressing, is similar to that hereafter described for *Crotalaria juncea*."

Dr. Roxburgh states, that he found the fibres to be stronger when obtained from full-grown plants that had ripened their seed, than when cut from plants in blossom. On the Coromandel coast he found it cultivated, and a coarse sackcloth made of its fibres.

In the Purneya district, Dr. Buchanan found it called *Ambya Pata*, on account of the acidity of its leaves, but in other parts *chandana*. In the southern parts the common cordage of the country was almost entirely made from its fibre. It was said to be sown in fields, which produce nothing else; a practice which Dr. Buchanan had observed nowhere else in India. It appeared to him a coarse material in comparison with the fibre of the Corchorus, but he had no opportunity of trying its strength. In some places a few of the seeds are scattered about among other crops on account of its leaves.

In Behar he found it called *Kudrum,* and cultivated only for being made into ropes, and not as an acid seasoning. About 2000 begahs were occupied with it. In Bhagulpore he found it cultivated nearly as much as the Corchorus. The natives considered ropes made of it stronger and more durable than those of the Jute; but its fibres are harsher, and, as he thought, could be reduced to fine thread.

In Goruckpore it was cultivated to the greatest extent, but always intermixed with the *urhur* or *Cytisus Cajan,* and ropes made of it were used for agricultural purposes.

In the Dinajepore district, Dr. Buchanan found it called *Mesta,* but its bark never used for making ropes; the leaves only being used as an acid green, the taste being pleasantly acid, and not unlike sorrel.

We find it equally cultivated in Central and Western India. It is mentioned as one of the plants employed for cordage at Hyderabad.

Colonel Sykes, in his 'Statistical Report of the Dukhun' (British Assoc., 1837, p. 241), enumerates it as one of the plants cultivated in the wet season; and among his drawings of cordage plants there is an excellent one of this plant, as well as of *Agave vivipara,* there called *gayal.* Among dry or spring season cultivation, the Colonel enumerates the *Taag* or *Crotalaria juncea,* its fibres being employed for ropes and for coarse canvas.

In the Madras Presidency, a number of fibre-yielding plants are mentioned by their native names, but as these differ in every district, and are not accompanied by Botanical names, it is impossible to determine to what plants they refer. We know that Dr. Roxburgh found *Hibiscus cannabinus* in cultivation on the Coromandel coast, and that a coarse sackcloth was made of its fibres. In Vizagapatam it is called Gunny fibre, and coarse sackcloth and rope made of it. So Dr. Ainslie says, "with the nar, or tough stringy fibre of the bark of the Hemp-leaved Hibiscus, a valuable kind of cordage is made, of various thickness." In a late Minute (19th Sept., 1854) by the Madras Government on the subject of fibres, we find it stated, that "the fibres of the roselle (*Hibiscus cannabinus*), which is known to grow readily and without much care all over the Madras territories, have been found to be an excellent substitute for tow, now imported from Europe." As the plant is so universally cultivated over a vast tract of country for home consumption, nothing would be easier than to obtain a very large supply of its fibres, if they were required for any of the ordinary purposes of cordage. The natives would have nothing to do but to increase a cultivation to which they are already well accustomed in all parts of the country.

Dr. Buchanan states, as the result of his experience in the lower provinces, that it is cultivated everywhere in India, on account of its leaves, which are eaten as a vegetable, and for its bark, which is most useful for making cordage. The Author has seen it in the same way very generally cultivated in the North-Western provinces, chiefly for cordage for domestic and agricultural purposes.

Though so generally cultivated, its fibre is hardly if at all known as a distinct article of commerce,—the exports of Indian fibres from the three Presidencies being entered as Hemp, those from Calcutta only being sometimes distinguished as Sunn. With regard to its strength, it may be said that, speaking generally, the fibres of the species of Hibiscus are not so remarkable for strength as for fineness.

Dr. Roxburgh, in his experiments, found that a line made of this fibre, from plants in blossom, broke with 115 lb., but with 110 lb. when the seeds were ripe; Sunn fibre, under the same circumstances, breaking with 130 and 160 lb. So in Dr. Wight's experiments, the fibre of *Hibiscus cannabinus*, which is sometimes called the Jute of Madras, broke with 290 lb., when Sunn (*Crotalaria juncea*) broke with 404 lb. Both these, like Dr. Roxburgh's specimens, were probably grown in the same climate. But in the Author's experiments, Sunn broke with 150 lb., when Brown Hemp broke with 190 lb.; but the Sunn was from Bengal, and the Brown Hemp from Bombay. There is, however, some uncertainty about this, because though no fibres can well appear more distinct than these two, yet the Author has in his possession fibres of a Crotalaria which are hardly to be distinguished from Hibiscus Brown Hemp. The Sunn fibre of Bombay was, even in Dr. Roxburgh's time, remarkable for its dark colour. But some specimens of *Ambaree* fibre, sent by Dr. Gibson as those of *Hibiscus cannabinus*, and which closely resemble those of some kinds of ordinary Brown Hemp, were favorably reported upon as follows, by Messrs. Enderby, then of the rope-manufactory at Greenwich. The Author has lately received an equally fine, if not finer, because softer specimen, from Messrs. Noble; but this is probably the produce of *Crotalaria juncea*. Unfortunately the best specimens of fibre come tied up in the same bundle with some ordinary Brown Hemp, and with some dirty, uncleaned fibre.

September 26th, 1844.

We have received your samples of Indian Hemp, and are pleased to observe that we are likely to obtain an article from thence, that will go far to make England independent of Russia for the supply of that important commodity. The samples supplied have much the character of Italian Hemp, but is inferior to it in colour and softness of fibre. It will not, therefore, in its present state be applicable for fine purposes.

We send you a sample of some of the East Indian Hemp we have had dressed; it appears very good, but not equal in strength to the generality of Russia Hemp; we feel, however, assured that it is capable of being got up in better condition.

The present price of Italian Hemp is £32 per ton; Russia Hemp, £28 per ton; Manilla, £23 per ton; New Zealand, £15 per ton; and Jute, about £13 per ton. The Indian Hemp, as per sample, £20 per ton; at which price we should at this period be prepared to purchase.

Yours very truly,

To Dr. J. F. Royle. C. H. G. Enderby.

The Ambaree Hemp is stated by Dr. Gibson to be treated like the Tag or Crotalaria, being cut in November, and stored away until leisure time arrives for stripping the bark. It is in common use for plough and cart ropes, and is esteemed by the natives as very inferior to that of the *Crotalaria juncea*.

Some of this fibre sent to Hull to be reported on in the year 1840, was thus spoken of: "A greater part of that by the 'Wanderer,' which is of similar quality to your Umbarree, or *Hibiscus cannabinus*, cannot be sold for £16 a ton in the Hull market, when Baltic Hemp meets a ready sale at £40. You will perceive how much depends on colour and staple. Prejudice is not wanting,—but that is giving way." (Agric. and Hortic. Soc. of Western India, 1842.)

The length of the fibres of carefully cultivated Ambaree Hemp is from five to six feet; they are of a paler brown than ordinary Brown Hemp, harsher in feel, and stick more together, as if all the gum had not been washed out; but they are divisible into fine fibrils, possessed of considerable strength, and well calculated for rope-making, as also for coarse fabrics. But, though esteemed by some of the natives of the West of India, it is not so good as the best Brown Hemp of Bombay—to be mentioned in connexion with Sunn.

As the fibres of this Hibiscus and of the *Sunn* are not distinguished from each other, or from others, in the account of the Exports from the Ports of India, we shall give these under the head of Sunn, and reserve also to that article some observations on the preparation of these Exogenous fibres in India, as well as on their prices, and the quantities in which they may be obtained.

Other Malvaceous Fibre-yielding Plants.

In connexion with *Hibiscus cannabinus* we may appropriately mention the other fibre-yielding species of the same genus. Among these we find those which are also used as articles of diet; as, for instance,—

Hibiscus esculentus, the *Okhro* of the West Indies, with which is now united the *H. longifolius* of the East Indies, the *Bandikai* of Madras, the *Ram turai* and *Dhenroos* of Bengal; and from both of which the *Bammia* of the west coast of Africa probably does not differ essentially. Of all these, the long, young pyramidal pods are filled when green, with a large proportion of mucilage, on which account they are gathered when green, and cooked as a vegetable, being much esteemed by many, though considered too viscid by others. The fruit is also used to thicken soups in the countries where it is indigenous and in the South of France and in the Levant. The seeds may also be added like barley to soups, and have been recommended to be roasted as a substitute for coffee. The bark of these plants also abounds in fibre, which is of fine quality, as in many others of the same genus. Dr. Roxburgh cut the stems when the seed was ripe, and committed them to the steep a few days after. (For results see p. 268.)

H. Abelmoschus, so named from the Arabic *hub-ool-mooshk*, in Hindee *mooshkdana*, or musk seed, is called *calee kustooree* in Bengal. The seeds have been so named on account of their odour. The plants abound in mucilage, and are much employed in the North-West of India in clarifying sugar. The stems were cut when in flower by Dr. Roxburgh, and steeped immediately: the result of his experiments is given in p. 268.

H. Sabdariffa, said to be so called from its Turkish name, while in the West Indies it is called Red Sorrel, and in the Madras territories *rozelle* and *rouselle.* It is cultivated in most gardens, because its calyxes as they ripen become fleshy, are of a pleasantly acid taste, and are much employed for making tarts, as well as an excellent jelly. Browne states that they are employed in the West Indies for making refreshing drinks. The stems having been cut when in flower, and the bark stripped off, and steeped immediately, display a mass of fibres in Dr. Roxburgh's specimens, some of which are still in the India House, with the ultimate fibres of a fine silky nature. The name *rouselle* is said to be a corruption of *oseille.*

The dietetical uses of these species have been mentioned, in order to show, that if cultivated on account of their fibre, they would also be useful for other purposes.

H. strictus was a new species described by Dr. Roxburgh, and which seems to be a native of the Rajmahl Hills, with a straight stem of from 6 to 14 feet in height, and a very smooth bark. It thrives luxuriantly with little or no care; seed-time the beginning of the rains; it is in blossom about their termination, and the seed ripens in December and January, soon after which the plants perish.

"Like many other of the Malvaceous tribe, the bark of this species abounds in flaxen fibres; but in none have I found so large a quantity, equally beautiful, long, glossy, white, fine, and strong, as in this. To these promising qualities may be added the luxuriant growth, and habit of the plant, rendering it an object deserving of every care and attention, at least until the real worth of the material is fairly ascertained.

"From several years' experience, I find the best season for sowing the seed in Bengal, is just when the first rains begin, which is generally in May, in beds; and when the plants are about six inches high, transplant them out in rows, about nine inches asunder, and about as much from each other in the rows. In 1801, I had forty square yards planted in this manner, which yielded thirty-three pounds weight of the naturally very clean fibres." Dr. Roxburgh's original specimens, still in the India House, are 9 and 10 feet in length, a fibrous mass, apparently easily stript off, and composed of fine and easily divisible fibres. (For strength, *v.* pp. 268-9.)

H. tiliaceus is the *Bola* of the Bengalese, common also on the Malabar coast, and supposed not to differ from *H. arboreus*, the *Maho tree* and *Mohaut* of the West Indies. These grow abundantly both in the West and East Indies.

Forster states, that the bark of this species is sucked in times of scarcity, when the bread-fruit fails. The mucilage with which all these plants abound, will no doubt afford some nourishment. The fibres of its inner bark are employed for cordage by the inhabitants of the South Sea Islands, and by the American Indians: it is said to gain in strength when tarred.

The Otaheitans make fine matting from it, and likewise manufacture it into ropes and cords. Voyagers relate that these filaments are adapted to any kind of cordage, even for the rigging of vessels, but rope thus made is not nearly so strong as that prepared from Hemp. The whips with which the negroes in the West Indies used to be punished, are said to have been made with the bark of this species. (*v.* p. 269.)

H. furcatus, a native of the interior of Bengal, growing to a height of from 6 to 8 feet. The bark yields abundance of strong white flaxen fibres, but the prickliness of the plant renders it very troublesome to handle. The stems were cut when in flower, and steeped immediately. (*v.* p. 268.)

H. mutabilis, a native of China, but common in gardens in India, and remarkable for the change in the colour of its flowers during the day. The fibres of the bark were found to be of a hard nature, and of a bad colour. (*v.* p. 269.)

H. collinus (*eriocarpus* of D. C.), a native of the mountainous parts of the Circars, where it is called *kanda-gang*, and where the natives use the bark as a substitute for Hemp. Under the head of this plant, Dr. Roxburgh states that he has often observed that most of the Indian plants of this family might be employed for the same purposes as Hemp, as the bark is tough, and may almost always be stripped off in long slips.

H. ficifolius is a species which Dr. Roxburgh so named, and of which he received the seeds from the Moluccas. It was an annual, growing very tall, often 12 to 14 feet high, growing straight, with few branches. The fibres he describes as uncommonly beautiful, and rather stronger than Sunn.

Besides these, other fibres of species of Hibiscus have been separated in India, as mentioned in 'Journ. Agri-Hortic. Soc.,' vi, App., 3, and vii, 193, though it is not easy to determine the plants intended; but this only proves how much the genus abounds in fibre-yielding plants.

So other species of this genus are similarly employed in other countries, as *Hibiscus clypeatus* and *elatus* in the West Indies; as *H.* (now *Thespesia*) *populneus* and *H. tiliaceus*, already mentioned, in the Society and South Sea Islands; *H. Manihot* in Japan; *H. heterophyllus* in New Holland; and *H. verrucosus* in Senegambia.

Sida is a genus of Malvaceous plants, which like others of the family contains many plants abounding in mucilage, and others with bark containing tough fibres, employed for cordage in different countries. One species, *S. tiliæfolia*, referred at first by Dr. Roxburgh to *S. abutilon*, is cultivated for this purpose in China. Some of its seeds were received many years ago at the Calcutta Botanic Garden, under the name of *King ma*, from Pekin, in the neighbourhood of which the plant is cultivated, for the sake of its fibre. Seeds were similarly received a few years ago by the Horticultural Society, and the Author saw a fine crop of the plants in their garden at Chiswick, which seemed about eight feet high. Some of these Dr. Lindley had steeped, in order to separate the fibres, and some were sent to Mr. Routledge in the year 1850, in order to try in his machine.

Dr. Roxburgh notices "the fibre of this plant as strong and pliable, very silky in its nature, and the plant of very rapid and luxuriant growth, three crops being obtained in one year. It may be brought into this country at the estimated price of £8 per ton, which is now about one fifth of the price of Hemp of the best quality." According to Dr. Clarke Abel, this plant is preferred for cordage in China Proper.

S. rhomboidea and *S. rhombifolia*, the *sufet* and *lal bariala* of the natives of Bengal, where the plants are indigenous in the rainy season. The bark of both, according to Dr. Roxburgh, yields abundance of very delicate flaxy fibres, which he thought might be advantageously employed for many purposes. When the seed is sown thick on a good soil, the plants grow tall and slender, without branches, and are every way fit for such purposes.

Major Hannay sent from Assam to the Agri-Hortic. Soc., in Dec., 1851, some of the fibre of *Sida rhomboidea,* which grows luxuriantly in that valley. Capt. Thompson thought from its length, its similarity to silk, and its great strength, that it would fetch a high price in England. The line (only half an inch in circumference) sustained, after exposure to wet and sun for ten days, 400 lb.

S. periplocifolia, a native of the Malay Islands, was also one of those subjected to experiment by Dr. Roxburgh, and who describes the plant as flowering and ripening its seed in the Botanic Garden at Calcutta, a great part of the year. "Its bark abounds in serviceable flaxen fibres, and as it shoots quickly into long, simple twigs, particularly if cut near the earth, it answers well for procuring the fibre of good length for most purposes."

Some of Dr. Roxburgh's original specimens, marked July, 1804, are still in the India House; the fibres are from four to five feet in length, and display a fine soft and silky fibre, as well adapted for spinning as the Jute, but are apparently superior.

Various species of Sida, as *S. asiatica, indica, graveolens,* and others, are extremely common in every part of India in the rainy season. Many of them, no doubt, contain fibre which might be turned to useful account.

Urena lobata and *U. sinuata,* two weeds also belonging to this family, the one called *bun-ochra* and the other *kungia,* and common in most parts of India, also abound in strong and a tolerably fine substitute for Flax.

If the common Mallow (*Malva sylvestris,* &c.) of Europe, or the Marsh-mallow (*Althæa officinalis*), are examined, it will be found that they abound in fibre; others of these genera are valued for their fibres in different countries, as *Malva crispa* is said by Cavanilles to have its fibre separated in Syria, and *Althæa cannabina,* is sometimes so employed in the South of Europe; so *Lavatera arborea,* or Tree Mallow, will be found to abound in fibre.

COTTON CORDAGE AND CANVAS (*Gossypium indicum, &c.; Malvaceæ*).

Though Cotton is a substance which is cellular in structure, and not fibrous, also sold by the pound, and not by the cwt. or ton, as the articles we have been treating of, yet it cannot be entirely omitted from a work on the Cordage and Clothing plants of India. But the Author may be excused from dilating on the subject, as he has so recently treated of it fully in his work on the 'Culture and Commerce of Cotton in India.'[1] Còtton, though used chiefly for clothing, is, in India, also employed to a considerable extent for cordage, as, for instance, for tent-ropes, of which so many are required for the use of the army, and made entirely of Cotton, as are the tents

[1] The Author has in the above work treated, first, of the Commercial causes which influence the irregular imports of Indian Cotton: secondly, of the Cultivation of Cotton, including the varieties of Commercial Cotton, and the species of Gossypium; Chemical Analyses of Cotton, its seed, and of Cotton soils; Climate of Cotton districts; and the Principles and Practice of Cotton Culture: thirdly, Experimental Culture of Cotton in India, in which all the different districts have been successively noticed. Some additional information has been published respecting Malwa, &c., in vol. vii of the 'Journ. of the Agri-Hortic. Soc. of Calcutta.'

There is only one point to which the Author wishes to refer, and that because it has been the subject of discussion, and because he ventured to doubt (pp. 449 to 454) the correctness of Mr. Davies's calculation of the cost of a candy of Cotton (20 begahs being required to produce it, or 784 lb.) in the district of Broach, which he made to be above seventy-five rupees. Mr. Landon, established as a cotton-merchant in Broach, and cleaning native Cotton by his saw gins moved by steam power; and who has lately taken out machinery for spinning Cotton, has stated by letter, and since, verbally to the Author, the following facts:

"About fifty patells and ryots who are now at my elbow with kuppas to sell, have this moment unanimously stated that the *average* cost of cultivating a bhar of kuppas in this district, including *rent* and *all* charges, is Rs. 15. The *average* quantity of kuppas which yields a candy of Cotton is 2½ bhars (this season it is 2$\frac{8}{20}$ bhars). Therefore, the cost of a candy of Cotton does not exceed, on an average, Rs. 15×2½=Rs. 37½! While the average price which I have paid the ryots, for a candy of Cotton in the seed, during the last six years, is Rs. 88¾! or Rs. 35½ per bhar. This I am prepared to show from my books, and to make oath of it if necessary. Again, I recently asked a ryot how many begahs of Cotton he cultivated: he replied forty; and that they produced ten bhars of kuppas. At the rate of Rs. 15 per bhar, the total cost to him of these ten bhars, including rent and *all* charges, was Rs. 150. The price which *I paid* him for it was Rs. 360! Others have repeatedly made similar statements to me, as to the produce and cost of production, in respect to greater and less quantities of land."

themselves. So, Cotton ropes are also employed for many domestic purposes. Specimens were sent to the Exhibition of 1851, both from Calcutta and Madras, and have considerable strength. Some of the native shipping, also, and even a few American ships, are rigged with Cotton ropes; while Cotton canvas is also employed for sails, especially on the coast of Cutch, where some very good is made, and sells for about three and a half annas per yard.

Silk Cotton Tree, and others (*Byttneriaceæ*).

The natural family of *Byttneriaceæ*, which includes such genera as *Bombax*, *Sterculia*, *Abroma*, *Guazuma*, &c., like that of the Mallow-worts, inhabits hot parts of the globe chiefly, and also like it contains a number of plants remarkable for abounding in mucilage and in fibrous bark. Of these some are employed for cordage in different parts of the world, and of them a few, as *Abroma augusta*, might probably be grown with greater profit, and yield a better product, than some of those which are now in cultivation.

Thus the species of Bombax, which are remarkable for their gigantic stature and their splendid inflorescence, are also so on account of their capsules, which, on bursting, display a flocculent substance, often mistaken by travellers for cotton, and the tree hence called *Cotton tree*. But as this substance is more silky than cotton, it has been distinguished by the name of *Silk Cotton*. It differs also in not spinning like cotton. Some difficulty, therefore, is experienced in making use of this very abundant cotton-like produce; but Mr. Williams, of Jubbulpore, has succeeded in spinning and weaving some of it so as to form a very good coverlet. It might be easily made use of for stuffing pillows, muffs, or coverlets, for wadding, or for conversion into half-stuff for paper-makers, perhaps for making gun-cotton.

In the 'Trans. of the Agri-Hortic. Soc.,' iii, p. 274, there is a report from the Society of Arts on two pieces of cloth made from the Simool or Silk Cotton tree; and it is observed that, from the shortness of the staple of the down, and its elasticity, it could not be spun by cotton-spinning machinery.

Several of this family abound in mucilage, thus a Guazuma is employed in South America in clarifying sugar; as a Kydia is in India. A species of Sterculia yields a tragacanth-like gum on the west coast of Africa, as another does in India. Several species of this genus are remarkable for the tenacity of the fibre of their bark, which is employed for cordage, as *Myrodia longiflora* in Guiana, and *Chorisia crispifolia* in Brazil, *Dombeya umbellata* in the Isle of Bourbon, and *Sterculia Ivria* in the West Indies. *Helicteres Isora* may be similarly employed in India.

Sterculia guttata is a tree, a native of Malabar, which was first made known by Capt. Dickenson, in the year 1802. The bark of the younger parts of the tree abounds with very strong, white, flaxen fibres, of which the inhabitants of Wynaad manufacture a kind of coarse cloth. It is not usual to make use of the bark until the tenth year, when its size will be equal to that of most forest trees. The tree is felled, the branches lopped off, and the trunk cut into pieces of six feet long, a perpendicular incision made in each piece, the bark opened, and taken off whole, chopped, washed, and dried in the sun. By these means, and without any further process, it is fit for the purposes of clothing.

Sterculia villosa, called *Oadal* in Assam, is another tree of this genus, which is a native of the mountainous countries to the eastward of Bengal. Trunk straight. The bark is smooth, but fibrous. Bags are made of it. Its fibres are made into cords by the natives of the eastern frontier of Bengal, to bind wild elephants with.

Of a coil of Oadal rope, Major Jenkins gave the following notice in the year 1847:

"The Oadal tree is very common, and the rope is made most readily; the bark, or rather all the layers, can be stripped off from the bottom to the top of the tree with the greatest facility, and fine pliable ropes may be made from the inner layers of bark, whilst the outer yield coarse ropes. The rope is very strong and very lasting—wet doing it little injury."

Oadhal is a creeper in Kemaon, with fine, strong fibres; and *Microlæna spectabilis* is a tree found at the foot of the Himalayas, which yields fibres fit for rope-making.

Guazuma ulmifolia is a South American tree, which was introduced into India, and largely cultivated at one time in the Madras Presidency under the name of Bastard Cedar, as fodder for cattle. The fibres of its straight, luxuriant, young branches were submitted to trial by Dr. Roxburgh. (*v.* p. 268.)

Abroma augusta, the *Woollet-comul* or *Ullat-kumul* of Bengal, and which Dr. Roxburgh at one time called Perennial Indian Hemp or Flax, is a native of various parts of India, growing luxuriantly in gardens even as far as 30° N. lat., and extending eastward to the Philippine Isles. It grows to a small tree, but may be cultivated as an annual, flowers profusely during the rainy season, and ripens its seed in the cold weather. It particularly attracted Dr. Roxburgh's attention; as the bark abounds with strong white fibres, which make a very good substitute for Hemp, affording good common cordage. The plant grows so quickly, as to yield two, three, or even four crops of cuttings annually fit for peeling; hence it may be advantageously cultivated, and is deserving of more than common attention on account of the beauty, fineness, and strength of its fibres. Dr. Roxburgh ventured to prognosticate as large a yearly produce as can be obtained from an acre of Danchee, Jute, Sunn, Hemp, or Flax; as it is a perennial, large, shrubby plant, in every respect easier to cultivate and to prepare the fibres than Sunn, and the produce much greater. Indeed, in an experimental culture, he obtained from three cuttings 271 lb. of clean fibre, which he states was three times greater than the average produce of Sunn.

To separate the bark from the shoots, maceration in stagnant water, from four to eight days, answers well during the warmer parts of the year, while three times as much is scarce sufficient during the cold season, indeed the process is scarcely practicable then; besides, the fibres are greatly weakened by prolonged maceration. The fibres being naturally very white and clean, they do not require to be cleaned. Dr. Roxburgh states that, in its native state, without being dressed in any way, it is about one tenth part stronger than Sunn, and in that state much more durable in water. A cord of its fibre bore 74 lb., when Sunn broke with 68 lb. (*v.* p. 269.)

In the following tables the results of some of Dr. Roxburgh's experiments are given:

Comparative Strength of Fibres, both dry and wet, ascertained by weights suspended to four-feet lengths of the several lines.

No.	NAMES OF THE PLANTS, And brief Remarks on the various Materials employed in these Experiments.	Average weight each line broke with when dry.	Average weight each line broke with when wet.	Average of weight gained by wetting the lines.
1	Hemp, the growth of 1800, from the Company's Hemp Farm near Calcutta . .	158	190	20
2	Jeetee (Asclepias tenacissima) . . .	248	343	38
4	Sunn (Crotalaria juncea), cut before the plants were in blossom, and steeped immediately .	112	158	41
5	The same as No 4, but dried, or rather kept for some time before they were steeped .	60	78	30
6	Sunn cut when in full blossom, and steeped immediately	130	185	42
7	No. 6, kept drying for some time . . .	100	166	66
8	Sunn cut when the seeds were perfectly ripe .	150	203	35
9	The same as No. 8, but dried . . .	110	163	48
10	Sunn, winter crop, cut when the seeds were ripe, and steeped immediately . . .	160	209	31
11	A var. of Corchorus capularis, Teetah Paat .	143	146	2
12	Reddish Corchorus capsularis, from China .	164	164	0
13	Corchorus olitorius, Bunghi Paat . . .	113	125	11
14	Æschynomone cannabina, Dancha, cut when the seed was nearly ripe	138	145	5
15	Abroma augusta, young shoots cut before the blossoms appeared	100	112	12
16	The same, from old ligneous plants, that had ripened their seed	121	121	0
17	Hibiscus strictus, from the Moluccas . .	104	115	10
18	No. 17, after it had ripened its seed . .	128	135	5
19	Hibiscus cannabinus, cut when in blossom, and steeped immediately	115	133	15
20	The same, cut when the seed was ripe . .	110	118	7
21	Hibiscus (No. 18 of the next table), cut when in flower, and steeped immediately . .	·116	123	6
22	Hibiscus Sabdariffa, cut when in flower, and steeped immediately	89	117	31
23	Hibiscus Abelmoschus, Calee Kustoree, cut when in full flower, and steeped immediately	107	107	0
24	Hibiscus esculentus, D'heroos, cut when the seed was ripe, and steeped a few days thereafter	79	95	20
25	Hibiscus furcatus, cut when in flower, and steeped immediately	89	92	3
26	Hibiscus pilosus, a large annual species, cut when in advanced flower, and steeped immediately.	97	130	34
27	Guazuma ulmifolia, stout young shoots of about six feet in height, from two years old roots, steeped immediately . . .	100	140	40
28	Fibres of the footstalks of the leaves of a large luxuriant wild Musa, or Plantain .	79		
29	A line made of fifteen threads of sail-twine, Calloee, Urtica tenacissima . . .	240	278	16

Comparative Statement of the effect of Maceration 116 *days in stagnant water, comparing the strength by weights suspended to four-feet lengths of the various cords therein mentioned, when fresh.*

No.	NAMES OF THE PLANTS, And brief Remarks on the various Materials employed in these Experiments.	Average Weight at which each sort of Line broke.					
		When fresh.			After 116 days' maceration.		
		White.	Tanned.	Tarred.	White.	Tanned.	Tarred.
1	English Hemp, a piece of a new tiller-rope .	105			rotten, as was also an English log-line		
2	Hemp, Cannabis, the growth of this season, from the Company's Hemp Farm near Calcutta	74	139	45	all rotten.		
3	Coir, the fibres of the husk of the Cocoa-nut .	87			54		
4	Ejoo, Saguerus Rumphii, Roxb.	96			94		
5	Æschynomene cannabina, Dansha of the Bengalese. The fibres of plants that had nearly ripened their seed	88	101	84	40	56	65
6	The fibres of the bark of No. 5, from plants coming into blossom	46	61	48	rotten	68	45
7	Crotalaria juncea, Sunn of the Bengalese .	68	69	60	rotten	51	65
8	Corchorus olitorius, Bunghi-Paat. The fibres of its bark called Jute	68	69	61	40	49	60
9	Corchorus capsularis, Ghee-Nalta-Paat. The fibres called Nalta-Jute	67			50		
10	Flax, Linum usitatissimum, the growth of the Company's Hemp Farm near Calcutta .	39			rotten		
11	Agave americana	110	79	78	rotten	rotten	15½
12	Sanseviera zeylanica; in Sanscrit Murva .	120	73	48	30	26	34
13	Abroma augusta. Woollet-comul of the Bengalese	74	58	44	38	54	50
14	Guazuma ulmifolia, Bastard-Cedar. The fibres of the bark of some straight luxuriant young plants	52	47	45	30	39	
15	Hibiscus tiliaceus, Bola of the Bengalese .	41	62	61	40	55	70
16	Hibiscus strictus, from the Moluccas, a tall, white-flowered variety of it	61			26		
17	Hibiscus mutabilis	45	53		rotten	45	
18	Hibiscus, from the Cape of Good Hope . .	22			17		
19	Bauhinia racemosa, Roxb., a large scandent species	69			rotten		
20	The same as No. 19, only maceration was used to help to take the bark off the twigs with more ease	56			rotten		
21	Sterculia villosa	53			30		

SUNN AND OTHER LEGUMINOUS PLANTS (*Leguminosæ*).

Sans., *Sana;* Hindee, *Sunn;* Bengalese, *Ghore Sun* and *Meesta pat;* Cing., *Kenna; Hemp* and *Sunn Hemp* in Calcutta; *Janapa, Shanapum,* also, *Madras Hemp; Taag* or *Conkanee Hemp, Salsette,* and *Bombay Hemp.* Some of the *Brown Hemp* of commerce.

The now well-known *Sunn* of India belongs to a family of plants, of which some, such as the Peas and Beans of Europe, are familiar to all; as are also the species of Phaseolus and Dolichos, yielding the pulses of India. The family has been named *Leguminosæ,* from the fruit of all consisting of a pod or Legume. Though very numerous in species, comparatively few are remarkable for their fibrous properties, though one of the oldest described cordage plants of Europe belongs to this family.

Under the head of *Esparto,* in the family of Grasses (p. 31), we have stated that *Stipa tenacissima* was no doubt one of the kinds of Spartum of the ancients, and that *Spartium junceum* was probably another. It was very common for the ancients to group substances together according to their properties rather than according to their external characters. Mr. Yates is of opinion, that this *Spartium junceum,* or Spanish Broom, was the original plant, and that the name Spartum, converted into Esparto, was afterwards applied to the grass. The *Spartium junceum,* or Spanish Broom, common in the sterile parts of the South of Europe, affords a fibrous thread which used to be made into cloth in Turkey, in Italy, and in the South of France. Near Lucca the twigs were formerly steeped in the thermal waters of Bagno a Acqua. After this process the bark is easily stript off, and it is then combed and otherwise treated like flax. In the vicinity of Pisa, also, the twigs were soaked in the thermal waters. In the South of France the Broom is grown in dry and unproductive parts, and also carefully prepared. The coarser thread is used to make bags for holding legumes, corn, &c.; the finer for making sheets, napkins, and shirts. (*v.* Yates's 'Textrin. Antiq.,' pp. 323-4.) A white-flowered plant has also been long used for the same purposes. This, there is little doubt, is the *Spartium monospermum,* or the white single-seed Broom; and probably also *S. multiflorum,* which is the Portugal white Broom. As these plants are naturalized in our gardens, it is easy to ascertain the toughness of their fibres by endeavouring to break one of their twigs.

In the subdivision of Leguminous plants with these Brooms we find the *Sunn* plant of India (*Crotalaria juncea*), which has so close a general resemblance to the Spanish Broom, that Mr. Yates has figured them together in the same plate, with the very object of showing their affinity.

The Sunn is probably the earliest of the distinctly named fibres, inasmuch as we find in the Hindoo 'Institutes of Menu,' that the sacrificial thread of the Cshatriya or Rajpoot is directed to be made of *Sana*; cotton being reserved for the Brahmins. Its name, *Shanapam* or *Janapa*, on the Madras side, is not very unlike *Canapa*, *Hampa*, *Hennip*, and *Hanf*. From these we derive our own name of *Hemp*. Under the name *Sana* it is mentioned in many Sanscrit works; and by that of *Sunn* it is known in most parts of India. The first notices in European works is, by Rheede ('Hort. Mal.,' v. ix, t. 26); by Ironside, in the 'Phil. Trans. of London,' lxiv, p. 99; and it is mentioned by Roxburgh in the early volumes of the Society of Arts' 'Transactions.' Towards the close of the last, and the beginning of this century, it attracted much attention both in India and in England; and much information respecting it is contained in Dr. Roxburgh's several works, as well as in Wisset's 'Treatise on Hemp and on the Sunn Plant,' 1804 and 1808. Dr. Buchanan in his 'Journey through Mysore,' mentions that Goni cloth for sacks is made of the fibre of *Crotalaria juncea*.

The annual stem is straight, smooth, striated, from four to eight (varieties even ten and twelve) feet high, branching towards the top, but more so when the plant stands single. Leaves scattered, short petioled, lanceolate, obtuse, with a small bristle-like point, from two to six inches long, both sides covered with soft, silver-coloured hairs. Stipules subulate, small. Flowers in terminal racemes, papilionaceous, of a beautiful bright yellow colour, each supported by an oval bract. Calyx two-lipped; the upper lip two-cleft; the under one two-parted in the middle. Of the yellow petals, the banner is obtuse, erect; the two wings oblong obtuse; the keel much pointed, slightly twisted at the apex, and closely shut. Filaments ten, their lower half united into one body, with a fissure down the upper side, which has a circular gape at the base; extremities free, and the alternate ones shorter than the others. Anthers on these linear; on the larger filaments ovate and two-lobed. Legumes sessile, club-shaped, turgid, from one to two inches long. Seeds numerous, kidney-shaped. (Roxb., 'Flora Indica,' iii, p. 261; 'Corom. Pl.,' t. 192.)

The seeds when ripe and loosened rattle within the pods, as in the other species, whence the genus has been named from the Greek word *krotalos*.

It is an annual plant, very generally cultivated in the southern parts of Asia, and everywhere in India, on account of the fibres of its bark, so well known as *Sunn* and *Sunn Hemp,* often erroneously called Hemp, though the true plant is also most common in India, but valued in the plains only for its intoxicating properties. The Sunn is exported from different parts of India, as from Calcutta, by the name of Sunn; that from Madras is known here as Madras Hemp; that from Bombay as Brown Hemp, being known there as *Taag* or Conkanee Hemp. It being a common practice to name it from the province where it has been grown. The late Dr. Stocks informed the Author that it was cultivated in Sindh, and that the species named *Crotalaria Burhia,* which grows wild in the most arid places, is also employed in Sindh as a cordage plant. The Author may mention that he has seen it thickly sown and carefully cultivated in the most northern provinces of India. The time of flowering and ripening its seed, as stated by Dr. Roxburgh, depend on the season it is sown; though in most parts it is raised during the rainy season, in others it is not sown until their cessation.

Culture.—The general time of cultivation is during the rains; and in Bengal a rather elevated rich soil is required, which ought to be well ploughed, or otherwise dressed to free it of weeds, and bring it into good tilth. In Wisset's treatise, pp. 38 and 39, it is stated that clayey soils are injurious, and that in a rich soil the fibre produced is of a coarser quality than that from high, dry situations. The quantity of seed, Dr. Roxburgh states, should be from eighty to a hundred pounds weight to the acre. In some districts less, in others a larger quantity is sown. (*v.* Wisset.) The natives say, the thicker the Sunn grows the better, and so thick as to prevent the air from passing through it. (l. c., p. 73.) At Commercolly it is stated that there are two kinds of Sunn; one being sown in June, the other in October, though they are nearly similar in quality. That sown in June is generally cut about August or September, and the other about April; but it is also sown in October in parts of the Dacca district. (*v.* Wisset, pp. 59 and 82.) The cause of the difference in the time of cultivation, is supposed by some to be that during the periodical rains the face of the country is under water.

In most places the seed is sown when the first showers fall, in May or June, and covered in by the harrow, or by any other mode. Little more is required, as the plant grows so rapidly as to keep down the weeds itself; otherwise it requires to be freed from weeds, when about nine inches high. By August the plant will be in flower, and from five to eight or more feet high. When the fibre is required of a fine and soft quality, it is pulled in this stage of its growth; if greater strength is the object, it must stand till in seed, or even till the seed is ripe. A portion of the crop always requires to be left for the sake of ripening some seed. The natives make use also of the fibres of such plants, and consider them strong. When ready for the purposes intended, the plant is cut or pulled up by the roots. At Hurriaul it is cut down as close to the ground as possible, and laid in ridges, care being taken to place the plants so that the leafy parts be one upon another. In this state they continue five, six, or ten to twelve days, or until the leaves begin to rot and fall from the stalks on being shaken about. (l. c., p. 113.) For culture in Madras and Bombay, see pp. 279, 282.

Produce, &c., per acre.—The produce of the cultivation of this plant per acre is most fully detailed in the abstracts of reports given by Mr. Wisset, and varies from 3 cwt. to 10 cwt. per acre; or on a medium probably about 700 lb. an acre. But there is difficulty in determining the point with exactness, from the difference in the begah as well as in the maund. The cultivation was said to yield tolerable profit, inasmuch as the plant requires scarce any attention, and consequently little labour or expense; and it may be off the ground in time to allow this to be prepared for any cold-season crop. But the expenses and the profit are as variously stated as the produce. The price is also given as varying from R. 1 8, and R. 1 12, to Rs. 3 per maund, at the same time; which it is difficult to account for, except from the habitual carelessness of the natives of India in all such statements. (*v.* 'Wisset,' pp. 146—155.)

Steeping.—Having grown and cut the plant, as well as removed its leaves, it is ready for the next process, that of committing to water, or other operation for separating its fibre. The length of time required for steeping depends on the season of the year, the heat of the weather, and consequently of the water. In August and September, from two to three days is generally sufficient. When the required effect has been attained, which will generally be known by the bark separating freely from the stalk, the people employed in the work stand in the water in which the plant has been steeped; each takes a handful thereof, which he breaks in one or more places, after having washed off any mud or filth; then grasps it by one end between both hands, and beats it against the surface of the water, which quickly removes the reed from the fibres; when the parcel is turned, and the other end treated in the same manner. Care must be taken not to over-steep, as this much weakens the fibre. (Wisset and Roxburgh.)

With respect to the proper time for steeping, and the period during which the stems should be steeped, great differences of opinion prevailed during the experiments at the beginning of the century. Mr. Fleming, disapproving of the native method of steeping the plants immediately after they were cut, and for three or four days, recommended that the plants, after pulling, be *first dried in the sun for two days;* after which, they should not be let remain in the water more than *forty* hours. Mr. Frushard objected, first, to the drying the article before watering; secondly, to the insufficiency of the time for watering; and lastly, to the manner of separating the fibre from the reed after watering. The general practice, he observes, is to set the plant upright in the water, immersed about one third only from the bottom, for one day before the complete immersion, in order that the thicker may be immersed longer than the thinner parts. Of the natives one said, "to dry before steeping was doing to undo." Another observed that it seemed to be "wanted to make difficult what was easy." Others exclaimed: "You may imprison our persons; you may strike our necks; but never will we make Sunn according to the advertisement." (*v.* Wisset, pp. 162, 195, and 202.) The whole forms an interesting commentary on attempts to improve native processes, before principles are thoroughly understood, or the superiority of European practices carefully established. (*v.* Table, p. 268.)

At Commercolly, when the plants of *Phool Sun* have been pulled and tied in bundles, they are for a day or two kept standing on their roots in an inch or two of water, which allows the fibre to obtain a proper degree of firmness, without suffering it to be parched by the heat of the sun.

Dr. Roxburgh observes, "all that seems necessary is to caution the cultivators against oversteeping the plant, which they are apt to do, because it renders the separation of the bark from the stalks easier, but weakens its fibres. Small pools of clear water, well exposed to the sun's beams, seem best suited for steeping in, because heat hastens maceration, consequently preserves the strength of the fibres, while the clean water preserves their colour. Deep water, being cooler, requires more time for the operation." He further states, that the result of many experiments leads him to think that steeping immediately after the plant is pulled is the best, at least in Bengal during the rains, for then it is very difficult to dry it, and the fibre becomes weakened and the colour injured. He found no advantage, but the reverse, by drying the plant, after maceration, and before the bark was removed, as often practised with Hemp and Flax in Europe.[1] But in his 'Fl. Ind.,' iii, p. 262, he says: "Others, and I believe with good reason, recommend its being dried for some time previous to its being steeped." When the seed is ripe the fibre is stronger, but requires a much longer time for steeping.

If the Sunn be dressed before it is shipped for England, the commodity will be rendered more valuable; but considerable loss of weight (probably about one third) having ensued from the combing or heckling removing much short fibre or tow, it is of course increased in price. The Sunn of Bengal is always whiter than that of Bombay, owing to the mode in which it is prepared.

Drying.—When the Sunn has been thoroughly washed, it is usually hung up on lines or bamboos to dry. When dry, it is combed, if intended for fishing nets or small lines; but if for common use, they merely separate the fibres a little with their fingers, and make it up into bundles for market. The use of the Hemp-brake is unknown in India, but the Sunn might in many cases, after watering, be bruised with a brake and then scutched.

It is in cleaning the fibres Mr. Frushard considers that the

[1] See also 'Observations on Fibrous Veg. Substitutes for Flax and Hemp,' p. 45.

natives are most liable to fail. He thinks it ought to be strongly insisted that they beat the plant (by handfuls at a time) on the surface of river water, in order to get rid more readily of the filth and mucus with which it abounds after steeping. But when the fibre is separated it must be thoroughly washed, by repeatedly squeezing the water out of it, and ultimately well wrung, to accelerate the essential process of careful drying. The cylinders for pressing Flax when moist (*v.* p. 206) would be useful, as also scutching mills properly suited to the fibres to be separated and prepared.

After the fibrous parts are well separated and well washed, they are in some places in Bengal laid in the sun to dry, before stripping them. At Jungypore, after washing and beating in the water, the *Sunn* is laid in the sun an hour or two, and the stalks are separated when half dried. Mr. Fleming recommended that after watering the plants forty hours, they should be taken out and dried gently in the sun for three or four hours, before the fibres are separated. The natives say, that to dry the plant on taking it out of the water before separating the fibre from the seed, will occasion a much greater loss in tow; so that they never practise this method but when distressed for time, and under the dread of leaving it too long in the water, when any parcel proves too much for the labourers employed in one day. Mr. Frushard also objected, that such drying must be insufficient, and that in Europe, generally, the plant is most thoroughly dried before it is put under the brakes, and that in Livonia the Hemp is heaped up, and covered up with straw, &c., in order to make it *sweat*, and that the Livonians say, it is in this operation of *sweating* that the good or bad quality of their Hemp depends.

Mr. Frushard observes, that "the natives get through the whole business with so much celerity that their mode of practice is highly in favour of the fibre retaining its strength; and should *sweating* be found to answer, it will be found much more congenial to its execution than the doing it while the fibre is still on the reed."

The measures adopted were successful to a great extent. Though the natives did not adopt all the innovations which had been proposed to them, yet from the supervision practised, they prepared the Sunn carefully according to their own methods, and that of itself was a great advantage; as only the good specimens were purchased by the commercial agents.

STRENGTH OF SUNN FIBRE.

In the anonymous pamphlet entitled, 'Observations on the Sunn Hemp of Bengal,' 1806, it is stated, that "the Court of Directors having sent orders to Bengal for the cultivation of Sunn with increased attention, tolerable success was attained in most places, but a superiority has certainly been manifested in particular spots, such as Dacca, Luckipore, Chittagong. Hurriall, Malda, Budaul, Rungpore, Radnagore, and Soonamooky"—but Commercolly and Cuttorah are not particularised, though good Sunn was no doubt produced at both places. These places have been mentioned now, to show that the experiments were carried on chiefly in Bengal, though it is by no means proved that the soil and climate of that province are better suited than those of many other parts of India for the production of good fibre. Indeed, there is little doubt that, whether owing to differences of soil and climate, or of preparation, the fibre of the same plant as grown in the West of India is stronger than as grown in Bengal. In the anonymous 'Obs.' it is further stated, that "the culture has not only been attended to by the most scientific men in India, but the means of dressing it so as to preserve the greatest strength to the fibre, &c.; and it is satisfactory to state, that some of the Sunn has exhibited a very considerable proportion of strength beyond the common expectation."

But the above pamphlet is chiefly valuable for giving the results of various "Experiments, made from 1802 to 1806, to ascertain the comparative strength of Sunn with Russian Hemp," made at Messrs. Huddart's rope-manufactory. "But in order to ascertain its comparative merit therewith, it is necessary first to state, that the difference in strength between the best and ordinary Russian Hemp is in the proportion of 5 to 4, sometimes as 6 to 4: that the strength of the best Russian Hemp to the best Sunn bears a proportion as 6 to 4." (p. 5.) "From hence it must be admitted, the Sunn, manufactured in the usual mode for cordage, cannot be put in competition for strength with Russian Hemp;" but when prepared by Huddart's Warm Register, "the proportion between Sunn so manufactured and the best cordage made in the common mode, when above six-inch, is in favour of the Sunn cordage, progressively as the size is increased." Instances are then given of "a sixteen-inch cable made from Sunn in 1802, laid down as a mooring cable at Gravesend the whole winter; and after various examinations, by cutting off the clinches, upon different ships taking it in as moorings, for five months in succession, it was found so fresh and good, that it went by the last ship that rode by it, to India, as a working cable." (p. 6.) It was also made into canvas and other cloth with success. "This has been manifested in a topsail made for one of the Indiamen, put on board here without any intimation of its difference; and the sail is returned not worse than the other sails of the ship."[1] (p. 7.)

But it must be remembered that these experiments were made with the Sunn which had been grown and carefully prepared under the supervision of the East India Company's commercial agents. A specimen of one of these *Sunns* is still in the India House, marked per *David Scott,* 1802; which, though having the light colour and showing the appearance of ordinary Sunn, is from four to five feet in length, much cleaner, both strong and flexible, and also divisible into fine fibrils. A salvage of it bore 175 lb., when some Sunn sent to the Exhibition of 1851 bore only 150 lb. There is a specimen also of the heckled Sunn, per *Wellesley,* 1802, about three feet long, a bright-looking fibre, but with a good deal of the cellular part still adhering to the fibres. Ordinary Sunn is, moreover, only about three feet in length, rather dirty; fibres entangled and intermixed with portions of the boon, as well as with many short fibres; hence much loss is sustained in heckling, and the men complain of the irritating particles which are given off during this process.

The want of strength is not surprising, for though three days is thought sufficient for the steeping, we learn that the natives, from the press of other work or from indolence, sometimes allow the stems to remain in steep for fifteen days. (*v.* Wisset, p. 195.) It has already been mentioned that Dr.

[1] Its weft only was Sunn, the warp Flax.

Roxburgh, in heckling, found it lost about one third; though the tow is of course of use for some purposes.

But that some good Sunn is also prepared in the present day is evident from the difference in price which it brings in the English market. Mr. Dickson also having passed some of it through his machine; the Sunn has become light-coloured and clean, with the fibres lying parallel to one another, and showing them as well fitted for spinning. Parties who have seen it have pronounced it well worth £35 a ton.

That good Sunn may also be produced in some of the old localities is evident, for Mr. Sconce, when Collector of Chittagong, having grown some Hemp and Flax in this district, as already mentioned at p. 177, grew also some Sunn, which was thus reported on by the Hemp and Flax Committee of the Agri-Horticultural Society, 1843.

"G. *Sample of Sunn* (*Crotalaria juncea*) *or Indian Hemp.*—Quality in every respect superior; clean, strong, of even fibre; would meet with an extensive and ready sale in Europe; it would pay better if not heckled, but merely scutched.

"In addition to the above, your Committee would beg to call the attention of the Society to the memorandum appended to this Report, obligingly furnished by Mr. Deneef."

"G. This is also a good-quality sample; but, like samples B and E (dressed Hemp and dressed Flax), it has been prepared in too expensive a manner to admit of its being profitable. It is much better than my sample of Sunn, and perhaps would fetch £20 per ton in the English market." The sample of true Hemp grown at Chittagong, Mr. Deneef says, would have fetched £18, but if better prepared, £25 per ton.

CULTURE IN MADRAS TERRITORIES.

Dr. Roxburgh, in describing the culture about Rajahmundry, and in the Northern Circars, states that the seed is sown towards the close of the rains, in October or November. A strong clayey soil suits it best, the farmers say. About 120 lb. of seed to the acre is the usual allowance. It requires no further care than being covered with the soil, which is done with the common Hindoo harrow. In February or March soon after the flowers drop, and before the seeds are ripe (when the Telinga people consider the fibre to be in the greatest perfection), it is pulled up by the roots, like Hemp in Europe; half dried in the sun, then tied up in bundles, and committed to the water, where it is steeped, &c. This plant, he further mentions—and it is the only one—is also cultivated there by some natives to feed their milch cows with during the dry season. It is very nourishing, and causes them to give more milk than most other food. It only bears two or three cuttings; after that, the plants perish. ('Corom. Plants,' v. ii, t. 193.)

Sunn is also cultivated in Rajahmundry as a second crop, on wet lands, with profit to the ryut; and is even exported from that and other Northern districts in some quantity.

Dr. Buchanan, in his 'Journey through Mysore,' mentions that, at Bangalore, Goni is a considerable article of manufacture, and that it is a coarse, but very strong sackcloth, from eighteen to twenty-two cubits in length, and from a half to a quarter of a cubit broad, and that it is made from the *Janupa*, or *Crotalaria juncea.* The *Goni* maker hires from some farmer as much high ground as he thinks will raise a quantity of *Janupa* sufficient to employ his family in manufacturing for the year. The soil may be red or black, but is not manured. The soil is sown broadcast when the rains become heavy. But it is also cultivated on rice-ground in the dry season, with the aid of irrigation. It requires four months to ripen. When cut down it is spread out to the sun and dried. The seed is then beaten out by striking the pods with a stick. The stems are then tied up in large bundles, and preserved in stacks or under sheds. The bundles are taken out as wanted, and put in the water, at which time their bands are cut, and the stems, being opened out, are kept down to the bottom by stones or mud. According to circumstances, they require to be kept in the water from six to eight days. When the bark separates easily from the stems they are taken out of the water, and a man taking them by handfuls beats them on the ground, and occasionally washes them, until they are clean, and at the same time picks out with his hand the remainder of the boon, until nothing except the bark be left. This is then dried, and, being taken up by handfuls, is beaten with a stick to separate and clean the fibres. ('Journ.,' i, p. 226.)

But when at Bhawani Kudal, in the Coimbatore district, he found a great deal of the *Shanapu*. This was grown by the farmers, who, when it is fit for steeping, sell it to the people called Telinga Chitties, who make the Hemp, and work it up into *goni* or sackcloth. There it thrives best on a poor, sandy soil, which, however, is manured any day between the 12th of July and the same day of August. The seed is sown broadcast after rain, and very thick—rather more than two bushels for an acre. The stems are sold by the thousand handfuls. Tall plants sell at two rupees for the thousand handfuls; short ones for a rupee and a half.

But the same plant is also cultivated on fields that have produced a crop of rice, between the 12th of January and the 12th of February. In the following month the field is watered, the seed sown, and covered with the plough. Once a month it requires to be watered, and it takes four months to ripen. This is more valuable than the Hemp cultivated on dry field. An acre requires $4\frac{8}{10}$ bushels of seed, and its produce was in those days worth about £1 2*s*. $10\frac{1}{2}$*d*.

Of these two notices the first is interesting, as showing that the natives of Mysore adopt a practice, that of drying their Sunn stems, which is objected to by those of Bengal. The second showing a separation of the occupations of growing and of preparing the fibre; and this may, perhaps, with a congenial climate, account for the goodness of the fibre of the Western coast.

Dr. Wight states that on the Madras side of India, not only the bark of this species, but of *Crotalaria retusa* is employed as Hemp in the manufacture of cordage and canvas. He further found the Janapa or Sunn plant cultivated at Coimbatore. The stems, cut and dried, were afterwards steeped. This loosens the bark, which is then easily stripped off, and undergoes but little further preparation. He found its fibres were next in strength to the *yerkum* or *mudar*, sustaining 407 lb., when the latter bore 552 lb., and has since observed to the Author that the *Sunn*, grown in the Pass of Poonany, open to both monsoons, is stronger than that grown in the interior.

Dr. Hunter has given the following account of the preparation of such fibres near Madras: "The native process of cleaning plants having bark and woody fibres"—of which kind are many of the cordage plants—"is very similar to that followed in cleaning fleshy and pulpy plants, viz., by burying in sand or mud at the edge of a tank or in a river, and leaving them to rot. There is this difference, however, that the plants are steeped longer, and are never exposed to the sun to dry, or stacked and covered with matting to be cleaned by dry beating. If this were done, the woody fibre would get hard and brittle, and would again adhere to the other fibre, which being partially rotten would break in the cleaning. To obviate this the rotted plant is taken up in large handfuls, and beaten on flat stones, first at one end and then at the other, in the same way as clothes are washed by the Dhobee; they are next well rubbed and washed to separate the impurities, and are spread out on the ground to dry. We can hardly wonder that most of the string and rope made from fibres prepared in this rude, coarse way, should be dark in colour, possessed of no strength, and of little value. As a general rule, every day's steeping of a fibre takes from its strength and imparts more or less colour. To obviate this, woody plants should be first well beaten with a mallet; then the bark should be separated from the stalk, for it is on the inner part of the bark that the fibres for cordage usually occur. When the bark is brought to a pulpy state, it must be well washed in clean water to remove as much of the sap as possible; for this is the distinctive agent which soon causes putrefaction."

CULTURE IN THE WEST OF INDIA.

On the Bombay side *Sunn* is also extensively cultivated, and attracted some attention at the beginning of this century in the island of Salsette, whence it was called Salsette Hemp, which is probably the same substance now called Brown Hemp. On that side of India, Dr. Roxburgh says, as in some other parts of India, the seed is sown towards the close of the rains, when a stronger soil is said to be required. We have seen that Col. Sykes enumerates the Sunn among the spring crops; that is, among those sown in autumn and reaped in spring. This Bombay Hemp or Sunn has always been highly esteemed. Dr. Roxburgh says it is reckoned particularly good—not inferior to the best Russian Hemp ('Fl. Ind.,' iii, p. 263); which he conceives is due to the mode of preparation, which we shall immediately notice. But something must also be owing to climate.

So long ago as the year 1802, some fibre was imported by Capt. Isaacke, of the *Skelton Castle,* which was at first considered to be the real Hemp, and called *Malabar Hemp.* Capt. Eastwick, one of the Directors of the East India Company has informed the Author that Major J. D. Watson, also paid great attention at this period to Malabar Hemp. Dr. H. Scott writes of it, that he does not know whether it be the same plant as the *Sunn* of Bengal, but where very great strength is necessary, the substance obtained from it is preferred to the Bengal Sunn, and is very superior to anything of the kind he has seen in the Guzerat. This, he thinks, may depend more on the steeping of the plant and the preparation, than on any difference in the vegetables that produce it; and this opinion was proved to be correct, for Dr. Roxburgh, having obtained some of the seed, found it to be *Crotalaria juncea.*

It was about the time that Dr. Roxburgh was employed in the culture of fibres in Bengal, he learnt that in the island of Salsette, where the best Sunn is said to be prepared, little or no maceration is employed; that the plant while moist is peeled by the hand, and immediately dried, in the open air or under cover, according to the state of the weather. By peeling, the fibres are better kept in their natural state of arrangement, and give support and strength to each other; whereas, by the process of the Bengalese, they get so materially entangled, that a great loss is always sustained. If they are restored to their natural situation by the heckle, there is a loss of nearly one half of the original quantity, which renders the heckled Sunn of Bengal of a high price.

Dr. Roxburgh further says, in 'Fl. Ind.,' p. 283: "Numerous experiments made by me induce a belief that the superiority of the Hemp depends upon the peeling; but it is probable that the climate of the West of India may be more favorable than that of Bengal for the production of a stronger fibre. For no great attention seems to be paid to the culture, according to recent accounts."

More recently, Capt. Thompson, of the firm of Thompson and Co., rope-makers, of Calcutta, in sending three samples of fibre from the Malabar coast, writes: "Allow me also to hand you three specimens of Hemp and rope made of them that I had brought from the west side of India, grown at the places named on the labels (Calicut, Ghote, and the Concan). These have been tested both at the Arsenal and Government Dockyards, and proved perfectly equal to any and all purposes that cordage made of Russian Hemp has hitherto been used for. From the encouraging reports upon this cordage from the heads of both the Naval and Military Departments, there seems no reason to doubt that this Hemp, and others that are being daily discovered, will completely supersede the importation of Europe-made cordage." Capt. Thompson adds, in a note: "This Hemp is no new discovery. I saw it in England, which led me to try it here (*i. e.*, Calcutta). 31st Dec., 1847."

Dr. Gibson, in a Report on the Agriculture and Horticulture of the districts near Bombay, states, that both the *taag* and *umbaree*, or *Crotalaria juncea* and *Hibiscus cannabinus*, are both reaped in the month of November, and both are stored to await the advent and leisure of the warm weather for stripping. The Tag is most usually pulled up, instead of being cut off; as in the latter way it leaves a strong and dangerous stubble. It is in the Deccan, he adds, reckoned a species of cultivation unworthy of a thorough-bred husbandman, and only to be grown by the Ghat people and the wilder tribes. The Wunjaras not unfrequently hire land to grow it on, as it is essential for affording them twine and materials for their gunnies. The seeds are beaten out with a stick, a part is reserved for future sowing, and the overplus is used to feed buffaloes. Its cultivation is more attended to in the Concan and Ghat districts than in the Deccan. It appears to suit any soil, and clears the ground of weeds. Having cultivated the plant to some extent in 1841, he found that it gave a return quite equal, if not superior, to that of the common grains of the country. Its chief expense consists in stripping the fibre. He had tried to separate the fibre by beating, after a slight immersion, but found the interior pith too soft to admit the separation of the fibre by that means. It is first steeped in water for five days

—in running water—and the fibre is afterwards separated by the fingers.

It is used by the natives for articles requiring much strength, as fishing nets, &c. (Agric. and Hortic. Soc. of Western India, 1842.)

Some specimens of the fibre of the *taag*, or *Crotalaria juncea*, having been sent to England to be reported on, were spoken of in the following terms, though the name of the reporter at Hull is not given (1840):

"This sample, No. 2 (*Crotalaria juncea* or *tag*), appears to me of the same quality as the Baltic. I return a part of it, made ready for spinning. You will see the great similarity of the two. My twine-spinner assures me that by taking it sooner, and by using more care in the steeping and exposure, it will be *fully equal to the Baltic*. Surely, by attention, this may be accomplished. It may require Englishmen to direct, and our implements (which are truly simple) to be used—when I have no doubt of the successful result, alike to the grower, the merchant, and our country. Your Hemp is very clean—a material point,—but it wants more beating and dressing; and I think the natives have not proper implements to do it with. You cannot improve in your mode of packing; it is decidedly superior to the Baltic. I do not despair of seeing the produce of the Baltic supplanted by that of India; as the defect appears to me solely to arise in the management of it: it stands too long before it is pulled or cut, or is too much steeped or exposed, to get the fibre to separate from the stalk." (Agric. and Hortic. Soc. of Western India, 1842.)

Wuckoo nar (or fibre), or *Travancore Flax*, as it has been proposed to be called, is another instance of the effects of locality and of climate, combined with variations in the mode of preparation, in making it impossible, from the appearance of fibres, to know the plants producing them. To the Exhibition of 1851, some specimens of strong canvas were sent from Travancore, which have been much approved of by competent judges, from the compactness and strength of the manufacture. On trial, it was found that a piece of this canvas, containing *eleven* threads, was equal in strength to canvas containing *fourteen* threads of Polish rein. Along with the canvas, a few small heads of the fibre were sent, and labelled *Wuckoo* and *Wucknoo nar*, or fibre, from Travancore. The appearance of this fibre is totally different from any other which comes from India; as it is in the state as if prepared for spinning into thread, and must have been combed or heckled. The fibres are brownish in colour, about 3 to 4 feet in length, clean, and shining, not so fine as Flax, but still resembling some of the coarser kinds. A very competent judge informed the Author that it might be sold for the purposes of Flax, or as a kind of Flax, and was worth £35 a ton. So, some specimens sent to Dundee were valued at the same sum, and it was said could be used for the same purposes as Flax, though rather too dry.

As the Wuckoo nar was so highly thought of, and the Author was unable to form any opinion respecting the plant which produced it, he requested his friend, Dr. Wight, so well acquainted with the Botany of the Peninsula, to ascertain the botanical name of the Wuckoo plant. The more so, as Travancore, with Cochin as a harbour which large ships can enter, is a favorable locality for the export of an article which seems a very desirable object of commerce. Dr. Wight having written to friends in the locality to ascertain this point, was surprised on hearing, as was the Author on being informed, that the Wuckoo plant of Travancore was nothing but the Taag of the Western ghauts, and which further north yields the so well-known Brown Hemp of Bombay. The Author may mention as a curious confirmation of the result obtained, that specimens of the Brown Hemp, passed through Mr. Dickson's machine, are exactly like the fibres of the Wuckoo nar, as sent from Travancore.

The whole subject forms a striking confirmation of the importance of what the Author has frequently endeavoured to impress upon planters and experimentalists, that is, the effects of climate and of physical agents on the products of plants. As these will be found to be quite as important as seed from particular localities, or the adoption of methods of culture which may be suitable to one and not to another locality where it is attempted to introduce them.

Besides Bengal, Madras, and the West of India, Sunn, that is, *Crotalaria juncea,* is also extensively cultivated in North-

West India, for ordinary use. The cultivation may be much increased, and it is probable with considerable addition to the strength and flexibility of the fibre, by the aid of irrigation; and this is easily managed in some, and will be so in most places when the great Ganges Canal is in active operation. It will be found there, as elsewhere, that, as stated by Mr. Deneef as his declared opinion, nothing is wanted but an improved preparation to make it a desirable article for the English market.

Enough has been said respecting the value of common Sunn for most of the ordinary purposes of cordage, and also of the invaluable properties of the fibre of the same plant as grown in the Western ghauts, and where its culture may be indefinitely extended, and easily exported by sea. Though some recent Sunn broke with 150 lb., and some old Sunn bore 170 lb., when Petersburgh broke with 160 lb., the two former may not be able to bear the same degree of twisting as the latter, but see the experiments at pp. 268, 289.

Brown Hemp has, by competent judges, been considered equal to many of the purposes of Petersburgh Hemp; and the Wuckoo nar bore 175 lb. in the same experiments. Dr. Roxburgh made and published a very valuable set of experiments on Sunn, as grown in Bengal. (*v.* Table, p. 268.) In Dr. Wight's recent experiments, the Janapa or Sunn bore 407 lb., and Cotton ropes 346 lb.; but the Ambaree or *Hibiscus cannabinus*, 290 lb., and Coir, 224 lb. The Janapa, or Madras Hemp, as it is called in the markets here, is thus mentioned by Mr. Dickson, as already quoted at p 133.

"Madras Hemp, valued when imported at £24 per ton, 2 cwt. 3 qrs. 3 lb:

Produced by the machines:

	cwt.	qr.	lb.	
Clean, long fibre, good, valued at £45 per ton	1	1	7½	
Clean tow, valued at £30 per ton .	1	1	9	
Waste	0	0	14½	
				2 3 3

Cost of preparation . 6*s.* 1½*d.*

"This Hemp, when prepared with the Patent Liquid, became soft, white, and so fine when heckled, as to bear the closest comparison with Flax at £80 per ton. It is better than any Russian Flax for fine spinning.

"Bombay Hemp, rough and dark, and valued at £20 per ton:

"This article, being similarly prepared, was considered equal in value with the Madras Hemp."

Though the importation of Sunn for a time diminished, it has again, during the last ten or twelve years, been imported in increasing quantities; and though here it is avowedly used only for ordinary purposes, Mr. J. Kyd, ship-builder, of Kidderpore, near Calcutta, maintained that the Sunn, if properly cured and dressed, would prove equal to Russian Hemp, and even as it was then produced, it was little inferior to it. All that he considered was required to bring this Hemp to a state of perfection, was European superintendence in the growth and manufacture of the material. The natives, moreover, who have many good fibres within their reach, usually make use of Sunn twine, well tanned with the bark of a species of Rhizophora. (*v.* Table of Exports, p. 299.)

The prices of these fibres in the interior, are stated to be from R. 1 8 to Rs. 2 8 per bazar maund; that is, from 3*s.* to 5*s.* for a maund of 84 lb., which is just three fourths of a hundredweight. So, in the Madras territories, it is stated that these fibres may be obtained at 2*s.* a maund in the interior. In Calcutta, Sunn is quoted at about Rs. 5 per maund; and in Bombay at Rs. 4 8 to Rs. 5½ per cwt. in Oct., to Rs. 8 per cwt. in June, but at Rs. 11 in June, 1854.

In the year 1844, when Petersburgh Hemp was selling here for £38 per ton, Indian Brown Hemp was sold for £20, Sunn from £16 to £18, and Jute from £10 to £12.

In Dec., 1854, Bombay Hemp was quoted at £35 to £48, Sunn £27 to £33, Jute £21 to £25, in the same 'Price Current,' when Petersburgh Hemp was selling at £58 to £63.

Comparative Strength between Sunn Cordage, when first made, and three years after, to ascertain the deterioration by Age, and the supposed effects of Tar.

Species of Rope.	Growth of Sunn.	When made.	Where made.	When tried.	Size.	Weight to break. 1803.				Weight to break. 1806.				The average of five trials.
					Inches.	Tons.	cwt.	qrs.	lb.	Tons.	cwt.	qrs.	lb.	per cent.
Hawser-laid Whale-line	Malda	1803	London	1803	6½	6	0	3	11	5	17	0	0	2½
Common Yarn	Ditto	Ditto	Ditto	Ditto	4	2	6	3	0	2	2	2	0	11
	Ditto	Ditto	Ditto	Ditto	3	1	14	2	0	1	9	2	0	14
	Ditto	Ditto	Ditto	Ditto	2½	1	4	1	14	0	19	0	0	20
	Ditto	Ditto	Ditto	Ditto	2	0	17	3	14	0	14	1	0	16

Comparative Strength between Cordage made in the common way, from the best Petersburgh clean and ordinary Hemp, and the Sunn Cordage made by Huddart's Warm Register.

Size.	COMMON MAKE.								Cuttorah Sunn in 1802.				
	Best Petersburgh.				Ordinary.								
Inches.	Tons.	cwt.	qrs.	lb.	Tons.	cwt.	qrs.	lb.	Tons.	cwt.	qrs.	lb.	
8	14	8	1	20	12	4	0	0	15	7	1	24	Warm Registered.
7	12	17	1	8	10	16	3	20	10	18	1	8	
6½	9	17	0	0	9	10	2	0	8	2	2	0	
5	6	7	1	8	5	17	0	0	5	17	2	8	
4½	5	19	2	10	4	17	0	0	4	10	1	20	
4	4	13	1	20	3	7	0	0	3	3	1	14	
3	2	15	0	14	2	6	3	7	2	2	2	24	
2½	1	19	1	14	1	10	0	0	No Warm Registered of these sizes.				
2	1	7	2	14	1	6	0	14					

Comparative Strength of the above best Petersburgh clean Hemp Cordage, in December, 1802, and May, 1806.

8	14	8	1	20	12	19	2	0	The depreciation of strength would be in greater proportion with ordinary Hemp.
7	12	17	1	8	11	13	2	0	
5	6	7	1	8	5	16	0	0	

Jubbulpore Hemp (*Crotalaria tenuifolia*, Roxb.)

Among the cordage sent to the Great Exhibition of 1851, there were some specimens sent by Messrs. Harton and Co., rope-makers, of Calcutta. These appeared to be of excellent quality, and were said to be made of Jubbulpore Hemp. The first notice which we have of this substance is in the 'Proceedings of the Agri-Horticultural Society,' where some Hemp grown in the Jubbulpore Garden from country seed sown at the end of June, 1840, and cut in October, and of canvas woven from the fibre in the School of Industry at Jubbulpore, were presented to the Society by Dr. F. M'Leod, Esq. When Mr. Williams, Superintendent of the above School, and by whom the plant had been grown and the fibre prepared, visited England in the summer of 1853, he presented the Author with a specimen of this fibre. This is long, that is, upwards of five feet in length, of the colour of Petersburgh Hemp, rather roughly prepared, inasmuch as some of the bast is still in the form of narrow ribands, but most of it separated into fine and strong fibres. In the experiments which the Author had made with it, its strength was proved to be at least equal, if not superior, to that of Russian Hemp, inasmuch as when a selvage of Petersburgh Hemp broke with 160 lb., one of Jubbulpore Hemp did not break with less than 190 lb. When examined by experienced brokers and manufacturers, it was considered an excellent substitute for Russian Hemp, and if a little more carefully prepared would leave hardly anything more to be desired, and was valued as worth at from £30 to £35 a ton, that is before any rise took place in the price of fibres.

The plant yielding this fibre having been discovered, we subjoin a description by Dr. Roxburgh, and though some botanists unite it with *Crotalaria juncea*, we keep it separate, until its identity has been determined by experiment. We also add the first notice of this fibre, and of rope made from it.

Crotalaria tenuifolia is a native of Coromandel, which is perennial, ramous, straight, furrowed, hoary. Leaves linear, sericeous underneath. Stipules minute, subulate. Racemes terminal. Legumes sessile, clavate, many-seeded.

In the Botanic Garden (Calcutta) it is perennial, growing to the height of nine feet, with numerous, slender, furrowed, straight branches, which are again more ramous at the top. During the cool season, each twig ends in a long raceme of large, yellow flowers, and the seed ripens in two months.

In the 'Proceedings of the Agri-Horticultural Society' for April, 1851, we find Captain Thompson presenting some dressed samples of the fibre from Jubbulpore, and a piece of rope made of it, part of the rigging made for some ships that were dismantled in the Bay of Bengal the year before, and which has proved equal to any Europe-made rope.

A good account of this fibre and its uses having appeared in the 'Journ. of the Agri-Hortic. Society,' and referring to the plant producing it, we here subjoin extracts from the paper.

At a meeting of the Agricultural and Horticultural Society of India, held on the 12th June, 1852, Messrs. Harton and Co. submitted specimens of the Jubbulpore Hemp fibre in a raw state; as also of fishing lines and tarred rigging made from it. A quantity of this raw material, procured from Jubbulpore by Messrs. Harton and Co. and the late Capt. Thompson about three years ago, was considered so well adapted for cordage purposes, owing to its excellent quality and great strength, that they have been willing to pay a high price for it, to meet the heavy cost entailed by the transport of so bulky an article from Jubbulpore to Calcutta. In consequence of an impression on their part, that the fibre in question was the produce of *Cannabis sativa*—it being so similar in many respects to Russian Hemp—the subject was deemed by the Society deserving of further inquiry.

An application was accordingly made to Mr. Williams, Superintendent of the School of Industry at Jubbulpore, for a small quantity of seed, which was sown immediately on its receipt on the 23d of June, 1852, in the Society's garden. In the course of nine weeks the seedlings had attained the height of 8½ feet, *without branching*—an important point in a fibrous-yielding plant—and commenced flowering in three months from the date of sowing.

Dr. Falconer, to whom a specimen was referred, has pronounced it to be *Crotalaria tenuifolia* of Roxburgh, which Wight and Arnott, and some other botanists, regard as merely a variety of *C. juncea*, the plant affording the well-known "Sunn Hemp" of commerce. But their opinion, it may be observed, is founded on dried specimens. The habit differs very much from that of *C. juncea*.

Messrs. W. H. Harton and Co. have been kind enough to furnish the following memorandum regarding the above fibre:

"This material has been tested several times in the Government Service, both Military and Marine, and some ropes have been found equal to the staple cordage of Europe. A coil of bolt rope, manufactured by us from Jubbulpore Hemp, tested last year in the Marine Department, broke with a strain of 57 cwt. A coil of the same size, taken from one of H.M.'s vessels, was tested shortly after, and broke with a strain of 59 cwt. It may be observed, that the Hemp used in the Naval yards of the British Government, is all selected from the fleet of hemp-laden vessels, before any is permitted to be delivered to private parties. This Jubbulpore Hemp can no doubt be considerably improved, were the preparing process in the hands of Europeans, manufactured according to the Russian method, instead of being left, as at present, so entirely to the careless and ignorant natives."

The following extract from Mr. Williams's letter, dated Jubbulpore, the 19th Nov., 1852, will close this brief notice of a fibre, which, no doubt, will be better appreciated when its merits become more generally known:

"I am pleased to learn that the seed of the 'Jubbulpore Hemp,' sent down by me in June last, has germinated so well in Calcutta. I can only grow it to advantage here along the ridges of the neighbouring hills (where it attains the height of from six to seven feet); that grown in the plains turning out weak in fibre when made into Hemp. I have lost considerably by sending this Hemp down to Calcutta for sale, having had the misfortune to have had several boats burnt while going down the river; and the steamers decline taking a cargo of it, in consequence of its combustible nature. The native insurance offices at Mirzapore also object to insure it, except at such high rates as to prevent all chance of profit; so that if it could be cultivated along the banks of the river, I have no doubt but that in a few years it would turn out a profitable source of export."

A copy of the official Report on the Experiments made in the Arsenal of Fort William having been subsequently published, is here subjoined.

Report of several kinds of Rope, the manufacture of Messrs. W. H. Harton and Co., of Calcutta, tested in the Arsenal of Fort William, 3d June, 1853.

Kind and quality of Rope.	Size.	Government proof.			Breaking weight.		
	Inches.	cwt.	qr.	lb.	cwt.	qr.	lb.
Oiled Jubbulpore Hemp (*Crotalaria tenuifolia*), Artillery Traces . .	3	36	0	0	43	2	0
Untarred do., superior four-strand, plain laid	3¼	42	0	0	83	0	0
Untarred Dunchee (*Æschynomene cannabina*), do., do. . . .	3½	49	0	0	75	0	0
Pine-apple Fibre, do., do. . .	3¼	42	0	0	57	0	0

(Signed) J. WILKINS,
Officiating Prin. Conductor,
Rear Godowns.

Some of the properties of this fibre may no doubt be due to the peculiar characteristics of the plant; but a good deal is no doubt also due to the soil and climate in which it is grown, and something probably to its having been grown and prepared under Mr. Williams's personal superintendence. This is obvious from the fact, stated by Mr. Williams, that he was only able to grow it on the sides of the hills; that grown in the plains below, he observes, was weaker in the fibre. Mr. Henley having grown some of this plant from the seed sent from

Jubbulpore, has observed to the Author, that, when grown in the lower provinces, although it attains a great height and grows luxuriantly, it is weaker in fibre and the produce smaller in quantity than when grown higher up the country.

The following reports have been made of this fibre by practical men:

"The Jubbulpore Hemp is a very strong article, and would take well if it could be sold cheap enough. A considerable quantity could be sold in Dundee." In another note it is stated to be "of considerable value, and that a good price could be got both for it and for good Sunn, valued at £30 and £35 a ton." Some of it sold, in the summer of 1853, for £27 a ton; when it was said to be worth £30 a ton, if a little better prepared.

DHUNCHEE FIBRE, *Sesbania aculeata* (formerly *Æschynomene cannabina*, Roxb., 'Fl. Ind.,' iii, p. 335, and *Æ. spinulosa*, do., p. 333; *Leguminosæ*).

The natives of Bengal familiarly employ and highly esteem a fibre which is known to them by the name of *Dhunchee*, *Dhunicha*, and *Dhunsha*. It is produced by a plant which Dr. Roxburgh thought was the same as the *Æschynomene cannabina* of König. This was described by Retz, and stated to be a native of the Malabar coast, and that its stems yielded a strong and useful fibre, as a substitute for Hemp. Messrs. Wight and Arnott, in their 'Flora of the Indian Peninsula,' consider it to be identical with *Sesbania cochinchinensis*, which they have from China.

Dr. Roxburgh states that he had not found his plant in a wild state, but that, in various parts of Bengal, it was cultivated for the fibres of its bark, which form a coarse substitute for Hemp. Messrs. Wight and Arnott (l. c.) unite the plant described by Dr. Roxburgh with one which is very common in all parts of India in the rainy season, the *Sesbania aculeata* of Persoon, and which is called Juyunti in Bengal, and *dhundain* in North-West India. It springs up in rice-fields, and other wet cultivation, during the rainy season. These two varieties are thus described by Messrs. Wight and Arnott, under the name of—

Sesbania aculeata, herbaceous, annual, erect, sparingly branched, glabrous; stem and petioles usually sprinkled with minute cartilaginous points; leaves eight to ten times longer than broad; leaflets twenty to forty pairs, linear, obtuse, mucronate; racemes axillary, peduncled, erect, lax, often about half the length of the leaves; few-flowered; flowers pretty large (more than half an inch long), on slender pedicels; corolla about four times the length of the calyx; legumes erect, nearly terete, sharp-pointed.

Dr. Roxburgh gives the following general directions for its culture. The soil is generally low and wet, and not requiring much preparation, as the plant is hardy, growing from six to ten feet, and rapid in growth. This renders it advantageous to cultivate, especially as it is considered a meliorating crop. The time of sowing is when the soil has been moistened by the first showers of April or May. About thirty pounds of seed are allowed to the acre, and less weeding is required than for *Jute*. The crop is ready to cut in September and October, though the fibre does not suffer if left standing till the seed is ripe, in November. The process of steeping and cleaning the fibre is similar to that required for *Sunn*, that is, *Crotalaria juncea*. The general produce of an acre is from one hundred to one thousand pounds of ill-cleaned fibre, the current price somewhat less than that of *Paut*, viz., *Corchorus olitorius* and *capsularis*. The expense of cultivation, including land-rent, is about nine rupees.

This plant, generally cultivated about Calcutta during the rains, grows to the height of from six to ten feet, the fibres are long (six to seven feet), but coarser and more harsh than those of Hemp, unless cut at a very early period. From its great strength it is well calculated for the manufacture of cordage and cables. In Bengal, the fishermen make drag-ropes to their nets of this substance, on account of its strength, and durability in water. Indeed, by the Bengalese it is considered more durable in water than either *Sunn* or *Paut*.

It has been observed to the Author by one gentleman well acquainted with this fibre in India, that he was at a loss to know why the Dhunchee remained so much neglected in this country, as it is really a very excellent fibre for common cord and twine purposes, and certainly very much superior in strength and durability to Jute. It is also a much hardier plant than Jute; the latter, indeed, being rather an uncertain crop, for the production of the fine, long, silky fibre, so much called for in this country. Another gentleman observed, that thoughr ather wiry it was strong, and chiefly remarkable for its contraction when wetted, so much so, that it would even carry away the mainmast of a ship by mere contraction.

Mr. Deneef, the Belgian farmer, presented samples of the Bengal Hemp, called *Dhuncha,* to the Agri-Horticultural Society, in November, 1840, and stated that they had been dressed after the Belgian mode. A begah, he says, will yield 173 lb. of cleaned fibre, and 92 lb. of seed. A woman can dress about 4 lb. a day. In April, 1851, Captain Thompson presented a dressed sample of the fibre of the *Dhuncha* of Bengal, and a piece of rope made of it. This rope, he stated, had been used in various ways for nearly two years, and from various reports upon it, he thought it likely to come into extensive use. Specimens of the fibre and rope were also sent to the Exhibition of 1851, and we have already given (at p. 292) the result of the trial made with this rope in the Arsenal of Fort William, whence it appears that a three and a half inch rope of Dhunchee broke with not less than 75 cwt., though the Government Proof, required for such rope, was only 49 cwt.

The price of the Dhunchee, in the interior, has long been about R. 1 8 per maund. The following are reports upon this fibre:

"The Dhunchee is very suitable for ropes, and if it will take in tar, is of considerable value. It would probably fetch from £30 to £35 a ton, and after being introduced and known, perhaps £5 more." It was also valued by others at £35 in 1853.

These fibres, in fact all the fibres from the East, would be much more valuable if properly scutched; and if scutching mills were sent out, these fibres could be brought in a greatly improved state to market.

Maljhun, or Maloo Climber, *Bauhinia racemosa* (*Leguminosæ*).

Along the forests of the Sewaliks and the hot valleys of the Himalayas, from the doons of the North-West to the valley of Assam, may be seen a magnificent climber, called *Maljhun* or *Maloo,* with a two-lobed leaf. Of this, the Author observed, in his 'Himalayan Botany,' p. 184, that *Bauhinia racemosa* hangs in elegant festoons from the tops of lofty trees, which one is at a loss to conceive how, from the distance of its root from the stems, it could ever have ascended; but occasionally a half-killed tree displays the mode of its progress, and indicates the destruction it must have created in the forest.

With the bark of this plant, which, when stripped off, is of a reddish-brown colour, the natives of these mountains make ropes. It was one of those to which Dr. Roxburgh turned his attention, and which has been frequently noticed by travellers in the Himalayas. Capt. Huddleston states that the stems are usually cut in July and August; the outer bark being stripped off, is thrown away, and the inner is used for ropes, as wanted, by being previously soaked in water, and twisted when wet. It is also said to be boiled, and beaten with mallets, which renders it soft and pliable for being twisted into ropes and strings for charpaes. Though the fibre makes very strong ropes, it is not over-durable, and rots if kept constantly in water. Though not collected for sale, it is very abundant all along the foot of the mountains.

Major Swetenham, formerly of the Bengal Engineers, on the 11th of November, 1840, despatched to the late Mr. Thomason some of the fibres of the Maloo creeper, and a specimen of a rope made from it, which he obtained from the valley of the Jumna River within the hills. He describes it as making strong coarse ropes, which he had found to answer well for suspension bridges, though he was unable to say how long they would bear exposure to moisture, for "they had been in use only for two or three years, and iron suspension bridges substituted." Specimens of the fibre, and rope made from it, were sent to the Exhibition of 1851, from Bhagulpore, and called *Patwa* or *Mawal* fibre.

Bauhinia scandens, similar in properties and uses to the above, is another species of the same genus, of which we find the following notice in the 'Journal of the Agri-Hortic. Society,' vi, p. 185. Specimens of the fibre of *Bauhinia scandens*, and cloth made therefrom, were sent to Major Jenkins by Major Hannay, who mentions that the fibre is used by the Nagas. The plant, Major Jenkins adds, is not uncommon about Gowhatti. It was recognized by Dr. Falconer, from a few leaves forwarded by Major Jenkins, to belong to *Bauhinia scandens*, a common species in Silhet. Captain Thomson having tested this fibre, reports on it to the following effect:

"The line made from the fibre sent by Major Jenkins, sustained for forty-five minutes, 168 lb., having stretched six inches only in three feet, and therefore is about the same strength with our best *Sunn* Hemp. But, whether from the mode of preparation or the nature of the material, is so harsh and stubborn, and the fibres stick so close together, that the heckles tear it to pieces, and injure its strength."

Dr. Buchanan, in his 'Survey,' mentions both these species as used for many of the same purposes.

DHAK, OR PULAS FIBRE, *Butea frondosa*, also *B. superba* (*Leguminosæ*).

One of the most generally diffused plants is the *Dhak* or *Pulas*, as it may be found near many villages, forming their tracts of apparently useless because jungle-like land, but which, in fact, is a place of pasturage for their cattle. The Dhak, which is the most usual shrub, yields them firewood, and its bark and roots fibrous matter, which is used as cordage, or beaten to a kind of oakum used for caulking boats. Though such fibre is unimportant as an object of commerce, it is of great use to the natives themselves, for agricultural and domestic purposes, as it is possessed of a good deal of strength. Some Pulas fibre was sent to the Exhibition of 1851, from Beerbhoom.

A ruby-coloured gum, which has been called *Butea kino*, exudes from incisions into the bark, which, though it abounds in astringent matter, Mr. Teil, of Calcutta, has found difficult to apply to the tanning of leather, but its colouring matter is powerful and permanent. In the jungles, where the Dhak is allowed to grow into a small tree, it is highly ornamental from the splendour of its inflorescence, and is further useful from its large flowers, called *teesoo* and *keesoo*, yielding a beautiful dye, which is likely to come into extensive use. This plant is further interesting, as that from which the name of the Pelasgi has been supposed to be derived by Mr. Peacock, in his 'Greece in India.'

PARKINSONIA ACULEATA.—Though this is an American plant, it may, like the Agave, be enumerated among Indian products, because it may now be met with as one of the most common trees in villages and cantonments, flourishing with less care than any other. Some of its fibre, of a beautiful white colour, was sent to the Exhibition of 1851, as a material for paper-making, and which could probably be afforded at a cheap rate, from the cuttings of the shoots of this plant. It, however, has been considered in this country as wanting in strength. It might, nevertheless, be found useful in mixing with other fibrous substances, and beaten up into half-stuff.

BOKHARA CLOVER.—A plant under this name has attracted some notice in Ireland, on account of its fibre. It is the *Melilotus arborca*, and is nearly allied to *M. leucantha*, and therefore not a true Clover. It grows so freely as to yield five or six cuttings in the season of green herbage, from which, it is said, a considerable proportion of strong fibre may be obtained; but the Committee of the Irish Flax Society state, that the trials made in steeping this plant were unsuccessful with them.

EXPORTS OF SUNN AND OTHER HEMP-LIKE FIBRES, ETC., FROM INDIA.

In the beginning of this work, when referring to the great increase which had taken place in the commerce of Indian fibres, a tabular statement was given (p. 9) of the exports of fibrous substances from the three Presidencies. In subsequent pages, the detailed exports of Coir and of Jute have been separately given, and under the head of *Ambaree* or *Hibiscus* fibre, it was stated that the detailed exports of this fibre would be given along with those of Sunn, because the two are not distinguished in the Reports of the Exports from India or in the Imports into this country. Indeed, in the latter, Jute has not hitherto been separated from the others; though it will be so in future reports. In the following table, therefore, the details of the Exports of Indian substitutes for Hemp are given, consisting chiefly of Sunn (Crotalaria); but some Hibiscus, and perhaps a little of Dhunchee, may be included.

Exports.	Hemp. (Sunn.)	Canvas bolts.	Hemp Twine.	Log lines.
From Calcutta—				
To United Kingdom	Mds. 5,641	—	137	—
„ North America	1,885	—	1,593	—
„ Hamburgh	80	—	—	—
„ Mauritius	12	348	490	85
„ New South Wales	17	150	1,097	653
„ Cape of Good Hope	—	15	—	—
„ Guam	—	102	—	—
„ Pegu	—	272	447	69
„ Coast of Coromandel	—	314	1,225	15
„ Coast of Malabar	—	728	2,987	39
„ Penang, Singapore, &c.	—	68	868	437
„ Ceylon	—	—	407	74
„ China	—	—	50	—
Total	Mds. 7,635	1,997	10,301	1,372
Value	Rs. 15,276	12,672	93,284	9,716
				Gunny bags (of Sunn?)
From Madras—				
To United Kingdom	Cwt. 294	—	—	—
„ Indian French ports	—	—	—	27,750
„ Arabian and Persian Gulfs	75	77	—	—
„ Ceylon	—	—	—	25,000
„ Maldives	—	60	—	
„ Pegu	—	—	—	3,500
„ Bombay	1,709	333	—	—
„ Cape of Good Hope	—	—	—	2,700
„ Travancore	17	—	—	—
Total	Cwt. 2,095	470	—	58,950
Value	Rs. 10,577	3,711	—	6,644
	Hemp and Hemp Rope.			
From Bombay—				
To United Kingdom	Cwt. 7,851	—	—	—
„ African Coast	16	—	—	—
„ Arabian and Persian Gulfs	2,925	—	—	—
„ Guzerat	500	—	} 144	—
„ Other Home ports	85	—	}	—
„ „ Foreign ports	—	—	65	—
Total	Cwt. 11,856	—	209	—
Value	Rs. 72,483	—	1,503	—

In a late Minute, published by the Madras Government (19th September, 1854) for the express purpose of directing attention to the fibrous productions of that Presidency, the exports are given as valued at the following sums, in the respective years from 1847 to 1852, excluding Coir and Coir rope. The year selected in this work, in consequence of the published accounts of the three Presidencies being complete, is that in which the exports were the smallest.

	Hemp.
1847-48 . . .	Rs. 19,819
1848-49 . . .	23,242
1849-50 . . .	23,076
1850-51 . . .	10,577
1851-52 . . .	46,683

Among the Imports of the three Presidencies, we find Cordage and Canvas; but excellent cordage is now made in Calcutta, both by Messrs. Thompson and by Messrs. Harton, as evidenced by the specimens which both sent to the Exhibition of 1851. Some of the canvas also is of excellent quality, as that sent from Travancore (*v.* p. 285).

Bombay, from its insular situation, requires both its Imports (some by sea, others by causeway) and Exports to be noticed. Among the Imports we find Canvas, 9367 bolts,[1] from the United Kingdom, Calcutta, Malabar, and Canara; Gunny bags, 2,729,407, from Calcutta, Malabar, Canara, and Concan. The first are no doubt made of Jute; but the others, probably, of Sunn. Hemp, 57,126 cwt., from Malabar and Canara, Concan, Guzerat, Goa, and the Arabian and Persian Gulfs. This probably includes both *Sunn* and *Ambaree,* or Crotalaria and Hibiscus fibre. Twine, 9738 cwt., from the United Kingdom, Calcutta, and Guzerat; Fishing Nets from the Concan, probably made of Conkanee Hemp; and Grass cloth from China. Of these, we find among the Re-exports, some Hemp, Canvas, Gunnies, and Twine, as well as China-grass cloth.

[1] Europe Canvas is generally preferred in India, though much dearer, that is, Rs. 24 5 6 per bolt of thirty-nine yards each, and country Canvas being only Rs. 16; because the former is so much more durable, and therefore cheaper in the end. But there is no doubt that some of the Indian Canvas is of much better quality than others; and it is desirable to ascertain where the best qualities are made, as well as of Twine and of Cordage; for though much depends upon manufacture, something is due to the fibre, and not a little to the soil and climate where the plant is grown.

Fibrous Plants of different kinds.

Following, as we have done, an arrangement according to the natural families of plants, for the express purpose of bringing together a number of plants which are allied in properties as they are in structure, we shall pass rapidly from the Leguminous plants to the Nettles and their allies, because few of the plants in the intervening families yield fibres which are as yet of commercial importance, though there are some well qualified to become so, from their great strength and fineness, as well as from the abundance in which they may be procured.

In the West Indies, cordage is made of the bark of a species of Mangrove, which is hence called Rope Mangrove. The coasts of the Bay of Bengal and of the Indian islands abound in the Mangrove, which is found also at the mouths of the Indus. Its bark has been used for tanning purposes, for which it is probably more suitable than for cordage.

Among the *Myrtaceæ*, or Myrtle tribe, we have species of Eucalyptus, called, by the colonists of Australia, "stringy bark," and "box-tree," and remarkable for the stringiness of their bark, which is therefore employed for making canvas and cordage by the aborigines, as mentioned by Bennett, in his 'Wanderings,' i, p. 169. In India the stringy bark of a tree called *koombhee* (*Careya arborea*) is employed by the natives of the countries along the foot of the Himalayas as a slow match for their match-lock guns. Among the fibrous barks sent from Assam to the Exhibition of 1851, was one that is named Roxburghia in the Catalogues. This is no doubt a mistake for some plant called after Dr. Roxburgh, probably *Poivrea Roxburghii*, one of the *Combretaceæ*, of which several are remarkable for tough wood as well as bark.

The *Cucurbitaceæ*, again, or the Cucumber and Melon tribe, which are so extensively cultivated in all tropical countries as food for the natives, abound, according to Dr. Hunter, in fibres of great length.

Indeed, many of the plants which are cultivated in fields or gardens would yield fibre in considerable quantities, which would be useful to the paper-maker, instead of being wasted or burnt. Of these we may instance, among the large family called *Compositæ*, the plant called Jerusalem artichoke, the stems of which abound in fibres. So probably does also the extensively cultivated *Carthamus* or Safflower.

Belonging to this family, we may mention a plant which is remarkable for the under surface of its leaves being covered with a cotton-like tomentum; hence it is called *kupassee*, from *kupas* (a name of cotton). The people in the Himalayas use it as tinder. It is also spun into thread and woven into cloth, of which bags are made. The string, until examined, looks as if formed of fibre. A coarse kind of blanket, called *kurkee*, is said to be made of this substance by the Hill people north of Deyrah. Though curious, this substance is not of much importance.

COROLLIFLORALS (*Corollifloræ*).

In a previous page (131) we have referred to the distinction between Exogenous plants, as having their floral envelopes composed of several or of a single piece. Having now passed through all the former families of plants, we have arrived at those which have the corol composed of a single piece or petal, into which the stamens are inserted. Hence, by botanists they are called *Corolliflorœ*. The arrangement may be useful, in enabling observers abroad, who are unacquainted with Botany, to ascertain the group to which any plant may belong which they find possessed of fibrous, or of any other useful properties.

DOGBANES (*Apocynaceæ*).

Among the division of plants which we have just noticed, there are comparatively few which are known to be useful for fibrous properties; yet there are some which are most conspicuous for the strength of their fibres. These belong to two families of plants which are so nearly allied to each other, that they were united together by the celebrated Jussieu. Both are remarkable for abounding in milky juice; and some of them in caoutchouc, or some analogous products. Of these, the Apocynaceæ or Dogbanes are composed chiefly of trees and shrubs, of which the Oleander is a conspicuous example. But some are herbaceous, as in the case of the Vinca, or Periwinkle as it is called, which shows another characteristic, that is, the climbing habit of many of these plants, as well as the toughness of their fibre, as may easily be ascertained by trying to break any of the long, trailing twigs of this plant, so common in gardens and shrubberies. Among these, is a plant called *Nerium piscidium*, by Dr. Roxburgh, 'Fl. Ind.,' ii, p. 7, common in the Khasya or Silhet Mountains, and there called *Echalat*. It there forms an extensive perennial climber. Its bark contains a large quantity of fibre, which the natives use for the same purposes as Hemp. Dr. Roxburgh, in steeping some of the young shoots in a fish-pond, in order to facilitate the removal of the bark and to clean the fibres, found that many, if not all the fishes, were killed. Hence the specific name which he applied. Dr. Wight has formed the plant into a new genus, Echaltum.

It is probable that there are many other fibre-yielding plants in this and the next family among the climbing species.

Asclepiads (*Asclepiadeæ*).

Closely allied to the *Apocynaceæ* is the family of plants which has been named *Asclepiaceæ* and *Asclepiadeæ*, from the genus *Asclepias*, to which most of the species formerly belonged. Among these, there are several remarkable for their fibrous properties, and many more probably remain to be discovered. Though many of this family of plants abound in the hottest and moistest parts of the world, others are also found in the driest and most barren parts of Asia, with a few species extending even to the North of Africa and to the South of Europe, Siberia, North America, and Japan; and southwards, to the Cape of Good Hope and New Holland. The great majority are distinguished by their twining habit; though their flowers are often inconspicuous, their seed-vessels are remarkable for being in pairs, and which, on bursting, display a quantity of thistle-like down attached to each seed, which floats them about as those of thistles and dandelions. This down may no doubt be turned to some useful purposes, and therefore makes the plants abounding in fibre more valuable, as thus yielding a double product; though it is probably only in dry and barren parts of a country, that it would be desirable to attend to these, instead of to the numerous other fibrous plants which may either be more easily cultivated, or the fibre separated with greater facility.

Syrian Dogbane, *Asclepias syriaca* (*Asclepiadeæ*).

Of the plants of this family, useful both for its down and for its fibrous stem, we may first mention that called Syrian Dogbane, which, although a native of the burning plains of Syria, will grow in colder climes, and is indeed cultivated as far north as Upper Silesia. It is easily propagated either by seed, or by parting the roots. The plants thrive luxuriantly in light soil, but will flourish on any poor land.

The silk-like down which surmounts the seed of this plant, is not more than an inch or two in length; but it has, nevertheless, been usefully applied for articles of dress manufactured of it both in France and in Russia. The fibres of the stem, prepared in the same manner as those of Hemp and Flax, furnish a very long fine thread of a glossy whiteness.

Jetee Fibre, Rajmahl Bowstring Creeper, *Asclepias*, now *Marsdenia tenacissima* (*Asclepiadeæ*).

This comparatively small climbing plant, with greenish-yellow flowers, was found by Dr. Roxburgh's son growing in dry and barren places in the Rajmahl Hills; since then also near Chittagong. Of the fibres of the bark of this plant, the Rajmahl mountaineers make their bowstrings. These are said to last for five years, though in constant use and exposed to all sorts of weather. A drawing and full description of this plant is given by Dr. Roxburgh in his 'Coromandel Plants,' iii, t. 240.

In preparing the fibres of this plant, the Hill people do not put the stems in water, but let them stand in the sun for a day till drier; from the ends, when cut, there exudes a milky juice, which thickens into an elastic substance, like, indeed forming one kind of caoutchouc, acting in the same way in removing black lead marks.

According to Dr. Roxburgh, the fibres of this plant are

not only beautiful in appearance and durable, but the strongest of any he had met with. Some twine made with it bearing 248 and 343 lb. in the dry and wetted states, when Hemp twine bore only 158 and 190 lb. in the same states.

Mr. W. C. Taylor since then met with the same plant near the Palamow coal-mines, having observed his boatmen twisting a substance into thread, which they called *chittee*, of which they made nets, finding it much stronger and more durable than Hemp, and not so liable to rot by being kept in water. Mr. Taylor mentions that the stems are cut into lengths, and then cut down the middle; then dried, and afterwards steeped in water for about an hour or more, which enables the bark to be separated with greater ease; when the fine silky filaments are separated. A 1½-inch rope having been made and sent to Calcutta, was there tested in the Master-Attendant's Office, and found to break with 903 lb., when even Europe rope broke with 1203 lb., and others with greater weights. Its elasticity was considerable, as it stood ninth in strength, but second in elasticity. It was supposed that this might possibly be caused by its being laid up by hand; and it was also observed that the result might have been better, if the yarns had been more easily (evenly?) laid up." But the plant is suited for better purposes than rope-making, besides not being eligible for this purpose, from its comparative rarity and mode of preparation. Mr. Taylor states it might be easily cultivated. (*v.* 'Journ. Agri-Hortic. Soc.,' 1844, p. 221.)

Specimens of the fibre of another species of *Marsdenia*, which has by Dr. Wight been named *M. Roylei*, are stated in the Catalogues to have been sent from Nepal to the Exhibition of 1851. Though the specimens have not been found, we may infer that the fibres of this species are made use of in Nepal.

Orthanthera viminea is another plant of this family well calculated to yield fibre. The Author found it growing at the foot of the Himalayan Mountains, and mentioned it in the following terms in his 'Himalayan Botany,' p. 274. "Another plant of this family, *Orthanthera viminea*, attaining a height of ten feet, is also remarkable for the length and tenacity of its fibres. This grows luxuriantly along the foot of the mountains;

and its long, straight, leafless, slender, and wand-like stems, point it out as seemingly well suited for rope-making."

Other plants of this family, useful for the same purposes, are *Hoya viridiflora*, which yields an excellent fibre, and probably also *Leptadenia spartea*. The fibre of another species of the genus, *L. Jacquemontiana*, was described to the Author, by his late lamented friend Dr. Stocks, as employed in Sindh with *Periploca aphyllum* for making into ropes and bands used for wells, as water does not rot them.

Specimens of the flowers, leaves, immature pods, and stem, of a fibre-yielding plant, were presented by Capt. Hannyington, Political Agent at Purulea in Chota Nagpore, to the Agri-Hortic. Society in 1841.

Capt. H. mentions that this plant is very abundant in the Hills about Purulea, and is also found in the neighbouring plains. It is known to the Coles by the name of *Apoong*. The fibre is said to attain its best condition after the rains. The Secretary mentioned that this plant was introduced into the Botanic Garden from Western India, and is well known to Dr. Wallich, who immediately recognized it as *Holostemma Rheedianum* of Sprengel, the *Ada-Modien* of the Hortus Malabaricus.

But there is no doubt that this family of plants contains many others possessed of useful fibrous properties; but we will conclude with one which is likely to be the most important of all, that is, the *Mudar* or *Yercum*.

MUDAR OR YERCUM FIBRE, *Asclepias* now *Calotropis gigantea*, and *C. Hamiltonii* (*Asclepiadeæ*).

Sans., *Arka* and *Akund*; Arab., *Ashur*; Hindee, *Ak*, *Mudar*, and *Muddar*; Madras, *Yercum*, *Tella Jilladdoo*.

In the Southern, as in the Northern parts of India, there is met with in considerable quantities in all uncultivated, and encroaching even on cultivated grounds, a plant with broad, rather fleshy, glaucous-coloured leaves; and which, on being wounded, gives out a milky juice from every part. This is called *Ak* and *Mudar* in Northern, and *Yercum* in Southern India. Its juice, and the powdered bark of its roots, have long been employed as an alterative by the natives of India, in leprosy and other cutaneous affections, and are no doubt possessed of active properties. Dr. Duncan obtained from it a principle which he called *Mudarine.* In Arabic authors on Materia Medica it is even supposed to have been known to the Greeks. It has long been famous for yielding a kind of Manna, which is called *Sukkur-al-ashur,* and *Ak* or *Mudar ke shukur* (sugar). ('Himal. Bot.,' p. 275.) Lately its milky juice has been collected by making incisions into the plant, and prepared as a substitute for Caoutchouc and Gutta Percha. (*v.* 'Journ. of the Agri-Hortic. Soc. of India,' viii, pp. 107 and 226.) Dr. Riddel calculated that ten average-sized plants will yield as much juice as will make a pound of Gutta-Percha-like substance. This is evaporated in a shallow dish, either in the sun or in the shade; when dry, it may be worked up in hot water with a wooden kneader, as this process removes the acridity of the gum. It becomes immediately flexible in hot water, but is said to become hard in cold water, and is soluble in oil of turpentine, takes impressions, and will no doubt prove a valuable product, either alone or mixed with other substances.

Mr. Moncton, C.S., has proposed making use of the downy substance contained in the follicles of the Mudar; and, indeed, has had paper made of it, as well pure as when mixed with two fifths of the pulp of the Hemp (Sunn?), such as the natives use for making paper. As the glossy and silky, but comparatively short fibre, is difficult to spin, a mixture of one fifth of cotton was made, in order to enable it to be worked. A good wearing cloth, which stands washing and takes a dye, was produced. It is, however, well suited for stuffing pillows or coverlets. Mr. Moncton calculated that its cost would be one rupee a maund. This silky down of the pods is used by the natives on the Madras side in making a soft, cotton-like thread.

The Mudar, Mr. Moncton observes, grows all over India; it seems to thrive on soils that either reject or destroy everything else. It is difficult to conceive anything less productive than dry sand, and yet the Mudar thrives in it. Should its cotton be found useful, the waste lands of India could be covered with it, as it requires no *culture* and no *water.* It comes to maturity in a year, but is perennial; and when once planted or sown, would require no further care; and where thickly planted, might be made the means of reclaimiug poor soils, as the leaves and some of the upper branches rot, while the root and stem remain. Col. Tremenheere, of the Engineers, has suggested that the Mudar should be used as a hedge to protect desert land brought under cultivation from the encroachment of drift sand. This would give a healthful impetus to the cultivation of the plant itself.

We have not entered on these details, in a work on Fibres, on account of the medicinal qualities, or of the down, or of the milky juice of this plant, but because it is one yielding a very excellent fibre. Of this, some beautiful specimens were sent to the Exhibition of 1851, by Dr. Wight, who made experiments upon its great strength. The late Dr. Stocks enumerated it in a list sent some years since to the Author, among the cordage plants of Sindh; and Capt. G. J. Hollings, Deputy-Commissioner of Leia, in the Punjab, has published an account of this fibre being used for fishing nets, and as cordage, at Dehra Ghazee Khan, on the Indus. The species, however, is not the same in all these places. *Calotropis gigantea* is that common in the Southern, and *C. Hamiltonii* in the Northern parts of India, and *C. procera* in Persia; the last extends even to Syria.

The mode of separation of the fibre is tedious, and may for the present oppose some obstacles to the ready supply of this material. Capt. Hollings states that the sticks of the Mudar were cut about twelve or eighteen inches in length; the outer bark was then carefully peeled off, and the fibre picked from the inner part of it. Several threads were then placed side by side, and twisted into a twine by rubbing them between the hands. No water is used (indeed is injurious); everything is done by manipulation. In a subsequent paper, Capt. Hollings observes, that the best plan is to select the straightest branches, which are always the largest; to let them dry for at least twenty-four hours, before any attempt is made to separate the fibre. On the second or third day the sticks are slightly beaten, especially at the joints, which ensures the bark, with the fibre attached, being peeled off without breaking. The workmen then bite through the bark, about the centre of its length; they then hold the tissue of threads in one hand, and separate the bark with the other. He did not find that any of the ordinary methods of separating fibre were useful; but it is probable that some of the mechanical methods of separating Flax would be effectual with this fibre when in a dry state.

Dr. Wight's specimens, which are those of *C. gigantea*, he describes as being merely stripped off from the stalk, and slightly prepared, to remove the epidermis. He observes, that as it is a most common plant, it may become a valuable article of commerce, if a less costly mode of separating it can be devised, without injuring its quality. The colour, when fresh, is of a greenish-white.

Dr. Wight, from his experiments, considered it the strongest fibre on the Madras side of India, where it is used for fishing lines. It bore 552 lb., when the Janapa or Sunn of Coimbatore bore 404 lb. A small cord, made of the specimens from the Punjab, examined by Capt. Thompson, at Calcutta, bore 3 cwt., "without showing symptoms of distress," and was therefore equal to the best cordage; but it seemed to him still better adapted for the purposes of Flax than of Hemp. Mr. Willis considered the fibre to possess extraordinary merit, which would be valued by spinners for use in their finer fabrics. So, when examined by practical men in this country, it has been pronounced to be well calculated for supplying the place of good Flax, for making prime yarns. One gentleman observed that it twists all up at the end, and therefore could not be heckled. But this is probably owing to the mode of preparation; as the natives are described as twisting it between their hands. It was considered well worth £30, or rather £35 a ton. Capt. Thompson thought, in Calcutta, that it would be valued at from £30 to £40 per ton in England; perhaps more.

Though the Mudar or Yercum fibre, from its fineness, seems well calculated to answer for many of the purposes of Flax; yet, from its strength, it is also well suited to supply the place of Hemp. In the Author's experiments, when Petersburgh Hemp bore 160 lb., and the Brown Hemp of Bombay and Jubbulpore Hemp bore 190 lb., the Yercum also bore 190 lb. Dr. Wight has given the following as the results of his experiments:

Coir	. 224 lb.
Pooley Mungee (*Hibiscus cannabinus*)	. 290 „
Marool (*Sanseviera zeylanica*) .	. 316 „
Cotton (*Gossypium herbaceum*) .	. 346 „
Cutthalay nar (*Agave americana*) .	. 362 „
Janapa (*Crotalaria juncea*), Sunn, hindee	. 407 „
Yercum (*Calotropis gigantea*) .	. 552 „

In considering the varied useful properties of these plants, we cannot but be struck with the fact, of how wonderfully the Creator of all has furnished every part of the world with plants and animals suited to its diversified soils and climates. So that if the people residing near these barren places would make use of the natural riches within their reach, they have the means, by commercial interchange, of commanding comforts to which they are now strangers; and we might then apply literally the words of the Prophet: "The wilderness and the solitary place shall be glad for them; and the desert shall rejoice, and blossom as the rose." ('Isaiah,' xxxv, 1.)

Aroosha Fibre of Chittagong, *Callicarpa cana* (*Verbenaceæ*).

The family of plants to which the above belongs is not remarkable for any fibrous bark, but it is so from the great diversity of appearance in the plants placed in it, inasmuch as it includes the lowly Vervein and the lofty Teak. The latter conspicuous among plants for the strength and durability of its wood; but its flower is small, and therefore not so much out of place among the Verbenaceæ, because it is by the structure of the flowers and fruit that plants are arranged. Mr. Sconce, when at Chittagong, had some of the fibres of a plant, which he says is there called Aroosha, prepared, first by cutting the stems, which grew three or four feet high, and then steeping. The inner bark was then easily stripped off. This was afterwards heckled, and a portion of the fibre spun into thread, but it does not appear of much value in a country where so many others abound.

Capt. Thompson reports as follows, on the fibre:

"The line I now send you, made from the fibre forwarded from Chittagong, broke at once, without stretching, with only 127 lb.; only the finest and largest of the material was made into this line. A line of Russian Hemp of the same size with the two herewith sent, will sustain with ease 400 lb.; so that this fibre is much too weak for either sail-cloth or cordage. It however possesses all the free and kindly nature of Flax, and even smells like Flax. It is easily worked, with little or no waste, and I think must have been prepared with vegetable oil."

NARAVALI FIBRE, *Cordia angustifolia* (*Cordiaceæ*).

Dr. Buchanan, in his 'Journey through Mysore,' mentions that ropes are made of the bark of the *Narwuli*, which is the *Cordia angustifolia*, and which he found common near Severndroog. Its fruit is esculent, but tasteless. The plant belongs to the same family as the Sebestens, formerly famous in medicine; but which, when ripe, seems only remarkable for containing much mawkish mucilaginous pulp. It is possible that the bark of some of the species, when young, may yield a useful fibre.

APETALOUS PLANTS.

Having at p. 131 pointed out that as some of the Exogenous families of plants have only a single floral envelope, we need here only note that the following families belong to this subdivision.

NEPAL PAPER PLANT, *Daphne cannabina* (*Thymelææ*).

At the Great Exhibition of 1851, many were much interested about a huge sheet of Nepal paper exhibited by Col. Sykes. This was curious, not only on account of its size, but also on account of the plant from which it was made. This belongs to a genus and family containing plants remarkable for their fibrous bark. Thus the Lace-bark tree (*Daphne Lagetta*, now *Lagetta lintearia*) of the West Indies is "remarkable for the beautiful net-like appearance of its several easily separable layers of bark, whence it has received its English name. As the fibres of other species possess considerable tenacity, they have been employed in making cordage; and the toughness, as well as fineness of the inner bark of these plants, may be seen in a plant common in our gardens, and used in medicine on account of its acridity, that is, the Mezereon, *Daphne Mezereum* of botanists. It is from the inner bark of one of these plants, the *D. Bholua* (*D. cannabina* of Loureiro, and which is supposed to be identical with the *D. odora* of Thunberg), which is extremely abundant in the Himalayas, that this Nepal paper is made, as from other species in other countries. Another plant of the same, or of an allied genus, as it is called both *Daphne* and *Gnidia eriocephala*, is very common on the ghauts of the West of India, and in the hilly parts of the Southern Mahratta country and of the Dukhun. Several specimens, from various localities, are in Col. Sykes's collection. It is probable that it might be turned to the same use as the Nepal plant.

Of the uses of this plant good accounts have been given by Mr. Hodgson ('Journ. As. Soc.,' i, p. 8, 1832) and Dr. Campbell. The former describes the process as consisting, first, in boiling slips of the inner bark of the paper plant in a ley of wood-ashes for about half an hour, by which time the slips will be quite soft. These are then beaten in a stone mortar with a wooden mallet till they are reduced to a homogeneous pulp. This is then diffused through water, and taken up in sieves and paper frames, as in the ordinary process for making paper by hand. When dry, the sheet of paper is folded up; sometimes it is smoothed and polished by being rubbed on wood with the convex side of a conch shell: but Mr. Hodgson does not explain how the very large sheets of several yards square are made. Though called Nepalese, the paper is not manufactured in Nepal, but in Cis-Himalayan Bhote, in the midst of its immense forests, where there is an abundant supply of the plant, of wood for ashes and for firewood, as well as a constant supply of clean water. This paper is remarkable for its toughness, as well as its smoothness. Some of it, in the form of bricks of half-stuff, was sent to this country previous to the year 1829. As the quantity sent was not sufficient for a complete experiment, a small portion of it was made into paper by hand. An engraver, to whom it was given for trial, stated that "it affords finer impressions than any English-made paper, and nearly as good as the fine Chinese paper which is employed for what are called India paper proofs." ('Gleanings in Science,' i, p. 210.) Dr. Campbell describes the paper, as made by the Bhoteahs, "as strong, and durable as leather almost, and quite smooth enough to write on; and for office records, incomparably better than any India paper. It is occasionally poisoned by being washed with preparations of arsenic, in order to prevent the destruction caused by insects. Many of the books in Nepal, written on this paper, are said to be of considerable age, and that the art of making paper seems to have been introduced about 500 years ago from China, and not from India." He states that this paper may easily be procured at Patna, Purneah, and other places in the plains of both Southern and North-Western India.

Celtis orientalis (*Ulmaceæ*).

Capt. Reynolds, who, like several of the other officers in Assam, has paid much attention to the natural products of the province, sent to the Agri-Hortic. Society a specimen of a primitive cloth made by the Garrows from the bark of a tree, whose leaves were enclosed in the parcel. "They make several such cloths of different colours from various barks, and though these manufactures would seem cheap enough, they are not usually at the expense or labour of even such rough clothing for themselves, preferring apparently to go naked; they import at least 100,000 mds. of Cotton, but to my knowledge do not weave a seer for themselves. The Garrows who come to the plains have generally some small ends of cloths; but these are bought from the Bengalees, apparently to attend the *hauts* (fairs) in, not as clothing to protect them from wind and weather."

Dr. Falconer, to whom the specimens were referred, pronounced them to be those of *Celtis orientalis*, a tree which is pretty common all over India, and known under the name of Chakan in Bengal. The cloth is probably called "Yangfung" in Assam: Capt. Reynolds names it "Amfuk." Dr. Buchanan Hamilton says, the under bark of this tree, like that of the West India kind, consisting of numerous reticulated fibres, forms a kind of natural cloth, used by the Garrows for covering their nakedness. ('Lin. Trans.,' xvii, p. 209.) He also describes it in his report on Assam as a kind of rug worn by the Garrows in the cold weather, and serving them as a blanket by night.

But the specimens of this, as well as some of others, are chiefly interesting as showing the probability of the existence of numerous plants, of which the useful properties still remain unknown—for the fibrous properties of this are not mentioned by Dr. Roxburgh; and of him, it is justly observed in the 'Journ. of the Agri-Hortic. Soc.,' vi, p. 188: "From this circumstance it may be inferred he was not aware of it, as he appears never to have allowed an opportunity to pass of drawing attention to the useful properties of plants described by him, but, on the contrary, to have ever been desirous of rendering his botanical acquirements subservient to the dissemination of useful information in connection with every department of the vegetable kingdom."

Hemp.

Sans., *Bhanga*, *Ganjica*; Hind., *Ganja*; Arab., *Kinnub*; Pers., *Bung*.

Though so many fibres have been mentioned under the name of Hemp, it is only now, as we approach the end of our labours, following an arrangement according to the natural affinities of plants, that we have arrived at the true Hemp plant, the *Cannabis sativa* of botanists. The fibre of which is so generally employed for cordage in Europe, that the value of all other fibres is estimated, not so much from their intrinsic properties, as from their greater or less resemblance to Hemp, and especially to Russian Hemp. There is every reason for believing that the plant is of Eastern origin, while there is no sufficient reason for thinking that the climate of Europe is so peculiarly suited to the production of its fibre, as to exclude those of its native climes. Especially where attention is paid to those where the plant is grown on account of its fibre, and these distinguished from the others where it is cultivated for its resinous and intoxicating secretion. The latter requires exposure to light and air. These are obtained by thin sowing, while the growth of fibre is promoted by shade and moisture, which are procured by thick sowing. But before we proceed to consider these points, we may first notice the botanical affinities of the plant.

By the celebrated Jussieu, the Hemp and the Hop plants were placed in the same natural family (*Urticeæ*) with the Nettles. In more modern works, they are either continued as a tribe of the same family, under the name of *Cannabineæ*, or these containing only the genera *Cannabis* and *Lupulus* are separated into a distinct family, under the same or a nearly similar name. These two plants are closely connected in properties, as in structure.

The Hop (*Humulus Lupulus*), besides a bitter, secretes a resinous principle: Hop bines abounding in fibre, have often been proposed to be turned to useful account, for cordage or paper, but as yet to little extent.

The Hemp plant likewise secretes a resinous principle in its leaves, on which account these, as well as the *churrus* collected from off the young tops of the stem and flowers, is highly esteemed in all Eastern countries, on account of its exhilarating and intoxicating properties. Hence, among the Arabs the Hemp has a variety of names, as "the increaser of pleasure," "the cementer of friendship," &c. By its name of *Hasheesh* it is often mentioned in the works of travellers in Egypt, Arabia, and Syria; while the name of *Bhang* is not less celebrated in the far East. The Author has treated together of these two plants, in his 'Manual of Materia Medica,' pp. 622—629, 2d ed., from which he extracts the following description of the plant:

The Hemp is a diœcious (occasionally monœcious) annual, from 3 to 10 feet high, according to soil and climate. Root white, fusiform, furnished with fibres. The stem erect; when crowded, simple; but when growing apart, branched even from the bottom, angular, and, like the whole plant, covered with fine but rough pubescence. This stem is hollow within, or only filled with a soft pith. This pith is surrounded by a tender, brittle substance, consisting chiefly of cellular texture, with some woody fibres, which is called the *reed, boon,* and *shove* of the Hemp. Over this we have the thin bark, composed of fibres, extending in a parallel direction all along the stalk. These fibres consist of delicate fibrils, united together by cellular tissue, and all covered by the thin membrane or cuticle.

The leaves are opposite or alternate, on long petioles, scabrous, digitate, composed of from 5 to 7 narrow, lanceolate, sharply serrated leaflets, of which the lower are the smallest, all tapering at the apex into a long entire point. Stipules subulate. *Males* on a separate plant. Flowers in drooping, axillary, or racemose panicles, with subulate bracts. Perianth 5-parted; segments not quite equal, downy. Stamens 5; filaments short; anthers large, pendulous, 2-celled; cells united by their backs, opening by a longitudinal slit. *Females* in a crowded spike-like raceme, with leafy bracts. The perianth consists of a single, small, spathe-like sepal, which is persistent, acuminate, ventricose at the base, embraces the ovary, and is covered with short brownish glands. Ovary subglobular, 1-celled, with one pendulous ovule. Style short. Stigmas 2, elongated, glandular. Nut ovate, greyish-coloured, smooth, covered by the calycine sepal, bivalved but not dehiscing, and inclosing a single oily seed. Seed pendulous. Testa thin, membranous, marked at the apex with a coloured hilum. Embryo without albumen, doubled upon itself. Radicle elongated, turned towards the hilum, and the apex of the nut separated from the incumbent plano-convex cotyledons by a small quantity of albumen.

The Author having for many years been of opinion that Hemp fibre might be advantageously produced in India in much larger quantities than has ever yet been the case, wrote a report on the subject, in the year 1839, which was sent to India, and published in the 'Trans. of the Agri-Hortic. Soc.,' vol. viii, p. 15. From this he will now make some extracts, and then adduce some of the valuable information which it was the means of eliciting:

"The cultivation of Hemp in India obtained very great attention from the Court of Directors, and instructions were sent to the Governments there to encourage its growth, as well as that of other cordage plants. As the natives of India employ between forty and fifty different kinds of plants for the fibre which they yield, fitted for this purpose in different degrees, the subject of investigation was sufficiently extensive, and received great attention from Dr. Roxburgh."

"On the present occasion I confine myself to the Hemp plant itself (the *Cannabis sativa* of botanists), as being the most valuable of the whole; and because it is in general erroneously supposed that it can only be successfully cultivated in European regions, though there is every reason to believe that it is originally a native of Asia, and even that its Greek and Latin name *Cannabis* is derived from the Arabic *kinnub*. It is well known to be common in Arabia and Persia, as well as in every part of China and of India, and likewise in Egypt and Turkey; but in all these countries it is valued chiefly, if not only, for yielding an intoxicating drug commonly called *bhang*. In European countries, it is on the contrary cultivated only on account of its ligneous fibre, so extensively employed in the manufacture of the strongest ropes, and of coarse but strong kinds of cloth. The wide distribution of this plant throughout Europe and Asia is remarkable, but easily explained, when we consider that it is an annual, which requires only a few months of summer temperature to bring it to full perfection. The requisites for its successful cultivation, it is, however, necessary to notice, when endeavouring to introduce elsewhere its culture.

"Hemp is cultivated in almost every part of Europe for home consumption, but only in large quantities for export in Russia and Poland, though the finest quality of Hemp comes from Italy. French Hemp is also much esteemed, as well as that grown in both England and Ireland; but for the present purpose it is necessary only to notice the culture of the chief kinds which enter into commerce.

"Hemp is cultivated in almost every province of Russia, but in the largest quantities in the interior, beyond Moscow, as well as nearer Petersburgh, and in the Polish provinces which belong to Russia. The soil must not be over rich nor too sterile, of moderate depth, and friable. The time of sowing varies from the middle of May to the end of June; by some it is recommended not to be sown until the latter end of June, as frosts are very injurious to its growth. The season of reaping is from the end of August to the end of September, and it is therefore between three and four months in a state of vegetation; the male plants being pulled some weeks before the female. The Russian summer, though short, is regular while it lasts, and the temperature sufficiently high to bring it to full perfection.

"That the northern latitudes of Russia are not essential for the successful cultivation of Hemp is, however, evident, from the large quantities which are grown in the southern climate of Italy, both in Bologna and Romagna, and along the banks of the Po, as well as in the neighbourhood of Naples. The Italians have a saying, that 'Hemp may be grown everywhere, but it cannot be produced fit for use, either in heaven or earth, without manure.' The climate of Italy, it is well known, is remarkable for its clearness, regularity, dryness, and warmth, and that irrigation is essentially necessary for much of its agriculture. The Italian Hemp is fine, soft, light-coloured, and strong, as well as long in the staple; and it is important to remark that it brings the highest price in the English market, as, for instance, it sells for 50 shillings per cwt. when the best Russia sells at 47 shillings for the same quantity.

"If we compare the summer temperature of the northern with these southern situations, we shall not find so great a difference as we might be led to expect by considering only their latitudes, or their mean annual temperatures. Thus Petersburgh and Moscow, in N. latitude 59° 56′ and 56° 45′, have mean summer temperatures of 62° 06′ and 67° 10′ of Fahr., while Milan and Rome, in N. latitude 45° 28′ and 41° 53′, have summer temperatures of 73° 04′ and 75° 20′."

"Without entering into details, it might be inferred as probable, that as Italy grows Rice, and so many other plants of India, so might the latter cultivate a plant like the Hemp, which succeeds so well even so far south as Naples, and which requires only a few months to bring it to perfection; and this even if India did not already possess it. But so far from this being the case, the reverse is the fact; and it is well known that no plant is so commonly cultivated in so many parts of India as the true Hemp plant, which is there called *ganja*, but which differs in no respect from the European plant, though the natives employ it only for the purpose of yielding *bhang*. But cultivated for this purpose, instead of being sown thick, as it ought to be when intended for cordage, it is sown thin by the natives, who afterwards transplant the young plants, and place them at distances of nine or ten feet from each other. The effect of this is to expose them more freely to light, heat, and air, by the agency of which the plant is enabled to perfect its secretions in a more complete manner, and the bhang will consequently be of a more intoxicating nature. The fibrous and woody parts at the same time attain a greater degree of stiffness and solidity, as is found to be the case with timber trees similarly exposed. The Hemp plant, thus grown, will branch much. It may be small in dry situations, and large in rich and moist ones, but in either case its fibres are found, both in Europe and India, to be rougher, stiffer, and more difficultly separated from the woody part than is desirable, but seed is produced in larger quantity and of better quality. This mode of cultivation has, moreover, the disadvantage of being more expensive, from taking up more space than is desirable when the plants are required to yield the best quality of fibre for cordage.

"Plants, when grown in moist situations, in shade, or set thickly together, are well known to run into leaf, shoot up, and to become more lax in texture, while their secretions are imperfectly formed, as is exemplified in the growing of Lettuce, Celery, &c. Hemp and Flax, when cultivated for their fibres, are sown thickly together, and they shoot up into long, wand-like plants, which are much less branched than when freely exposed. Air and light having less free admission, and heat having less influence in evaporating the sap, the effect is to produce a longer fibre, which is at the same time soft and pliable, as well as more easily separated, and in larger quantity on the same space, than when they are set widely apart.

"The natives of India also sow their *Sunn* and *Jute* very thickly together when, for the sake of their fibres, they form the exclusive crop. The effect is to produce a long and flexible fibre, though this is not sufficiently strong to form a good substitute for the true Hemp. This might be cultivated in suitable situations in India, in a manner similar to that adopted in Europe, or like that practised with its substitutes in India. The effect would undoubtedly be to produce a sufficiently long fibre, which would also be softer and more pliable, at the same time that it retained a great portion of its original strength, and probably in as large a quantity as is yielded by the *Sunn* plant. Thus an article might be produced, which, judging from the Italian samples, might enter into competition with the Russian product, and, at all events, afford much more valuable cordage than the several (usually considered) inefficient substitutes which are so extensively cultivated in India, and which, imported into this country, sell only for 15 to 20 shillings per cwt., at the same time that the Russian, Polish, and Italian Hemps are selling for 42 to 50 shillings per cwt.

"The difference in price would appear a sufficient inducement to attempt the culture of the true Hemp in India, especially as there could be no doubt respecting its growth, as it is already so common in every part of that country, and requiring, if anything, only a little modification of its properties. This could be ensured, most probably, by a change in the mode of cultivation. Dr. Roxburgh, as long since as the year 1800, thought Rohilcund and the neighbouring hills suited to the cultivation of Hemp. I have seen it in great abundance, in a wild state, in the Deyra Doon, and also in the Khadir land of the Saharunpore district, especially along the upper part of the Doab Canal, and where it was chiefly valued for its leaves, being made into *bhang* and *subjee*, and the stems, when dried up, being burnt for firewood.

"There would be little difficulty in cultivating this plant in the low *Khadir* land, where it is wild; nor in converting it into merchantable Hemp. For the natives of the neighbourhood already make use of it, partially for the manufacture of ropes; and the inhabitants of Malabar are said by Dr. H. Scott to employ the Hemp for making their fishing nets.

"The natives of the Himalayas likewise possess the plant, from which though they prepare an intoxicating drug, which they call *churrus*, they likewise value it for its ligneous fibre, from which they prepare a coarse kind of cloth, which they send into the plains for making very durable *grain-sacks*, as well as the strongest ropes (called *sel*), for crossing their rivers.

"This fact, though not generally known, is mentioned by Kirkpatrick in his account of Nepal, and was ascertained by General Hardwick, in his visit to Srinuggur, as well as by myself, when travelling in the Himalayas ('Illust.,' p. 333). I also obtained specimens of the rope and cloth when travelling there, but which I regret I am unable now to find. The plant I have seen in a very luxuriant state at least ten or twelve feet high, in the Himalayas, at elevations of 6000 and 7000 feet, especially in the neighbourhood of buffalo-sheds. In such situations and near villages it could no doubt be easily cultivated to a great extent, and yield a valuable and profitable product.

"The Hemp could likewise be cultivated in the plains at two seasons of the year; that is, during the rainy season, as is now the case, but likewise along with the cold-weather cultivation, which is so similar to that of the summer culture of European countries. But experiments require to be made and specimens procured in order to determine which season is most proper for the culture of this plant in order to yield Hemp of the best quality.

"Hill people might no doubt easily be obtained for preparing the Hemp according to their own method, and teaching the people in the plains, who are already practised in the art of preparing *Sunn*. It would, however, be desirable to procure, if practicable, the assistance of some European (and such might be found among the soldiery) who had seen and practised the preparation of Hemp in this country. The experiment might be made with little expense, and probably great advantage, from the useful information which would be obtained for the use of cultivators, in the Botanic Garden at Saharunpore, if instructions were given to this effect to Dr. Falconer, Superintendent of that Institution.

"For due attention being paid to the details of this subject, it would be extremely desirable to send out to India specimens, with prices of the different qualities of Hemp found in the markets of this country, so that cultivators in India might know what they had to imitate and rival. It would also be extremely desirable, in order to ascertain the present quality of the Himalayan Hemp, that specimens, in different states of preparation, were sent here, as prepared by the Hill people, together with specimens of the Hempen Rope and Sackcloth of the Himalayas."

Subsequent to the publication of the foregoing report, several papers were sent to the Agri-Horticultural Society of Calcutta, and which are published in vol. viii of their 'Transactions,' and in vol. i of their 'Journal.' These were from Majors Swetenham and Corbett, Captains Kirke and Huddleston, and from the distinguished naturalist, Mr. Hodgson. The substance of the last two we here republish, as containing much of the information on culture contained in the others, while Major Corbett and Capt. Kirke give valuable information respecting the cost and the expense of conveyance to Calcutta; which will be immediately noticed.

Extracts from a Report on Hemp Cultivation, &c., in British Gurhwal, by Captain H. Huddleston, 14th July, 1840.

2. There are two kinds of Hemp, "*Bhang*," indigenous to the Himalayas;—that called "Khur-Bhunga," or Jungle Bhang, growing wild throughout the whole of these Hills in all situations, and attaining a very considerable height during the season of the periodical rains, is of no use whatever, for the very insignificant quantity of "churrus" (the inspissated juice of the leaves obtained from the plant by rubbing between the hands) does not remunerate even the poorest class for the trouble bestowed upon it, and as

it does not yield a fibre that can be turned to any use, I need not of course make any further remarks regarding it.

3. The real Hemp, or cultivated kind, is grown chiefly on high lands, and principally on the northern faces of the mountains, in well prepared and abundantly manured soils close to villages, or in recently cleared lands by burning the primeval forests, the soil of which, from the accumulated decomposed vegetable matter of years, is rich enough to ensure the superior growth of the plant and an abundant crop without any manure for one season. No irrigation is ever resorted to, and very little is produced under an elevation of 3000 feet, the heat of the valleys being detrimental to its quality, and the plant appears to flourish best at elevations of from between 4000 to 7000 feet.

The middling district situated between the "Pindur" to the north and the "Nyar" or "Samee" rivers to the south, and centrically with regard to the province of Kumaon and Gurhwal, may be termed the chief Hemp-producing districts of British Gurhwal. The fields nearest to villages, as being the easiest for manuring, and the culturable wastes with a rich soil of accumulated rotten vegetation, or recently cleared forest lands, being those in which the Hemp plant is alone cultivated to advantage with respect to its quality.

4. The culture of "Bhang" or Hemp, as practised in this district, is as follows: After the ground has been well cleared and prepared, the seed is sown, towards the end of May, or early in June, at the rate of 20 or 25 *pathas*, equal to about 26 or 33 seers (from 52 lb. to 66 lb. avoirdupois) per beesee, which latter is the common denomination now used in Gurhwal, and very near equal to an English acre. During the early growth of the plant the ground is kept free from all weeds, and the young plants are thinned, leaving a few inches between each, and until the crop has attained a good height, the ground is kept clean from all rank vegetation—after which it attains to the height of twelve and fourteen feet, and is cut in September and November.

5. Of this cultivated Bhang there are two kinds, the plant called *Goolanga* or *Goolbhanga* which produces seed (the female), and the one which only flowers, but has no seed; and this latter is called "Phoolbhang" (the male), from which the best sort of Hemp is prepared; the plants being cut a month or six weeks earlier, and producing a stronger and superior fibre to the other. On the stalks being cut green, they are dried for several days in the sun, by being piled against the walls of the terraced fields until they become quite brown. The plants have the seed extracted by rubbing between the hands, which produces the "Churrus," and this is scraped off and made into rolls for sale. The leaves also are pounded, from which "Ganjah" and "Subzee" are manufactured in small quantities. When the stalks are sufficiently dry they are tied up into bundles, and steeped for fifteen or sixteen days (eight days, Swetenham) in tanks or running streams, being kept under water by pressure—on being taken out they are beaten with wooden mallets, and dried again in the sun, when the fibre is stripped off from the thickest end of the stalk, and after being again beaten, this fibre is made up into twists for sale and manufactured into sackcloth for wear, bags, and ropes.

6. The total money return from the produce of the cultivation of the Hemp plant would be considerable, if there were any demand for exportation, though the average return even now is amply remunerating to the grower, and were it not from the well-known dislike which the Hill people have to extra labour, it would be more extensively cultivated than it is. The limited cultivation at present, however, supplies the wants of the population for sackcloth, bags, and ropes, nearly the whole of which, in considerable quantities, is consumed in the district—the lower classes of the Gurhwal population dressing themselves in the cloth manufactured from the Hemp, and this still encourages the cultivation in a great measure. The average return per beesee (or English acre) may be stated as follows:—three seers (6 lb.) of churrus, value

Rs. 6 (or twelve shillings); four maunds (or 320 lb.) of Hemp, value Rs. 8 (sixteen shillings); and about thirty to thirty-five seers (60 to 70 lb.) of seed, yielding about five seers (10 lb.) of oil, value R. 1 (two shillings). Giving a total of Rs. 15 per beesee.

7. The seed sells generally at 20 *pathas* per rupee, or from twenty-seven to thirty seers (as this wooden measure varies in different places), and the seed being light, I have found that the average weight of each patha is about one seer and five chittacks. The Hemp sells at 2 rupees a maund amongst themselves, and the Dooms (or lowest class of the agricultural community) are the chief cultivators of the plant.

8. When Dr. Rutherford held a contract for the supply of Hemp to the Honorable Company, and also made extensive purchases of it with other staple articles of produce of the Hills on his own account, the cultivation of Hemp was very considerable indeed in this district; and in case of any demand being again created, immense tracts would no doubt be sown with it, provided the same plan of advances to cultivators were adopted.

9. The plan adopted by Dr. Rutherford appears to have been thus: advances through his agents to the landed proprietors and individual cultivators were made during the early part of the year, stipulating for the Hemp being delivered at their own doors at 4 rupees a maund, and the carriage during the cold season to the marts of Kotedwarra in Gurhwal, and Chilkeea in Kumaon at the foot of the Hills (where Goomashtas or agents were ready to receive the Hemp), being defrayed extra—which did not, I imagine, on an average exceed a rupee a maund—so that the raw material was and is capable of being delivered at those marts for 5 rupees a maund; and as only a few miles further of land carriage would be required to ship the Hemp into boats on the Ganges or Ram Gunga for transit to Calcutta, this would not, I should think, double the cost of it.

Hemp Cultivation in Nepaul: by H. B. Hodgson, Esq.

Mr. Hodgson states, that the cultivation is peculiar to the Northern districts of Nepaul, but only, as he suspects, because the tribes inhabiting them are less scrupulous than the people of the great valley, and other Central and Southern tracts; for, at least in the valley, the plant flourishes greatly, if properly tended, as Mr. Hodgson has proved in his own garden; and the spring crops of the valley are almost choked with *spontaneous* growth of Hemp, which, however, being uncultivated, is stunted and virtueless. The Northern districts (popularly called Cachar) are nevertheless the prime seats of culture, and there alone is the plant manufactured into rope or cloth; though the edible extracts are sometimes prepared nearer to and around Katmandhoo.

The season of sowing Bhang seed in Nepaul is from Chyett to Bysack (March to April).

Damp soils, comprising black earth, are fittest for this crop. Before ploughing the field, sufficient manure is to be sprinkled over it, then completing the work of the plough, the seeds are to be sprinkled, and having broken the clods into dust, the field is to be made even.

At seven or eight days after sowing the seeds the plants come up, but their rapidity of growth and their size and strength depend on the abundance of the rains or artificial watering. If the plants be very thick, they must be thinned, so as to stand three inches distance from each other. They flower and fruit in Sawun (July); and at the beginning of Bhadoon (August) are in their full growth; but while yet succulent and in flower, they are to be cut, with exception of some seed plants, which are not to be reaped till October. It is the bark of the young but full-grown or Sawun plants, which is soft, that is used for making Bhangela. That of the old or October plants is hard and not suitable for manufacture.

After the plants have been cut off at the ground, they must be placed in the sun for eight or ten days, or until they be dried sufficiently. They must then be steeped in water for three days, and on the fourth day the plants must be taken out of the water and peeled. The peelings are to be washed and put in the sun; and when quite dried, they are ready for manipulation. They are then to be torn into thin threads with the nails of the hands; next twisted with a spinning-wheel (Tikuli), and when the threads are thus prepared, they are to be boiled with ashes of wood and water in a pot, for four hours, and to be washed again for the purpose of whitening. This is the way of preparing Bhangela thread, out of which blankets are woven.

One mana (half a kucha seer) of seed is sufficient for a ropini of land (one fifth of Badshahi bigah), which produces ten or twelve loads of bhang. Hemp grows equally well on slopes or flats, and near the tops as well as on the sides of the mountains, if not too low. But a moist rich soil is indispensable. The plant attains to a height of eight to ten feet, and should be cut when the flower is falling and the seed forming.

Before proceeding to consider the prospect of obtaining merchantable Hemp from the heights of the Himalayas, we may notice what is practicable in regard to—

Hemp Culture in the Plains of India.—Though the production of Hemp in the Himalayas, and in the low lands at their foot, is chiefly contemplated, that of its culture in the plains may also be mentioned. This was attempted by Dr. Roxburgh, and though probably in the least favorable situation in India, yet with some success; as he observes:

"In many parts of Bengal, particularly where the land is so low as to remain humid through the dry season, Hemp thrives luxuriantly during the cold season; at Soonamooky it did well on a sandy soil, manured with dung from stables. Prolonged immersion much injures the quality of the Hemp, the rainy season is therefore preferable for the cultivation and maceration of the plant, and we must content ourselves with one crop in the year, for it is a very false, though prevailing notion, that the fertile fields of Asia produce at least two crops annually. The burning heats of Asia, while they last, are as unfavorable for vegetation as the frosts of winter are in Europe." And in Wisset it is stated:

"A native, who had an opportunity of observing the mode of cultivating and preparing the Hemp raised by Mr. Douglas, at Rishera, has offered to the Board of Trade to contract with them for supplying a very considerable quantity, I believe 500 maunds (about 17 tons), of properly dressed Hemp next season, at the rate of ten sicca rupees per maund (this is equal to 300 sicca rupees, or, at 2*s*. 6*d*. = £35 per ton, and at 2*s*. = £30 per ton)."

The next important notice which we have respecting the culture of Hemp in the plains of India, is from Mr. Deneef, already mentioned at p. 174, &c., and of and from whom we have the following communication :

Sample of Hemp grown and manufactured in Bengal, after the manner pursued in Belgium. Presented by Mr. H. Woollaston, on behalf of Mr. G. Deneef, Belgian farmer.

Calcutta, Oe. 8, 7630, 1840.

Monsieur Spry, Secrétaire de la Societé d'Agriculture et d'Horticulture du Bengale,

J'ai l'honneur de vous envoyer par l'entremise de Monsieur Woollaston, membre de votre Société, un échantillon de chanvre, qui me semble mériter beaucoup d'attention, il me parait aussi avantageux que le chanvre de Russie et de Manille qui se vendent à Londres £22 à £27 le tonneau. La manufacture en est tres simple et n'exige aucun instrument; elle est faite en Belgique par des vieillards et des enfants. Aucun ouvrage ne saurait être plus convenable pour les bras inactifs des familles pauvres de cette contrée, il n'est nullement fatigant et se fait par assis; de plus, chaque livre de chanvre, procure au teilleur 3 lb. de matière a brûler.

La préparation du sol ne demande pas de grands soins ni par conséquent de grandes dépenses ; sa végétation est superbe, la plante n'occupe le sol que pendant 80 jours (du commencement de Juin, à la fin d'Août). J'en ai a peu prés 4 beegas, qui me donneront environ 1000 lb. de fibres, que je prepare en ce moment; et que je me propose d'envoyer le plutôt possible, pour échantillon, à la Société expérimentale du Lin a Londres, et aprés en avoir reçu une reponse, concernant sa valeur reélle; je m'empresserai de vous envoyer un rapport exact sur la mode de sa culture.

Il serait étonnant que l'Inde, qui a tant de moyens en terrain et en hommes, ne pourrait pas concourir avec la Russie, qui est obligée de payer £2 0 0 par tonneau pour frais d'exportation au gouvernement Russe meme, et 6*s*. per tonneau au passage du Sond, et ne pourrait réclamer sa part, des millions d'espèces, que la mère patrie est obligée de payer annuellement à la Russie sa puissante rivale.

J'ai l'honneur de vous saluer avec la plus parfaite considération,

Votré trés devoué serviteur,

G. Deneef, Belgian Farmer.

The Hemp produced by so little labour and care, and which only occupied the ground for eighty days from the beginning of June to the end of August, according to Mr. Deneef, was pronounced good by the members of the Flax and Hemp Committee; by Mr. Fergusson, as "uncommonly strong, and if it can be produced cheaply and abundantly, it is likely to be a most important article." Mr. Hodgkinson, who doubted of its being the true Hemp—though without sufficient grounds—

pronounced "the article as superior, be it what it may, and deserving of the first attention."

With respect to the interchange of seed, or to the kind which is most desirable, we have the following fact, though it is probable that some of the Himalayan seed would answer equally well:

"A few fresh stalks of Hemp raised from Russian seed received last year from Dr. Royle, and corresponding specimens of the indigenous Hemp plant of Bengal. *Presented by Mr. Deneef.* The superiority of the former in texture was very apparent."

In treating of both Flax and Sunn, mention was made of Mr. Sconce's experiments with both of these plants at Chittagong, in the year 1843. He at the same time grew some Hemp from country seed (*ganza*) sown in November. Of the fibre, the Hemp and Flax Committee reported: The Fibre is exceedingly strong and clean, but the admixture of Tow spoils the appearance and deteriorates the quality; while of the dressed Hemp it was said, that some of the fibres were strong, others weak, and as only partially heckled. These defects, being those of management, might easily be remedied.

From the far Southern we proceed to the North-Western provinces; here the late Mr. Bell, of Agra, on hearing of the above experiments in Bengal, writes, that there "can be no difficulty in the cultivation of the *bhang* or *ganja*, which is now sown only for the intoxicating drug the natives obtain from it; but the vigour the plant shows, and the height it reaches when thus sown, much scattered to admit of its throwing out its branches, satisfied me that, sown more densely, it would at least run the height of Sunn, and this I suppose sufficient for the desired length of fibre in the Hemp."

There is no doubt that the Hemp plant will grow to a great height even in the plains of India. The Author received a letter from his friend, Capt., now Sir Proby Cautley, dated from Saharunpore (10th Aug., 1840), stating that the Hemp was in cultivation in the Botanic Garden, and looking as fine as any that he had ever seen, nearly twelve feet high, with a natural healthy look of dark green. Dr. Falconer, however, afterwards reported that the Hemp fibre did not retain the strength or flexibility which characterise it in the Himalayas. But the Author has been informed that they are able to use some of the Hemp growing spontaneously along the upper part of the Himalayan base, for the general purposes of cordage. The Hemp growing in the Goruckpore district at the foot of the Hills, is considered of good quality, and some is being sent to this country on purpose to have its properties tested. It is probable that Mr. Williams might succeed in the cultivation of Hemp in the soil and climate of Jubbulpore.

Quality and Cost of Himalayan Hemp.—From the account which has been given above, by local officers, of the cultivation, and the other testimony which we have respecting the plant, there is no doubt that the Ganja of the Himalayas is the true Hemp plant of Europe (the *Cannabis sativa* of botanists). As the plant has ceased to be as extensively cultivated as formerly chiefly from the want of any external demand, there would seem to be no difficulty in again increasing the culture, and to a still greater extent, if this requisite for all culture was again restored. The only questions which remain to be determined are the quality of the Hemp and the cost at which it could be conveyed to Indian ports, where, if not required for export to Europe, it could be beneficially employed for naval and other purposes. This would be preferable to their continuing, as in some places is still the case, to import Hemp and Tow from Europe, when India produces at least as good, if not a superior article, and at a cheaper rate. This is evident from the following abstract of the information on the subject.

"In the Himalayas the Hemp grows wild, and is, moreover, carefully cultivated, both on account of its exhilarating secretions, and its strong and flexible fibre. With the properties of this the Hillmen are well acquainted, as they make with it both twine and rope, and a coarse cloth (*bhangela*) with which they clothe themselves, as well as make sacks and bags. Their hempen wrappers they wear much as a Highlander does his plaid, fixing it in front with a wooden skewer, instead of a brooch. A traveller in the Himalayas, some years since, described the natives as applying Hemp 'extensively to purposes of a domestic nature, such as hanging their supernumerary female children, administering rope's-end to their wives, penning up cattle, and making a sort of netted, or knitted, or knotted shoes, to which a sole of untanned leather is sometimes, but by no means generally, affixed.'

"The culture seems to be very well understood in most parts, though the best methods are not always practised either of planting, or of picking, or of preparing their Hemp. All along the Himalayas—that is in Nepaul, in Kemaon, in Gurhwal, and up to the newly acquired hills of the Punjab, at elevations of from 3000 and 4000 to 7000 feet—Hemp is cultivated by the Hillmen, though chiefly for their own use, the plants growing to eight or ten, some say twelve or fourteen, feet in height. They sow about the month of May, carefully prepare, and usually manure the ground, weed and thin the plants to within three or four inches, and cut the male plants, '*phoolbhanga*, which flowers, but has no seed,' a month or six weeks before the female plant, '*goolanga*, or *goolbhanga*, which has seed,' the latter being harvested about the end of September. The stems, when cut down, are dried in the sun, and then steeped in water for three or more days. Beaten with wooden mallets, the fibre is then stripped off, and again beaten. In some places it is said to be boiled with wood ashes—that is, potash,—and sometimes bleached before being spun into thread. The stalks are made into torches. The culture is described to be the most profitable of any, as the *churrus* and *ganja*, different forms of *bhang*, are said of themselves to pay the expenses of culture. The Hemp they sell among themselves for Rs. 2 a maund—that is, 4s. for about 82 lb. The seed is even roasted and eaten, or expressed for its oil, and the oilcake given to their cattle. The culture is not much extended, for it is more laborious than they like, and there is said to be a prejudice among the Brahmins and Rajpoots against the cultivation of this plant, which is therefore confined to the Doom class. But there is no doubt that the culture could be immensely extended if the inducements of price were greater."

There being no doubt of this being the genuine Hemp plant, the next point to ascertain is the quality of the fibre which the Hillmen produce with their own unaided efforts. On this point the information is most satisfactory. Mr. Hodgkinson, a Calcutta merchant, who was well acquainted with this staple, and had personal knowledge of the produce on the Continent, pronounced some Hemp sent from the Deyra Doon to be "equal in colour, cleanness, length, and strength to the best Russian."

Mr. Deneef, a Belgian farmer, sent to India by the Flax Experiment Company, said: "Ces échantillons sont de vrai *Cannabis sativa*, pareil à celui du nord de l'Europe. J'ai été enchanté de voir une si charmante vegetation de cette plante produite dans l'Inde; mais cet article n'est pas preparé comme on le desire dans les marchés Anglais; d'abord chanvre mâle et chanvre femelle ont été coupés ensemble, et ensuite dressés dans l'etat humide d'apres la methode des Indiens. S'il était dressé à la manière des Européens du nord, qui consiste à tirer le chanvre mâle, cinq semaines avant celui qui produit la sémence, à ne rouir que bien peu chaque genre séparément, la chanvre mâle ne pouvant pas séjourner dans l'eau aussi longtemps que l'autre; ensuite à ne le dresser que quand il est bien sec et lorsque les fibres se separent aisément; il formerat une belle matière première pour les cordages solides. Au contraire, dressé et rincé dans l'eau il perd'une certaine graisse qui lui est naturelle, et qui est cause que la poix s'imbibe plus facilement avec lui, ce qui le rend fort contre la pluie et la chaleur, et fait en même temps bénéfice du manufacturier, qui sait si bien distinguer la différence de la préparation."[1] ('Journ. Agric. Soc. of India,' i, p. 46.)

Some specimens of Hemp from the Himalayas recently tried in this country have been found to bear a greater weight and strain than the best Petersburgh Hemp. Some of it is also very fine and soft, more like Flax than Hemp.

There is little doubt, therefore, of the good quality of this Hemp, even without any improvement from European instruction. It is a not less important point to ascertain the price at which it could be brought to this

[1] In preparing Hemp for the European market, care should be taken not to twist or tie the ends together, but having laid the fibres parallel to each other, simply to tie them together near the thicker end, so as to form *heads*, as seen in Petersburgh Hemp.

country. In the 'Journal of the Agri-Horticultural Society of India, (vol. i, p. 45), may be observed a memorandum by the late Lord Auckland, when Governor-General of India, in which it is stated:

	£	s.	d.
Prime cost of Hemp at Deyra, Rs. 54 per ton	£5	8	0
Carriage to Calcutta (about 1000 miles), Rs. 24 per ton .	2	8	0
Total cost and charges of Hemp at Calcutta . . .	£7	16	0
Prime cost of Hemp seed at Deyra, Rs. 36 per ton . . .	3	12	0
Carriage to Calcutta, Rs. 24 per ton	2	8	0
	£6	0	0

Though the above are deduced from the rates at which the natives sell Hemp and Hemp seed among themselves, large quantities could not be obtained at the above prices, for the natives would not extend their crop, or take much trouble in preparing it for market, unless some greater inducements were held out to them. Others, therefore, have calculated that the price of the Hemp might be doubled to the natives, and that one rupee more should be given for their bringing it down to the foot of the hills, whence it could be readily conveyed to the Ganges, either from Kemaon or Gurhwal, or from Sirmore to the Jumna, and from the Kangra Hills to the Sutlej. Therefore Capt. Kirke calculated the cost of 500 maunds of Hemp from Deyra Doon, a valley within the Himalayas, to be about Rs. 2500; carriage on bullocks to the Ganges (but carts have been much introduced since then), Rs. 125; a 600 maund boat from Sookertal, Rs. 130; together Rs. 2755; this, with the addition of ten per cent. for contingencies, making the total cost to Calcutta, Rs. 3030 for 500 maunds of Hemp, or for something more than seventeen tons, or about £17 14*s*. a ton in Calcutta.

Capt. Kirke's memorandum further states that 22½ feet of the fine sail-cloth which he forwarded could be bought for 9½ annas; 22½ feet of the coarse sackcloth for six annas; 20 seers of the rough Hemp for one rupee; and 29 seers of the Hemp seed for one rupee.

Major Corbett gives three calculations of the cost of Hemp from the district of Kemaon to Calcutta, all expenses included:

From Kotedwarra, 37 tons, £661—£17	17	per ton.
,, Chilkeea	13	15	,,
,, Sunea	13	4	,,

He also sent some Hemp cloth or canvas made in the Hills, which was 7¼ yards long, and 22½ inches wide, of which the price was one rupee.

The above facts being sufficiently favorable, both respecting the quality and the cost of the Himalayan Hemp, and the Author having been informed by good practical judges that the best plan to make the peculiar qualities of any of these Indian fibres known to manufacturers here would be to have a few tons of each sent into the market for two or three years, he was induced to recommend that this should be done with the Himalayan Hemp.

"As it is quite practicable to give an impulse to the growth of Hemp in the Himalayas, and as the price is so moderate and the quality so good, I believe it might be established as a regular article of export from India, or, at all events, of consumption in the dockyards of that country. I would therefore suggest that the local officers of the districts of Kemaon, Deyra Doon, Sirmore, and Kote Kangra (more properly Kooloo), should be authorised to purchase certain quantities of the Hemp (say from 5 to 10 tons), and send it down to Calcutta, for transmission to and sale in the markets of this country, taking care that while they give sufficient encouragement to the cultivators, they do not so far increase the cost, either by raising the price or by enhancing the expense, as to interfere with its subsequent profitable sale by merchants. It is probable that the Himalayan Hemp would sell here for £35 a ton."

The Author has lately received a letter from Dr. Jameson, dated 6th Nov., 1854, referring to this fibre, and also to the order which had been sent by the Court of Directors to India for the purchase of some of this Himalayan Hemp, in order to make it known in the markets here. He states that the Civil Authorities had "issued orders to purchase ten tons of the Hemp grown in Gurhwal and Kemaon, which they were procuring at the rate of from Rs. 4 to Rs. 6 per maund, or £10 16*s*. to £16 4*s*. per ton. Carriage to Calcutta will cost about £5, and to England, with other incidental charges, say £10 per ton[1] more, which will bring the article up to £25 16*s*. to £31 4*s*. Of course, when it is exported on a larger scale the price of carriage will be greatly decreased." "This country possesses immense advantage in abundance of land, &c., and the Calcutta and Bombay merchants could always have their Hemp to ship in December." With regard to the quality of the Hemp he observes: "Moreover, the Hemp grown in our mountains and in the Doons (valleys) is far superior in strength to the Russian samples of Russian Hemp which have been sent by the Court of Directors. On showing these to the Puharee (Hill) growers of Hemp, they declared that were they to produce such an inferior article it would scarcely find a sale." The specimens were obtained from one of the most respectable houses in London, and bought for their own use. They were sent for the purpose of showing how the Hemp of commerce comes into market, instead of being twisted, tied, or platted, as is much of the fibre from

[1] Mr. Henley (*v.* p. 86) estimates all such charges at £7 a ton.

India. But if the Himalayan Hemp generally resembles that which has been referred to as from Kangra, no Russian Hemp will come near it in point of strength.

The essentially good qualities of the Hemp grown in the Himalayas, consisting in the strength, divisibility, fineness, and softness of the fibres of much of what is grown there, will make it, when known, very desirable for many purposes. That grown at the lower elevations is also possessed of considerable strength, as proved from the experiments made on a 2-inch rope in the Master-Attendant's office at Calcutta. The results given in the accompanying table (p. 332) are a portion of an extensive series of experiments, undertaken in the year 1840, in compliance with the orders of the Marine Board, dated 7th October, 1839.

The samples of Deyra and Arracan Hemp were forwarded for experiment from the Agri-Horticultural Society, and were laid up in a 2-inch rope, in November 1841, but the experiments were interrupted by the death of the Master-Attendant, and these samples were not submitted for trial till the 18th of December, 1844, so that the rope was three years old. At the same time, the small samples of *jetee* (*v.* p. 304) were tried.

It will be seen from the abstract, that amongst the thirteen samples of the 2-inch rope, the Deyrah Hemp stands the fifth in strength and the twelfth in elasticity. ('Journ. Agri-Hortic. Soc.,' iii, p. 227.) Further details are given in other tables, at pp. 224-25 of the Journal.

But Hemp of far greater strength is produced in these, which are probably the native hills of the plant. Mr. Williams, of Jubbulpore, gave to the Author, in the year 1853, a sample of Hemp, which he stated had been forwarded to him by D. F. Macleod, Esq., as the produce of Kote Kangra, in the Sikh Himalayas. This the Author has, in his Lecture and Experiments, as well as in communications with various individuals, called Kote Kangra Hemp. It is the fibre which is mentioned (at p. 133) as not breaking with a weight of 400 lb., when China-grass from Assam broke with 320 lb., and Petersburgh Hemp with only 160 lb. It has, moreover, appeared to all the practical men who have since then examined it, as the strongest fibre with which they were acquainted.

Abstract of Report of Proof of Moorgahvi, Arracan, Deyra, and Jetee Rope, compared with Europe, Manilla, New Zealand, Sunn, and Coir Rope, in the order of Strength and Elasticity.

No. of Sample.	STRENGTH.				ELASTICITY.			
	2-inch Rope.		1½-inch Rope.		2-inch Rope.		1½-inch Rope.	
	Names.	Weight at which broken.	Names.	Weight at which broken.	Names.	Length stretched before breaking.	Names.	Length stretched before breaking.
		lb.		lb.		Inches.		Inches.
1	Manilla, (white,) .	2731	New Zealand . .	2231	Sunn, (white,) . .	17½	Coir, (plain,) . .	32
2	Sunn, (ditto,) . .	2679	Europe, (1839,) . .	1967	Ditto, (tarred,) . .	13⅝	Jeetee . . .	15
3	Europe, (Pat,) . .	2655	Ditto, (Pat,) . .	1743	Manilla, (tarred,) .	13½	Sunn, (white,) . .	13½
4	New Zealand . .	2591	Sunn, (tarred,) . .	1703	Moorgahvi, (white,) .	13	Manilla, (white,) .	13
5	Deyrah	2519	Ditto, (white,) . .	1607	Manilla, (white,) .	11½	Sunn, (tarred,) . .	11⅓
6	Europe, (1839,) . .	2463	Manilla, (tarred) .	1463	Europe, (1839,) . .	10⅔	Europe, (Pat,) . .	10¼
7	Sunn, (tarred,) . .	2239	Ditto, (white,) . .	1431	New Zealand . .	10½	Moorgahvi, (tarred,)	10
8	Arracan . . .	2231	Europe, (twice laid,)	1214	Europe, (Pat,) . .	10⅓	Ditto, (white,) . .	9½
9	Manilla, (tarred,) .	1712	Jeetee	903	Moorgahvi, (tarred,)	9½	Europe, (1839,) . .	9½
10	Europe, (twice laid,)	1351	Moorgahvi, (white)	875	Arracan . . .	9	Manilla, (tarred,) .	9
11	Ditto, ditto . .	1295	Europe, (twice laid)	871	Europe, (twice laid,)	8⅔	New Zealand . .	8
12	Moorgahvi, (white,)	1175	Coir, (plain,) . . .	823	Deyrah . . .	7½	Europe, (twice laid,)	6½
13	Ditto, (tarred,) . .	1063	Moorgahvi, (tarred,)	711	Europe, (twice laid,)	7	Ditto, ditto . . .	6

Master-Attendant's Office,
30th Dec., 1844.

A. B. Clapperton,
1st Assist. to the Master-Attendant.

Dr. Jameson, in the above letter, observes, with regard to the so-called Kote Kangra Hemp, that he himself had brought it to Mr. Macleod's notice, and that it was not produced in the Kangra district, but in Kooloo and Lahoul, which are a little farther in the interior.

Before concluding, we have to detail the method of cultivating and preparing Hemp in Europe, in order to contrast them with the practice of the East, and for the information of those who may wish to cultivate it in this country. We are indebted for the directions to some of the most approved writers on the subject, and have contrasted them with those of Mr. Rowlandson in his paper in vol. x of the 'Journ. of the Royal Agricultural Society.'

CULTURE AND PREPARATION OF HEMP IN EUROPE.

Hemp being one of the few plants cultivated in Europe, which has the male and female flowers in different plants, affords some anomalies in its culture, especially that of having two harvests in the same crop. In some older works the male is frequently named the female plant, and *vice versa*.

Soil.—The soil in which Hemp thrives, is a deep, rich, moist soil, five or six inches deep; besides the alluvial, where sand and clay are intimately mixed, and having the above characteristics, also the friable loams, which contain much vegetable matter. All should contain a fair portion of sand, as this keeps the soil open and light for the roots to spread in. Hemp thrives well in Holland and Lincolnshire. Stiff, cold clays are unsuitable, for even if the plant should grow well, it is not easy to pull it, "for when strong clay becomes saturated with rain, the soil runs together, and on drying sets as hard as a pavement." If the soil be over-rich, the plant grows too luxuriantly, and produces a coarse but strong fibre. But Hemp is sometimes sown in such soils to meliorate them for the cereals, which would otherwise run too much to straw. But as many soils are too poor, they require to be raised to a suitable state by the addition of manure; and with this, it is said that Hemp may be grown in the same soil for many years. When a fine quality of fibre is required, of course, only the most suitable soil should be selected, or that in which the growth of the plant is neither excessive nor stunted. In Italy, Hemp is sown in their best lands, which are rich and strong loams, and made fine and friable. In Romagna, where the best Hemp is produced, they say it may be grown anywhere with manure. In the Himalayas, the Author has seen the Hemp growing most luxuriantly in the neighbourhood of bullock-sheds, and producing fibre of great strength. In India, spots near the habitations of natives are the best adapted for the growth of Hemp; but in these they generally grow Tobacco. At Soonamooky it grew luxuriantly in sand, which was manured with stable-dung. Hence, Hemp grown in the plains will be dearer than the other fibres.

Culture and Manure.—But the richness of the soil, and the quantity of manure required, must vary, not only according to the nature of the soil and its requirements, but also to the warmth of the soil and the nature of the climate. Warm, moist ones require less than cold, whether dry or moist climates. In England, Mr. Rowlandson says, the generality of soil will require a dressing of ten tons of well-rotted farm-yard dung per acre, ploughed and harrowed in early in April. He quotes an extensive grower, who says twenty-five tons of well-rotted, mixed stable and feeding-shed manure, should be applied per acre. The land should, of course, be in the first instance well ploughed and properly drained; also, well harrowed and rolled, to get the top-soil into good tilth; and weeds, as horse-mint, or twitch, destroyed. The manure must be carefully and evenly spread, and the plough follow close to the spreader.

Seed.—Of seed, that from Holland is the most esteemed, ripens soon, yields abundant crops, and of a fine quality; but well-grown English seed is also of good quality. Indian seed, from external appearance, appears fine; but may not be so well suited in the first crop for fibre; but the Himalayan seed, both from its appearance and the nature of its produce, is probably inferior to none, and perhaps only requires interchanging with different districts. The seed should be of a bright, grey colour, and plump; and must not have undergone heating in any way, and therefore the taste, when bitten, should be sweet, and not bitter or acrid.

The quantity of seed may vary from two to two and a half, others say to three bushels an acre. The last, if a fine fibre is required for weaving into cloth. But the larger quantity cannot be sown on very rich soils. The thicker it is on suitable land, the finer it will grow. The fresh-ploughed land should be sown very evenly, care being taken to scare away birds. The best time for sowing, in England, is from the 1st to the 15th of May; but it is sown even in June, as frosts are apt to injure the young plant; but late-sown plants are apt to grow thin and weak.

After-culture.—Hemp seed is sown both broadcast and in drills. When grown on account, chiefly, of the seed, it is sown thin. Sinclair says, by sowing Hemp in drills, a coarser and stronger bark or fibre, fit for cordage, will be produced, and a less quantity of seed is required than by sowing it broadcast. This latter mode is to be preferred, when Hemp is wanted for textile purposes. The stems rise slender and fine, according to their proximity; but they require to be weeded or hoed out to within a foot of each other, and may require a second hoeing, to destroy weeds; but in general the Hemp will, itself, smother all weeds, except in the spaces between drills. During its season of rapid growth, the plant necessarily requires moisture, and therefore, in some countries, irrigation is practised.

Pulling.—As already observed, Hemp has usually two harvests; but when grown on account of the fibre only, it may be pulled when in flower, and no distinction made between the male and female plants. But as it is usually desirable to get both the seed and the fibre of both plants, the male plants, or *white Hemp*, are pulled as soon as they have shed their pollen, usually about thirteen weeks after they have been sown. They may then be easily recognised by their leaves becoming yellow, and the stem of a whitish colour, and the flowers faded. Each plant is pulled up singly by the root, care being taken not to break or cramp the stem in the hand. The ripeness of the female plant is known not only by many of the same signs as those of the male, but also by the seeds beginning to turn of a grey colour, being firm inside, and some of the capsules to open. This is generally about Michaelmas in England. When the seed has become perfectly ripe, the bark is apt to become woody and coarse, and to separate with difficulty. But the seed which is required for sowing, ought to be taken from plants allowed enough of room to spread and then to fully ripen their seed.

Drying.—When the plants are pulled, it is recommended to hold the root end upppermost, and with a wooden sword dress off the flowers and leaves, as they assist in manuring the land. They are then bound in small bundles with bands at each end, of such a size that you can grasp with both hands, or sometimes into bundles of twelve handfuls each, and arranged along the borders of the field. If not done before, with a fork knock and shake off the soil from the roots, and scrape off the undergrowth of leaves. It is then set up like wheat in shocks, for a week or so. The stalks which form each handful should be as nearly as possible of an equal length, and the roots in particular should be placed as even as possible. If the crop is kept till spring, it is tied in larger bundles, and stacked and thatched.

Gathering Seed.—When the female Hemp is gathered, it is allowed to stand eight or ten days in the air, to allow the seed to dry and ripen; the tops being covered with undergrowth, to keep off the birds. After which, they cut off the heads, or gently beat out or thrash them to get out the seed, on a cloth. Care must be taken in conveying the bundles of seeded stems, as by passing a rope round the bundles and under the heads, and dragging the rope over the shoulder. The seed which remains after this operation, is got out by combing the heads on the teeth of a ripple; but the seed is inferior to that which first falls out, and is unfit for sowing. The female plant is generally stacked during the winter, and not steeped till the spring.

Drying.—When the Hemp has been pulled, it ought, according to some authorities, to be dried in the sun for one or two days, but Du Hamel observes, that it is a matter of doubt whether the plant should be dried before it is steeped; so Mills, in his 'Husbandry,' like the natives of India with their Sunn (*v.* p. 274), thinks that this drying appears needless trouble. So Marcandier directs, that when the Hemp is perfectly ripe, it must be put into the water as soon as it is pulled out of the ground; and Sinclair says, that Hemp should be watered as soon as possible. In this state, it is said to require only four days, but, when it has been dried, eight days of steeping. The time must, moreover, depend a good deal on the temperature of the water.

Steeping.—The steeping of Hemp, called *Water-retting*, is a very important part of its preparation, and is to be distinguished from another method, which is called *Dew-retting*. The steeping places are often only ditches, three or four feet deep, varying in breadth and length, dug for the purpose on the margins of rivers. The bundles of Hemp are laid at the bottom of the water, and covered with straw, and sometimes with sods, and loaded with pieces of wood and large stones to keep them down. The object, as in the case of Flax, is by a slight degree of fermentation to enable the epidermis, or outer skin, to separate readily from the bark, and this from the boon or reed. This is readily ascertained, by taking out one of the steeped stems and holding it by the root end, and drawing the thumb-nail up the stem to the top. If the fibre slip up the stem, it is a proof that it has been sufficiently retted.

Du Hamel, having steeped Hemp in different sorts of water, observes, that the fibres steeped in putrid standing water were softer than those which had been steeped in running water. But in water which does not run, the fibres contract a disagreeable colour: they are, however, notwithstanding this, easily bleached; it is desirable, however, to make a small stream of water pass through the steeping place.

Du Hamel, referring to the common opinion, that Hemp intended for fine cloths should be retted more than that for coarse cloths, and that for making of ropes should be steeped least of all, observes, that though there may be some truth in this, it is in vain to hope greatly to improve, by this process, fibres which are naturally coarse. A fine fibre cannot be obtained without the concurrence of soil, of seasons, and of climate, the mode of sowing and of culture, and the degree of ripeness.

Drying after Watering.—When the Hemp is sufficiently retted, it is taken carefully out of the water, and then carried to a field of aftermath or any other grass (hence called *grassing*) that is clean and free from cattle. Here it is spread out very evenly, and will probably require to lie there for three weeks or more, in order to bleach, and the fibre to become free; during which time it must be carefully turned over, with light long poles, every three or four days. Mr. Rowlandson says it is sufficiently bleached when pink spots appear on the stem. It is sometimes dried along a wall, or on rocky ground, and sometimes artificially, in ovens and kilns. When dry, the Hemp is tied up in bundles again, and carried to the barn or rick.

Peeling and Breaking.—When the Hemp is sufficiently dried, the next process is either to *peel* it, by taking one stalk after the other, breaking the reed, and slipping off the bark. The process is simple but tedious, and will give occupation to those who are without any. But it comes off in ribbons, which do not heckle so well as Hemp that has been broken, and they are apt to retain some of the thick parts next the root, hence the saying, that this mode is better for the seller than the buyer.

The term of breaking or braking Hemp, applies rather to the boon or reed than to the fibre, for this only bends under the hand of the dresser, and does not break. The operation is performed either by beating the Hemp, which is a laborious and tedious work, or by the break, which may be moved either by hand or by a spring or treddle attached to the upper jaw of the break, or by fluted rollers, worked by horse-, wind-, or water-, and now sometimes by steam-power. When Hemp has undergone the process of breaking, it is ready, like Flax, for the process of scutching, in which scutching mills are now used, as in the case of Flax. By rubbing, beetling, and striking the Hemp with reiterated blows, the longitudinal fibres are separated from one another, and in proportion to the greater or less degree of that separation the Hemp becomes more or less fine, elastic, and soft to the touch. (Du Hamel.)

Dew-retting (p. 199), Mr. Rowlandson says (l. c., p. 180) will produce the most valuable white Hemp. The stems, after being pulled, are allowed to stand in the stooks for two or three days; they are then spread out on land where the grass is plentiful, and may require to be there for six weeks, and to be frequently turned. The process will be completed when the pink spots appear, as before noticed, which must be carefully looked for, when it will be ready to gather and tie up in bundles, to form stooks, in order to dry; the fibre will not sustain any damage before the pink spots appear. *Snow-retting* is practised in Russia and Sweden. After the first fall, they spread the Hemp (which has been dried in the sun or otherwise) on the snow, and leave it there to be covered with other falls of snow, until spring, when it is usually found to be sufficiently retted. (Wisset, p. 194.) In Livonia they steep their Hemp in a manner which is a medium between still and running water, in a series of basins, one above the other, but as has already been observed, the French, for whom this information was originally obtained, do not avail themselves of it. (*v.* l. c., p. 204.)

In addition to the ordinary methods of preparation of Hemp, we may briefly refer to others, most of which, however, have in improved forms been already noticed under the head of Flax.

The Abbé Brulles recommended the use of soap in the proportion of one part to forty-eight of water, at a temperature of about 200° F., and the water to be about forty times the weight of the Hemp. Du Hamel tried boiling the Hemp stems in water, but he did not find that the peeling was facilitated. Marcandier recommended a second watering, and also the use of a warm alkaline ley. (l. c., pp. 243 and 245.)

But as we have seen the use of hot water successfully applied to Flax in recent times, and soap has been used in several processes, and in a very ingenious manner in one which we omitted to notice,—that in which a little acid is afterwards added, so that decomposition takes place, in consequence of the acid uniting with the alkaline base, when the oil which is set free assists in softening the fibre.

In the article on Sunn we have already referred (p. 276) to a peculiar method of drying, to which the Livonians are said to ascribe the good or bad quality of their Hemp. The stems are first set up to *drain*, and then spread out for a day to *dry*; after which they are made up in heaps, and covered over with straw, or other similar material of any kind, to make them *sweat*. When they have sweated *enough*, they are laid again in small heaps, so that the air may dry them in the shade by blowing through them; after which they are next effectually dried by fire, kiln, or oven, and immediately put under the breakers whilst yet hot. It is probable that this method, when skilfully practised, must produce some of the same effects in Hemp as in some other vegetable substances. Mr. Frushard observes, with regard to the natives of India: "The reason why their tobacco falls so much to dust, is owing to its not being *sweated* enough. When properly *sweated*, as they manage it in America, it becomes tough like a bladder; and toughness and suppleness are the qualities wanted in Hemp." (Wisset, p. 223.)

Besides these, we have also the dry method of separating Hemp in some places, as related by Mr. Durno, who was the British Consul at Memel, and who states that in the southern parts of Poland, steeping is not practised at all, on the supposition that the harle is thereby weakened, and the colour darkened. Instead of steeping, they there *dry the stalks in the sun*. But the dressing is more laborious, and consequently more expensive. (Wissèt, p. 177.) Mr. Dickson, as in the case of Flax, has succeeded admirably in separating Hemp fibre by passing dried stems from Italy under the rollers of his machine (*v.* p. 224), and the Author has no doubt that the method may be successfully practised with several fibres for many purposes.

Crop and Profit.—Mr. Rowlandson says the best land for obtaining fibre of the strongest description is a fat loam, not too heavy with clay, and a portion of sand intermixed. On such land, succeeding a crop of beans, Hemp will grow six or seven feet high, and bean-stalks in such make good manure for Hemp. He adds: "I have known 9 quarters of beans per acre after Hemp, weighing 21 stone per sack. Hemp after beans will produce 30 stone more per acre, of the strongest and heaviest fibre, than by any other mode of culture; the weight of fibre in ordinary culture and circumstances will produce 60 to 70 stone per acre." A good crop of Hemp after beans will produce 28 to 30 bushels of seed per acre; in the ordinary way, 20 to 22 bushels per acre. But only particular circumstances or prices render Hemp a desirable culture in England; for, in general, it cannot be considered a productive crop—though it may bring 5*s.* per stone, and good seed 5*s.* per bushel,—as it requires much manure, and "Hemp land will grow other crops of equal or superior value at a less cost." But other countries, such as parts of India and the Himalayas, which prefer any exportable product like Flax or Hemp, will be glad to cultivate both, if they get any reasonable encouragement. The co-operation of a purely manufacturing establishment might facilitate and give advantages to the production of Hemp, as to that of Flax.

IMPORTS, ETC., OF HEMP FROM INDIA.

It is not impossible therefore that as India now supplies England with the cheapest of fibrous materials, Jute, that the country will also be able to supply the strongest and best, that is, Himalayan Hemp. The greater distance which this has to travel, but chiefly by the Ganges River, may be easily paid for by its greater value. We also believe that as Mr. Deneef succeeded in growing some good Hemp even in the plains of Bengal in the rainy season, so others will be able to do so in other parts of India. The expenses of transit from distant parts will, no doubt, be diminished when larger quantities are operated upon and the arrangements are made by mercantile men. All such transactions in the Hills would be facilitated if it were found possible to make the road from the Kemaon Hills into the plains practicable for light carts, as this has been done with the Sikh hills to some extent, but these are there less precipitous. That there is nothing chimerical in the expectation of greatly increased quantities of fibre being imported, even from so distant a country as India, is evident from what has already taken place. If this has been possible with the cheaper it cannot be impracticable with the better. Though the information is not very certain, we find from the published reports that Hemp was exported from India to the following extent:

HEMP IMPORTED FROM INDIA, AND SOLD IN ENGLAND.

	Cwt.		Cwt.
1803	4820	1807	4738
1804	8335	1808	4023
1805	3399	1809	1543
1806	6421	1810	2555

In 1850-51, Imported into Bombay, of *Ganza* (Hemp-herb), 514 cwt. from Concan; and Exported to the United Kingdom 15,896 lb.=Rs. 5796.

How greatly and rapidly the increase of fibrous materials has gone on within the last few years from India is evident from the following table of the imports from Russia and the British territories in India, from 1847 to 1851; while in the year 1831, 506,803 cwt. were imported from Russia, and only 9472 cwt. from the East Indies.

Quantities of Hemp Imported into the United Kingdom from—

	1847	1848	1849	1850	1851
Russia	544,844	540,207	641,548	614,535	672,342
Br. Ter. in East Indies	185,788	258,239	360,362	399,345	590,923

As soon as Hemp is brought down in the spring, or in the course of the summer, it is selected and made up into bundles by sworn selectors (*brackers*), who are said to act with impartiality and exactness; and tickets are affixed to every bundle as selected, &c.

Hemp at Petersburgh is assorted into clean Hemp, or firsts; outshot Hemp, or seconds; half-cleaned Hemp, or thirds; and Hemp Codilla. Riga Hemp is distinguished as rein (or clean), outshot, and pass Hemp.

Particular care is taken to ship Hemp and Flax in fine, dry weather. If either get wet, they are apt to heat, and to be totally spoiled. For this reason every vessel taking in Hemp and Flax is furnished with mats to prevent their getting damp.

A bundle of clean Hemp weighs from 56 to 65 poods; ditto outshot, 48 to 55 poods; ditto half-clean, 40 to 55 ditto. (1 pood=36 lb. avoirdupois.) 63 poods are about equal to an English ton; the fixed charges on which in Petersburgh amount to 45 roub. 32 cop.; also commission and stamps, and on import into London, about £10 *5s. 8d.*, freight included; when the price is £40 a ton. (*v.* M'Culloch, from Mr. Borrison on the Commerce of Petersburgh.)

With regard to prices, those of Hemp will of course vary at different times, like those of all other products. It is usually highest in the summer months, and lowest in September.

In December, 1833, Petersburgh clean Hemp was 25*s.* to 26*s.*; Riga Rein at 29*s.* per cwt.

In the year 1840, Italian Hemp was at 50*s.* the cwt.; Polish Rein, 48*s.*; Petersburgh clean, 47*s.*; clean for cordage, 46*s.*; Polish Pass Hemp, 46*s.*; Petersburgh half-clean, 42*s.*

In the year 1844, the price of Petersburgh Hemp was 38*s.* per cwt., or £38 per ton.

At the end of 1854, Petersburgh clean, £60 10*s.* to £63; outshot, £59 to £61; half-clean, £57 10*s.*; Riga Rein, £61 to £64; do. outshot, £58 to £63. But we cannot do better than conclude with an extract from the 'Commercial Circular' of the Messrs. Lindsay.

"As regards Hemp, the rates for this article advanced in the early months of the year, and obtained their highest point in March, when £75 per ton was paid for clean. They then gradually fell to £58 to £60—about its present value—it having become apparent that supplies to a much larger extent than were anticipated would be received *viâ* Memel, &c. The future range of prices will, of course, necessarily depend on the action of our Government as respects Prussian neutrality. It, however, must not be lost sight of that the variety and extent of substitutes in the course of introduction will, under any circumstances, for some time to come diminish the consumption of Russian Hemp."

BREAD-FRUIT TRIBE (*Artocarpeæ*).

Though in general appearance no plants seem to differ more than the Mulberry and Bread-fruit trees from the Nettles, yet if we examine the actual flowers of all these plants, we shall find that the resemblances are much greater than the differences. Hence Jussieu united them together into the natural family of Urticeæ; but as some are distinguished by their milky juice, and flowers aggregated into heads, these have been separated from the others under the name of Artocarpeæ.

Among these we find the Bread-fruit, Fig, and Mulberry, genera of extensive distribution, numerous in species, growing to a great size, and many of them of the greatest utility to mankind: though we have only to notice them with reference to their fibrous properties. These are probably much more important than is generally supposed; if we look to them as sources of material for paper-making, since the bark of some of the species is already applied to this purpose in some countries.

Thus the Bread-fruit tree (*Artocarpus incisa*), so famous for affording the chief article of food to the inhabitants of the South Sea Islands, and for which an expedition was sent by George III, under the celebrated Bligh, to introduce it into the West Indies, has bark which is also useful to the people from its fibrous qualities: for being stripped and then beaten and prepared, it makes a kind of cloth, with which the South Sea Islanders clothe themselves. At Taiti, clothing made of it, and worn chiefly by the common people, was more common than that made with the Paper Mulberry, though inferior to it in softness and whiteness.

Some of the Indian species of Artocarpus, as the *Jak* tree, *Kantal*, or *A. integrifolius*, and the *Dephal* or *A. Lakoocha*, and others, are probably possessed of similar properties; they are very abundant, grow to a great size, and are frequently cut down on account of their wood.

There were sent to the Exhibition of 1851, bark and bark *cloth*, which may all be produced by species of Artocarpus, as one of them is said to be bark of the

Trap tree, a species of *Artocarpus*, which furnishes the Gutta used as birdlime. The fibre of the bark is used for fishing lines, cordage, and nets at Singapore.

Chowat Kurnat, similar to the above, from Baram River.

Glam tree bark, from Borneo, furnishes a paper-like bark much used in caulking the seams of vessels.

Kumut or bark cloth worn by the Kayans when mourning for the dead—River Baram.

The Paper Mulberry, formerly Morus, now *Broussonetia papyrifera*, is a tree of this family which has long been famous for its fibrous bark, as this is made into a kind of cloth as well as into paper. It is a native of the isles of the Southern Ocean, as well as of China and of Japan. In Taiti, or Otaheite, and other islands, they make cloth of its bark; and it is said that the finest and whitest cloth and mantles worn by the principal people at Otaheite and in the Sandwich Islands is made of the bark of this tree, and this when dyed red takes a good colour. It is called *Kaili* on the west coast of Celebes. Some of the cloth made of its bark was sent to the Exhibition of 1851.

The manufacture of paper from this bark was long since accurately described by Kæmpfer, as seen by him in Japan, where they are said to cultivate this plant much as osiers are cultivated in Europe; the young shoots being cut down in December, after the leaves have fallen. These are then cut into good long pieces, and are boiled until the separation of the bark displays the naked wood, from which it is then easily separable with the aid of a longitudinal incision.

In order to make paper, the dried bark is soaked for a few hours in water, after which the outer cuticle and the internal green layer are scraped off. The stronger and firmer pieces are separated from the youngest shoots, which are of inferior quality. The selected bark is boiled in a ley of wood-ashes till the fibres can be separated by a touch of the finger. The pulp so produced is then agitated in water till it resembles tufts of tow. If not sufficiently washed the paper will be coarse, but strong; if too much boiled it will be weaker, but white. It is then beaten on a table, with batons of hard wood, into a pulp. Mucilage obtained from boiled rice, or from a plant called *oreni*, is added to the pulp. These three are stirred with a clean reed till reduced into a homogeneous liquor, and when of a due consistence are ready for conversion into sheets of paper. This process is interesting, from its resemblance to that adopted with the Nepal Paper plant, showing the probable introduction of the art from China.

Specimens of Paper Mulberry cloth, or rather paper used for the purposes of cloth, and made from the bark of the Paper Mulberry, as well as paper made from the same bark, were sent to the Exhibition of 1851 from Singapore.

The fibrous properties of the foregoing plant are interesting not only on its own account but also because it is allied to the Mulberries, a genus (*Morus*) numerous in species, and abounding in individuals, many of which are cultivated on account of their fruit, but still more for their leaves as food for the silk-worm. It is probable that most of the species of the genus Morus have bark of a sufficiently fibrous nature. But few, if any, seem to be turned to useful account. Yet the bark of the White Mulberry seems from very early times to have been made into paper in China; for Marco Polo informs us that "the Grand Khan causes the bark to be stripped from those Mulberry trees, the leaves of which are used for feeding silk-worms, and takes from it that thin rind which lies between the coarse bark and the wood of the tree. This being steeped, and afterwards pounded in a mortar until reduced to a pulp, is made into paper, resembling that which is made from cotton." This fact directs attention to the bush cultivation of the Mulberry in Bengal, for feeding silk-worms. This culture consists in planting cuttings of the Mulberry, which, as they grow, are cut down about four times in the year, in order to produce young leaves for the successive broods of silk-worms. The countless number of shoots which are thus thrown away, or used as fuel, would probably, under the agency of the dhenkee, yield good half-stuff for the paper-maker. Mr. Henley, indeed, informs us that, before leaving India, he had produced very satisfactory specimens of half-stuff from the bark of these rejected stems. The bark separates when the cut stems are steeped in water, and when pounded up, the greater part of the mucilaginous matter passes off, leaving a mass, having much of the good qualities of linen rag half-stuff.

The genus *Ficus*, celebrated for one of the species yielding the Fig, one of the most early cultivated of fruits, and another the Caoutchouc of Assam, while the Bur and the Peepul are, in India, two of the most highly esteemed of trees, is also a genus numerous in species which abound in all parts of India. It is probable that the bark of some of the species, like that of the Mulberry, may be converted into half-stuff, as Mr. Ostandje states that the bark of one of the species is used for paper-making in the Island of Ceylon.

A stately forest tree, called Chandul, which has been placed here and called *Lepurandra saccadora*, is indigenous on the West side of India, as in the ravines at Kandalla and in the jungles near Coorg, where people manufacture sacks from the bark by a very simple process. A branch is cut, corresponding to the length and diameter of the sack wanted. It is soaked a little, and then beaten with clubs until the inner bark separates from the wood. This done, the sack formed of the bark is turned inside out and pulled down, until the wood is sawed off, with the exception of a small piece left to form the bottom of the sack, and which is carefully left untouched. These sacks are in general use among the villagers for carrying rice, and are sold for about six annas each.

Nettles (*Urticaceæ*).

In treating of Hemp, it was stated that it belonged to the natural family of the Nettles, or *Urticeæ*. These are widely diffused throughout both tropical and temperate climates, though they generally occur where there is considerable moisture either of soil or of climate. Though small and herbaceous in Europe, they grow to a gigantic size in the hot moist parts of Asia, and extend from its warm tropical islands, all along the Malayan Peninsula, to the foot of the Himalayas, and along which, and in its valleys, they flourish, even near to the banks of the Sutlej. Species are also found around the Neilgherries, and along the Malabar coast to the Concan. Though the flowers of all are inconspicuous, some of the species (as *Urtica pulcherrima*) are remarkable for the beauty of their foliage; one of them (*U. tuberosa*) is distinguished by its tuberous rootstock, which is eaten by some of the natives of India, either in its raw or cooked state. Every one, however, knows that the great characteristic of the Nettles is their sting. Some of the Indian species are remarkable, even among Nettles, for this quality; as, for instance, *U. crenulata* and *U. heterophylla*, the latter "a most ferocious-looking plant." Many of the Nettles formerly placed in the genus *Urtica* have been removed to the genus *Boehmeria*, which includes what are sometimes called stingless Nettles. But many of each have long been famous for the tenacity of their fibre.

Thus, of the European species, thread and cloth, as also paper, have been made from the fibre of the common Nettle (*Urtica dioica*). So, of the Siberian species, *U. cannabina*, thread and cord is made for the use especially of fishermen. In the Society Islands, also, cord is made with the fibres of *U. argentea;* and in Japan, the bark of the species called *U. Japonica,* is employed in making lines, cordage, and cloth.

China-grass, Rheea, or Ramee Fibre (*Urticaceæ*).

China, *Chû* or *Tchou Ma;* Japan, *Tsjo, Karao;* Sumatra, *Caloee;* Malay, *Ramee;* in Bonoa, *Inan;* on East Celebes, *Gambe;* Rungpore, *Kunkhoora* and *Kunchoora;* Assam, *Rheea;* in Shaw, *Pan.*

The species which is most famous among these Nettles for its fibre is that called *Urtica nivea,* but now *Boehmeria nivea.* Kæmpfer, in his 'Amœnitates Exot.,' gives *Mao, Tsjo, Karao,* as the Japan names of the plant; and Thunberg says of it, copying from him: "Cortex pro funibus conficiendis, et filis validis ad texturas, expetitur;" and "E seminibus oleum causticum exprimitur."

Though we have now abundance of information on the subject, in place of the hints we formerly had, it is only within the last few years that Sir W. Hooker has published, in the 'Kew Journ. of Botany,' vol. i, p. 25, and vol. iii, p. 313, that he has obtained satisfactory information, through Sir George Staunton and Dr. Wallich, that the so-called China-grass is the fibre of this *Urtica nivea* of Linnæus, the *Boehmeria nivea* of Gaudichaud.

Though the beautiful fabric known as China-grass cloth has long been known, its fibre has only in comparatively recent times attracted much attention, and the plant producing it was long unknown. When imported, however, into this country, it sold for 60 to 80, and even for £120 a ton. It can be, at most times, had at Ningpo for about 6 dollars a picul of 133 pounds. The above high prices following every demand, have prevented this fibre from coming into general use for our manufactures. But a small black, almost invisible spot, which occasionally occurs on the fibre has also prevented its use for fine purposes.

Though the plant was not known botanically, full descriptions of the mode of preparing the fibre are given in Chinese works. One of these accounts was translated and transferred to the 'Journ. of the Hortic. Soc. of London,' in vol. iv, part iv, under the head of the Cultivation and Preparation of the *Tchou Ma*, or Chinese Flax; and this we propose republishing, for reasons which will be obvious.

By this account we learn that the plant is cultivated with considerable care; that it may be obtained from seeds, but more quickly by parting the roots, as it throws up numerous shoots; that these may be cut down, and that fresh ones will spring up, so that three several crops are obtained in the season. Great care is also taken in the scraping, peeling, steeping, and bleaching of the fibre. We also learn that the first crop yields strong and coarse fibres, and the second and third crops, delicate fibres for the finer fabrics.

This China-grass fibre has of late years attracted considerable attention, and no less than three Prize Medals were given at the Exhibition of 1851, for the finely prepared specimens of this fibre. These looked like fine white silk or asbestos, some dyed of different colours, and some woven into cloth. The Jury Report of Class IV thus mentions them:

"The process of Messrs. L. W. Wright and Co., for the preparation of China-grass, &c., for which a patent was obtained in 1849, consists, essentially, in a very ingenious arrangement for boiling the stems in an alkaline solution, after they have previously been steeped for twenty-four hours in water of a temperature of 90°. The fibre is then thoroughly washed with pure water, and finally subjected to the action of a current of high-pressure steam till nearly dry. A very beautiful series of specimens, illustrating the preparation of this fibre, the various stages of the process, the bleaching of it, and the uses to which it may be applied, both alone and in conjunction with other fibrous materials in the formation of mixed fabrics, is shown by Messrs. Wright.

"Very beautiful samples of China-grass fibre are likewise shown by Messrs. Hives and Atkinson.

"Equally fine specimens are exhibited by Messrs. Marshall and Co., of Leeds.

"For all these samples, the Jury have awarded Prize Medals."

Caloee or Ramee (*Urtica tenacissima*, Roxb.)

Dr. Roxburgh, when making his experiments on Fibres at the beginning of this century, took much pains with one of a species of Urtica, which he named *U. tenacissima*, because he considered it one of the strongest fibres he had ever met with. He first became acquainted with it in consequence of four plants having been sent to him by Mr. Ewer from Bencoolen, in Sumatra. He afterwards wrote that "some thousand plants have been reared from these four, so readily does it grow and multiply;" in fact, that "it may be grown from cuttings as readily as the willow." He further describes it as thriving anywhere, but most luxuriantly in shade, where there is much moisture. In four months it attains the height of eight or ten feet, when its shoots flower and can be cut down. Other shoots then spring up, which are also soon fit to be cut; and so on successively for almost any period. If left alone, the plant will in a short time produce a complete jungle. He, however, experienced considerable difficulty in separating the fibre. The Malays, he learned, merely steep the shoots in water for ten or twelve days, peel off the bark, and dry it in the sun.

Besides its strength, he considered that the beauty, fineness, and softness of the fibre, are also greatly in its favour. In Sumatra it is called *Caloee;* but the Malays call it *Ramee,* and use the fibre for sewing thread, for twine, and for making fishing nets. Marsden states, that the shoots are cut down, dried, and beaten, after which the rind is stripped off; but Dr. Roxburgh did not find this method to succeed with him. He was afterwards informed by a friend at Canton that the grass cloth of China was made from the fibres of this plant.

In the year 1810 three bales of this Caloee fibre were sent to the India House, having been produced in the Botanic Garden at Calcutta. In December, 1811, one of these bales was sent to Messrs. Sharpe, then of Mark Lane. On the 4th Feb., 1812, they reported, that having brought the Caloee fibre to the state of Hemp for the use of cordage, a thread was spun, of the size of those spun in the King's Rope-yards, which bore 252 lb., whereas the weight required to be borne in his Majesty's yards by Russian Hemp of the same size is only 82 lb.

Other bales were subsequently received on several occasions, and in 1815 one was sent to Dr. Taylor, of the Society of Arts. The Society voted one of their medals to Capt. J. Cotton, of the East India Company, for his efforts in introducing this fibre into this country.

A bale of this fibre having been given to Mr. Lee, the inventor of the machine mentioned at p. 221, he observed that the fibre appeared to have been peeled off the plant while it was in a green state, and that this rendered it of less value. He conceived that it would be more easily cleaned if the plants were taken dry, without water-steeping or dew-retting. But when cleaned the fibre is strong, soft, and fine, and of more value than the best Russian Hemp.

Two more bales were sent in December, 1814, to the Court of Directors by Dr. F. Buchanan, who had succeeded Dr. Roxburgh, with a letter, dated 16th December, 1814, from which the following is an extract: "I beg leave to mention that the Caloee plant is by no means a new species of Urtica, as Dr. Roxburgh supposed. It is the *Urtica nivea* of Willdenow and the *Ramium majus* of Rumphius."[1] ('Flora Amboin.,' v, t. 79, fig. 1.) "The plant under the name of Kankora has from time immemorial been cultivated in the Dinagpur and Rongypur districts of Bengal, and its fibres are used for a few purposes that require great strength with little thickness, but the expense of cleaning the fibrous part has always prevented it from coming into general use." He therefore proposed discontinuing the cultivation. But if we refer to Roxburgh's 'Flora Indica,' iii, p. 591, then, certainly, in manuscript, we find that he was quite aware of his plant being identical with that of Rumphius, though it appeared to him to differ from the description of the *U. nivea* of Willdenow.

We observe that it was considered at that time that Indian fibres could never be introduced into this country, as the freight could not be calculated on at less than £12 per ton, of fifty cubic feet. Now about 30,000 tons weight are imported.

The Court, in a dispatch dated 8th May, 1816, in sending out some of Lee's machines (p. 222), and referring to this plant, observed: "The Caloee is a plant that appears to be com-

[1] Rumphius observes, respecting the separation of the fibre, that it is more easily effected when the stem is in a dry state: "Caulium cortex tenuis est, inque fila findi potest præsertim in siccata planta;" and, again, "Caules autem isti sponte siccari debent tum facile separatur ipsorum cortex, qui in fila commode findi potest." "Alii adultos sumunt viridis herbæ caules, ipsorumque deglubunt exteriorem viridem, et succosum, corticem ad interiorem album librum qui ligno incumbit, quum in tenuissima findunt fila." (l. c., p. 214.) He further says, "It is diligently cultivated in all places inhabited by the Orang Badjos."

paratively in its infancy as to cultivation, but being a perennial the expense attending other fibrous plants is not incurred; and if this process, instead of scraping and peeling, will furnish its fibre clear of its mucilaginous coat, you may rejoice in the acquisition of the invention: for we have found the fibre stronger than Russian Hemp of the best description; and by some further improvements of this person's invention it has been brought to a thread, preferable to the best material in Europe for Brussels lace."

So that at that time one of the most important applications of this fibre was well known.

Rheea of Assam; *Kunkhoora* of Rungpore. (*Urtica tenncessimi.*)

The above very valuable plant was for some time lost sight of. But attention having been directed, by Major Jenkins and the officers employed with him in Assam, to the fibrous plants of that valley, Major Hannay and Capt. Dalton were induced to cultivate a small portion of land with this fibre; and the former having prepared ten bales of a fibre which he called Rheea fibre, and five bales of another called Bon Rheea, and eleven of these having been sent to the Court of Directors of the East India Company, were referred to the Author to report upon. This he did to the following effect:

" The Rheea fibre forwarded by the Government of Bengal as the produce of Assam in order that its properties and value may be correctly ascertained in this country, appears to me likely to prove one of the most valuable products of India, for in strength it far exceeds the best Hemp, and in fineness it rivals superior kinds of Flax. Its culture is well known to the natives of Assam as well as of the districts of Rungpore, of Dinagepore, also in Burma, Siam, and of other Eastern countries and islands. It can now be produced and sold with profit at as cheap a rate as Russian Hemp.[1] If any machine could be invented for facilitating the separation of the fibre from the woody part of the stalks, the Rheea would speedily undersell all other fibres, as from four to five crops of fibre can be obtained from the same plants within the year.

[1] This is probably at present incorrect, from the Author misunderstanding a passage in Major Hannay's report. (*v.* p. 352.)

"The Rheea fibre, though a new import from Assam, is well known under another name, being identical with the highly valued article of commerce, known by the name of China-grass, the Chu-Mâ of the Chinese, and from which the famed Grass cloth of China is manufactured. The proof is very complete of the identity of the plants from which these two differently named fibres are obtained. One of the educated Chinese introduced into Upper Assam on the establishment of the Tea Manufactory in that valley, recognised the *Rheea* as identical with the *Chû Mâ* of his own country.[1] The Rheea of Assam had been ascertained by botanists to be the same plant as the *Urtica tenacissima* of Dr. Roxburgh, who half a century ago was informed by a friend at Canton that the plant which he had obtained as the *Caloee* of Sumatra, and to which he had given the above botanical name, was that from which the Chinese grass cloth was made. Lately, Dr. Macgowan, settled at Ningpo, sent specimens of the Chû Mâ to Calcutta. These Dr. Falconer found to be the same plant as the *Boehmeria nivea* of botanists, described under the name of *Urtica tenacissima* by Roxburgh. He says: 'The specimens from China correspond exactly with those grown in the Botanic Garden, with which I have compared them.' (May 5, 1849.) Sir W. Hooker has also identified these two plants as being identical, and has described the former as yielding what is called *China-grass*. Further, manufacturers in this country have found the two fibres to be the same for all practical purposes."

Mr. Sangster, who has paid much attention to this fibre, writes, that "our engineer, who prepared all our China-grass, is satisfied that your samples are equal to the best sorts from China." So Mr. Marshall, of Leeds, who is the largest consumer of China grass in this country, is satisfied that the Assam is the same for all practical purposes, as will afterwards clearly appear.

"The identity of the Rheea fibre with China-grass, or the

[1] "I went this morning to the old Chinese Doctor of Medicine here, with a good grass cloth handkerchief in my hand; and on seeing which he immediately said it was the *Hengchung Hapo* of China, and identical with the *Rheea* of the Doms of Upper Assam, the stuff being whitened by bleaching. I can trust to what this old man says, as he is an intelligent man and a great reader; his acount was corroborated by another intelligent Chinese, formerly one of the Government head tea-makers." (Major Hannay.)

Chû Mâ, and consequently its value having been proved, it is important to find that it is a plant very widely diffused in the East. Dr. M'Gowan writes from Ningpo ('Agri-Hortic. Soc.,' vi, p. 241), that 'the Chû Mâ is found at the base of hills from Cochin China to the Yellow River, and from Chusan to the farthest west that researches can for the present extend.' We find that it is known in Celebes and Borneo, cultivated in Java and Sumatra, and many other of the islands of the East, where it seems to be known chiefly by the names *Rami* and *Caloee*. It is known in Siam and at Singapore; the string made of it is called *tali rami*, and the fishing nets manufactured with it are conspicuous for their elegance and strength. Col. Burney, in 1836, obtained it from Pivela and Youkyouk, in the Shan province of Ava, where it is called *Pan*, and where Mr. Landers afterwards found it. Plants sent by the Colonel to Moulmein and to Tavoy succeeded well, but required much water. It has long been known as cultivated by fishermen in the Bengal districts of Rungpore and of Dinagepore, where it is called *Kunkhoora*. Col. Jenkins first sent it from Cochin in 1836; and it is found in different parts of Assam, where it is called *Rheea*, and from whence specimens have frequently been sent to the Agri-Hortic. Society of Calcutta, and whose 'Journal,' vols. iii to viii, contain numerous notices respecting it.

"In Assam, Rungpore, and Dinagepore, this plant seems to be very generally cultivated, though only in small quantities, by the Dooms or fishermen, near their huts. The climate of Assam, and of these districts, being moist, is very suitable to the plant. Manure is useful, moisture essential for quick growth, as well as shade and protection from storms to allow it to grow to the height of eight feet, from which a six-feet fibre may be extracted. Hence it is most common in the districts along the foot of hills. It is grown from the separated roots, and may be cut down several times, so that four or five crops may easily be obtained during the year, and the aggregate produce of an acre of ground be about twelve maunds. The different crops vary in strength and fineness. All the officers of the district state that the culture is perfectly understood, and though cultivated only in small quantities by the fishermen for their own use, it is susceptible of easy and rapid extension, if the cultivators had any inducement to grow it. The expense seems to be about five rupees a maund; for Major Hannay, referring to the fact of £20 a ton having been offered for any quantity in Calcutta, observes that, as 'it costs at least five rupees per maund, you will see that it can scarce be sent to Calcutta at the price offered.' He says, also, that if any cheaper method of separation from the stalk could be discovered it would undersell all other fibres."

From the mode of expression adopted as above by Major Hannay, the Author was led to think that the whole expense for the production of the fibre was five rupees a maund. But in another place he says, the expenses of cultivation are ten rupees a maund. Capt. Jenkins ('Journ. Agri-Hort. Soc.,' viii, p. 379) also says, the present cost is ten rupees a maund; but as the plant can be grown with the least possible trouble, and the preparation of the Flax from it is a very facile process, he states, that "there is no doubt the Flax can be grown at half this price." The dearness is no doubt owing partly to only small quantities being produced for the use of the fishermen, who do not for their purposes require very large quantities. Mr. Henley, in a letter in the 'Journ. Agri-Hort. Society,' says, that "it must necessarily be a much more expensive article than either Sunn or Jute, inasmuch as a labourer can prepare one and a half to two maunds of Jute per day's work, whilst of the *Kunchoora* he cannot manufacture more than as many seers." It is evident that some improved method of separation is the most essential requisite.

"Various attempts have been made to make this fibre more generally known, and to bring it into demand as an article of commerce." (The early experiments have already been mentioned.) "It has frequently been sent by Col. Jenkins, and the officers employed in Assam, to the Agri-Horticultural Society of Calcutta. Mr. Henley, and others, have sent small quantities to the markets of this country, but without attracting much attention, or selling it at remunerating prices. Samples were sent by Major Hannay, Capt. Reynolds, Baboos Deena Nath, and Lokenath, to the Exhibition of 1851, when honorable mention was made of their exertions.

"A Prize Medal was, however, awarded for some beautifully white and silky looking fibre sent by the Singapore Committee, from M. Weber, of Java, as the produce of a plant which he called *Boehmeria candicans*, and also *Linum usitatissimum* on the same label. The former is probably only another name for our plant, as it is said to be the *Rami* or *Ramee* of the Malays. The plant is cultivated by the Dutch in Java, and its fibre has been introduced into Holland, and gold medals awarded to Messrs. Meerburg, of Leyden, for specimens of sail-cloth, ropes, cables, &c., and also for some finer kinds of cloth and table-cloths. The plant producing this fibre was called *Boehmeria candicans*, and also *B. utilis* by Professor Blume, but it is probably only a variety of *B. nivea*, or perhaps a nearly allied species.

"Major Hannay, who has long paid attention to this fibre, and to whom much praise is due, was induced to grow, and prepare the present samples together with some grown by Capt. Dalton (six bales of Dom Rheea and five of Bon Rheea), in consequence of applications from this country by merchants, who, however, did not offer a sum (£20 a ton at Calcutta) which would pay for the expenses of culture and preparation.

"Since the samples arrived in this country, I have endeavoured to make the fibre known, and its value appreciated. Specimens of both the Rheea and the Wild Rheea were sent to the Society of Arts, and an account of them published in their 'Journal' for the 9th of December, 1853. Specimens were also sent to Mr. Marshall, of Leeds; likewise to the Commercial Association of Manchester, to Belfast, to Paris, and to the Chamber of Commerce at Dundee. Its fibres have been shown to, and specimens given to numerous individuals well acquainted with such subjects.

"The letter of Mr. Marshall is most satisfactory, as he is himself a spinner of the finest yarns, and the largest if not the only consumer of China-grass:"

Dear Sir,—We have examined the samples you sent to us, and I now give you the result.

No. 1. Cultivated Rheea.—This is evidently just the same fibre we are using, imported from China, under the name of China-grass. It is not so fine in quality as the best descriptions we obtain from China, which are still longer than this sample, and of a green colour. We should class it with the middle or coarse quality, and estimate its value, delivered in England, at £48 to £50 per ton. It appears to be clean and regular in colour, and free from dead fibres, which are often a great detriment; and would be an useful quality of fibre, of which we could take a regular supply.

No. 2. Rheea fibre, sent to the Exhibition of 1851.—The same as No. 1, but coarser in quality.

No. 3. Fibre from Java.—We think this is the Rheea fibre prepared, but can hardly judge from so small a sample: it seems to be a good, clean fibre, and worth further inquiry.

No. 4. Wild Rheea fibre.—Very coarse; only fit for rope-making.

I hope this report will be satisfactory to you. It would certainly be an important advantage to us, as consumers of China-grass or Rheea fibre, to be able to obtain a supply from Assam. If it could be supplied at lower rates than those I have mentioned, that would, of course, much encourage the consumption of it in this country. I have stated what we consider the *full* value at present in our market here. At present there is not much consumed in England, but a good supply from a nearer market than China might enlarge the demand.

I am, sir, very truly,
J. G. Marshall.

Leeds; *Dec.* 10, 1853.

Major Hannay, in one of his papers to the Agri-Horticultural Society of Calcutta, mentions that some specimens of his Rheea fibre having been sent direct to Leeds were valued at £50 a ton. Mr. Sangster, of the firm of Wright and Co., to whom one of the Prize Medals was awarded, has no doubt of the identity of the Assam produce with that of China, and therefore of its being of equal value. Mr. Dickson, who has had much experience with different fibres and the finer kinds of Flax, pronounced it to be a splendid fibre. Mr. Norrie, of Dundee, who has also examined many of these Indian fibres, finds it a very superior article, which can be brought to different qualities of fineness to suit the market it is sent to. It can be prepared to a quality suitable for the Dundee market, and also to a much finer quality, suitable for the markets requiring it finer; but says it must be kept soft and silky, which no mere mechanical means will do. These are very different opinions from one given a few years ago by a practical man, who stated that it might answer for carpet warps. Within the last year many have applied to the Author for information respecting this fibre, and how it could be obtained. One house in Belfast applied, through the Secretary of the Commercial Association of Manchester, for fifty tons of the fibre, and one gentleman, who has long paid attention to China-grass, and has carefully examined the Rheea fibre of Assam, addressed a letter to the Court of Directors of the East India Company, stating that he wished to obtain it to the extent of fifty tons monthly for a Continental house.

" *The Rheea Fibres for Rope-making.*—Though I have no doubt that, when the peculiarities of the Rheea fibre, or China-grass, are more generally known, its excellent qualities will be fully appreciated, and it will come into more general use as a rival to the finer kinds of Flax; yet at present there are, I believe, but few spinners who thoroughly understand its management or have machinery to do it justice. It is not likely therefore to realise its full value in the market at present. Hence it was desirable to have its strength tested as a substitute for Hemp, as it might not all be required to supply the place of Flax. Mr. W. Cotton has been good enough to have a bale of Rheea fibre, and also one of the Wild Rheea, twisted into five-inch rope, and prepared by the warm register in Messrs. Huddart's rope-manufactory at Limehouse; the strength of each was carefully tried and compared with similar rope made of Russian Hemp. I am happy to state that the experiments which I this day (16th Jan., 1854) witnessed were most satisfactory, neither rope breaking until the Rheea fibre bore above nine tons weight, and the Wild Rheea, within a few pounds, nearly as much. The results of the experiments are stated in the accompanying memorandum, with which I have been favoured by Messrs. Huddart. (*v.* p. 373.)

"*Bon Rheea or Jungle Rheea.*—Though it is to be hoped that the Rheea fibre will prove too valuable to be only employed for rope-making, the Wild Rheea, on the contrary, is well calculated, and is indeed sent, for this purpose. No information has been sent respecting the plant yielding it, but it is no doubt one of the Nettle tribe, and from being called Bon or Jungle Rheea, it has been inferred that it is the Rheea in a wild state. But though we have no proof of this, it is satisfactory to find that Major Hannay describes it as 'uncultivated, but very common in all parts of the province:' and again, 'common in most of our forests; by proper management, any quantity of young shoots can be obtained, and as the divided roots afford numerous shoots, and the plant can be propagated by slips as well as by seed, its cultivation for its fibre might be carried on with facility.' He further says, 'it is cultivated largely by the Hill tribes on the west of Yeunan, and by the Singpoos and Dhoanncas of our own north-eastern frontier, to a small extent only for a coarse cloth, but chiefly for nets.' It is recognised by the Nepaulese as the Leepeeah of Nepal. Capt.

A. Thompson, of the firm of Thompson and Co., rope-makers, of Calcutta, says of it, that it is all that can be desired for either canvas or lines, and only requires to be known to be generally used for that purpose."

"Having ascertained in the most satisfactory manner that the fibres in question are possessed of the requisite degree of strength, and the Rheea fibre of fineness in addition, the next point to determine is how to make their good qualities so known in the market, that the fibres may not be condemned as new things and of no value. I am informed by the best judges, that, having taken the best means to determine the real value of the articles, they must next be sent into the market for three or four years in sufficient quantities to attract the notice of the best manufacturers; and for this purpose I am told that from ten to twenty tons annually would be sufficient: others say twice a year, but this in the case of India would be needlessly troublesome. The time, however, is extremely favorable for such an experiment, from the high price of Russian Hemp, which I am told will not come down to its ordinary price for two years, if the supply of money from this country is stopped for even this season."

"The next difficulty is to induce the natives of the districts containing these valuable fibres to extend their ordinary cultivation of the Rheea or of the Hemp, or to collect the Wild Rheea in increased quantities, and to prepare them all as carefully as possible for the English market. The officiating Commissioner of Revenue in Assam recommends that, as the culture of the Rheea fibre is sufficiently well understood, 'the best way to encourage its extension would be to secure to the ryots a sure market at remunerating prices.' Capt. Dalton, Collector of Debrooghur, states, 'that the best method would be for Government to offer a premium of so much a ton on all that is produced for three or four years.' Both recommendations might be united in one, if the officers who take so zealous an interest in the improvement of their districts were authorised to purchase (unless they find individuals willing to do so) from ten to twenty tons of these fibres in their respective districts, taking care that they were as carefully and cleanly prepared as possible, and as closely resembling as possible the specimens of Petersburgh Hemp which Mr. W. Cotton has been good enough to send for transmission to India. The improved appearance of the Rheea fibre sent by Major Hannay is owing to specimens sent out to him by Mr. W. Sangster. I would include in this direction for the Rheea fibre also the districts of Rungpore and of Dinagepore, where the same fibre is cultivated under the name of Kunkhoora, and where labour is more abundant than in Assam."

TRANSMISSION OF RHEEA FIBRE FROM ASSAM.

In conformity to the orders of the Court of Directors, directions were sent by the Governor-General of India with printed copies of the papers to the Commissioners in Assam and Rajeshaye, and to Singapore.

Colonel Jenkins, in his reply, dated 2d August, 1854, reports that Capt. Dalton, Collector of Luckimpore, did not expect to be able to obtain more than two or three tons, as the cultivation of the Rheea is at present confined to a few villages of fishermen, and that Major Hannay some time since abandoned the experimental cultivation which he had commenced, on account of the low prices then offered, which would not pay the cultivators.

But it is stated—"As the large introduction of this article amongst our articles of commerce is likely to be a matter of great importance, I would beg to recommend that Government should buy up any quantity, up to ten tons, procurable each season for the next three years." This has been sanctioned by the Indian Government.

Capt. Dalton writes: "The lowest price at which it is likely to be procurable is six annas a seer, or about £42 sterling a ton. When it is more extensively cultivated, and the best method of preparation thoroughly understood, so that, as in the reeling of silk, women and children may be employed as well as men, it ought not to cost more than four annas a seer, or £28 a ton." He continues:

"The process described in Dr. Royle's paper, quoting from Major Hannay, is that commonly used by the natives of the province. Major Hannay practised a different method, which he calls the Indo-Chinese, which is not only the most cleansing, but also the cheapest." (*v.* p. 363.)

Major Hannay, besides describing this method as below, states that he had been requested to forward to England some of the Rheea as stripped from the stalk, and without any further scraping or cleaning. But he is of opinion that if the Rheea is not immediately deprived of its gummy and mucilaginous matter, it would most probably rot before reaching England. (This, however, would only be the case if it were not perfectly dry, and this may be difficult to effect in a moist climate like that of Assam.) "A cleaning factory established in the Rheea-growing districts, and capital employed to encourage the ryots to cultivate, would be the most likely means to cheapen the article in the market and increase its subsequent consumption." Ten bales of the Dom Rheea had, however, been sent off to this country.

Dr. Oxley, in reply to the requisition for some of the fibre from Singapore, writes (19th July, 1854) that the *Ramee* is indigenous all over the Malayan Archipelago; it grows freely at Singapore, but is not cultivated or planted to any extent, and therefore it could not be obtained in any quantity, though it is used by the Malays as twine, their common name for which is "*tali ramee.*" They make their fishing lines of it, and prefer their own lines to any of European manufacture. The refuse in preparing the fibre is admirably adapted for making paper, and is used for this purpose in Java. As this fibre is remarkable for fineness, flexibility, and strength, it seems well worthy of cultivation, especially if any cheaper method of cleaning can be devised, as it is an object of attention in Java, whence it is imported into Holland, and various goods made of it, as we have already stated, by the Messrs. Meerburg, at Leyden.

The Ramee, that is, the *Rheea* of Assam, yielding four or five cuttings in the year, amounting to about twelve maunds of valuable fibre, must, therefore, be well worth cultivation in many localities from Assam to Arracan, also in Pegu, and down to Singapore, and perhaps also on the Malabar Coast. We therefore republish modes of cultivation and of preparation. The first, from Chinese works, is very similar to the directions from similar sources given by Dr. M'Gowan, of Ningpo (*v.* 'Journ. Agri-Hortic. Soc.,' vol. vi, p. 209); while the second is that which Major Hannay so successfully practises in Assam.

CHINESE CULTIVATION.—THE TCHOU MA, OR CHINESE FLAX (URTICA NIVEA).

Translated from the Chinese, by M. Stanislas Julien, and retranslated from the French.

[The following extract possesses much interest, in addition to what it derives from its Chinese origin, in consequence of its being not impossible that attempts may be made to introduce the cultivation of Tchou-ma into Great Britain. Its delicate fibre forms the Flax from which the finest of the Chinese linen fabrics are manufactured.]

Amongst the products of Chinese industry which were exhibited a few years ago in the Rue St. Laurent, were some pieces of a fine silky tissue, called by the Chinese *hia-pou* or summer cloth, and made of the fibres of the plant called by botanists *Urtica nivea.* Some seeds of this plant were sent from Canton in 1843, by M. Hébert, but they never arrived; and I was at that time told that they would probably not grow in our climate. I am sorry that I was not then able to translate the papers which I now lay before the public. After reading the following account of the cultivation of the plant in question, it will be readily seen, by those who are competent judges of the matter, that the supposed want of success was owing to nothing but ignorance of the care and delicate treatment which are necessary for the culture of the plant now before us. The way in which its valuable threads are peeled, steeped, and bleached, is, as will be seen, described by the Chinese authors, with a precision and minuteness amply sufficient to enable any person to pursue this new branch of industry in our own country. Until a new supply of seeds is received from China, roots or young plants of the *Urtica nivea* may be obtained from the Garden of Plants, and be propagated in the way mentioned below: and thus may a substance be given to our manufacturers, which will, in their hands, be made into a tissue as soft as silk, and as fine as, but stronger and tougher than the best French cambric.

Cultivation of the Tchou-ma (Urtica nivea).

('Imperial Treatise of Chinese Agriculture,' lib. lxxviii, fol. 3.)

For the purpose of sowing the *tchou-ma* in the third or fourth month, a light sandy soil is preferred. The seeds are sown in a garden, or where there is no garden, in a piece of ground near a river or a well. The ground is dug once or twice, then beds one foot broad, and four feet long are made; and after that the earth is again dug. The ground is then pressed down, either with the foot or the back of a spade. When it is a little firm, its surface is raked smooth. The next night the beds are watered, and on the following morning the earth is loosened with a small-toothed rake, and then again levelled.

After that half a *ching* (four pints and a half) of moist earth and a *ho* (one pint) of seeds are taken and well mixed together. One *ho* of seeds is enough for six or seven beds. After having sown the seeds it is not necessary that they should be covered with earth; indeed, if that were done, they would not germinate.

The next thing to be done is to procure four sticks, sharp at one end, and to place them in the ground in a slanting position, two on one side of the bed and two on the opposite side; they are for the purpose of supporting a sort of little roof two or three feet high, and covered with a thin mat.

In the fifth or sixth month, when the rays of the sun are powerful, this light mat is covered with a thick layer of straw. If this precaution were not adopted, the young plants would be destroyed by the heat.

Before the seed begins to germinate, or when the young leaves first appear, the beds must not be watered. By means of a broom dipped in water the roof of matting is wetted so as to keep the ground underneath moist. At night the roof is removed in order that the young plants may catch the dew.

As soon as the first leaves have appeared, if parasitical plants appear they must be immediately pulled up. When the plant is an inch or two high, the roof may be laid aside. If the earth is rather dry, it must be slightly moistened to the depth of about three inches.

A stiffer soil is now chosen and thrown into beds, to which the young plants are to be transferred. The following night the first beds, in which the young plants are, are to be watered, the next morning the new beds are to be watered also. The young plants are then dug up with a spade, care being taken to keep a small ball of earth round their roots, and are pricked out at a distance of four inches the one from the other. The ground is often hoed.

At the end of three or five days the earth must be watered, and again at the end of ten days, fifteen days, and twenty days.

After the tenth month the plants must be covered with a foot of fresh horse, ass, or cow dung.

(Extract from the General Treatise on Agriculture, intituled 'Nong-tching-tsiouen-chou.)

When the *tchou-ma* is cultivated for the first time it is raised from seed. The roots of the seedling plants give of themselves new shoots. At the end of a few years the roots cross each other and intertwine, when the stems must be separated and replanted.

At the present day it is very common in the countries of 'An-king and Kien-ning, to disentangle the roots with a knife, and to replant them. Those who cannot procure seeds follow the plan adopted for obtaining young mulberry trees from layers.

This plan is a very quick one.

In those countries, however, where there are no roots of the *tchou-ma*, and where it is not easy to procure them from other places, the seed is had recourse to.

As soon as the young plants are a few inches high they are watered with a mixture of equal quantities of water and liquid manure. Immediately after the stems are cut the ground must be watered, and this ought to be done at night or on a cloudy day; for if the plants were watered in the sunshine, they would rust. Great care must be taken not to make use of pig's dung.

The *tchou-ma* may be planted every month; but it is necessary that *the ground be moist.*

Transplantation and Propagation of the Tchou-ma.

('Imperial Treatise on Agriculture,' lib. lxxviii, fol. 5.)

When the tufts of the *Tchou-ma* are strong enough the earth around is dug, and new stocks are detached and transplanted elsewhere. The principal stock then grows more vigorously. At the end of four or five years, the old stock becoming excessively strong, they are divided and replanted in other beds.

Some persons are satisfied with bending the long stems down and obtaining layers in the ordinary way.

When a bed becomes too crowded, another must be formed, and then another and another. In this way the plants may be propagated to any extent.

A stiff soil that has been well worked in autumn is chosen and manured with fine muck. In the following spring the plants are transplanted. The best time for carrying on this operation is when vegetation commences; the next best is when the new shoots appear; and the worst is when the stems have attained a considerable size.

The new plants are placed a foot and a half from each other, and when they have been well surrounded with earth they are watered.

In summer as well as in autumn advantage must be taken of the time when the earth has just been moistened by rain. The offsets can be transplanted to places near at hand; but it is essential to have a ball of earth around each plant.

To propagate the *tchou-ma*, proportions of its roots two or three inches long are detached by a knife, and are placed by twos and threes in little trenches that are about a foot and a half from each other. The roots are then surrounded with good earth and watered; the watering is renewed three or five days afterwards. When the new stems have attained a certain height, the earth must be often hoed.

If the earth is dry it must be watered. If the plants have to be carried to a distance, their roots ought to be surrounded by the soil in which they have been growing, well enveloped in leaves of the reed. They are placed, in addition to this, in a mat folded so as to exclude them from air and light. They may then be carried without danger to a distance of many hundred miles.

The first year, when the plants are a foot high, they are gathered; they are gathered again in the second year. The fibres of the cut stems are fit for spinning.

In the tenth month of every year, before cutting the offsets which pass beyond the roots, the earth is covered with a thick layer of cow or horse dung. In the second month the manure is raked off, in order to allow the new plants to come up freely. At the end of three years the roots become excessively strong. If part of the plants which come up in close tufts were not removed, the others would be smothered.

Gathering the Tchou-ma.

The *tchou-ma* may be gathered three times a year. When the stems are cut, the little shoots springing from the rootstock should be about half an inch high. As soon as the large stems are cut, the suckers spring up with more vigour, and soon furnish a second crop. If the young shoots be too long, the large stems ought not to be cut; but the ground shoots would not become vigorous, and would be prejudicial to the development of the larger stems.

The first crop is got in towards the commencement of the fifth month; the second in the middle of the sixth, or at the beginning of the seventh month; and the third and last in the middle of the eighth or the beginning of the ninth month. The stems of the second crop grow much faster than the others, and are by far the best.

After the crop, the stocks of *tchou-ma* are covered with manure and immediately watered.

Peeling the Fibres of the Tchou-ma.

When the stems are all got in they are split longitudinally with knives of iron or of bamboo. The bark is first removed; then the lower layer (which is white, and covered with a shrivelled pellicle which comes off by itself) is scraped off with a knife. The interior fibres are then seen; they are to be removed and softened in boiling water. If the *tchou-ma* be peeled in winter, the stems must be previously steeped in tepid water in order that they may be the more easily split.

The first layer of *tchou-ma* is coarse and hard, and is only good for making common materials; the second is a little more supple and fine; the third, which is the best, is used for making extremely fine light articles.

Steeping and Bleaching the Tchou-ma.

The stems are tied up in little sheaves and placed on the roof of a house, in order that they may be moistened by the dew at night, and dried again by the sun in the day.

In the course of from five to seven days they become perfectly white. If the weather be cloudy or rainy the stems are placed under cover in a current of air. If they are wetted by the rain they immediately turn black.

Another author says, after peeling the fibres they are tied in skeins, arranged in a circle, and steeped for a night in a pan of water; they are then spun on a wheel. This done, they are again steeped in water containing the ashes of burnt mulberry wood.

Having taken them from the pans they are divided into packets of 5 oz. weight each; the packets are placed for a night in a tub of a mixture consisting of a cup of pure water and an equal quantity of powdered chalk to each packet.

The next day the chalk is got rid of, and the fibres are boiled in water containing straw ashes, by which process they become white and supple. Being now dried in the sun they are again boiled in pure water; they are then stirred about in more water, which finishes the cleansing process, and lastly they are dried in the sun.

This done, the fibres are joined end to end on the wheel so as to make long threads, which form the warp and the woof, and are manufactured into stuff in the usual way.

Another author says, after having spun the fibres of *tchou-ma*, they are boiled in lime water, and when cool, carefully washed in pure water. Then by means of a bamboo sieve, placed on the surface of the water, they are spread out in equal layers in order that they may be as it were half wetted below, and half dried above. As night approaches, they are taken out, strained and dried: the same process is repeated the next and following days, until the threads are perfectly white. They are then, but not before, fit for being made up.

According to another process, the *tchou-ma* is first soaked, then spun and made up, instead of being soaked after the spinning.

Other persons again take the fresh fibres, expose them at night to the dew, and in the day to the sun; then spin and weave, bleaching last of all.

Others, lastly, following those who employ the plant *Ko*, cut the stems, soften the fibres in the steam of boiling water, then weave, and do not bleach at all. Fibres thus prepared give a material that is more supple and fibrous.

Mode of gathering the best seeds of Tchou-ma.

When seeds of *tchou-ma* are wanted for the purpose of sowing, those which are found on the main shoots are to be preferred. In the ninth month, after the period *choang-kiang* (after the 2d of October), the seeds are collected and dried in the sun; they are then mixed with damp sand, and put in a bamboo basket, carefully covered with straw. This precaution is needed, for if the seeds are frozen they will not grow. The seeds of the lateral shoots are not fit for sowing. Before sowing, the seeds are thrown into water, and those that sink are used, while the others are of no use.

The seeds are sown before the first half of the first month. The best seeds are those which are spotted black. After they are sown they are covered with ashes. If they are sown thick the plants coming from them will be weak and sickly; they will be strong and healthy, on the contrary, if the seeds are thinly sown. As soon as the leaves appear the plants are watered with liquid manure. In the seventh month the seeds are collected, put on canvas, and hung in a strong current of air; this aids and hastens germination. ('Journal of the Horticultural Society of London,' vol. iv, part iv.)

INDO-CHINESE METHOD *for preparing the Rheea Fibre, as practised in Upper Assam. By Major Hannay.*

To cut the Rheea.—The Rheea is fit for cutting when the stems become of a brown colour for about six inches upwards from the root.

Hold the top of the stalk in the left hand, and with the right hand strip off the leaves by passing it quickly down to the root, and cut off with a sharp knife, taking care to be above the hairy network of the roots, as these should be covered up with manure immediately to ensure another crop quickly; lop off the tender top to the stalk, and make the reeds up into bundles of 200 or 250, if the stripping process is not to be carried on in the field or garden, but it is best to strip off the bark and fibre on the spot, as the burnt ashes of the stem afford a good dressing for the roots along with dry cow dung.

To strip off the Bark and Fibre.—The operator holds the stalk in both hands nearly in the middle, and pressing the forefinger and thumb of both hands firmly, gives it a peculiar twist, the inner pith is broken through; and then passing the fingers of his right and left hand rapidly, alternately, towards each end, the bark and fibre is completely separated from the stalk, in two strands.

Making up into Bundles.—The strands of bark and fibre are now made up into bundles of convenient size, tied at the smaller end with a shred of fibre, and put into clean water for a few hours, which I think deprives the plant of its tannin or colouring matter, the water becoming quite red in a short time.

Cleaning Process.—The cleaning process is as follows:

The bundles are put on a hook fastened in a post, by means of the tie at the smaller end, at a convenient height for the operator, who takes each strand separately of the larger end in his left hand, passes the thumb of his right hand quickly along the inner side, by which operation the outer bark is completely separated from the fibre, and the riband of fibre is then thoroughly cleaned by two or three scrapings with a small knife. This completes the operation, with some loss, however, say one fifth, and if quickly dried in the sun it might at once be made up for exportation; but the appearance of the fibre is much improved by exposure (immediately after cleaning) on the grass to a night's heavy dew, in September or October, or a shower of rain during the rainy season. After drying, the colour improves, and there is no risk from mildew on the voyage homewards.

OTHER SPECIES OF URTICA AND BOEHMERIA (*Urticeæ*).

BON RHEEA, Wild or Jungle Rheea, Boehmeriæ species.

In the preceding observations, the *Bon* or *Bun Rheea*, that is, Jungle Rheea, is so called as if it were the Dom Rheea or China Nettle in a wild state. Of this there is no proof, but considerable probability that it is a distinct species, possessed of many of the same properties as the Ramee or Rheea Nettle.

Indeed, Major Hannay, who has chiefly brought it into notice, says of Bon or Jungle Rheea (*Boehmeriæ* species) that it is a jungle plant, common in the Assam forests, and thriving best in the vicinity of water or of running streams. When unmolested it grows to a tree, but, by proper management, any quantity of young shoots can be obtained; and as the divided roots afford numerous shoots, the plant can be propagated by slips as well as by the seed. Its cultivation for its fibre might be carried on as with the Willow in Europe.

By the Chinese in Assam it is said to be exported into Southern from Northern China. It is cultivated largely by the Hill tribes, north-west of Yeunan, and by the Singpoos and Dhoanncas of our own north-eastern frontier, to a small extent only for a coarse cloth, but chiefly for nets. The Nepaulese recognise it as the *Leepeeah* of Nepaul. ('Journ. Agri-Hortic. Soc.,' vii, p. 222.)

This fibre, in the state in which it has been sent, is well adapted for rope-making. It is about five feet in length, brown in colour, strong, and flexible. Capt. W. Thompson, of the house of Messrs. Thompson, rope-makers, of Calcutta, says of it: "It is all that can be desired either for canvas or lines, and only requires to be known to be generally used for such purposes." It was the kind which was made into a five-inch rope by Messrs. Huddart (p. 373,) along with the Dom Rheea or China-grass, and broke with a weight of about nine tons, or precisely 21,025 lb. Since then, it has been made up into ropes of various sizes, which have been carefully tested, and found in every case greatly to exceed in tenacity those made of Russian Hemp of the same size, as shown in the Table at p. 374. It has also been made up into lines and cords, some of them almost fine enough for fishing lines: in all which it displays its fitness for all such purposes, from the union of strength and flexibility. There is no doubt that it would command a market as soon as its good qualities become known. It would be desirable to ascertain whether, by pressing it between grooved rollers, or something of that kind, it could not be sent in a still cleaner state, and command a still higher price. It was valued at £35 a ton.

Mesakhee Fibre, Boehmeriæ species (*Urticeæ*).

Another fibre is enumerated by Major Hannay ('Journ. Agri-Hortic. Soc.,' vii, p. 217), which he says is called *Mesakhee*, and is an *Urtica*, but not a stinging one. It is a shrubby tree, probably a species of *Boehmeria*, and is very abundant. Its young branches, which are tender and red-coloured, as well as its leaves, are edible. Only a small quantity was at first sent, but afterwards three maunds of the fibre, to Messrs. Gouger and Co., to ascertain the value of the fibre in the Home market. Capt. Thompson says of it, in a report to the Agri-Horticultural Society: "I forward a log-line made of the fibre of the *red Mesakhee* plant, as also the remainder of the fibre itself. I find the strength of it quite equal to Russia Hemp, but for want of being properly harvested, the fibres cling so close together that great loss of material takes place in hackling it. I think it well adapted for cordage, and if brought into general use ought to bring as much as Petersburgh Hemp." ('Journ. Agri-Hortic. Soc.,' viii, p. 90.)

Major Hannay says: "The Murrees and others might be induced to bring the fibre for sale; but as the value of this Nettle in the market has not been ascertained, I have only offered at the rate of Rs. 5 per maund, which, however, on account of the slow method of manipulation, has not been considered remunerative." (l. c., p. 89.)

Of Major Hannay's Nos. 6, 7, and 8, the first, which is the foregoing, he says is called *Mesakhee* or *Mejingah*, the other *Mesakhee*. No. 6 has but little fibre and very rough stem. No. 7 has much the same habits as Bon Rheea, and can be cultivated like it. Its fibre is also of the same character, but white, strong, and durable. It is used for the same purposes.

Capt. Dalton, in a letter, dated 20th July, 1854, referring to what the Author had said respecting the Wild or Bon Rheea, writes: "As he alludes to the batch sent through this office by Major Hannay in 1853, he must refer to the 'Mesakhee,' of which large quantities are procurable, growing wild in Upper Muttock and elsewhere in the district. The instructions regarding the specimen of Petersburg Hemp sent out as a sample are more applicable to this fibre than to the Dom Rheea.

I propose to take measures for collecting as much of it as I can get prepared. The cost will be from three to four annas a seer. This might be accompanied by samples of the *Bon Rheea, Bon Surat,* and other fibres, all prepared to resemble the Petersburgh Hemp. If for these wild fibres we had a good market, the frontier tribes, Singphoos, &c., who understand how to prepare them, might be induced to assist in supplying them." The specimens which the Author had referred to in the above communication were sent under the name of Bon Rheea from India. The two plants, *Bon Rheea* and *Mesakhee,* may be identical or nearly allied species, but this cannot be ascertained without authentic Botanical specimens. Major Hannay distinguishes the two kinds—the *Bon Rheea* being his No. 2, and *Mesakhee* No. 6—in his paper in the 'Journ. Agri-Hortic. Soc.,' vii, p. 215.

Chor Putta, or Surat, *Urtica crenulata* (*Urticeæ*).

This plant is a native of the hills and valleys on the east of Bengal. Dr. Roxburgh obtained it first near Luckipore. It has since been found near the Pundua Hills. Major Hannay enumerates it among the fibrous plants of Assam. It has an erect shrubby stem, with oblong acute leaves, having the margins crenulate or slightly dentate, both sides alike the bark armed with acute burning hairs. The sting produces great pain, extending to the armpit; abates after two or three days, but does not disappear entirely for nine days. Major Hannay says of this and another, which he enumerates as Nos. 3 and 4, and calls gigantic stinging Nettles, that they afford a quantity of fine white fibre, but apparently of no great strength, and, by report, not very lasting. Some of the Hill tribes use the fibre for fabricating coarse cloths.

Horoo Surat of Assam, or Neilgherry Nettle, *Urtica heterophylla* (*Urticeæ*).

The *Horoo Surat* of Assam, said to be the *Urtica heterophylla* of Dr. Roxburgh, is the most widely diffused of the large Indian Nettles, inasmuch as it is found in the Southern Concan, on the Malabar coast, and specimens of fibre of what was called *Neilgherry Nettle,* produced by *Urtica heterophylla,* were sent by Dr. Wight to the Exhibition of 1851. It is also found in Burmah and in Assam; and along the foot of the hills extends to the DeyraDoon. It may be seen even in the northern valleys of the Himalayas. It is an annual, with erect angular stems, marked with small white specks, in which are inserted stiff, most acute bristles. The leaves are long, petioled, caudate at the base, variously lobed, and towards the top of the plant almost palmate; all are grossly serrate, armed with the same bristles as the stem and branches, from four to eight inches long and nearly as broad. Dr. Roxburgh says of it, that it is the most ferocious-looking plant he has seen, and it acts up to its appearance: the least touch of any part producing most acute pain, but fortunately of short duration. The bark abounds in fine, white, glossy, silk-like, strong fibre. Major Hannay says of it, that it is the *Horoo Surat* of the Assamese, and known to the Bhotecas as the *Serpah* or *Herpah,*—that the fibre is extensively used by them in the manufacture of cloth. It was recognized by the Chinese as the *Theng Mah,* and said to be prized for the softness of its fibre, as well as for its strength. As the seeds are quick of vegetation, the cultivation of this plant can be carried to any extent.

The fibre of this Nettle, sent from the Neilgherries, is very long, soft, white, and silky, and has been much admired by many of the best judges of fibres. The specimens were sent by Dr. Wight, and prepared in a rude way by boiling by the Todawars of the Neilgherry Mountains. Dr. Wight says of it, that "it produces a beautifully fine and soft flax-like fibre, which the Todawars use as a thread material, and if well prepared fitted to compete with Flax for the manufacture of even very fine textile fabrics."

This fibre could of course be equally well prepared in a multitude of other places, some near, others distant from the sea. Mr. Marshall did not consider it well suited for his purpose. At Dundee, it was thought a very good fibre, but rather dry. Mr. Dickson, who has passed it through his machine and liquid, has rendered it like a beautiful, soft, silky kind of Flax, and calls it a wonderful fibre, of which the tow would be useful for mixing with wool, as has been done with the China-grass, and the fibre used for the finest purposes. If this should be proved to be the case on trial, it might no doubt be produced abundantly, and, with some improved process of separation, very cheaply, at easily accessible places on the Western Coast of the Indian Peninsula.

POOAH FIBRE, *Boehmeria frutescens* (*Urticeæ*).

Dr. Campbell, Superintendent of Darjeeling, addressed a letter to the Agri-Hortic. Soc., forwarding a new description of Wild Hemp from Eastern Nipal and Sikkim, on behalf of Sergeant Crutcher, who used the fibre in his craft of sewing leather.

" *Description of the Plant.*—The plant from which the Hemp is made is called 'Pooah' by the Parbuttias; 'Kienki' by the Lepchas; and 'Yenki' by the Limboos. It grows to the height of six or eight feet, and varies in the thickness of the stem from the size of a quill to that of the thumb. The leaf is serrated, of a dark green colour above, silvery white below, not hairy or stinging; and has a reddish pedicle of about three inches long. The seed forms in small currant-like clusters along the top of the plant, and on alternate sides about an inch apart. Two small leaves spring from the stem at the centre of and above each cluster of seed.

" *Habitat.*—The 'Pooah' is not cultivated, but grows wild and abundantly in the valleys throughout the mountains of Eastern Nipal and Sikkim, at the foot of the Hills skirting the Tarai to the elevation of 1000 or 1200 feet; and within the mountains up to 3000 feet. It is considered a hill plant, and not suited to the plains or found in them. It does not grow in the forest, but is chiefly found in open clear places, and in some situations overruns the abandoned fields of the Hill people within the elevations which suit it. It sheds its leaves in the winter, throws them out in April and May, and flowers and seeds in August and September. The exact period altering of necessity with the elevation.

" *When used.*—It is cut down for use when the seed is formed; this is the case with the common Flax, in Europe. At this time the bark is most easily removed and the produce is best. After the seed is ripe it is not fit for use, at least it is deteriorated.

"*How prepared.*—As soon as the plant is cut, the bark or skin is removed. This is very easily done. It is then dried in the sun for a few days; when quite dry it is boiled with wood-ashes for four or five hours; when cold, it is beaten with a mallet on a flat stone until it becomes rather pulpy, and all the woody portion of the bark has disappeared; then it is well washed in pure spring water and spread out to dry. After exposure for a day or two to a bright sun it is ready for use. When the finest description of fibre is wanted, the stuff after being boiled and beaten, is daubed over with wet clay, and spread out to dry. When thoroughly dry the clay is rubbed and beaten out; the fibre is then ready for spinning into thread, which is done with the common distaff.

"*Uses.*—The 'Pooah' is principally used for fishing nets, for which it is admirably adapted on account of its great strength of fibre and its extraordinary power of long resisting the effects of water. It is also used for making game-bags, twine, and ropes. It is considered well adapted for making cloth, but is not much used in this way."

Dr. Falconer recognized the "Pooah" as the "*Boehmeria frutescens* of Botanists, common at lower elevations on the Himalayas from Gurhwal to the Sikkim hills (Ganges to Burrampooter). In the outer hills of Gurhwal and Kumaon it is called 'Poee,' and the tough fibre is used there for making nets. In Darjeeling, *B. frutescens* goes by a similar name, 'Pooah,' and the fibre is used for similar purposes. It was first described by Thunberg, who distinguishes it from the textile species, *Boehmeria* (or *Urtica*) *nivea*, which grows there in abundance."

Capt. Thompson, to whom the specimens of Pooah fibre were sent, says of it, that, "when properly dressed, it is quite equal to the best Europe Flax, and will produce better sailcloth than any other substance I have seen in India. I observe, from Dr. Campbell's communication, that mud is used in the preparation, which clogs it too much, &c. My superintendent, Mr. W. Rownee, who understands the nature of these substances, tells me, that if potash were used in the preparation (which is invariably done with Russian Hemp and Flax) instead of clay or mud, that the colour would be improved, the substance rendered easy to dress, and not liable to so much waste in manufacturing." Sergeant Crutcher thought that the fibre might be supplied for four rupees a maund, when large quantities were prepared. Capt. Thompson thought that it would be worth twelve rupees a maund in Calcutta.

Other Himalayan Nettles.

Major Swetenham, when writing respecting the Maloo Creeper (*v.*p. 296), mentions the large Nettle of Gurhwal—which he says is considered by the natives as superior to Bhang, or the true Hemp—thus: "There is another plant that grows in the interior of the Hills from which stronger ropes even than the Hemp are said to be made—I allude to the large Nettle plant. I have seen this growing to the height of fourteen or fifteen feet; the Hill people in preparing ropes from this plant, steep it for *three* days *only*, and then strip off the fibre; this is done in a contrary method to the Hemp stripping, *i. e.*, the top of the Nettle is broken off, and the fibre pulled down from the thin end."

Capt. Huddleston, in his paper on the Hemp of the Himalayas, mentions also other fibres. Among these—"The larger Nettle called *Jurkundaloo, Kundaloo,* and *Kubra,* grows chiefly in the northern parts of the district, in great quantities; it also grows in the middle ones; and from its fibres the natives make rope for tying up their cattle and snow-sandals. One bundle will produce about a seer of fibre, but it is not collected for sale. The plant grows about eight or nine feet high, and the stalks are about the size of a finger in thickness. It is cut in the cold season, and the stalks are soaked a few days in water before the fibre is stripped off from the thick end like Hemp." ('Trans. Agri-Hortic. Soc.,' viii, p. 275.)

Dr. Campbell also mentions the gigantic stinging Nettle of the Nipal and Sikkim Hills, as made into Hemp and used in making the cloth called "Bangra." The preparation is the same as the "Pooah." The Bangra is harder and stiffer than the "Pooah," and not adapted to making cordage and nets.

Mr. C. Gubbins, C.S., when at Simla, forwarded some specimens of fibrous material produced by a species of Urtica growing about and below Simla, used by the natives of those parts for making string. The process, which he describes as employed for separating this fibre, is interesting from its simplicity. The plant is cut in October, and dried in the sun; when brittle it is beaten, and the fibres separate easily. He observes: "Seeing it stated that there was considerable labour required in cleaning the fibre, I made particular inquiries on this head; and as far as I can learn, there is no greater trouble in cleaning the fibre of the Urtica when merely dried, than is experienced with the Hemp of the Hills which is not rotted in water." Hence the separation would seem to be effected entirely by the dry process and mechanical means.

Capt. Rainey, when Assist. Pol. Agent at Subathoo, sent a net formed from the fibre of a Stinging Nettle, which grows in the same locality as that described by Mr. Gubbins, as he says:

"1st. The Nettles from which this sample was wove, grew in the low valleys adjacent to the Hill Station of Simla in the Himalaya Mountains.

"2d. The vegetable abounds in all the ravines and valleys of those mountains, and forms one of the most rank weeds of these places, during the rainy months.

"3d. In August and September, when it is in perfection, it can be obtained in any quantity, running from five to six and seven feet in height.

"4th. As far as I have been able to ascertain, it is chiefly in demand, if not at present wholly so, for fishing nets; in consequence of the virtue ascribed to the cord wove from it, of gaining increased strength by constant immersion in water, and resisting decay from that element longer than any other description of cords.

"5th. The weed is known throughout the lower and centre ranges of the Himalayas by the names Babar, or Allow, or Bichoo; the last evidently consequent on its stinging property, being the common designation of the scorpion.

"6th. The following is the preparation to which the article is subjected by the natives of the place; but, I doubt not, much of the process might be omitted or simplified—

"1st. Being cut in August or September, the weed is exposed for *one* night in the open air.

"2d. The stalk is then stripped of leaves and dried in the sun.

"3d. When well dried it is deposited in an earthen pot which contains water mixed with ashes (the refuse remains of any wood fire), and boiled for four and twenty hours.

"4th. The stalk thus boiled is then taken to a stream and well washed.

"5th. The Hemp is then brought home, and being sprinkled with flour (otta) (of the grain called Koda), it is again dried in the sun, and afterwards spun at any time into cord for nets of every description."

As no distinctive characters are given of these Nettles, it is impossible to determine the respective species. In Gurhwal and near Simla, *Urtica virulenta* and *U. heterophylla* are common as stinging Nettles, as well as some others; while of species of Boehmeria, the *B. frutescens, macrostachya, Goglado, salicifolia*, are found, and all probably abound in fibre, though a few only have been as yet ascertained to do so, as has been mentioned in the preceding pages.

STRENGTH OF THE RHEEA OR NETTLE FIBRES.

With regard to the strength of these Nettle fibres, it has already been stated that Dr. Roxburgh found the Rami or Caloee bore 240 lb., when Hemp bore 158 lb., and Sunn 150 lb., *v.* Table, p. 268. Messrs. Sharpe, in 1815, found a cord bore 252 lb., when Russian Hemp was only required to bear 82 lb. So in our experiments with these fibres in an untwisted state (already quoted at p. 131), Petersburgh Hemp bore only 160 lb., when China-grass bore 250 lb., the Rheea 320 lb., and the Wild Rheea 343 lb. Mr. Henley had previously found the Kunkhoora or Rheea to bear about three times the weight of Russian Hemp. Capt. Thompson also thought it about three times as strong; and though rather too wiry, he considered it would make excellent cordage, as well as canvas. But though this is too valuable to be applied to such purposes, we have in the Wild Rheea equal strength with greater flexibility, and all that is required, as is apparent from the following abstract of the experiments made at Messrs. Huddart's, referred to at p. 355.

Experiments on Strength of Rope made from samples of Fibre of the growth of India, received from Dr. Royle, at Messrs. Huddart's Rope-manufactory, Limehouse, Feb. 13, 1854.

Description of Hemp.	Size of Rope.	Number of Yarns per strand.	Total number of Yarns in Rope.	Strength of Rope in pounds.	Strength of Rope per inch, circumf. squared.	Size of Rope at breaking.	Tar absorbed.	Amount of stretching.
	Inc.							
Wild Rheea, 1st expt. .	$4\frac{7}{8}$	44	132	19,032	*844	$4\frac{3}{8}$	1-7th	1 in 16
Ditto, 2d expt. . .	$4\frac{7}{8}$	44	132	21,025	*894	$4\frac{5}{8}$	1-7th	1 in 16
Rheea Fibre . . .	$4\frac{7}{8}$	44	132	20,488	*910	$4\frac{5}{8}$	1-9th	1 in 16

So Messrs. Morgan, having made some rope for Mr. Sangster with the Rheea sent him by Major Hannay from Assam, found it to be at least 50 per cent. better than similar rope made of Russian Hemp. This is conspicuous also in the following experiments. The excellence of the fibre for lines and fine cordage is particularly observable in the fine thread called *Talli Rami* from Singapore, as likewise in the delicate nets, some of which seem fine enough for lace instead of for catching fish. The fitness of the Wild Rheea, from its strength, flexibility, and durability, is seen in the various kinds of line and cord which the Author has had made of it in this country, as well for fishing lines, as bowstrings, clewlines for hammocks, &c., in order to show its fitness for all and every purpose to which fibrous substances require to be applied.

A subsequent report was made on the strength of these fibres, when twisted into cords and rope of different sizes.

"In continuation of the experiments which I made on the strength of some Indian fibres in their untwisted state, I beg leave to subjoin an account of some others that I thought it desirable to have made on some of these fibres after they had been twisted into twine, cord, and rope, of different kinds, by a regular rope-maker. This I have had done in order to obviate the objections which are made against new articles by ignorance or prejudice, or from the opposition of interested parties.

"These cords and ropes having been subjected to a fresh set of experiments, and compared with others made of Russian

Hemp and of as nearly as possible the same size, I am happy to report that in every instance the Wild Rheea has proved stronger than Russian Hemp, and in the case of the two-inch rope the Indian fibre bore 1000 lb. more than the Russian. The cultivated Rheea, which is equally strong, will, I hope, be applied to better purposes than rope-making; but it is important that the Wild Rheea is proved by these experiments to be fit for every purpose for which strong fibre is required, either in Europe or in India."

A few experiments were also made with rope made of other Indian fibres.

"Plantain and Pine-apple fibres, though less strong, are capable of bearing considerable weights, and might be used for many ordinary purposes. But the fibre of the Agave, commonly called American Aloe, is capable of bearing a great strain, and the plants have the peculiarity of being able to flourish in a dry soil and climate, such as that of the Deccan and of Mysore. The Dhunchee fibre of Bengal, which is hardly known in this country, appears to be as strong as Russian Hemp, and is, I understand, as easily cultivated and as cheap as Jute. The results which have been obtained will be incorporated in my forthcoming account of Indian fibres."

		lb.
Wuckoo Fibre small Cord	broke at	86
Petersburgh Hemp Cord		170
Wild Rheea Cord, same size as Russian		190
Rheea Fibre Cord, one thread larger		230
Pound line of Wild Rheea		510
Six-thread Cord of *Petersburgh Hemp*		505
Six-thread Ratline of Rheea, tarred		525
Six-thread do. of Wild Rheea, do.		530
Nine-thread do. of Wild Rheea, do.		860
Twelve-thread do. of Wild Rheea, do.		1120
One-inch Rope of Wild Rheea		1350
One-and-half-inch Rope of Wild Rheea, tarred		1900
One-and-half-inch Rope of Wild Rheea, do.		1900
Two-inch Cord of *Russia Hemp*		1800
Two-inch Rope of Rheea Fibre, tarred		2800
Twelve-thread Rope of Plantain, made in India		864
Twelve-thread do. of Pine-apple, do.		924
Two-inch Cord of *Russia Hemp*		1800
Two-inch Rope of Dhunchee fibre, made in India		1850
Two-inch Rope of Agave, usually called Aloe, do.		1900

For the sake of comparison we reprint the experiments made with the untwisted selvages of some of the same fibres, and of which the specimens were very carefully prepared by George Aston, and their strength tried in the office of the Military Stores.

Petersburgh Clean Hemp	broke with	160 lb.
A fibre from Travancore, called Wukka	„	175
Yercum fibre	„	190
Jubbulpore Hemp	„	190
China grass, from China	„	250
Rheea fibre or China grass, from Assam	„	320
Wild Rheea, also from Assam	„	343

Hemp from Kote Kangra, in the Himalayas, bore 400 lb. without breaking.

The other tables, in which the strength of various Indian fibres is given, as tested by different experimentalists, are to be seen, of Pine-apple fibre at p. 41; of Agave, &c., p. 49; of Moorva, p. 56; of Plantain, p. 88; of different fibres, pp. 268, 269; of Sunn, pp. 277, 289; Jubbulpore Hemp and Dhunchee fibre, p. 292; of Mudar, p. 310; of Himalayan Hemp, p. 331; and of other fibres, p. 332; of Rheea and other Nettles, pp. 347, 355, 364, 372.

We have thus carried our investigation of fibre-yielding plants from Grasses in the Endogens to Nettles among the Exogens. We have found that in following an arrangement according to the Botanical affinities of plants, we have obtained some important practical results. Inasmuch, as we have seen different plants with their products, possessed of the same properties, grouped together in the same natural families; and have been led to infer how appropriately we may search among these very groups, for other fibrous plants in whatever country we may be in, though none exceed India in such natural riches.

We may congratulate our readers that the arrangement has brought us to conclude with a family like that of the Nettles, of which so many of the species are conspicuous for fibrous properties, each consisting of numerous individuals widely distributed, and which are easily cultivated. They appear useless only because so few take the trouble, or, we should rather say, enjoy the pleasure of reading the wide-spread book of Nature. When some of the improved methods of separating fibre are successfully applied to such plants as the Rheea and Wild Rheea, the benefits to India and the world will be incalculable. For they are exceeded by none in fineness, excel all others in strength, and may be fitly compared to the trunk of the elephant, which can pick up a needle or root up a tree.

CONCLUDING OBSERVATIONS.

The Author having endeavoured to carry out what he stated to be his opinion in his Lecture before the Society of Arts, finds he cannot do better than conclude as he did then :

"The foregoing enumeration will, I hope, be considered sufficiently extended to prove that India possesses a number of plants, many of them valuable as articles of food, or for other properties, and which are capable of yielding very excellent kinds of fibre, useful either for Paper-making, for Textile fabrics, or for Cordage. They vary in fineness and in strength, as is required for the various wants of the arts and manufactures of civilised life. It would be easy to extend the list (as has been done in this work) with the names of many other plants which are already employed by the natives of India, or which have been subjected to experiment by Europeans. But it will, perhaps, be better to recapitulate the most important of the subjects which I have brought before your notice. Neglecting the Grasses, which, however, are not to be forgotten, if we want a cheap material for paper-making—and this is far from an unimportant object, considering the constantly increasing demands and the rising prices, of the raw material required for this indispensable requisite of civilised life. That paper so made will not be devoid of many useful properties I feel well assured, from the pleasure I have myself experienced in writing these notes on paper made from straw. But it is among the white-fibred plants, such as the Moorva, the Aloe, and the Agave, also in the Pine-apple, and, above all, in the Plantain, that we have boundless supplies of material, not only for paper-making, but for the finest as well as the coarsest textile fabrics, and for cordage which may rival Manilla Hemp, or the American Agave, which bridges over broad rivers. The oakum of these plants may be converted into paper; and that made from the Plantain is remarkable as well for fineness as for toughness. The fibres may be woven into fabrics of different qualities; and though they may not be well fitted for making knots, they may yet be twisted into ropes which are capable of bearing considerable strains, and possess the advantage in their white colour, of not being likely to deceive the purchaser by a semblance to Hemp. So if we require a fibre which shall unite with strength the property of being almost indestructible under water, we have only to employ the black horsehair-like fibres of the Ejoo or Sago Palm, which has also all the lightness of the Coir of the Cocoa-nut.[1]

"Among the Malvaceous and Leguminous plants, or those among which the Brown Hemp, the Dhunchee, and Sunn of India are found, with the Jute among the Linden tribe, we have a variety of cheap products, because the plants can be grown with ease, and their fibres separated with facility. The supply may, moreover, be indefinitely and rapidly expanded, because they form a part of the ordinary culture. Though these do not possess all the strength, they have the colour of Hemp, which I am told is an advantage; and they are admirably adapted for many coarse fabrics, as well as for cordage for ordinary purposes. Many of them also are edible, like the Okhro of the West Indies and the Ram turai of India; and, therefore, we may, as in the case of the Plantain, be multiplying the supply of food for the body, at the same time that we are increasing the means for diffusing information for the mind."

[Though numerous attempts have been made to produce merchantable Flax in India and without much success, chiefly from inattention to physical desiderata, I believe there is at present a very favorable prospect of getting some good Flax

[1] Since the articles on Moorva, Pine-apple, Manilla Hemp, and Plantain were written, the Author has received specimens from Bombay, from Dr. Gibson, of cord made from the first, under his direction, who states that the plant is abundant on that side of India, and yields one of their strongest fibres. Dr. Oxley, at Singapore, writes that thousands of acres of Pine-apple plant cover the adjacent islands; so that the supply might be considered inexhaustible, of a fibre remarkable as well for fineness as for strength; and also, that the *Musa textilis* of Manilla grows freely there, and would thrive well in the low lands, if these were drained. Dr. Hunter, of Madras, has stated that Plantain fibre has begun to be exported from the West or Malabar coast of India. Indeed, several of the fibres mentioned in the above Lecture and in this work have been imported during the year into this country; or have been sent as specimens, from new sources.

from the North-Western provinces, from whence the successful example may spread to other parts. As Jute has come to be an important article of commerce for textile purposes, so I believe that several other fibres might become so, as they have also the characteristic of fineness with the property of being spun, and that much more easily than either the Plantain or Pine-apple fibre, employed for textile purposes by the islanders of the great Indian Ocean.]

"But, if we require fibres possessed of all, or even more than the strength of Russian or of Polish Hemp, we shall find this a property, not only of the Hemp of the Himalayas, but of the various Nettles which clothe the foot of these mountains, from Assam to the Sutlej; and if we pay a price proportioned to the quality of the article, I have no fears but that the supply will increase in proportion to the demand. If we want them still cheaper than they can at present be furnished, we have only to supply the cultivators with some simple machinery, by which the fibre may be separated more easily than by the present primitive methods. In that case I feel assured that the Rheea fibre will not only undersell every other fibre, but, in point of strength, take a position which will be second to none of those which are at present imported. India is in many respects so well suited to the growth of fibres, that the supply not only of this, but of many others, may easily become more abundant than from any other country.

"In addition to affording such facilities, I hope the day is not distant when something will be done to encourage, instead of depressing the efforts of planters and colonists when they send a new thing to market. Because some account of the properties and value of the article as suited to different purposes would be more encouraging than a statement that it is of 'no value' because 'unknown in the market.' While the fact very often is that the substance is well known in many markets, though not in the one to which it has unfortunately been sent. I feel confident that the Collections of Raw Products which are being established will have considerable effects; but they should be multiplied so as to extend to every large commercial town, or at least to the principal sea-ports; and as in the city, time is counted by minutes, I would have one in the very heart of the city. But to be fully useful such Collections should be connected with Societies interested in the investigation of such subjects, and publishing Journals where the learning, the science, and the practical applications connected with each subject should be published. I could almost hope that the time is come (or very nearly so) in which knowledge of Natural Subjects should be considered a part of General Education, and that what is called the study of Geography be connected with a general knowledge of the Soils, the Climates, the Plants, and the Animals of the different regions of the globe, and not be confined, as it often is, to boundaries, to the height of mountains, the length of rivers, and to a bare enumeration of places. Some of the improved views now entertained on such subjects must be ascribed to the discovery that so many made of their own ignorance at the Great Exhibition of 1851, which in this, as in so many points, will continue to be, as it has already been, of immense benefit both to producers and consumers in all parts of the world."

Finally, the Author may say, that if there is any truth in the information which he has brought together, or in the inferences which he has drawn, there need be no want of, but an abundant supply of cheap and effective materials for Paper-making, and our textile manufactures from the vegetable kingdom need not be confined to Flax and to Cotton. While with regard to cordage, neither our Royal nor our Mercantile Marine need restrict themselves to European sources of supply. So if, for fishing nets, track-ropes, and mine-ropes, we require the utmost degree of strength in the smallest amount of space, the requisites are to be found in some of these Oriental fibres, as, for example, in the Rheeas of Assam, the Rami of the Malays, or the Chû Ma of China. These produce fibres of different degrees of fineness, according as they are taken from the later or the earlier crops; so, while the one may rival the softest Flax in fineness, the other may exceed the Russian, or any other except Himalayan Hemp, in strength.

APPENDIX.

A.

An Account of the Total Quantities of Flax and Hemp respectively IMPORTED *into the* UNITED KINGDOM *in each Year, from* 1801 *to* 1853, *both inclusive; distinguishing the Quantities received from the Russian Empire from those received from all other parts.*

YEARS.	FLAX AND TOW, OR CODILLA OF HEMP AND FLAX.			HEMP DRESSED.		
	From Russia.	From other parts.	From all parts.	From Russia.	From other parts.	From all parts.
	Cwt.	Cwt.	Cwt.	Cwt.	Cwt.	Cwt.
1801	188,106	85,613	273,719	682,175	67,171	749,346
1802	215,086	67,528	282,614	445,759	61,634	507,393
1803	215,201	76,431	291,632	686,777	70,912	757,689
1804	261,814	90,786	352,600	716,013	23,124	739,137
1805	369,871	101,877	471,748	615,771	15,932	631,703
1806	306,119	52,793	358,912	742,382	5,691	748,073
1807	378,362	44,414	422,776	751,828	25,869	777,697
1808	136,481	80,311	216,792	240,146	22,294	262,440
1809	395,217	134,868	530,085	796,076	59,765	855,841
1810	476,100	38,383	514,483	844,308	116,302	960,610
1811	224,037	10,734	234,771	452,588	16,296	468,884
1812	356,267	6,329	362,596	733,991	129,632	863,623
1813	The Records of the year 1813 were destroyed by fire.					
1814	389,948	110,585	500,533	526,488	42,235	568,723
1815	233,423	92,453	325,876	722,692	30,094	752,786
1816	150,321	62,350	212,671	369,177	6,280	375,457
1817	294,456	120,300	414,756	458,531	16,758	475,289
1818	286,603	141,045	427,648	659,431	24,777	684,208
1819	335,491	74,290	409,781	485,006	7,788	492,794
1820	315,481	66,907	382,388	415,813	10,350	426,163
1821	365,087	133,466	498,553	253,425	2,372	255,797
1822	419,860	190,246	610,106	583,761	32,694	616,455
1823	297,845	256,093	553,938	653,161	13,980	667,141
1824	448,894	293,637	742,531	557,365	14,571	571,936
1825	666,279	388,954	1,055,233	578,647	16,443	595,090
1826	527,905	160,717	688,622	465,088	24,242	489,330
1827	669,937	237,142	907,079	524,868	48,525	573,393
1828	643,153	233,036	876,189	454,303	49,817	504,120
1829	683,956	238,084	922,040	327,379	47,553	374,932
1830	703,582	240,514	944,096	461,099	45,671	506,770
1831	623,257	313,154	936,411	506,803	24,017	530,820
1832	667,868	314,648	982,516	492,355	101,209	593,564
1833	776,856	352,777	1,129,633	469,960	57,499	527,459
1834	562,816	248,906	811,722	583,841	89,970	673,811
1835	438,483	302,331	740,814	610,519	77,040	687,559
1836	1,037,021	492,095	1,529,116	556,458	29,574	586,032
1837	682,025	318,840	1,000,865	591,675	181,946	773,621
1838	1,089,559	536,718	1,626,277	580,999	149,377	730,376
1839	705,708	517,993	1,223,701	781,462	214,231	995,693
1840	870,401	382,839	1,253,240	599,078	84,990	684,068
1841	969,455	377,388	1,346,843	542,764	109,401	652,165
1842	844,725	301,034	1,145,759	415,565	170,340	585,905
1843	1,089,386	347,764	1,437,150	463,061	272,682	735,743
1844	1,112,024	471,470	1,583,494	655,954	257,279	913,233
1845	859,627	558,696	1,418,323	603,286	328,564	931,850
1846	740,396	406,696	1,147,092	620,656	262,238	882,894
1847	681,167	370,922	1,052,089	542,857	268,708	811,565
1848	1,085,732	377,929	1,463,661	536,400	309,371	845,771
1849	1,352,334	454,339	1,806,673	636,938	424,955	1,061,893
1850	1,240,766	582,152	1,822,918	600,992	447,643	1,048,635
1851	818,676	375,508	1,194,184	664,580	628,831	1,293,411
1852	949,907	458,807	1,408,714	537,132	531,024	1,068,156
1853	1,294,827	607,650	1,902,477	806,396	412,374	1,218,770

B.

MATERIALS FOR PAPER-MAKING.

The deficient supply of and an increasing price for, the materials for making paper, with the prospect of a still greater consumption, having for some time excited the attention of manufacturers and of the public, the Author has, like others, been requested to state what probable sources of supply were open to the manufacturer.

In histories of the manufacture of paper, the Chinese are generally acknowledged to have been the first to have made paper from pulp. The Egyptian paper, or Papyrus, was made by gumming slices of vegetable tissue together under pressure. So what is called Rice paper consists only of thin slices of cellular tissue of a little-known plant. The Arabs are supposed to have learnt the art in the eighth century from the Chinese, but much more probably from the Hindoos, as they translated many of their works and adopted much of their science. (*v.* the Author's 'Essay on the Antiquity of Hindoo Medicine.') The Arabs are further said to have introduced the art of paper-making into Spain in the ninth or tenth century. Paper was first made at Nuremburg in the year 1390, but in England not till the year 1450.

There is no doubt that the manufacture of paper from pulp has been known in China from very early times: it is said for at least 2000 years. They employ a vast variety of fibrous substances for this manufacture, and apply paper to a variety of uses little thought of in other countries. They make up an infinite variety of kinds, from the coarse, heavy, half-inch-thick touch-paper, for retaining a slow, enduring fire, to the beautiful so-called India paper suited for our finest proof engravings. In the tea-chests there is a lavish use of many thicknesses of paper. If a hut or boat is leaky over-head, the bed is protected by a large sheet of oiled paper. If a shopkeeper wants to tie up a parcel, he seizes a strip of tough paper, and by rolling it on his thigh at once converts it into a strong pack-thread. Even patches on a torn sail are at times made of tough paper, as we have been informed by an intelligent visitor to that country. It is the cheapest of materials in daily use, and the manufacturers are very numerous. They make it of Rice straw, of young Bamboos, of different fibres, and of the bark of the Paper Mulberry. Showing that the inventors of the art make use chiefly of unwoven fibres, though they also employ refuse cloth and silk, &c.

So India, though hardly ever mentioned in histories of the art, is a country where considerable quantities of paper are made, though not generally of a good quality; their thick ink does not so much require this. There are small manufactories of it in most parts of the country, and to a considerable extent at such places as Ahmedabad, Lucnow, &c. As we have seen in the foregoing pages, a great variety of fibres, such as Jute, Sunn, Ambaree, Moorva, and old sacks and fishing nets are also employed, though in general the natives prefer the Sunn fibre. The Himalayan process with the inner bark of the Paper plant very much resembles that of the Chinese with the Paper Mulberry. It is probable therefore that the art was introduced from that country into the Himalayas, and not from India. Into which it was probably carried at a very early period, and from thence learnt by the Arabs; who would hardly else have used Cotton, an Indian product. The Hindoos themselves, as I am informed by Professor Wilson, still used, about the beginning of the Christian era, or as late as the age of the Dramas, the inner bark of the *Bhurja* or Birch (*Betula Bhojputtur*) for writing on. In Southern regions the leaves of the Palmira and of the Talipat are well known to have been long used, as they still are, for writing on with a style. But the manufacture of paper from pulp has long been established in India, and before the Arabs began to make translations from the Sanscrit, at the same time that they did so from Greek writers.

Dr. Buchanan, in his survey of the lower provinces of the Bengal Presidency, has given an account of the manufacture of paper from Pat or Jute (*Corchorus olitorius*) at Dinagepore, and in Behar, &c., from Sunn (*Crotalaria juncea*). It is also so made in other parts of the country, as well as from Hibiscus fibre. And there can be no difficulty in doing so with the numerous fibrous materials which India produces in such vast variety, and which we have already mentioned in so much detail.

It is objected that pulp from unwoven fibres does not draw through the present machinery so well as that made from rags. A modification of machinery would remedy this. But it is probable that if the half-stuff were made from the clean bark without first separating the fibres, these might probably be so entangled as to answer some of the effects of the weaving. As rags have to be collected, cut, cleaned, and bleached, the Author cannot but think that the primitive method of using the bark of suitable plants and trees will afford both a cheap and an effectual substitute. Besides which the supply of rags must come short of the increasing demands of the world for paper.

Bengal and the east coast of the Bay of Bengal, as well as the Malabar or west coast of India, are the places where the growth of suitable materials, from the warmth and moisture of the climate, is most abundant, and the conveyance by sea is at the same time most easy. In Arracan the price of Bast, even made into rope, is one rupee per maund. (*v.* p. 238.)

As the greatest natural riches would be of little value unless they could be made available at reasonable rates, the Author consulted Mr. Henley, who is practically well acquainted with the usages of the people and the rates at which their services may be obtained. He has favoured the Author with letters on the subject, and has also published a paper in the 'Journal of the Society of Arts' for 1854, p. 486. He there observes: "It is to India we must look for extensive and cheap supplies, for it is there alone we find the necessary conditions of very low-priced and intelligent labour, with an abundance of elementary suitable materials; and that as articles of small price are particularly sensitive of charges, such as of freight, &c., it is only by large operations that an average of low charges can be accomplished."

Suitable materials being abundant, he proposes that it should be reduced to the state of half-stuff by the aid of the Dhenkee, already mentioned at p. 86, as an instrument to be found in almost every house in Bengal, being used for husking rice, the preparation of tobacco, of drugs, dye-stuffs, and brick-dust.

The charges to London, including freight, insurance, exchange, dock, and in fact all commercial charges, he estimates at £7 per ton weight. It is necessary to specify the ton weight, as the ton for freight would be only 16 cwt. The cost of half-stuff, as already quoted at p. 86, of different qualities, would be about £4 4*s*. and £7; as contracts could be made at the rate of Rs. 1 8, or 3*s*., to Rs. 2 8, or 5*s*., per maund of 82 lb., deliverable at any central depôt within a radius of twenty miles. The expenses of agency, conveyance, &c., in India, about £2 2*s*., and of freight to London, and other expenses, about £7; so that the lower quality might be imported here for £13 4*s*., and the better quality, equal to linen rags, for £16 5*s*.

"It would be necessary to have recourse to the usual Indian system of making cash advances to contractors ere a pound of the goods had any existence. Such, however, is the universal system of the country. The natives, it must be admitted, are wonderfully faithful on the whole in adhering to their bargains."

"The method proposes to avail itself at once of their own simple arts; it brings the question as nearly as possible to the state of a domestic industry, ever the most economical in such countries; it reduces to the lowest point the charge of collecting from extensive districts the various elementary matters which might present themselves."

Dr. L. Playfair, in a communication on this subject, observes, that the price mentioned in the Treasury letter, of 2*d*. to 2½*d*. per lb. for a partially prepared pulp, is by most makers considered to be too high, and that materials should be looked for at the price of 1*d*. to 1½*d*. per lb. for roughly prepared pulp; but if bleached, or in as far an advanced state with regard to colour and texture as cotton or linen rag, then 2½*d*. to 4*d*. per lb. might be obtained. "The quantity of any promising material sent home for experiment should not be less than half a ton in weight," though in some cases a cwt. will give satisfactory results.

To serve as points of comparison we may here insert a notice of the ordinary and the increased prices of rags from the 'Journal of the Society of Arts.'

A.	26*s*. . . .	32*s*. to 34*s*. per cwt.
B.	16*s*. . . .	20*s*. "
C.	11*s*. 6*d*. . . .	15*s*. "
D.	7*s*. . . .	10*s*. "

Bleaching salts, alkali, alum, hide pieces for size, are other articles required; and all have increased in price.

Of the quantity of material that is required, we may form

some idea from the fact that 177,633,009 lb. weight of paper were produced in 1853 in Great Britain.

C.

The Author having been requested to give his opinion respecting an increased supply of Materials for Paper-making, did so in the Report which is subjoined to the following—

Copy of Correspondence between the Departments of the Treasury and Board of Trade, in regard to the increasing Scarcity of the Materials for the Fabrication of Paper.

(Printed by order of the House of Commons.)

Treasury Chambers, February 13, 1854.

Sir,—I am commanded by the Lords Commissioners of Her Majesty's Treasury to acquaint you that it has been represented to their Lordships that great and increasing scarcity has been felt of late in obtaining supplies of the raw material of paper, consisting not only of rags, but also largely of the refuse of cotton- and flax-mills. It is stated that within the last ten years the prices of these articles have greatly advanced, that rags can be imported from only a few parts of Europe, and that as there is no regular and open market for rags and the other materials used in the manufacture of paper, increased demand and high price do not call forth increased supply, as in other articles of commerce from abroad.

With a view to diminish the inconvenience thus felt, it has been suggested to my Lords, that Her Majesty's Consuls abroad might be instructed to obtain information, and procure samples of vegetable fibre in their respective localities, applicable to the manufacture of paper. In doing this, it would have to be borne in mind that the great essential of such an article must be its cheapness, to cover the high freights now prevailing, and which, it may be anticipated, will prevail for some time. As regards the nature of the articles, my Lords are informed, that with the exception of jute canvas and gunny bagging, every description of vegetable fibre is now capable of being bleached, and is available for fine papers. Fibrous reeds and rushes, the inner bark of many trees, and several kinds of vegetable fibre in warm or tropical countries, are substances likely to be of service, especially where they could be imported as dunnage among the cargo, or in compressed bales, but quantity and steadiness of supply are essential. As regards price, my Lords understand that if the article could be laid down so as to cost from 2*d.* to 2½*d.* per lb. when purified and bleached, without reckoning the cost of preparation, it would be sufficiently low to answer the purpose in view.

My Lords request that you will bring this subject under the consideration of the Lords of the Committee of Privy Council for Trade, and move their Lordships, if they concur in the expediency of the inquiry here suggested, to communicate on the subject with the Foreign Office, in order that the necessary circular instructions may be issued to Her Majesty's Consuls abroad, to carry out the objects adverted to.

I am, &c.,

James Booth, Esq., &c. (Signed) JAMES WILSON.

Board of Trade, April 19, 1854.

Sir,—I am directed by the Lords of the Committee of Privy Council for Trade to forward to you a copy of a communication received from the Lords of Her Majesty's Treasury, and to request that the Commissioners for the Affairs of India may bring it under the notice of the Chairman and Directors of the Honorable East India Company, with a view to obtaining the opinion of Dr. Forbes Royle, the officer in charge of the scientific correspondence relating to the vegetable productions of India.

I have, &c.,

Sir T. N. Redington, &c. (Signed) J. EMERSON TENNENT.

India Board, May 15, 1854.

Sir,—In reply to your letter of the 19th ult., enclosing a letter addressed to the Board of Trade by the Treasury respecting the procuration of raw material for the manufacture of paper, I am directed by the Commissioners for the Affairs of India to transmit to you a report by Dr. Royle, received from the East India House upon this subject, in compliance with the object expressed in your letter.

I have, &c.,

Sir J. E. Tennent, &c. (Signed) T. N. REDINGTON.

Memorandum on Materials for the manufacture of Paper procurable from India.

In reply to the reference from the Lords of the Committee of Privy Council for Trade, requiring my opinion respecting increased supplies of raw material for Paper-making, I beg to be allowed to observe that it is a subject on which I have of late been frequently consulted, and have communicated much of the following information.[1]

Paper, it is well known, is in Europe made chiefly from linen or cotton rags, but also from the refuse and sweepings of cotton- and flax-mills, as also of the coverings of our cotton bales and of worn-out ropes. But paper is also made from the stems and leaves of many grasses, as from rice straw, and from the bamboo by the Chinese, and of late from common straw in this country, and even from wood shavings. The fibrous part of many Lily- and Aloe-leaved plants have been converted into excellent paper in India, where the fibres of Tiliaceous, Malvaceous, and Leguminous plants are employed for the same purpose: as in the Himalayas, one of the Lace-bark tribe (p. 310) is similarly employed, and in China one of the Mulberry tribe, and the Nettle in Holland. I mention these various sources, because plants belonging to the same families as the above abound in India and other warm countries, and are capable of yielding a very abundant and never-failing supply of sufficiently cheap and very excellent material for paper-making of all kinds. Some may be used without any further process of bleaching, but all are capable of having any colour they may possess destroyed by chemical means. I would not except the jute canvas or gunny bagging, because I have seen specimens of jute of a beautiful silky white, both plain and manufactured into fabrics for furniture, &c., &c., as shown by the late Colonel Calvert at the East India House.

As the Chinese make paper of rice straw, and of the young shoots of the bamboo, while the Hindoos make ropes of different grasses (such as *Saccharum Munja* and *S. Sara*) strong enough for their Persian wheels as well as for towing lines, it is evident that these and probably many others contain a suffi-

[1] Some of it was published about the same time in the 'Gardener's Chronicle.'

ciency of fibrous material for paper-making (p. 30). The cultivated Cereals cannot well be turned to much account, for their straw forms the chief food for cattle; but as the country abounds with grass jungles, which are in the autumn of every year burnt down in order that the young blades may spring up and afford pasturage for cattle, it is evident that there are many situations where a sufficiency might be cut down before it has become perfectly dried up, and converted into half-stuff for paper-makers [as might also the refuse of the Sugar-cane].

Of the Sedges (p. 33) also some are, in India, employed for making ropes, as the Bhabhur or *Eriophorum cannabinum*, for making rope bridges for crossing some of the hill torrents. The Papyrus we know was used by the Egyptians for making their paper, but this was by cutting the material into thin slices and making these adhere together under pressure. But others of the genus, as the *Cyperus tegetum*, is used in India for mat-making. As these plants as well as Rushes grow together in large quantities, it would be quite possible in many places to turn them to profitable account.

Many parts of the world abound in the Lily- and Aloe-leaved plants which have been alluded to above, and of which the leaves contain much easily separable fibrous materials. These belong to the genera Agave, Aloe, Yucca, Sanseviera, Bromelia, and others, all of which abound in white-coloured fibres, applicable to various useful purposes, and of which the tow might be used for paper-making, and considerable supplies obtained. Paper used to be made from the Sanseviera in Trichinopoly, and some has been made at Madras, of the unbleached Agave alone, and also mixed with old gunny bags. (pp. 37, 41, 51, 57.) [Recently, also, from the leaf of the Pandanus, p. 35.]

[The Arrow-root (p. 60) and Ginger tribes (p. 61), containing such plants as those yielding the fecula called Arrow-root, Tous les Mois, Tikkur, &c., and Ginger, Turmeric, Cardamoms, &c., all have annual stems and leaves, which are the refuse of the present culture, and might yield an abundant supply of half-stuff.]

Among cultivated plants there is probably nothing so well calculated to yield a large supply of material fit for making paper of almost every quality as the Plantain (*Musa paradisiaca*) (*v.* p. 61), so extensively cultivated in all tropical countries on account of its fruit, and of which the fibre-yielding stems are applied to no useful purpose. The plant, as every one acquainted with tropical countries knows, is common near the poorest huts and in the largest gardens, and is considered to yield by far the largest quantity of nutritious matter. Its fruit in many places supplying the place of bread, and in composition and nutritious value approaching most nearly to the potato, may, if produced in too large a quantity, be preserved in the same way as figs, or the meal may be separated, as it resembles rice most nearly in composition. Each rootstock throws up from six to eight stems, each of which must be yearly cut down, and will yield from three to four pounds of the fibre fit for textile fabrics, for rope-making, or for the manufacture of paper. As the fruit already pays the expenses of the culture, this fibre could be afforded at a cheap rate, as from the nature of the plant, consisting almost only of water and fibre, the latter might easily be separated. One planter calculates that it could be afforded for £9 13*s*. 4*d*. per ton. Some very useful and tough kinds of paper have been made in India from the fibres of the Plantain, and some of finer quality from the same material both in France and in this country.[1]

All the plants which have been already mentioned are devoid of true bark, and are called Endògenous in structure. Simple pressure between rollers, and washing, would appear to be sufficient for the separation of the fibres of most of them. But the following families of plants are all possessed of true bark which requires to be stripped off, usually after the stems have been steeped in water, before their respective fibres can be separated from the rest of the vegetable matter.

The Flax plant (p. 133) abounds in fibre, but this is too valuable to be converted into paper. India, however, grows immense quantities of the plant, on account of its seed (linseed) which is both consumed in the country and exported in enormous quantities. But nowhere is the fibre turned to any account. This is no doubt owing to the climate not favouring the formation of soft and flexible fibre; but the short fibre which is formed, and might be easily separated, would be valu-

[1] Specimens of these and of the other Papers made in India, were sent with the original communication, and were afterwards shown at some Scientific Meetings.

able for paper-making, and might add to the agriculturists' profits without much additional outlay.

So some Malvaceous (p. 253) plants are cultivated on account of their fruits being used as articles of diet, as Okhro (p. 259) (*Hibiscus esculentus*), in the West Indies and in the United States. The *Ram-turai* of India is closely allied to it, and is cultivated for the same purpose. Both plants abound in fine flexible fibre, which is not, but might be easily separated, and afford a considerable supply, especially if the cultivation was extended in the neighbourhood of towns. Paper is made from a species of *Hibiscus* in Japan, and *H. Sabdariffa* is cultivated in India on account of its jelly-yielding calices. Numerous other species of Hibiscus, of Sida, and of other genera of this family, abound in warm climates; several are cultivated in different countries, as *Hibiscus cannabinus* in India, and *Sida titiæfolia* in China: more might be so. They grow quickly, and to a large size, and abound in fibrous material of a fine, soft, flexible quality: on which account they might be cultivated with profit, and the tow be useful to the paper-maker. (p. 200.) [The stems of Cotton plants would also yield a supply.]

The Tiliaceæ (p. 232) are likewise remarkable for the abundance and fine quality of fibre which many of them contain. *Tilia europea* produces the enormous quantities of bast exported from Russia. *Corchorus olitorius* and *C. capsularis*, the leaves of both of which are used as a vegetable, yield the large supply of Jute (p. 239) imported into this country, as well as the gunny cloth and bags exported even to America. Several species of Grewia yield edible fruit, on which account they are cultivated. Others abound in the jungles, and most would yield a valuable fibre, as some of them already do, for commercial purposes. [The Indian Basts, p. 239, are cheap, and abound in fibre.]

Some of the Leguminosæ also abound in valuable fibre. *Crotalaria juncea* yields the common *Sunn* of India. *Sesbania aculeata* or *cannabina* yields the *Dhanchi* of Bengal; while *Bauhinia racemosa* is used for making rope bridges in the Himalayas. The fibre of *Parkinsonia aculeata* was sent to the Exhibition in 1851, expressly as being fitted for paper-making: though colourless, it wants strength. (pp. 270—298.) [Some paper is made from gunny bags in India.]

Several plants produce large quantities of a silky cotton-like substance, not applied to any use, such as the Silk Cotton tree (p. 264), the Mudar of India (p. 306), several species of Saccharum (p. 32), &c., which might be collected where labour is cheap, and would no doubt be well fitted for conversion into pulp for paper. [So also the Dogbanes and Asclepiads, pp. 302-3.]

[The Nepal Paper plant (*Daphne cannabina*) has been mentioned above, and is treated of at p. 311.]

Among the Nettle, the Mulberry, and Bread-fruit tribes of plants (p. 340), there are many which seem well calculated to yield material for paper-making. The Chinese we know employ the inner bark of *Morus*, now *Broussonetia papyrifera* (p. 341). This, no doubt, produces some of the Chinese paper, which is remarkable for toughness. I believe that the refuse cuttings of the bush cultivation of the Mulberry in Bengal (p. 343) might be turned to profitable account. The barks of many stinging (*Urtica*), and of stingless (*Boehmeria*) Nettles (p. 344), abound in fibres remarkable for strength; the tow of these might be converted into paper-stuff if not required for mixing with wool (p. 358) [as might also the bark cloths, p. 342].

The weeds of tropical countries which grow in such luxuriance, and among which are species of Sida (p. 262), of Grewia, of Corchorus, of Triumfetta (p. 233), and of many other genera, might all yield an abundance of fibrous material, if the refuse of the above cultivated plants were found not to be sufficient. Some simple machinery for separating the fibre would greatly facilitate operations, while the expenses of freight might be diminished by compression, or, as suggested, by packing the material as dunnage. The cheapness of labour, as of everything else in many of these countries, would enable material for paper-making to be brought here in great abundance and at a sufficiently cheap rate, if ordinary pains were taken by the consumers in Europe, to encourage the planter or colonists of a distant region.

I have, &c.,

(Signed) J. FORBES ROYLE.

East India House, May 3, 1854.

INDEX.

ERRATA.

Page 32, line 38, *for* "Mr. Burns," *read* "Mr. Barns;" so also in pp. 33 and 144.
„ 33, „ 29, *for* "Cyperacæ," *read* "Cyperaceæ."
„ 254, „ 17, *for* "Numajee," *read* "Munjee."
„ 341, „ 9, *for* "ineisa," *read* "incisa."
„ 343, „ 37, *for* "saccadora," *read* "saccidora."
„ 345, „ 8, *for* "Shon," *read* "Shan."
„ 349, „ 12, *for* "tencessime," *read* "tenacissima."
„ 375, „ 4, *after* "Military Stores," *add* "the strength of the large ropes was tried at the Rope-works of Messrs. Mathews, in Bermondsey."